CHICANA FEMINISMS

. . . . .

POST-CONTEMPORARY

INTERVENTIONS

Series Editors: Stanley Fish

and Fredric Jameson

. . . . .

CHICANA FEMINISMS

• • • • •

A CRITICAL READER

Edited by Gabriela F. Arredondo,

Aída Hurtado, Norma Klahn,

Olga Nájera-Ramírez,

and Patricia Zavella

Duke University Press

Durham and London 2003

© 2003

Duke University Press

All rights reserved

Printed in the United States

of America on acid-free paper ⊗

Designed by Rebecca Giménez

Typeset in Trump Medieval by

Tseng Information Systems, Inc.

Library of Congress Cataloging-

in-Publication Data appear

on the last printed page

of this book.

We dedicate this book to

Sonia Saldívar-Hull, feminist,

scholar, and activist, for her

generous contributions

to the development

of this project.

CONTENTS

· · · · ·

PREFACE

· · · · ·

This book emerged from an interdisciplinary collective linked by a common concern with theorizing and in some cases reinterpreting Chicana/o experiences and their representations. As five Chicanas trained in varied scholarly disciplines—anthropology, folklore, psychology, literature, and history—and from different generations with diverse backgrounds and histories, we developed this transdisciplinary project to capture the new challenges posed by feminist dialogues. The fissures and tensions generated from our distinct backgrounds and approaches forced us to confront the essentialism that has been stereotypically imposed on us as "Chicanas" and to negotiate a multidisciplinary framework that integrated our respective interests. Furthermore, our commitment to a collective enterprise compelled us to find productive ways of engaging our differences.

The Chicano/Latino Research Center (CLRC) at the University of California, Santa Cruz proved critical to our pursuit. With support from State Senate Concurrent Resolution 43 funds and under the leadership of Norma Klahn and Pedro Castillo, we founded this campuswide research unit in 1992 to foster interchange among UCSC faculty to encourage and promote more nuanced understandings of transnational Chicano/Latino communities. Mindful of the multiple changes generated by globalization, increased transnational migrations from Latin America, and complex processes of identity and cultural formation, the CLRC selected "cross-border perspectives linking the Americas" as its organizing principle. Through activities such as colloquia, the working paper series, conferences, visiting scholars, and research clusters that include faculty and graduate students, the CLRC has become an internationally recognized site for transdisciplinary and cross-border scholarship on Chicano and Latino issues. (For further information, see the CLRC Web site: http://lals.ucsc.edu/clrc.)

In 1996 we established the Chicana Feminisms Research Cluster at the CLRC. The book began as a series of questions we raised as we investigated Chicana feminisms through interrogating a range of texts, including history and film as well as recent theoretical and creative pieces. Our aim was to explore Chicana feminist thought and the way it is articulated in a variety of venues. We sought to capture the process of debate and dialogue that has always been integral to Chicana feminist theory and praxis, and to illustrate how Chicana feminists have instigated passionate responses —dialogue, disagreement, alternative formulations—with each other and from others.

With these goals in mind, we invited eight women to present their research at the Chicano/Latino Research Center in a colloquium series on Chicana feminisms in 1997 in conjunction with a course taught by Aída Hurtado on Chicana feminisms. The scholars were chosen to represent a variety of issues and approaches and included Elba Sánchez, Norma E. Cantú, Beatriz Pesquera, Carla Trujillo, Patricia Zavella, Rosa Linda Fregoso, Sonia Saldívar-Hull, and Norma Alarcón. We then invited them to submit essays and suggest possible respondents. In addition to those who submitted their manuscripts, we expanded the contributors to include others whose work is central to Chicana feminist thought. The respondents were intentionally selected to open up dialogue with a variety of perspectives, to air disagreements, and to explore points of convergence with other political projects. We are gratified by the thoughtful commentaries submitted by the respondents, who engaged the authors with profound questions and complicated the discussions further. We hope that this book will encourage other women to make explicit their dialogues with feminists and nonfeminists alike.

ACKNOWLEDGMENTS

· · · · ·

We are grateful to our friends and colleagues who read early versions of the introduction and gave us helpful suggestions for revisions: Lionel Cantú, Norma E. Cantú, Rosa Linda Fregoso, and Alexandra Minna Stern. We appreciate the support of the Chicano/Latino Research Center for providing an intellectual home for this project and innumerable other means of support throughout the years that helped bring this book to fruition. Special thanks to Sonia Saldívar-Hull for her support. Thank you also to Erin Morimoto, Denika Hernández, Jessica Vazquez, and Shane Fisher for their assistance with mundane but necessary tasks. Finally, a very warm thank you to Cheryl Van De Veer and Zoe Sodja of the Document Publishing and Editing Center at UCSC for editorial assistance.

INTRODUCTION

Chicana Feminisms at the Crossroads:

Disruptions in Dialogue

· · · · ·

Su cuerpo es una bocacalle [her body is an intersection].
—Gloria Anzaldúa, *Borderlands/La Frontera*

In her groundbreaking anthology, *Making Face/Making Soul: Haciendo Caras*, Gloria Anzaldúa organized a collection of writings by women of color that reflect what she calls "our fragmented and interrupted dialogue which is said to be discontinued and incomplete discourse" and asked readers to participate "in the making of meaning . . .to connect the dots, the fragments" (1990, xvii–xviii). *Chicana Feminisms: A Critical Reader* represents our move to build on Anzaldúa's observation that the praxis of feminists of color is often not recognized or sanctioned in the academy. Specifically, we highlight the process of debate and dialogue that has always been integral to Chicana feminist theory and practice.

At times, the debate has been highly contentious, particularly in the struggle for a voice and space within masculinist projects, such as the Chicano movement, or within predominantly white, middle-class feminist circles.[1] Teresa Córdova summarizes the nature of these struggles: "Chicanas write in opposition to the symbolic representations of the Chicano movement that did not include them. Chicanas write in opposition to a hegemonic feminist discourse that places gender as a variable separate from that of race and class. Chicanas write in opposition to academics, whether mainstream or postmodern, who have never fully recognized them as subjects, as active agents" (1994, 194). In other words, Chicana feminisms are characterized by "finding absences and exclusions and arguing from that standpoint" (Hurtado 1998, 135). By occupying this "third space" (Pérez 1999; Sandoval 2000), Chicana feminists actively contest the silencing that has been used against us.[2] As it has been for other feminists of color, "talking back" (hooks 1989) has been an important form of disruption for Chicanas. Talking back creates waves of disturbance that establish women's humanity, agency, and worth.

Chicana feminisms constitute a political stance that confronts and undermines patriarchy as it cross-cuts forms of disempowerment and silencing such as racism, homophobia, class inequality, and nationalism. In this book, we show how Chicana feminist writings move discourse beyond binaries and toward intersectionality and hybridity. Grounded in our understanding of power as relational, we are working toward an explanatory matrix that confronts the shifting boundaries of discourse and captures ties to lived experiences. Our guiding metaphor for Chicana feminist writing expands on Anzaldúa's notion of Chicanas' bodies as *bocacalles*. Literally, bocacalle translates as an intersection where two streets cross one another. However, a more provocative translation of bocacalle as mouth/street evokes images of women shouting in the streets or the assertion of Chicana feminisms as public discourse demanding to be heard.

The experiences of Chicana feminists, speaking and living in complex social realities and crossing borders—physical and metaphorical—situate us as parts of multiple constituencies. This is a standpoint that can be arduous, for it entails multiple debates and critiques. However, it is one that Chicana feminist writers have used to articulate the historical specificity of the Chicana experience. Chicana feminists strategically engage and move fluidly among different constituencies, always risking the consequences of not aligning ourselves absolutely with any of them.

Our metaphor for capturing the multiple engagements by Chicana feminists is of women living and working in an intellectual *glorieta* (a roundabout), a space that centers on the Chicana experience and is a standpoint from which we engage in dialogue with different audiences and participants. The *avenidas* that we face in the glorieta allow Chicana feminists to make assessments of power in relation to our varied locations. Like a Mexico City glorieta, the dialogue is fast-paced, fluid, and flexible, at times unnerving; it forces intellectual dexterity. Such agility is foundational to the Chicana feminist political project, which intervenes in important ways to raise consciousness and further the struggle for decolonization against multiple oppressions. This anthology highlights the critical interventions that Chicanas and Mexicanas have made vis-à-vis gender politics in today's increasingly complex world.

Chicana feminist writers recognize that women of Mexican origin constitute a diverse community that requires varied theoretical frameworks and methodological approaches to understand all facets of Chicanas' experiences. Imbricated within various systems of inequality, Chicanas differ from one another on the basis of class, racialization, generation, sexual orientation, age, language use, region, and place of birth (Zavella 1994). Further, scholars use various terms to describe women of Mexican origin. How Chicanas/os identify themselves varies according to region, the changing historical, social, or political context, and/or whether individuals consider themselves to be biracial.[3] For example, the 1960s Chicano movement politicized and made the term Chicano respectable; however, it remains controversial (Limón 1981; Hurtado, Gurin, and Peng 1997). For historical reasons, many people of Mexican origin in New Mexico prefer the term Spanish or Hispana/o (Zavella 1996). We use the term Chicana to convey the politicized nature of our project. But regardless of whether one uses Chicana, Mexicana, Tejana, or another term, heterogeneity is critical to understanding the overall Chicana experience.

Nonetheless, Mexican women in the United States share some common structural locations and experiences. Chicanas are predominantly of working-class origin, disproportionately poor compared to Chicano men, and even after several generations do not experience significant social or economic mobility (Hayes-Bautista et al. 1992; Hurtado et al. 1992). Often the victims of uncaring schools, Chicanas, like other people of color, experience low educational attainment.[4] Chicanas are frequently concentrated in labor markets and work sites segregated by race and gender (Mauricio Gastón Institute 1994; Zavella 1987), with immigrant women (and men) at the bottom of the occupational structure in what Lisa Catanzarite (2000) calls "brown-collar jobs." These jobs are often nonunion, pay minimum (or below) wages, have few benefits, and are seasonal and/or subject to displacement, such as jobs in agriculture or garment manufacturing (Morales and Bonilla 1993). Chicanas who work in the informal sector (for example, as domestic workers or day care providers) face irregular working hours, with little or no regulation of their working conditions and few recourses if their employer underpays them or does not pay at all.[5]

Yet historically, there has always been some social mobility, however limited. Particularly after the struggles for civil rights in the 1960s and

1970s, there has been a growing population of Chicanas/os in business, politics, and professional occupations. Chicanas who have managed to achieve higher education and professional positions, however, often find themselves tokenized, with expectations that they will serve multiple constituencies (Segura 1992; Pesquera and Segura 1993).

Cultural forces, such as stereotypic representations of women of Mexican descent in popular culture, including film, literature, television, music, and the visual arts, produce other forms of disempowerment.[6] Just as such renderings can work to homogenize and codify the experiences of Chicanas, they can also flatten or erase the multiplicity and complexity of Chicana lives. Chicanas contest those representations and claim subjectivity on our own terms through diverse means, including activism, writing, and teaching as well as producing our own versions of popular culture or through deployment of popular cultures in subversive ways (Klahn 1994). In this light, the struggle for interpretive power occurs in varied venues.

Chicanas' experiences are rooted in Mexican history, with a legacy of colonialism, violence, discrimination, and complex class and racial hierarchies against the backdrop of Catholicism and language repression, especially toward indigenous peoples (Castañeda 1993; González 1999). Moreover, late twentieth-century changes, such as the end of the cold war and the passage of GATT and NAFTA, opened up trade restrictions and signaled shifts in the politics of globalization. In an age of information economies, globalization, and new opportunities for migration, the ongoing settlement of Mexicans in the United States is part of a worldwide reconfiguration of peoples that shows no sign of stopping.

Mexican migration and settlement is bringing about enormous changes that touch all aspects of women's lived realities. These include struggles over human rights, citizenship and linguistic rights, increasing class differences, the feminization of the labor force, and the lack of educational opportunities for a large sector of this population within increasingly nativist U.S. politics.[7]

The particularities of the histories of Mexico and the United States and the realities of continuous movement within and across social locations mean that Chicanas increasingly deploy a transnational perspective that enables us to confront the clash and confluence of cultural, political, and economic disparities. Acknowledging the border as a site of convergence, conflict, and creativity, Chicana feminists also recognize how increased globalization and migration have transformed the modern nation-state.[8] Cross-border perspectives taken up by Chicana feminists elucidate new social formations and explicate different lines of communication, disrupting Anglo/Eurocentric visions of "civilization" and imperialist conquest.

Chicana feminist writers have contributed original formulations for understanding the variegated experiences of women of Mexican origin under advanced capitalism. Theorizing and documenting the intersections of class, race, gender, sexual preference, and nationality, Chicana feminists offer critical insights into *mestizaje,* hybridity, and the "borderlands" (Anzaldúa 1987; Saldívar-Hull 2000), the continuum of color, phenotype, and privilege (Hurtado 1996a), as well as oppositional consciousness and practice (Sandoval 1991; Pardo 1998), notions of the decolonial imaginary (Pérez 1999), and the methodology of the oppressed (Sandoval 2000). These concepts mark a consciousness of resistance to the repression of language and culture, a recognition of a "third space" located within intersecting structures of power in which women construct claims to human agency. For example, contesting their marginalization, Chicana lesbians assert what Emma Pérez calls *una lengua y un sitio,* a discourse and social space "that rejects colonial ideology and the by-products of colonialism and capitalist patriarchy—sexism, racism, homophobia" (1991, 161).

In addition to decolonizing theory and representation, Chicanas have a long history of organized resistance and struggles for social justice. Under the cloak of protection of family and community, Mexican women have organized for access to state-funded resources such as recreation centers and cultural events, to prevent the construction of toxic waste centers and jails in their communities, and to curb gang violence (Orozco 1994; Pardo 1991). They have organized for union recognition, and in the process have constructed new identities with rights in American society.[9]

To capture the complexity of Chicanas' experiences, feminist scholars have used multiple epistemologies and methods. These include oral histories;[10] creative production such as poetry, theatrical performance, painting, dance, and music;[11] and social science surveys (Segura and Pesquera 1992; Pesquera and Segura 1993). Some Chicanas combine analytical tools and cross disciplinary boundaries. For example, literary critic Alvina Quintana (1989, 1996) uses Chicanas' creative writings as ethnographic texts, social psychologist Aída Hurtado (1996a) draws on fables proposed by race theorists, and creative writer Ana Castillo's (1995) book-length essays draw on varied genres to highlight Chicanas' condition. Regardless of the method, the struggle lies in documenting the intricacies of Chicanas' experiences as racialized women of color within their historical conditions. Clearly, Chicana feminists favor multidisciplinary approaches.[12]

Such multidisciplinarity can be challenging, problematic, and marginal.

Working at the interstices, Chicana feminists make visible subjugated knowledges and offer new theories and insights. Sonia Saldívar-Hull writes: "As a consequence, we have to look in nontraditional places for our theories: in the prefaces to anthologies, in the interstices of autobiographies, in our cultural artifacts (the *cuentos*), and if we are fortunate to have access to a good library, in the essays published in marginalized journals not widely distributed by the dominant institutions" (2000, 46).

An emergent body of Chicana feminist scholarship has surfaced in several disciplines as well and is represented to some extent in existing anthologies.[13] Cultural studies and feminist anthologies have incorporated Chicana authors, situating their contributions in projects whose purpose is to extend debates in cultural and gender studies.[14] In collaboration with other women of color, Chicana feminists have also contributed to rethinking feminism and cultural studies in general. Feminists of color have formulated notions of simultaneity of oppression, imbrication, and multiple subjectivities in a postcolonial context.[15] There is a rich collection of anthologies of creative writing and political essays that constructs a relational framework, exploring parallel historical experiences of Chicanas and Latinas.[16] *Chicana Feminisms* seeks to extend these important works by illustrating the relational experiences of Chicanas, highlighting the dialogue that feminist scholars engage in with various constituencies.

The essays in this anthology are written by scholars and creative writers who speak from diverse fields, situated knowledges, and ideological leanings, disrupting the notion of Chicana identity as monolithic and homogeneous. These authors contribute original interpretations that add nuance to our understanding of Chicana experiences. Ultimately, the essays constitute a project by "native" scholars engaged in theories, methods, and practices with broad political implications, where the representation of Chicanas and analyses of their conditions constitute sites of struggle. To foster dialogue at the point of production, we chose to open a space for a critical conversation within the text itself by inviting respondents to engage with contributors. The respondents were selected for the explicit purpose of generating a lively exchange; they could engage the work in dialogue, discussion, or debate, critically addressing the theories, analysis, and issues presented in the essay, or they could use the work as a point of departure to elaborate an alternative perspective or to explore points of convergence with their own work. The respondents represent various voices: the younger generation, those from different racial/ethnic groups or nationalities, cultural workers who are not located in the academy, and male critics.

Three overarching themes emerged in these pieces: lived realities, creative expression among a range of feminist practices, and the politics of representation. These themes are interlinked, conveying the layers of meaning of Chicanas' experiences. Often, the writers included here spanned more than one theme. Maylei Blackwell, Aída Hurtado, and Patricia Zavella theorize the lived experiences of Chicanas and grapple with the complications of being ethnographers, contesting the representation of their subjects as they give voice to practices or discourses seen as unconventional or even taboo. Elba Sánchez, Norma Cantú, Amalia Mesa-Bains, and Olga Nájera-Ramírez theorize creative expressions such as writing, visual arts, and performance, mindful that reception or interpretation of Chicanas' work is contested terrain. Norma Alarcón, Maylei Blackwell, Rosa Linda Fregoso, Ellie Hernández, Norma Klahn, and Olga Nájera-Ramírez theorize the politics of representation in dialogue with scholars and artists who do not focus primarily on Chicanas. Further, in dealing with previously silenced or unsanctioned ideas, concepts, and perspectives, many of our authors have coined new terms and created hybrid genres for articulating their views and ideas.

Elba Sánchez, a creative writer and poet, criss-crosses genres, using essays, poetry, and letters to delineate her trajectory as she immigrates to this country from Mexico. By using multiple metaphors—earth, water, ecosystems, cosmology—she outlines the complexity of forging a "mestiza consciousness" (Anzaldúa 1987). Her journey culminates in her becoming one of those "glorieta" writers who speaks truths to multiple constituencies. Renato Rosaldo, a poet and cultural anthropologist, becomes part of those constituencies as he "writes back" through a mix of letters and commentary. He suggests using the notion of *lengualidades* to underscore the languages, tensions, and translations of multiply situated identities that Sánchez describes. His blending of genres further complicates this metaphor of lengualidades and "speaks to" the multiplicity Sánchez captures in her writing.

Maylei Blackwell, a historian and cultural theorist, contests the masculinist histories of the Chicano movement through the memories and stories of women involved with Las Hijas de Cuauhtémoc, a Chicana feminist group active in the 1960s and 1970s. She explores how the telling of social movement history is political and has implications for current identity formations and boundaries. She argues that by disrupting the discursive terrain of political meaning, the Hijas de Cuauhtémoc were able to maneuver, contest, and negotiate a Chicana feminist project. Anna NietoGomez, one of the activists who contributed her oral history to Blackwell's project, responds. Using Blackwell's essay as a point of departure, she elaborates further the complex relations that Chicanas had in the community, with other Chicana groups, and with Women of Color.

Norma E. Cantú discloses the mental and physical processes that she underwent in writing her award-winning novel, *Canícula*. In her essay, Cantú shares with the reader the processes and influences that led her to stretch and skillfully combine conventional genres to create a new form that she names "fictional autobioethnography." Using photographs to trigger memories of, by, and about her family, *Canícula* tells a story of a girl's life experiences growing up along the U.S.–Mexico border. In so doing, Cantú joins a growing cadre of experimental writers who have purposefully drawn from multiple disciplines and challenged generic boundaries. Anthropologist Ruth Behar, herself a prominent figure among experimental writers, responds to Cantú's essay. Wholeheartedly endorsing and even celebrating Cantú's accomplishment, Behar nonetheless raises a concern that such writing often comes with certain "costs." Cantú and Behar's dialogue, like the novel, reaches beyond traditional genre structures and tells a story of the unreliable nature of memory.

Literary critic Norma Klahn situates women's autobiographical fictions and her own interpretation in Emma Pérez's (1999) "decolonial imaginary." In this creative literary space, subjects construct their identities, languages, and memories through the oppositional political formation of feminism. Going beyond cultural theory, Klahn historicizes and analyzes texts by Sandra Cisneros, Mary Helen Ponce, Norma E. Cantú, and Pat Mora and argues that they explicitly mark spatial configurations in their emplotments of identity. By focusing on the centrality of home and providing critical perspectives on the family, these Chicanas "talk back" to Chicano nationalist discourse and patriarchy more generally from what she defines as a differently constituted form of autobiography. Klahn reinserts these writers' agency, culture, and language into history through their own literary forms. Mexican cultural critic Claire Joysmith points out the transgressive nature of Klahn's intervention and the autobiographical texts of Chicanas who claim differently their Mexicanidades—Mexican identities. Particularly in Mexico, where Chicana literature is often not translated into Spanish and rarely is read, the politics of representation of Mexicanidades becomes more complex and contingent.

In her reading of *Gulf Dreams* by Emma Pérez, Ellie Hernández insightfully deconstructs this innovative novel, which she sees as disrupting traditional Chicana/Mexicana cultural representations. Studying it in dialogue with Pérez's theories on sexuality and desire, Hernández analyzes the ways in which Pérez writes outside of conventional autobiographical narratives by using a disembodied voice to represent the psychic fragmentation of Chicanas. Pérez sees Chicanas as subjects of colonial legacies that have denied Women of Color, specifically lesbians, a voice in history. In his response, film and cultural critic Sergio de la Mora recognizes Hernández's contribution to Chicana lesbian scholarship, placing her with other Chicana critics of her generation, such as Yvonne Yarbro-Bejarano, Alicia Gaspar de Alba, and Mary Patricia Brady. De la Mora furthers the discussion on the ways colonial violence, particularly sexual violence as depicted in the novel, has always been an effective strategy for mobilizing patriarchal property rights that exert and maintain domination.

In her study of the poetics of the *ranchera*, anthropologist and folklorist Olga Nájera-Ramírez analyzes the constructed nature of this popular form, focusing both on the melodramatic imagination that informs its content and its performative aspect, which women deploy subversively. Nájera-Ramírez's contribution complicates previous treatments of this genre, demonstrating that this form, especially when appropriated by women, is multivalent and challenges traditional gender roles. In his response (written in Spanish), Mexican cultural critic José Manuel Valenzuela Arce explores melodrama in relation to urban migrations and the ways the ranchera song emerges as a privileged expressive form. His analysis acknowledges the significance of gender and the ways Nájera-Ramírez's article calls attention to a feminist intervention in this predominantly patriarchal genre. Rebecca Gámez's translation into English of Valenzuela's response makes this dialogue accessible to other audiences.

Through a series of oral histories, anthropologist Patricia Zavella is literally in dialogue with Chicanas and Mexicanas. She explores how compliance through silence affirms repressive systems of sexuality based in Catholic and cultural prescriptions of normative sexual behaviors. Zavella transgresses these silences by inviting these women to talk about how heterosexual and lesbian Mexicanas/Chicanas disrupt these sexual ideologies through resistive practices and verbal expressions. She argues that by historicizing these women's experiences, we see the transnational nature of discourse and practice that links second-generation Chicanas and Mexicana immigrants regarding sexuality. Social psychologist Michelle Fine further underscores the intricate conversational ripples of "talkin' sex" by responding to Zavella in epistolary form. Crossing disciplines, spaces, and genres, this disruptive conversation engages readers as actors and provokes yet more talking.

Transgressing the disciplinary constraints of her training in quantitative social psychology, Aída Hurtado turns to the borderlands of oral history, feminist *testimonio*, and cultural studies to make sense of a Mexican woman's migrations between Mexico, South Texas, and the Midwest in the 1960s. Inocencia's story is a journey toward eventual redemption despite the many obstacles placed by family expectations, the labor market, and the social and personal travails that Mexican women have to negotiate. Hurtado makes a powerful argument that, despite what on the surface seem like conventional expectations of family bliss, Inocencia's life embodies the independence, autonomy, and strength that constitute a feminism unrecognized in academic theories. Historian Gabriela Arredondo finds remarkable parallels in the experiences of Mexicanas who migrated through Texas, dispersing throughout the Midwest two generations before Inocencia. Like Inocencia, they labored to create independent lives for themselves and their children. These earlier women also confronted racialization, violence, and discrimination, all of which worked to erase their particular experiences. By giving voice to the lives of these women, this dialogue across generations fights that erasure (historic and academic) and acknowledges the value of individually lived experiences.

Artist and scholar Amalia Mesa-Bains contributes an insightful essay on *domesticana*, a Chicana feminist aesthetic practice of taking scrap materials found in the everyday to create something new. The artistic production, offered with style and humor, becomes a subversive act that defiantly challenges patriarchy and colonization. Art historian Jennifer González responds to Mesa-Bains's essay by first underscoring the need to create new terms. She forcefully argues that the creation of new labels is crucial to fully appreciating the aesthetic innovations produced outside the narrow boundaries of mainstream art. Noting that the practice of domesticana is characterized by such principles as paradox, humor, biculturality, and subversion, González provocatively suggests that domesticana may be at play in other genres or venues as well.

Our intention in this book is to create dialogues between authors and discussants and to provoke a multidimensional rippling of talk among many scholars. Cultural critic Rosa Linda Fregoso analyzes the gender dynamics of the film *Lone Star* as read against the interpretation provided by Chicano folklorist José Limón, who initially read the film against Fregoso's interpretation. Both of these scholars are acting, reacting, and reconsidering the points in their subsequent productions in response to their debate, giving us, their readers, a multilayered interpretation of the film. Cultural critic Ann duCille weighs in with her response to both Fregoso's and Limón's essays and reacts to the multidimensional cacophony produced by their exchange. Read from her perspective as an African American woman, duCille inserts an analysis of the Africanist presence in the film. In the end, the richness of the dialogue moves beyond what is usually offered by one critic's interpretation.

In her essay, literary and cultural critic Norma Alarcón questions critical practices that continue to marginalize Women of Color as she engages contemporary critics such as Lacan, Derrida, Kristeva, and Butler. Opening a space for her own intervention, Alarcón studies Anzaldúa's text *Borderlands/La Frontera: The New Mestiza* as a deconstruction of colonizing Western paradigms and as an attempt to repossess the borderlands in polyvalent modes that go beyond earlier Chicano-coded appropriations. Alarcón argues that Anzaldúa reinscribes gynetics through the textual production and positionality of a "mestiza consciousness," mapping a third space outside hegemonic nationalist discourse as well as a patriarchal ethnonational oppositional consciousness. In response, cultural and literary critic Marcia Stephenson stresses the historicity of the term *mestiza* as she turns to the Andean region, another geopolitical space marked by the legacy of colonization. There the term *mestizo* is synonymous with ethnic and political acculturation. In this space where mestizaje is legitimized by modernization projects, the native Andean woman, says Stephenson, is excluded both as a historical presence and as a speaking subject. Nevertheless, Stephenson studies a recent text by an Aymara woman, María Eugenia Choque Quispe, and the ways she has retheorized the feminine both within and against the Bolivian and ethnonational "family romance."

Collectively, these essays point to the spaces of creative responses that signal women's refusal to be silenced as they emerge and speak out in interviews, art, music, and literature. The essays capture the lived realities, creative expressions, and politics of representation in Chicana feminisms. Through this anthology we hope to contribute to the growing research field of Chicana studies and to the ways it converses with Latina/o studies, Ethnic studies, Gender and Feminist studies, Gay and Lesbian studies, and Cultural studies. Indeed, we hope that by situating this project within critical debates that are addressing inter/intraethnic questions nationally and cross-border issues transnationally, we will create and expand a space of productive and continuing dialogue in an increasingly interconnected world.

NOTES

1. See Alarcón 1990; Hurtado 1989, 1996b, 1997; Orozco 1986; Sandoval 1990; Zavella 1989.

2. See Baca Zinn et al. 1986; Blackwell 2000; Córdova 1994; de la Torre and Pesquera 1993; A. García 1989; Hurtado 1996a, 1997; Zavella 1989.

3. See J. García 1981; Hurtado 1997; Hurtado and Arce 1987.

4. See Cuádraz 1997; Hurtado and García 1994; Valenzuela 1999; Gándara 1995.

5. See Chávez 1991; Hondagneu-Sotelo 1994; Romero 1992; Ruiz 1987.

6. See Ruiz 1998; Goldman 1994; Gaspar de Alba 1998; hooks 1995; Lipsitz 1990.

7. See Chávez 1991; Flores and Benmayor 1997; D. Gutiérrez 1995.

8. See Klahn 1994; Zavella 1997; Nájera-Ramírez 1989, 1994, 1996, 2002; Kaplan, Alarcón, and Moallem 1999.

9. See Coyle, Hershatter, and Honig 1984; Flores and Benmayor 1997; Friaz 2000; Romero 1992; Ruiz 1987; Soldatenko 2000.

10. See Ruiz 1987; Romero 1992; Zavella 1997; Pesquera 1997; Segura 1992.

11. See Baca 1990, 1993; Broyles 1986, 1989, 1994; Cantú 1995; Cisneros 1994; Mora 1993; Pérez 1996; Yarbro-Bejarano 1985, 1986, 1991, 1994; Mesa-Bains 1990.

12. This is captured in a number of multidisciplinary anthologies: Moraga and Anzaldúa 1983; Moraga 1983; Anzaldúa 1987, 1990; Del Castillo 1990; Trujillo 1991; Alarcón et al. 1993; de la Torre and Pesquera 1993; Cantú and Nájera-Ramírez 2002.

13. See Del Castillo 1990; Delgado Bernal 1998; M. Gutiérrez 1999.

14. See Gordon and Newfield 1996; Grewal and Kaplan 1994; Lamphere, Ragoné, and Zavella 1997; Mohanty, Russo, and Torres 1991; Warhol and Herndl 1997.

15. Alexander and Mohanty 1997; Crenshaw 1989; Davis 1981; Lowe 1996.

16. Acevedo et al. 2001; Alarcón, Castillo, and Moraga 1989; Anzaldúa 1990; Boza, Silva, and Valle 1986; Fernández 1994; Gómez, Moraga, and Romo-Carmona 1983; Ramos 1987; Rebolledo and Rivero 1993; Ruiz and DuBois 1994; Vigil 1987 [1983]; Fregoso 1984.

WORKS CITED

Acevedo, Luz del Alba, Norma Alarcón, Celia Alvarez, Ruth Behar, Rina Benmayor, Norma E. Cantú, Daisy Cocco de Filippis, Gloria Holguín Cuádraz, Liza Fiol-Matta, Yvette Flores-Ortiz, Inés Hernández-Avila, Aurora Levins Morales, Clara Lomas, Iris López, Mirtha N. Quintanales, Eliana Rivero, Caridad Souza, and Patricia Zavella. 2001. *Telling to Live: Latina Feminist Testimonios.* Durham, NC: Duke University Press.

Alarcón, Norma. 1990. "The Theoretical Subject(s) of *This Bridge Called My Back* and Anglo-American Feminism." Pp. 356–69 in *Making Face/Making Soul: Haciendo Caras,* ed. Gloria Anzaldúa. San Francisco: Aunt Lute Foundation Books.

Alarcón, Norma, Ana Castillo, and Cherríe Moraga. 1989. *The Sexuality of Latinas.* Special issue of *Third Woman* 4.

Alarcón, Norma, Rafaela Castro, Emma Pérez, Beatriz Pesquera, Adaljiza Sosa Riddell, and Patricia Zavella, eds. 1993. *Chicana Critical Issues: Mujeres Activas en Letras y Cambio Social.* Berkeley: Third Woman Press.

Alexander, M. Jacqui, and Chandra Talpade Mohanty, eds. 1997. *Feminist Genealogies, Colonial Legacies, Democratic Futures.* New York: Routledge.

Anzaldúa, Gloria. 1987. *Borderlands/La Frontera: The New Mestiza.* San Francisco: Spinsters/Aunt Lute.

————, ed. 1990. *Making Face/Making Soul: Haciendo Caras. Creative and Critical Perspectives by Feminists of Color.* San Francisco: Aunt Lute Foundation Books.

Baca, Judith. 1990. "World Wall: A Vision of the Future without Fear." *Frontiers* 14(2): 81–85.

————. 1993. "Uprising of the Mujeres." P. 272 in *Chicana Critical Issues,* ed. Norma Alarcón, Rafaela Castro, Emma Pérez, Beatriz Pesquera, Adaljiza Sosa Riddell, and Patricia Zavella. Berkeley: Third Woman Press.

Baca Zinn, Maxine, Lynn Weber Cannon, Elizabeth Higginbotham, and Bonnie Thornton Dill. 1986. "The Costs of Exclusionary Practices in Women's Studies." *Signs: Journal of Women in Culture and Society* 11(21): 290–303.

Blackwell, Maylei. 2000. "Geographies of Difference: Mapping Multiple Feminist Insurgencies and Transnational Public Cultures in the Americas." Ph.D. diss., University of California, Santa Cruz.

Boza, Maria del Carmen, Beverly Silva, and Carmen Valle, eds. 1986. *Nosotras: Latina Literature Today.* Binghamton, NY: Bilingual Review Press.

Broyles, Yolanda Julia. 1986. "Women in El Teatro Campesino: ¿Apoco Estaba Molacha La Virgen de Guadalupe?" Pp. 162–87 in *Chicana Voices: Intersections of Class, Race and Gender,* ed. Teresa Córdova, Norma Cantú, Gilberto Cárdenas, Juan García, and Christine M. Sierra. Austin: Center for Mexican-American Studies, University of Texas at Austin.

————. 1989. "Toward a Re-Vision of Chicano Theater History: The Women of El Teatro Campesino." Pp. 209–38 in *Making a Spectacle: Feminist Essays on Contemporary Women's Theater,* ed. Linda Hart. Ann Arbor: University of Michigan Press.

————. 1994. *El Teatro Campesino: Theater in the Chicano Movement.* Austin: University of Texas Press.

Cantú, Norma Elia. 1995. *Canícula: Snapshots of a Girlhood en la Frontera.* Albuquerque: University of New Mexico Press.

Cantú, Norma, and Olga Nájera-Ramírez. 2002. *Chicana Traditions: Continuity and Change.* Champaign: University of Illinois Press.

Castañeda, Antonia I. 1993. "Sexual Violence in the Politics and Policies of Conquest: Amerindian Women and the Spanish Conquest of Alta California." Pp. 15–33 in *Building with Our Hands: New Directions in Chicana Studies,* ed. Adela de la Torre and Beatriz M. Pesquera. Berkeley: University of California Press.

Castillo, Ana. 1995. *Massacre of the Dreamers: Essays on Xicanisma.* Albuquerque: University of New Mexico Press.

Catanzarite, Lisa. 2000. " 'Brown Collar Jobs': Occupational Segregation and Earnings of Recent-Immigrant Latinos." *Sociological Perspectives* 43(1): 45–75.

Chávez, Leo R. 1991. *Shadowed Lives: Mexican Undocumented Immigrants.* New York: Harcourt Brace Jovanovich.

Cisneros, Sandra. 1994. *Loose Woman.* New York: Knopf.

Córdova, Teresa. 1994. "The Emergent Writings of Twenty Years of Chicana Feminist Struggles: Roots and Resistance." Pp. 175–202 in *The Handbook of Hispanic Cultures in the United States,* ed. Félix Padilla. Houston: University of Houston, Arte Público Press.

Coyle, Laurie, Gail Hershatter, and Emily Honig. 1984. "Women at Farah: An Unfinished Story." Pp. 227–77 in *A Needle, a Bobbin, a Strike: Women Needleworkers in America*, ed. Joan M. Jensen and Sue Davidson. Philadelphia: Temple University Press.

Crenshaw, Kimberlé. 1989 "Demarginalizing the Intersection of Race and Sex: A Black Feminist Critique of Anti-discrimination Doctrine, Feminist Theory, and Anti-racist Politics." Pp. 383–95 in *Feminist Legal Theory: Foundations*, ed. D. Kelly Weisberg. Philadelphia: Temple University Press.

Cuádraz, Gloria. 1997. "Chicana/o Generations and the Horatio Alger Myth." *Thought and Action: NEA Journal of Higher Education* 23(1): 103–20.

Davis, Angela. 1981. *Women, Race and Class*. New York: Vintage Books.

de la Torre, Adela, and Beatriz M. Pesquera, eds. 1993. *Building with Our Hands: New Directions in Chicana Studies*. Berkeley: University of California Press.

Del Castillo, Adelaida, ed. 1990. *Between Borders: Essays on Mexicana/Chicana History*. Encino, CA: Floricanto Press.

Delgado Bernal, Dolores. 1998. "Using a Chicana Feminist Epistemology in Educational Research." *Harvard Educational Review* 68(4): 555–79.

Fernández, Roberta, ed. 1994. *In Other Words*. Houston: Arte Público Press.

Flores, William V., and Rina Benmayor, eds. 1997. *Latino Cultural Citizenship: Claiming Identity, Space, and Rights*. Boston: Beacon Press.

Fregoso, Rosa Linda, ed. 1984. *Bearing Witness/Sobreviviendo—An Anthology of Writing and Art by Native American/Latina Women*. Special issue of *Calyx (A Journal of Art and Literature by Women)* 8(2).

Friaz, Guadalupe M. 2000. " 'I Want to Be Treated as an Equal': Testimony from a Latina Union Activist." *Aztlán* 20(1–2): 195–202.

Gándara, Patricia. 1995. *Over the Ivy Walls: The Educational Mobility of Low-Income Chicanos*. Albany: State University of New York Press.

García, Alma. 1989. "The Development of Chicana Feminist Discourse, 1970–1980." *Gender and Society* 3(2): 217–38.

García, John A. 1981. " 'Yo Soy Mexicano'. . . : Self-Identity and Sociodemographic Correlates." *Social Science Quarterly* 62(1): 88–98.

Gaspar de Alba, Alicia. 1998. *Chicano Art: Inside/Outside the Master's House, Cultural Politics and the CARA Exhibition*. Houston: University of Texas Press.

Goldman, Shifra. 1994. *Dimensions of the Americas: Art and Social Change in Latin America and the United States*. Chicago: University of Chicago Press.

Gómez, Alma, Cherríe Moraga, and Mariana Romo-Carmona. 1983. *Cuentos: Stories by Latinas*. New York: Kitchen Table, Women of Color Press.

González, Deena. 1999. *Refusing the Favor: The Spanish-Mexican Women of Santa Fe, 1820–1880*. New York: Oxford University Press.

Gordon, Avery F., and Christopher Newfield, eds. 1996. *Mapping Multiculturalism*. Minneapolis: University of Minnesota Press.

Grewal, Inderpal, and Caren Kaplan, eds. 1994. *Scattered Hegemonies*. Minneapolis: University of Minnesota Press.

Gutiérrez, David. 1995. *Walls and Mirrors: Mexican Americans, Mexican Immigrants, and the Politics of Ethnicity*. Berkeley: University of California Press.

Gutiérrez, Maria Elena. 1999. "The Racial Politics of Reproduction: The Social Construction of Mexican-Origin Women's Fertility." Ph.D. diss., University of Michigan, Ann Arbor.

Hayes-Bautista, David E., Aída Hurtado, R. Burciaga Valdez, and A. C. R. Hernández. 1992. *No Longer a Minority: Latinos and Social Policy in California.* Los Angeles: University of California, Chicano Studies Research Center.

Herrera-Sobek, Maria, and Helena María Viramontes, eds. 1995. *Chicana (W)rites on Word and Film.* Berkeley: Third Woman Press.

Hondagneu-Sotelo, Pierette. 1994. *Gendered Transitions: Mexican Experiences of Immigration.* Berkeley: University of California Press.

hooks, bell. 1989. *Talking Back: Thinking Feminist, Thinking Black.* Boston: South End Press.

———. 1995. *Art on My Mind: Visual Politics.* New York: New Press.

Hurtado, Aída. 1989. "Reflections on White Feminism: A Perspective from a Woman of Color." Pp. 155–86 in *Social and Gender Boundaries in the United States*, ed. Sucheng Chan. Lewiston, NY: Edwin Mellen Press.

———. 1996a. *The Color of Privilege: Three Blasphemies on Race and Feminism.* Ann Arbor: University of Michigan Press.

———. 1996b. "Strategic Suspensions: Feminists of Color Theorize the Production of Knowledge." Pp. 372–92 in *Knowledge, Difference, and Power: Essays Inspired by Women's Ways of Knowing*, ed. Nancy Rule Goldberger, Jill Mattuck Tarule, Blythe McVicker Clinchy, and Mary Field Belenky. New York: Basic Books.

———. 1997. "Understanding Multiple Group Identities: Inserting Women into Cultural Transformations." *Journal of Social Issues* 53(2): 299–328.

———. 1998. "*Sitios y lenguas:* Chicanas Theorize Feminism." *Hypatia* 13(2): 135–59.

Hurtado, Aída, and Carlos H. Arce. 1987. "Mexicans, Chicanos, Mexican Americans, or Pochos . . . ¿Que Somos? The Impact of Language and Nativity on Ethnic Labeling." *Aztlan* 17: 103–29.

Hurtado, Aída, David E. Hayes-Bautista, R. Burciaga Valdez, and A. C. R. Hernández. 1992. *Redefining California: Latino Social Engagement in a Multicultural Society.* Los Angeles: University of California, Chicano Studies Research Center.

Hurtado, Aída, and Eugene E. García, eds. 1994. "The Educational Achievement of Latinos: Barriers and Successes." Santa Cruz: University of California Eligibility Study.

Hurtado, Aída, Patricia Gurin, and T. Peng. 1997. "Social Identities—A Framework for Studying the Adaptations of Immigrants and Ethnics: Mexicans in the United States." Pp. 243–267 in *New American Destinies: A Reader in Contemporary Asian and Latino Immigration*, ed. D. Y. Hamamoto and R. D. Torres. New York: Routledge.

Kaplan, Caren, Norma Alarcón, and Minoo Moallem, eds. 1999. *Between Woman and Nation: Nationalisms, Transnational Feminisms, and the State.* Durham, NC: Duke University Press.

Klahn, Norma. 1994. "Writing the Border: The Languages and Limits of Representation." *Journal of Latin American Cultural Studies* 3(1–2): 29–55.

Lamphere, Louise, Helena Ragoné, and Patricia Zavella, eds. 1997. *Situated Lives: Gender and Culture in Everyday Life.* New York: Routledge.

Limón, José E. 1981. "The Folk Performance of '*Chicano*' and the Cultural Limits of Political Ideology." Pp. 197–225 in "*And Other Neighborly Names": Social Process and Cultural Image in Texas Folklore,* ed. R. Bauman and R. D. Abrahams. Austin: University of Texas Press.

Lipsitz, George. 1990. *Time Passages: Collective Memory and American Popular Culture.* Minneapolis: University of Minnesota Press.

Lowe, Lisa. 1996. *Immigrant Acts: On Asian American Cultural Politics.* Durham, NC: Duke University Press.

Mauricio Gastón Institute for Latino Community Development and Public Policy. 1994. "Barriers to Employment and Work-Place Advancement of Latinos." Unpublished report to The Glass Ceiling Commission, U.S. Department of Labor.

Mesa-Bains, Amalia. 1990. "Quest for Identity: Profile of Two Chicana Muralists. Based on Interviews with Judith F. Baca and Patricia Rodriguez." Pp. 68–83 in *Signs from the Heart: California Chicano Murals,* ed. Eva Sperling Cockcroft and Holly Barnet-Sánchez. Venice, CA: Social and Public Art Resource Center.

Mohanty, Chandra Talpade, Ann Russo, and Lourdes Torres, eds. 1991. *Third World Women and the Politics of Feminism.* Bloomington: Indiana University Press.

Mora, Pat. 1993. *Nepantla: Essays from the Land in the Middle.* Albuquerque: University of New Mexico Press.

Moraga, Cherríe. 1983. *Loving in the War Years: lo que nunca pasó por sus labios.* Boston: South End Press.

Moraga, Cherríe, and Gloria Anzaldúa, eds. 1983. *This Bridge Called My Back: Writings by Radical Women of Color.* Watertown, MA: Persephone Press.

Morales, Rebecca, and Frank Bonilla, eds. 1993. *Latinos in a Changing U.S. Economy.* Newbury Park, CA: Sage Publications.

Nájera-Ramírez, Olga. 1989. "Social and Political Dimensions of Folklórico Dance: The Binational Dialectic of Residual and Emergent Culture." *Western Folklore* 48 (January): 15–32.

———. 1994. "Engendering Nationalism: Identity, Discourse, and the Mexican Charro." *Anthropological Quarterly* 67(1): 1–14.

———. 1996. "The Racialization of a Debate: The Charreada as Tradition or Torture?" *American Anthropologist* 98(3):505–11.

———.2002. "Mounting Traditions: The Origin and Evolution of the Escaramuza Charra." In *Chicana Traditions: Continuity and Change,* ed. Norma Cantú and Olga Nájera-Ramírez. Champaign: University of Illinois Press.

Orozco, Cynthia E. 1986. "Sexism in Chicano Studies and the Community." Pp. 11–18 in *Chicana Voices: Intersections of Class, Race, and Gender,* ed. Teresa Córdova, Norma Cantú, Gilberto Cárdenas, Juan García, and Christine M. Sierra. Austin: Center for Mexican American Studies, University of Texas Press.

———. 1994. "Beyond Machismo, La Familia and Ladies Auxiliaries: A Historiography of Mexican-Origin Women's Participation in Voluntary Associations and Politics in the United States, 1870–1990." Pp. 37–77 in *Renato Rosaldo Lecture Series Monograph* 10. Palo Alto: Stanford University.

Pardo, Mary S. 1991. "Creating Community: Mexican American Women in Eastside Los Angeles." *Aztlán* 20(1–2): 39–72.

———. 1998. *Mexican American Women Activists: Identity and Resistance in Two Los Angeles Communities*. Philadelphia: Temple University Press.

Pérez, Emma. 1991. "Sexuality and Discourse: Notes from a Chicana Survivor." Pp. 159–84 in *Chicana Lesbians: The Girls Our Mothers Warned Us About*, ed. Carla Trujillo. Berkeley: Third Woman Press.

———. 1996. *Gulf Dreams*. Berkeley: Third Woman Press.

———. 1999. *The Decolonial Imaginary: Writing Chicanas into History*. Bloomington: Indiana University Press.

Pesquera, Beatriz. 1997. "In the Beginning He Wouldn't Lift Even a Spoon." Pp. 208–22 in *Situated Lives*, ed. Louise Lamphere, Helena Ragoné, and Patricia Zavella. New York: Routledge.

Pesquera, Beatriz M., and Denise A. Segura. 1993. "There Is No Going Back: Chicanas and Feminism." Pp. 95–115 in *Chicana Critical Issues*, ed. Norma Alarcón, Rafaela Castro, Emma Pérez, Beatriz Pesquera, Adaljiza Sosa Riddell, and Patricia Zavella. Berkeley: Third Woman Press.

Quintana, Alvina E. 1989. "Challenge and Counter-Challenge: Chicana Literary Motifs." Pp. 187–203 in *Social and Gender Boundaries in the United States*, ed. Sucheng Chan. Lewiston, NY: Edwin Mellen Press.

———. 1996. *Home Girls: Chicana Literary Voices*. Philadelphia: Temple University Press.

Ramos, Juanita, ed. 1987. *Compañera: Latina Lesbians (an Anthology)*. New York: Latina Lesbian History Project.

Rebolledo, Tey Diana, and Eliana S. Rivero. 1993. *Infinite Divisions: An Anthology of Chicana Literature*. Tucson: University of Arizona Press.

Romero, Mary. 1992. *Maid in the U.S.A.* New York: Routledge.

Ruiz, Vicki L. 1987. *Cannery Women, Cannery Lives: Mexican Women, Unionization, and the California Food Processing Industry 1930–1950*. Albuquerque: University of New Mexico Press.

———. 1998. *From Out of the Shadows: Mexican Women in Twentieth-Century America*. New York: Oxford University Press.

Ruiz, Vicki L., and Ellen Carol Dubois. 1994. *Unequal Sisters: A Multicultural Reader in U.S. Women's History*. New York: Routledge.

Saldívar-Hull, Sonia. 2000. *Feminism on the Border: Chicana Gender Politics and Literature*. Berkeley: University of California Press.

Sandoval, Chela. 1990. "The Struggle Within: A Report on the 1981 N.W.S.A. Conference." Pp. 55–71 in *Making Face/Making Soul: Haciendo Caras. Creative and Critical Perspectives by Feminists of Color*, ed. Gloria Anzaldúa. San Francisco: Spinsters/Aunt Lute.

———. 1991. "U.S. Third World Feminism: The Theory and Method of Oppositional Consciousness in the Postmodern World." *Genders* 10 (spring): 1–24.

———. 2000. *Methodology of the Oppressed*. Minneapolis: University of Minnesota Press.

Segura, Denise A. 1992. "Chicanas in White Collar Jobs: You Have to Prove Yourself More." *Sociological Perspectives* 35(1): 163–82.

Segura, Denise, and Beatriz Pesquera. 1992. "Beyond Indifference and Antipathy: The

Chicana Movement and Chicana Feminist Discourse." *Aztlán: A Journal of Chicano Studies* 19(2): 69–93.

Soldatenko, María Angelina. 2000. "Organizing Latina Garment Workers in Los Angeles." *Aztlán: A Journal of Chicano Studies* 20(1–2): 73–96.

Trujillo, Carla, ed. 1991. *Chicana Lesbians: The Girls Our Mothers Warned Us About.* Berkeley: Third Woman Press.

Valenzuela, Angela. 1999. *Subtractive Schooling: U.S. Mexican Youth and the Politics of Caring.* Albany: State University of New York.

Vigil, Evangelina, ed. 1987 [1983]. *Woman of Her Word: Hispanic Women Write, Revista Chicano-Riqueña.* 2d ed. Houston: Arte Público Press.

Warhol, Robyn R., and Diane Price Herndl, eds. 1997. *Feminisms: An Anthology of Literary Theory and Criticism.* New Brunswick, NJ: Rutgers University Press.

Yarbro-Bejarano, Yvonne. 1985. "Chicanas' Experience in Collective Theater: Ideology and Form." *Women and Performance* 2(2): 45–58.

———. 1986. "The Female Subject in Chicano Theater: Sexuality, 'Race,' and Class." *Theater Journal* 38(1): 389–407.

———. 1991. "De-constructing the Lesbian Body: Cherríe Moraga's *Loving in the War Years.*" Pp. 143–55 in *Chicana Lesbians: The Girls Our Mothers Warned Us About,* ed. Carla Trujillo. Berkeley: Third Woman Press.

———. 1994. "Gloria Anzaldúa's *Borderlands/La Frontera:* Cultural Studies, 'Difference,' and the Non-Unitary Subject." *Cultural Critique* (Cary, NC) fall (28): 5–28.

Zavella, Patricia. 1987. *Women's Work and Chicano Families: Cannery Workers of the Santa Clara Valley.* Ithaca: Cornell University Press.

———. 1989. "The Problematic Relationship of Feminism and Chicana Studies." *Women's Studies* 17: 24–36.

———. 1994. "Reflections on Diversity among Chicanas." Pp. 199–212 in *Race,* ed. Steven Gregory and Roger Sanjek. New Brunswick, NJ: Rutgers University Press.

———. 1996. "Feminist Insider Dilemmas: Constructing Identity with 'Chicana' Informants." Pp. 138–69 in *Feminist Dilemmas in Fieldwork,* ed. Diane L. Wolf. Boulder, CO: Westview Press.

———. 1997. "'The Tables Are Turned': Immigration, Poverty, and Social Conflict in California Communities." Pp. 136–61 in *Immigrants Out! The New Nativism and the Anti-Immigrant Impulse in the United States,* ed. Juan Perea. New York: New York University Press.

CHAPTER ONE

Cartohistografía: Continente de una voz

Cartohistography: One Voice's Continent

ELBA ROSARIO SÁNCHEZ

• • • • •

It began with a dream where I was physically transformed. I was no longer body and flesh, eyes, hair, and teeth, but hills, valleys, orchards, forests. I had metamorphosed into a mountain range with caves and volcanoes and bodies of water surging through me. As I extended my arms, I was a whole coast, and then I stretched into a continent. I was my own continent with many geographies. I could see lush forests, fields of abundance, the sands of desert terrain that were me. This was my physical landscape.

I began to think about that continent in my dream, that self, and about how my writing and poetry have been a discovery, an ongoing exploration of that self-territory. My writing has been a way to name the landscapes of emotions, to recognize those layers of experiences that have sculpted my ecosystem and have chiseled my herstory. As well, writing has been a path to forging my spiritual cosmology.

I began to write because I love to read, and because I remember vividly as a young reader scanning library shelves and listings, looking for authors with Latino-sounding names who might come close to describing and feeling my reality, who might connect me with my own identity. Octavio Paz could never do that for me, but he was guaranteed to be in almost every library I checked out. I wanted to read about the everyday life of other young Mexicanas, Chicanas[1]—others like me who live between, entre culturas, languages y lenguas, friends, families, worlds. I wanted and needed to

Nopalitos, painting by Daniel Sánchez-Glazer.

write as a way to fill the void of voices that didn't speak to my experience. I wanted to write porque en mi familia, yo no hablaba, unless I was spoken to. And what was I going to do with all my feelings, ideas, dreams, and turmoil? I wanted to chronicle biographical and fictional relatos, to make real, to give flesh to the word, to my and our story. I had to write because clearly, for our voices to be heard through time, they need to be passed from mouth to mouth, and they also need to be written. That is why our Chicana writings are vital. Because they enter into the realm of historical and creative documentation of who we are and have been, all at the same time. Our writings, en nuestros idiomas, are the testament of our vibrant resistance, as our metaphors, code switching, theories, visions, and worlds—real and imagined—give shape, texture, and human depth to the history of our very presence and resistance.

"Cuando desaparezcan los libros, las lenguas recontarán las historias." Eso es lo que me dijo mi "agüelita" una vez. He cargado sus palabras y consejos tucked in my rebozo, desde que las sentí, es decir, desde que las entendí. Español es y ha sido mi primera lengua. It is my conscious resistance en este English-only state. Español es otra conciencia, otro mundo. Spanish is the language of my cognitive self, of my dreams y recuerdos. Aprendí a cantar en español, to play adivinanzas and other games. De chica aprendí a inventar cuentos para que mi hermanita por fin se duermiera. Al terminar el quinto grado, a la edad de once años ya contaba, multiplicaba, dividía, sumaba y resolvía problemas matemáticos en español. ¿Inglés?, eso fue después, when I came to the United States.

I remember well my aching jaw, my face muscles hot and tight, tongue feeling twisted, contorting in strange ways, as I learned to mimic with my new English-speaking tongue. Before I learned to speak English, to understand it, the world was a confusing and frustrating blur of face, body, and hand gestures. I felt totally isolated outside of my home. I learned to speak English in six months. This was due in part to my awareness of the urgent need to survive in what I perceived to be, almost immediately, a hostile environment. English became even more critical when I realized how limited my father's own English really was. My mother didn't speak English at all. Within a year, I learned to spell and write English well enough to become the official family translator and secretary.

My English, Spanish, Spanglish, and other lengualidades have danced around each other and together en mi boca, casi forever, like seasoned partners on the dance floor, se siguen bien, sus vueltas y pasos bien coreografiados. Otras veces, chocan y hasta se tropiezan, una lengua con las otras. As a Chicana, mis lengualidades y sus hermanas culturas have been energized and expanded by the urgency, the positive, heart-pulsing beats and and spoken word world of hip hop culture that is a part of my son and daughter. My life has been enriched by these constant encuentros con otras y otros whose español y cultura are distinctly different from my own. El diálogo que hemos compartido ha expandido no sólo mis horizontes lingüísticos sino mi sentido y entendimiento del mundo, de mi gente y mí misma.

I trust that readers of this work will be linguistically and culturally savvy, polylingüe, comfortable with a certain amount of code switching (in English, Spanish, standard and nonstandard varieties, and others). Despite what many literature profs and editors out there skeptically say, I am confident that there is a significant and, dare I say, large reading audience that is comfortable with an array of lenguas. I am talking about an audience that vive una realidad mestiza, en el sentido de mezclada, que se ha expuesto a varias culturas y gentes, one that eats, breathes, dreams, and lives every day en diferentes y múltiples mundos y habla en code-switching, multilingual conciencias. My Chicana voice is singular or unique by its "Chicano" definition, its sociopolitical and historical context. At the same time, even

Carnalita Dancing, painting by Daniel Sánchez-Glazer.
Courtesy of Elba R. Sánchez and her family.

in its Chicananess, my voice may strike a familiar chord with those who have experienced immigration, those who on a daily basis switch and juggle identities and tongues and tangle with cultural conflicts, as they skillfully maneuver making a living, being with family, having a personal life, y todo lo demás.

My exposure to multilingualismo and my experience as an interpreter and translator have shown me that there are some words that encompass such complex concepts or realities in one language that they cannot be translated into another. Something definitely gets lost in the translation! One such word is tepalcate. It is impossible to translate the deep stir- rings that are elicited inside me by the musical sound of the Nahuatl word tepalcate. It is the feel of the word on my tongue, the history, the senses, the emotions that the word evokes, that give it meaning and definition. The English-Spanish dictionary translates tepalcate as "shard." How can "shard" possibly translate or give meaning to a word that is my umbilical cord, that links me to my mestizo reality? How can the sounds and smells of the water as it fills the jar, the vivid red of the wet clay, that are deeply imprinted in my mind and heart when I hear that living breathing word, become a real experience for someone else in the translation?

Tepalcate a Tepalcate[2]
estos hombres
de ojos pálidos
llegaron un día
queriéndolo todo
nos forzaron
de nuestro lugar sagrado
nuestra naturaleza sabia
donde hasta la más
chiquita yerba
tiene su lugar
su alma
nos arrojaron
a este frío hostil
pavimento gris
de mediocridad
donde miedo nos tienen
y donde nos hostigan
y aquí
como en muchos otros lugares
sólo rotos pedazos dispersados
les parecemos
de nuestra naturaleza
quisieron apartarnos
y nosotros
de todos modos pasamos
de mano a mano
capas de ceniza
que arraigamos
entre huesos
piedras y caracoles
bajo nuestro techo
entre diente y lengua
vuela la pájara amparada
de nuestra naturaleza

somos tepalcates
de barro y física fuerza
perduramos en la montaña
en los barrios
en la selva
tepalcate a tepalcate
nos reconocemos
somos caras en relieve
de una misma pieza

I will not translate poems like "Tepalcate a tepalcate." I could not do justice a la realidad de la palabra. At times, translation is frustration; there is no discourse to turn to. Even after breaking the word down, the greatest challenge to the translator or interpreter is to come as close as possible to a dignified expression and meaning of the word. There are times, therefore, when I refuse to translate. This is a deliberate act on my part. The untranslatable has to be approached in a different manner. La palabra desconocida necesita a more sensual "reading," one that challenges the reading or listening audience to be open and resourceful, to resort to other ways of "reading" the words or of "listening" for other meanings.

There has to be more than one way to experience a voice and a poem. That is why I sometimes say that you don't have to speak or understand the language in order to feel poetry. Poetry is not just the act of putting the thought on paper or the linear reading and approach to the poem. Poetry is about engaging the senses, the lilt of the words, the rhythm of the verse, the musicality and tone, the energizing and vivid delivery of the poet, his or her body language and movement. It's about the smells in the room as you listen to the poem (or the smells that the poem itself elicits); it's about the live audience's reaction, about "listening" with a different ear, about "feeling" and imagining at another level.

In the process of detailing my creative landscape, my voice has renamed and defined my own language and "individual" experience. Yet this "individual" voice has reached others along the way and I have been privileged to engage in a meaningful dialogue with people who see themselves reflected in my poems. Through this encuentro I found that my reality is in some significant way a part of theirs too, que compartimos una esencia humana. Al escribir mi cartohistografía, what I once believed were individual relatos have become encuentros of shared emotion(s), a link that forms and connects my path with the meeting and merging of others. In this encuentro between writer and reader/listener, ser a ser, there occurs the possibility of a powerful process. Como escritora y poeta, es mi lengua, la todo poderosa, la que hace y deshace. My polylingual lengua habla mi realidad, es mi realidad. Cuando digo cilantro, lo pruebo. Mi lengua es como una metáfora, viste colores vibrantes, define mi identidad en español, en English y en espanglish, y sprinkled with other stuff, my tongue questions and explains my pocha reality, da voz a mi conciencia, protesta en las marchas. Es mi lengua la que besa apasionadamente en varios idiomas (pa' que se entienda la traducción). My tongue names injustices I witness, a veces en voz de poeta, a veces en mi native lengua pocha, from my pocha perspective. Sometimes I use my university-trained and degreed tongue, when it is necessary. My lengua recuenta en color y olor de carne propia. It is my tongue that boldly translates those injustices in English, para que entiendan los que no las viven y los que por miopes no las ven. Mi lengua es un órgano vital. It is a gift, my power.

A Gift of Tongues
this tongue of mine sets fires
licking hot all in its path
scorches the old
announces the new
this tongue of mine
breaks through walls
setting free
imagery of feelings
odors of dreams
tasting the bitter
the rancid
quenching its thirst
this tongue of mine
invents the words
creating familiar signs
draws my days in bold hues
celebrates
affirming my world
this tongue of mine
opens wounds
heals the hurt
with warm breath savors
the other
the you

that is also me
this tongue of mine

The aim of this essay is to set a framework that looks at Chicanas' work and, more specifically, my own Chicana work. I want to see, for example, how the development of my identities as Mexican, immigrant, Chicana, Latina, mujer, ser natural y espíritu, and so on reflect in that work.

Because my writing has been a way of mapping a life, necesitaba tomar de varias palabras y conceptos para nombrar este proceso. The first word I began to take apart was cartography. From cartography I borrowed carto- as the art or technique of making maps or charts—el arte de trazar mapas geográficos. I then took histo- from history / historia: (del griego historia), en su sentido de relato de los acontecimientos y de los hechos dignos de memoria. In other words, a narrative of events, a story, a chronicle. También reclamo histo de historia en el sentido de desarrollo de la humanidad. En este caso, desarrollo de mi propia humanidad. I wanted to utilize a distinct meaning of histo-: as a chronological record of events of the life or development of an individual, a people. In this case, my own chronological development as a woman, a Chicana, the development of my political conscience, and my humanity.

My work is a part of history. Yet, by nature, it is herstory, one that seeks to encompass other women's stories and, further, might possibly encompass the story of a community. When it is recorded, herstory has the potential of being both individual and collective biography. The last part of this constructed term consiste de la palabra: grafía, del griego, graphé, acción de escribir. Significa un sistema de escritura, o el empleo de signos determinados para expresar las ideas. In English, -graphy: a process or method of writing or other graphic representation.

It is through the reconstruction of these terms that I arrived at the term cartohistografía or cartohistography. Its definition follows: Documentación de una historia o experiencia individual por medio de escritos, dibujos, u otra representación cuyos signos y significados son compartidos; amplía la geografía del espacio individual al espacio comunal. The historiography of an experience is chronicled and shaped through the writer's use of language, metaphor, cultural signifiers, the content of the work, the sociopolitical, historical, and cultural context in which the work is produced. The instant the cartohistographer's experience or vision is documented, it creates a physical, material space with its own geography, ecology, and cosmology.

Cartohistography may be useful as a means to gain understanding about the development of multiple identities and the political consciousness that is a part of each level of identity development. For example, in my case, cartohistography may be useful in revealing the development of the political conscience in my work, as my identities expanded from the former Mexicana to the Chicana, madre, poeta, colega, educadora, entre otras.

Mi trabajo, "el nuestro," me y nos afirma a sí mismas. Our work confirms our constant migrations, transformations, visions, and will. Our Chicana production, both literary and critical, exposes myriad voices and a purposeful dialectic; it is a testament to our resistance as we move and act on our future. Our production delineates our heritage. Es una expresión de quienes somos, de nuestro ollín o movimiento, our sociopolitical, cultural, and human development. This cartohistographical frame fits the expression of my work, theory, and my Chicana feminist framework.

As cartohistography, my writings explore the longitudes and latitudes of an ever-shifting map of life, where my conciencia is affected by physical elements and vice versa. My landscape is at times eroding, but rebuilding as well, always renewing, changing once again. Each time I or we write and chronicle our real and imagined spaces, we are consciously naming, putting on the map, so to speak, previously unknown territory. My objective as cartohistographer is to explore, to understand the depth and range of this terrain.

Como cartohistógrafa, estoy observando y definiendo científica y sensiblemente todo eso que llena mi espacio. I am making real herstory by placing my voice, mis escritos, in the context of a timeline of the cartohistography of the Mexicano Chicano and polycultural peoples or pueblos to which I belong. Digo pueblos o comunidades porque mi geografía se mueve, se expande, es flexible. My borders are fluid and I am an active member of many comunidades. Por ejemplo, pertenezco a las comunidades Chicana y Latina, soy de familia trabajadora, mujer, educadora, madre, trabajadora cultural, y agrego a éstas, varias otras comunidades. As Chicana artists and writers, our work and expression become a physical mediation of our herstory. Nuestros escritos consideran, miden y explican experiencias individuales que forman parte del rompecabezas de nuestra comunidad. Al publicar estos escritos exigimos reconocimiento de esa realidad.

I have linked various poems and stories in this essay to illustrate my own cartohistography. Espero que este trabajo muestre más que todo, una conciencia y voz desenvolviéndose. Como cartohistógrafa me esfuerzo para unir territorios antes separados, ésos que engendran potencial de convertirse en territorios comunes, tierras hermanas a través de nuestra literatura. Por medio de éste y de nuestros otros escritos, reflexionamos, analizamos,

creamos conciencia y proseguimos a la siguiente etapa de nuestro desarrollo. Como escritoras y cartohistógrafas trazamos lazos comunes en nuestro
continente de mujer.

Me siento continente
en mi sueño
me veo
continente
tierra firme
y frondosa
masa geográfica
de curvas y cuevas
trenzas de ríos
por mi espalda
se escurren
me oigo
canción hirviente
de corazón volcánico
epicentro
senos reventando
lava candente
pezones que se hinchan
al rozarse con el cielo
me pruebo
continente de sal
de espuma de mar
olas de una lengua
en algas enredada
entre la contracorriente
y el rojo ruboroso
de corales
acaricio
a piel de flor
sentimientos como
alfombras de esmeraldas
sedientas niñas de
aguas que fluyen
por mi ser entero
empapando
junglas espesas

todo esto
mío
dulce olor
de cocoa llena el aire
mis brazos y piernas
encarnadas montañas
y cañones que
como arcos
se estiran
entretejiendo
sentido y razón
tierra segura
en una tormenta
trazo las líneas
definiendo el mapa
de mi geografía
territorio de todavía
desconocidos rincones
estoy nombrando
reclamando
soy un continente

I Feel Myself a Continent
In my dream
I see myself
a continent
tierra firme
lush and leafy
geographic mass
of curves and caves
braids of rivers
draping across my back
I hear myself
simmering song
volcanic core
and epicenter
breasts bursting
white-hot lava
nipples swelling
as they caress the sky

I taste myself
salty continent
of ocean foam
waves of a tongue
in seaweed beds tangled
between the undertow
and blush red corals
I stroke
a piel de flor
emerald carpets of feelings
thirsty daughters
of waters flowing
within me
soaking
dense jungles
all this
is me
sweet smell
of cocoa fills the air
as my arms and legs
fleshed mountains
and canyons
stretch
weaving and tugging
meaning and reason
tierra segura
in a storm
I trace the lines
defining the map
of my geography
territory of still
unknown spaces
I am naming
claiming
I am a continent

I came to this country in August 1960 at the age of 11. Llegué purita Mexicana. There were no questions or confusion about my identity. I knew where I came from, who I was. I was proud to be Mexicana, and my parents reinforced my nationalist loyalties. Almost immediately after arriving in the United States, however, I learned that this new land and climate were not so hospitable. I can still hear mi mamá's constant reminder: "Aquí la gente piensa que los mexicanos somos cochinos, unos flojos. Siempre que salgas a la calle, tienes que salir bien vestida y pórtate bien. ¡No quiero que nadie te diga nada nunca! [Here people think that Mexicans are dirty and lazy. You must always dress and behave well when you are out. I don't ever want anyone to say anything to you!]"

When my father brought us from the state of Jalisco, in 1960, to the Black or African American Fillmore District of San Francisco, a small community of five Mexican families came together on Divisadero Street, settling themselves between Bush and California Streets. We lived in a two-bedroom flat directly above the Flying Chicken & Pizza Take-Out Restaurant and a couple of buildings down from the popular ten-cent launderette; nuestros hogares were filled with the sounds of children, español, y música. The smell of frijoles and roasted chiles filled the air. Our families were from small towns outside of Guadalajara, namely, la Experiencia and Atemajac, and were now transported within doors of each other, in San Francisco. I was the oldest of about seven Mexican kids on the block. We played together in each other's houses because our parents rarely let us play outside.

I felt different and apart from those outside of the small five-family Mexican community because I did not speak English.

Uprooted
endless is the wait
sleepless and cold
my trembling spirit
I am dormant shadow now
risking the flame
of my life
I reach
the darkened gateway
seeking refuge
there are no doors here as
the night opens in flight
and I feel about to fall
into the abyss

My first day of school, that September in 1960, was a garbled memory of sensory perceptions. Emerson Elementary School on Pine Street was a segregated school, only half a block from my house. When I first walked into Mrs. Anderson's fifth-grade class, I noticed that she, like all the children in the class, was Black. Smiles and gestures were the extent of our communication. En mi mente, mi voz gritaba en español, mientras yo trataba de controlar la multitud de sonidos que me parecían garabatos, por primera vez muda, sin lengua.

Desterrada
larga es la espera
de esta sombra adormecida
y tembloroso espíritu
en el frío trasnochador
me encuentro sin cobija
arriesgando el calor
de mi vida
no existe puerta
en este portón oscuro
donde busco refugio
la noche se abre en vuelo
y me siento
a punto de caer
en el precipicio

Still, I managed to make a few friends with the girls in class and learned to read face and body language. In the first week of school, Mrs. Anderson gave me a picture dictionary and I began copying words and sentences from the dictionary every day. Though I did not understand anything that went on, after a while I felt comfortable in the classroom with my teacher and classmates.

Krystal became my friend soon after I stepped through the door of the fifth-grade classroom. A month or so later, Krystal and I were waiting in line to jump rope during recess when I saw a tall skinny girl coming toward us. I didn't need a translation to read the anger on her face. She was coming straight toward us, swinging her arm with force from her hip to a raised fist. I struggled to understand her words, but they were not yet part of my minimal English vocabulary. I looked around. She pushed me as she screamed at me, and then I heard the word "Patty." I understood the word Patty. That was a girl's name. There was a Patty in our class. I thought, that's it! She's confusing me with Patty. But the girl was now even more and more upset and getting angrier. In the best English I could utter, I said to her, "My name Elba, not Patty. My name is . . ." Then she lunged at me. After what seemed like a long time, I heard a bell clang in my ear, and a teacher was standing beside us. The teacher separated us. I saw Krystal and Jackie and several of the other girls in our class gesture as they spoke to the teacher. The girl who called me Patty pointed to me as she spoke. I could not say a word.

I saw that angry girl in the yard many times after, but she appeared to have lost interest in me. Months later, and still confused over the incident, I learned from Krystal what that girl had been yelling about that day in the yard. "She was calling you a white paddy," said Krystal, who then explained, "It was an insult she was yelling at you, when she called you a paddy." "But Krystal," I responded, "my name is not Patty. I am NOT a paddy. And I am NOT WHITE!" I knew what I was. The thought that someone could see me or think of me as "white" and not Mexican confused and concerned me for days. This was my first dialogue with myself about who I was, how I saw myself, and about how others saw me or thought of me. Este fue mi primer choque with issues of color, race, and ethnicity. There were feelings of anger and hurt stirring and churning within, feelings I could not describe because I had no words for them, no vocabulary to name them. Nevertheless, even without being named, they were already a part of my experience and conciencia.

Comencé a escribir cartas a la familia en México poco después de llegar. Eran mi vínculo, mi única conexión a la familia, a las fiestas de cumpleaños, a los ritos y celebraciones que habían sido parte de mi vida diaria. Airmailed letters between my mother and father, who immigrated to Chicago years before, had been the only way to maintain familial ties now stretched by the distance of miles, la separación de meses y años. Letters embraced and delivered the bits of intimate news, the daily challenges, fears, frustrations, y pequeños triunfos de esa nueva vida. Letters were also reminders of the painful physical separation, the empty vastness of distance between us.

It is not by coincidence, then, that I choose to write stories in the form of letters. In our family, as far back as three generations (that I know of), migration, physical distance, uprooting, and separation have been a constant. Esta experiencia es compartida por muchas otras familias, no es única.

Cruzando Fronteras

A mi mamá, quien esperaba las cartas de
Chicago, donde se encontraba su "viejito"

perseguida por tu ausencia
el pito del cartero me hace correr
mis manos se adelantan
vuelan

extendiéndose como pista
para que sobre ellas
aterrice el sobre esperado
las conocidas letras
quizás haya una mancha
un hilo
un cabello
una foto
algo que me acerque
más a ti
al otro lado
sudas a chorros
te despiertan y acuestan
retorcijones
de entrañas
hambrientas
algunas mañanas
y muchas noches
te sientes morir
tan lejos de tu suelo
de tu gente
yo busco tu aliento
en esas cartas
quizás al desdoblar
las hojas
sentiré el calor
de tus manos
quizás
así llegue a mí
el olor de tu sudor
el sabor de tus palabras
risas besos
vía aérea
vía aérea
vía aérea

Letters, traditionally written by the women of the house, have been and will continue to be vital to herstoricizing our reality, passing it down to those who come after us. As women, Chicanas, Salvadoreñas, Puertorri- queñas, or however we identify and name ourselves, though our individual story is singular and in that way unique, we share the same pain of uprooting, immigration, cultural conflict, and physical and emotional separation. That is the legacy that links us, links many other women's (and families') stories.

My letter-writing link to México y la familia after my arrival in San Francisco and the United States was my Tía Inés. Tía Inés was bilingual because she had married a "gringo," a retired U.S. Army man. She also lived in Arizona on and off for several years, so she understood what it meant to live on the outside, in the United States. We began writing letters soon after my arrival in San Francisco. Inés, my mother's eldest sister, had been like a second mother to us. Tía Inés, who never had children, was the only one patient enough to listen to my prepubescent yearnings, my self-discoveries, my dreams and nightmares, and, of course, ella estaba enterada de todo lo que pasaba en la familia.

Two years after moving to the United States, right before my fourteenth birthday, mi mami and papi planned our first return visit to Mexico. I didn't know then just how revealing this trip would be for me. Only later did I realize that this was to be a painful journey into questioning myself, that I would be forced to look at myself through my own Mexican family's eyes. Before, my identity was questioned by an outsider, someone not from within mi cultura, ahora sería diferente.

I couldn't wait to get there. Finally, a trip HOME, a mi México lindo, a chance to visit la familia, to be in our tierra, entre nuestra gente. I missed the family warmth and closeness. I missed the life I had known, donde me sentía bien y donde me conocían.

TÚ NO ERES COMO NOSOTRAS

19 de agosto de 1964

Querida Tía,

Ya no aguanto. No puedo guardar el coraje que siento Tía. ¡Esa Rosalba me hizo sentir tan tan mal! Me hizo casi odiarla. Sentí, como si cada una de sus palabras fuera una piedra. Siempre fuimos como hermanas— desde niñitas. Nunca lo esperé de mi propia prima. Not my own family! It makes me both mad and sad, real sad.

Hay palabras y escenas que quedan grabadas en la memoria, así con su propio olor y amargura. Se hacen como cicatriz y se llevan muy, muy adentro. ¿No fue usted quién me dijo esto? Pues, así es Tía. No olvidaré la manera como caía el sol, como su luz se reflejaba en la ventana, cómo

Rosalba frunció la cara, su tono de voz, lo fuerte de sus palabras y la manera cómo me arrojó cada una de ellas. Me acuerdo hasta del olor de esa tarde, porque había hecho mucho calor todo el día, y para entonces ya empezaba a anochecer. Parecía que iba a llover otra vez. Todo eso, y más quedará grabado en mi corazón para siempre. It has been branded in my mind. Porque Tía, si Rosalba ya no piensa que yo soy de allá, que yo no soy mexicana, y acá me dicen que no soy de aquí, pues tengo que preguntar, entonces, ¿de dónde soy? ¿Quién soy? Y, ¿quién es ella para decirme a mí quién soy yo? Sí, no lo olvidaré. No le miento Tía, it hurt me real, real bad!

Déjeme contarle, eran las 5 o 6 de la tarde. Llegamos a la casa de mi Tía Victoria, y Rosalba y Tere estaban enfrente, en la sala. Bueno, lo que antes era sala, porque ahora tienen su salón de belleza allí. Todo se veía muy diferente. We hugged real hard when we first saw each other, y después de saludarnos y platicar un poco en la cocina, nos fuimos a sentar en el patio.

I sat on the floor with my back to the wall and tucked my legs to the side. El azulejo se sentía fresco. Rosalba sat in front of me in one of those old canvas lounge chairs. We were just starting to warm up to each other. We could hardly believe it. Two years since we last saw each other! That's a long time. Especially because our families used to spend almost every Sunday together, ever since we were babies. We practically lived in each other's houses as we were growing up.

Lo que pasó es que estábamos hablando de cuánto nos extrañamos. De cómo es diferente la vida de allá. De cómo era muy duro vivir y ser quienes somos allá,—pero nosotras seguimos siendo mexicanas, le dije yo.

—Tú ya no eres mexicana. Me interrumpió Rosalba.

—¿Cómo que ya no soy mexicana? Y tú, ¿por qué me dices eso?

—Porque tú ya no eres como nosotras. Nomás no lo eres. Ya no eres mexicana. Aquí te voy a dar un ejemplo muy sencillo. ¡Mira nomás cómo estás sentada! Una mujer mexicana no se va a sentar en el piso durante una visita como tú lo estás haciendo ahorita. ¿Me entiendes méndez? Por eso y por otras razones, la manera cómo te vistes, la manera cómo te llevas con la gente ahora, y hasta lo que dices, tus palabras. Has cambiado. Tú ya no eres de aquí. ¡Ni lo creas! ¡Eres una pocha! ¡Ya no eres mexicana!

I got up at that point, Tía, porque entre nos, I wasn't going to take that from her.

———¿Y quién eres tú, pa' decirme a mí, quién soy yo? Tú no eres nadie pa' . . .

—Ya, ya párenle las dos. ¡Ni modo que se vayan a pelear! Si apenas se acaban de ver. ¡Ustedes dos como siempre! Luego luego empiezan a picarse una a la otra. Parecen hermanas. Vamos a la cocina a tomar un vaso de agua fresca muchachas. Mi Tía Victoria me agarró de un brazo, a Rosalba del otro, y nos llevó a la cocina, sin darnos oportunidad de continuar.

Yo sólo escuchaba el eco de las palabras de Rosalba. Se repetían una y otra, y otra vez en mi mente. It was too much. I was so angry! I almost felt like crying, because I was sooo sooo angry. I could hear a ringing in my ears. How dare she! Es que ellas no entienden, Tía. They don't know what it's like to live here.

Well, okay. I have changed a little since I came to San Pancho, but Tía, I ask you, ¿qué tiene que ver que yo me sienta en el piso durante una visita? ¡Si estábamos entre familia! She's right, though. Mexican women don't sit on the floor like I did, unless they're by themselves or with their kids, right Tía?

Maybe I am changing, then. Because I don't see anything wrong with sitting on the floor like I did. And frankly, there are some rules about what it means to be a "Mexican woman" that I can no longer accept. Ya no sé si puedo aceptar el criterio mexicano; se me hace muy limitado. Es que tengo problemas con lo que es y no es aceptable en una mujer. I don't know what it means to be a "real" Mexican woman. Una "verdadera mujer." You mean I could be an "un-real" Mexican woman? What does that mean? See what I mean, Tía?

Es que mire, vivo acá, pero eso no quiere decir que me siento parte de todo esto. Yo no me siento parte de esta vida gringa, de estas costumbres gringas. Por lo menos, no de todas ellas. Anyway, es obvio para mí, that even if I wanted to be a part of all this, I couldn't be, because I'm a Mexican. Here, they'll always see me as a Mexican. Y en mis ojos, Tía, yo sigo siendo mexicana. No sé qué otra cosa llamarme.

Bueno, Tía, gracias por escucharme. By now, you probably already heard Tía Victoria's version. ¿Alguna vez le pasó a usted algo así? Le mando muchos besitos a usted y sus pajaritos. Saludos al Tío Bob. Reciba muchos abrazos y todo el cariño de su sobrina quien la extraña y quien sigue siendo quien es y soy . . . YO!

—La Chayito

"You're not like us. Eres una pocha. ¡Tú ya no eres mexicana!" Those words from my cousin's mouth shook what I knew until then as my rock-solid Mexican foundation of identity. I was desperately searching for solid ground to stand on. I struggled to respond immediately, to build a sense of myself, to feel a sense of rootedness.

> . . . my ancestors knew their grains
> like each of their offspring
> once planted
> they watered and nurtured them
> growing cycles
> of sprouting sons and daughters
> predicting harvests to come
> (excerpted from "Sowing Seeds")

"¡Tú ya no eres mexicana!"

I was hurt and angry. I felt rejected. This was my cousin, almost my sister, my own family, rejecting me, pointing out to me how I had changed already, forcing me to reexamine my identity. In my landscape, this was an earthquake, shaking hard the strata of former layers of myself. I began feeling tremors around my roots. I had to closely sift through my home soils, my adopted soils, redefine my borders and reshape my self-definition. I had to come to grips with an evolving identidad. After those initial moments of shock, I took inventory of what I know to be true, what cannot be taken away from me.

> . . . my grandparents gathered
> their thirteen children
> to live with the land
> of the land
> for the land
> cycles marked
> year after year
> these brothers and sisters
> my uncles and aunts
> on warm nights
> sat in a circle
> on the rooftop of the house
> en el rancho
> guitars and harmonicas
> their favorite songs

rising to the stars
canciones de amor
love songs
like sighs and soft whispers
sung to the moon
in the fields
and on the rooftops
cycles marked
year after year
after year

I first came to my sociopolitical and activista conciencia during my sophomore year in high school, when my social science teacher, Sister Mary Margaret, assigned an article about the United Farm Workers and César Chávez. I read about the farmworkers and their efforts to organize, about their lived injustices, the conditions they endured and in which they labored for close-to-nothing pay. This had a profound effect on me. I remember both tears and rage welling up inside of me. I had the strongest sense at that moment that I was of these people, that their struggle was also mine.

Mi conciencia despertó y abrazó la realidad de su lucha, que también era mía. Esta era mi gente y yo de ellos. I saw myself reflected in the faces of the farmworkers and their families. I saw my father's face in the faces of the men; in their hands, my father's arthritis-gnarled, working hands. These people were my own, and I embraced fully my newly recognized link with the huelguistas and with la causa. When I embraced this community of Raza fighting for our rights, I began my participation in my future. That year began the exploration of my political map, el despertamiento de mi conciencia, on this side of the border.

LOS FARMWORKERS

16 de febrero de 1965

Querida Tía Inés,

Espero que esté bien, en compañía de todos sus periquitos y pájaros. Le mando muchos corazoncitos por el Día de San Valentín. Saludos al Tío Bob y a su horrorosa (no le diga que así hablo de su perra), horrorosa, Chiquita. Ojalá y no esté ladre y ladre como lo hace cada vez que la veo. Es obvio que la Chiquita y yo no nos caemos bien, ¿verdad?

Tengo tanto que contarle. Este segundo año de high school apenas ha empezado y ya han pasado tantas cosas acá (y no sólo en mi vida personal). A veces veo las noticias en la tele y me asombro.

Mi maestra de estudios sociales este año es la Sister Margaret. Muchas amigas me habían dicho que era muy difícil su clase, que no me iba a gustar, that she gives a lot of homework! Well, one thing is true. She does give a lot of homework! But you know what? I love her class! It is one of my favorites. She makes me want to know what's going on in the world and why. She makes me look at things I never looked at before. For a nun, she's boss! (you know, ¡muy suave!)

Cada semana, la Sister Margaret nos hace leer "current events," de *Newsweek* magazine. Después, nos hace escribir sobre ellos, she organizes discussions in class, and speaks to us about words and issues like civil rights, discrimination, freedom, justice. Lo que está pasando a los negros en este país no está bien, Tía. Me da coraje ver cómo les echan los perros, los insultan y maltratan, y cuando protestan, les tiran agua con mangueras de alta presión, los golpean y para el colmo, después de todo esto, hasta los meten a la cárcel. They are just demanding the right to vote, to be heard. Imagínese. When I see that happening, I feel like it could happen to me, like it is happening to me. Me da miedo y me da rabia.

Sigo leyendo artículos sobre César Chávez y los farmworkers (son los campesinos y sus familias) que cosechan la uva por todo el estado. Tía, los farmworkers son humildes campesinos mexicanos que vienen de allá y trabajan muy duro, en condiciones horribles, from season to season, para cosechar los files (son los campos—es una de esas palabras que no le gustan a usted porque es español pocho, pero así se dice). Los farmworkers quieren formar una unión para protegerse de los abusos que sufren en los valles de California. Tía, no se imagina las condiciones en las que han tenido que vivir los farmworkers. ¡Y los niños! Siento tanta rabia y a la vez hasta me dan ganas de llorar porque no sé qué hacer. A veces me enojo conmigo misma por ser tan chillona. Lloro cuando me siento triste y lloro cuando me da rabia. ¿Qué le voy a hacer, Tía? Pero en fin, no sé si le puedo explicar bien lo que siento.

Los farmworkers y su unión, le llaman la UFW (United Farm Workers union), están organizando un boicoteo de uvas (para que se reconozca su derecho a tener una unión), y para que mejoren sus condiciones de trabajo. Yo voy a apoyarlos. Les voy a contar a mi papi y mami de lo que he leído y aprendido y les voy a pedir que no compren uvas. No sé si se ha reportado esto en las noticias allá. ¿Cómo lo ve usted, Tía? ¿Qué piensa usted de todo esto? Escríbame pronto, su sobrina chula, quien la quiere mucho.

—Chayito

Esta concientización política o despertamiento social, el grito y la lucha for civil rights in the grip of the sixties, inspired me to write and publish my first poem in the high school yearbook.

. . .

With no one to help me or be my friend
With no one to guide me or hold my hand
Why do they hate even my shadow?
Don't they know man minus love is hollow?
If ever a wrong their heart has committed
There's always a reason. Their fault is permitted.
Man needs the time, the love, the grace,
Not to be prejudiced of my race.

I wrote "The Price of Color" in 1967 (only the last section is included here). It was the height of the civil rights movement, anti–Vietnam War demonstrations, and, of course, the UFW organizing efforts. En este poema, se expresa una naciente conciencia, a getting-bolder tongue, y las cartas a México continuaban . . .

A LAS ESCONDIDAS

Mayo 2 Querida Tia,

Espero que usted esté bien y contenta y manteniéndose ocupada con las flores de su jardín. Siento mucho que sus cotorritas se hayan muerto. I'm sooo, so sorry, Tía. They were the prettiest little things y muy platica-doras. But please remember that you have lots of other "children" to take care of, todos sus otros pajaritos, la necesitan, así como la necesitamos todas las sobrinas latosas como yo.

This school year has been hard! I'm anxious to put it behind me and to start working this summer. I'll be working at St. Joseph's again. My official job title is Summer Relief Hospital Operator. Qué título más largo, ¿que no?

I'm glad I don't have to worry about looking for a summer job. That's what a lot of my high school friends are doing. Pobrecitas. Since I fin-ished my operator training last summer, I already know what to do. I'm a very lucky girl, Tía, to have a job. Podré ahorrar una parte de mi pago and help pay for my tuition (like last year). I can save some money, too. Pero a ver si me compro unos zapatos (me encantan los zapatos) and a winter coat, too. The first coat I buy for myself will have to be good quality, so it lasts.

¿Se acuerda que le había dicho de los farmworkers y de su unión? Pues, voy a contarle algo, pero por favor le pido que no lo cuente a NADIE. Es que ya sabe, si por alguna razón se enteran mis padres, ¡chintole, me hacen PURO MOLE! Pero no estoy haciendo nada malo, Tía. I'm doing what I think is right. What I think is just. Mire, I continue to read and find out more about the farmworkers. About a month and a half ago, Papi and I went to Mi Lindo Mazatlán (donde compramos la fruta y verdura, ¿se acuerda?). Anyway, pues there was this flyer with a huge UFW black eagle on it. That's the first thing I noticed from far away. The flyer said people from the UFW would be at Dolores Park on Saturday afternoon.

Tía, I had to go! So, les conté una mentirita a mi papi y mamá. I told them I was going downtown for two hours to check out coats. That's the only thing I could think of telling them, para ver si me daban permiso de salir. I gave them a specific amount of time that I would be gone so they wouldn't get suspicious. Lo único gacho de mi plan fue que in order to go downtown, my parents won't let me go, unless I dress up, con medias y toda la cosa. Siempre andan con su "¿qué va a pensar la gente?"

I took the J streetcar from our house y me dejó en el mero Parque Dolores. Ya había bastante gente. It was windy and gray. There was this guy. He was an organizer who had been a farmworker all his life. También habló una trabajadora del campo. I really liked what she said and how she spoke. She looked like she was a strong woman, but she looked very aged. Ella contó lo que es vivir y tratar de mantener a su familia, trabajando en los campos.

Tía, me dolió escuchar de los tantos sacrificios y las inhumanidades que ella y otra gente ha sufrido. No es justo. Nomás no lo es. Me hizo pensar también de cómo mis propios padres trabajan muy duro. Mi papi dice que trabajamos como burros y camellos aquí. Pero Tía, ¡¡trabajar en el campo es todavía peor!! Los campesinos también tienen derechos. ¿No cree usted? Because it's the farmworkers who are getting paid the least and the ranchers, los dueños, are the ones getting richer on the backs of los farmworkers y otros trabajadores como mi papi y mamá.

I got very rattled, Tía, because everything that I heard made sense to me. Me sentí muy emocional. Sentí tantas cosas, coraje, tristeza, más coraje. Me emocioné tanto que hasta empecé a gritar: ¡Viva La Huelga!

¡Viva la UFW! Se me enchinó el pellejo y se me pararon los vellitos al escuchar mi propio grito por primera vez. ¡Imagínese! Meanwhile, I was trying to keep warm and looking around me all the time to make sure I didn't run into someone who might know mi familia. I also kept looking at my watch to make sure I wasn't going to be late getting back home, si no . . .

Desde que aprendí de su causa he sentido que los farmworkers son mi gente. Su causa también se ha hecho la mía, en ese momento en el parque, decidí apoyar su lucha de alguna manera. I had Boycott Grapes and UFW pins, flyers, and an announcement for picketers needed at local Safeways on the following weekend, all tucked away in my purse. Decidí que iba a compartir lo que había aprendido. Le iba a pedir a mi papá que no comprara uvas, para apoyar a los farmworkers. What a big mistake, Tía!! BIG!

(Ya me estoy cansando de escribir, siento la mano muy caliente, pero le quiero contar todo.) I thought a good time to share what I learned would be el domingo, durante la comida. That's the only day we can all be together as family.

—I want to show you something, les dije. Apenas acabábamos de comer. I came back to the table with the pins and the UFW flyer. Les conté de la clase de Sister Margaret, de que estábamos leyendo current events (I thought it might help if they knew that my teacher was talking about it in class) y que así me había enterado de los farmworkers, y que por casualidad, el otro día, cuando regresaba del centro, los había oído hablar, y que yo pensaba que era justo el boicoteo contra las uvas y que por qué no los apoyábamos nosotros también. It almost seemed to come out all in one breath.

Mi mamá inmediatamente dijo,—¡No seas ridícula! No te andes metiendo en esas cosas.

Mi papá agregó,—¡No quiero que andes en la refolufia! No te andes metiendo con esos tales chicanos. ¿Me entiendes?

Y hasta mi metiche hermana menor abrió su bocotota para reírse,— ¡Ja, ja, ja, mi hermana la comunista!

Allí se acabó todo Tía, con mi mamá gritando,—¡Y no queremos saber que andas metida en nada de esto! Me tomaría mucho explicarle la decepción que sentí. La única que no dijo nada fue mi hermanita. Ella solamente se me quedó viendo, parecía venadita asustada. My little sister, Tía, at least she supported me with her silence.

Desde entonces, yo salgo cada sábado, es lo máximo que me puedo safar de la casa por unas horas, para que mis padres no sospechen. Me voy a piquetear (así le dicen) a las escondidas. Piquetear es otro pochismo, Tía, viene de "to picket," se entiende, ¿verdad? Me voy a marchar para la UFW enfrente de la tienda de Safeway. While I picket back and forth in front of the Safeway, I try to talk to the shoppers about supporting the grape boycott. Como mi papi acostumbra ir de compras los sábados, yo me voy a piquetear a un Safeway que está allá por la calle Geary, muy lejos de donde él va y adonde no van muchos latinos. Every Saturday, I take the bus to the Safeway, picket for three hours, and then go home. Mi daddy is sometimes coming back from food shopping when I'm getting home too. So far, he hasn't questioned me about where I've been. It's strange doing this behind their back, but I don't understand why my own mom and dad don't see how important this is. That's hard for me, Tía, it's really hard sometimes.

Gracias por escucharme. I really have to stop now or my hand will fall off. Le manda muchos besitos su sobrina rebelde y comunista quien la quiere mucho. Por favor no le diga nada de lo que le he contado a mis padres. Yo seguiré a las escondidas. Gracias por quererme tanto, Tía . . .

—Chayito

I was determined. I believed in what I was doing. I had been watching the marches and demonstrations by the Black Panthers and other civil rights groups on television, had read about and witnessed the brutality and backlash against them. I knew in my heart that all those battles were righteous and necessary for change. My political conscience was fully awake and would not go back to its unknowing self. My parents must have suspected something because they seemed to warn me over and over. First my mother: "Mira, no quiero saber que tú andas metiéndote con esos tales chicanos. ¡No son más que puros troublemakers cochinos!"

—Mejor que no te vea con ellos. Ya vas a andar en la calle como los negros y ahora, que disque protestando con los chicanos. No chiquita, ¡eso no! Me advirtió mi papá.

A couple of days later, as we sat around the dinner table, my sister Terri said, "Ahí viene la revolucionaria. I mean, la comunista." These and other comments became a part of the family bantering, a psychological tug of war, as the challenges posed by the restrictive walls and prohibitive borders of growing up in a traditional, Mexican immigrant family clashed with the reality of a changing world and a growing conciencia.

Así como había despertado mi conciencia política y había comenzado a hacerme preguntas difíciles sobre mi propia familia, sobre mi rol y mis responsabilidades de hija mayor y el conflicto con mi rol de activista, también mi desarrollo físico me hizo enfrentarme a mi conciencia adolescente de mujer. Participar en las marchas y demostraciones del UFW también significaba tener que lidiar con la falta de respeto de los hombres hacia las mujeres. I had to figure out how to deal with the vulnerability I suddenly felt as a young woman. I wanted to look ugly so I would be ignored, left alone. Comentarios estúpidos como: "¡Ay, qué mamacita tan buena!" me fastidiaban y tenía que reprimir el coraje explosivo que sentía, porque era mejor no contestar. Though there was a growing and vociferous feminist movement, it was not possible for me to identify with the bra-burning women who wanted nothing to do with men. I had to find a way to deal with los hombres en mi comunidad. Sentía que de otra manera, nunca saldríamos adelante.

I have never thought of myself as strictly or solely a feminista. It is one of the many -istas that are a part of me. My own tracing and mapping as a feminist came about as a result of my activism, my political involvement, and my professional and cultural work. I have never belonged to a feminist movement per se, except for support and cultural groups para mujeres. Instead of participating in a feminist group, I have participated and worked with immigrant rights movements, worker and union movements, gay rights and solidarity movements, and national and international cultural movements. I have become a feminist in the process of my activismo, in the process and struggle of my relations with the men and women in all aspects of life, in the process of fighting for a just and equal society.

ESPEJISMO: MUJER POESÍA

ésta no viene
engalanada
vestida de encajes
ni tampoco viene
con pelos en la lengua
no
ésta no llega
adornada de florecitas
a rosa olorosa
no señor
ésta viene
vientre puño
raíces tallos
manos brazos

espinas le curten
la lengua
a veces ofrece
hilos de miel
flor de naranjo
a veces
arroja veneno
ésta viene
a dar testimonio
a expresar su dolor
abriendo la puerta
a su realidad
gritando verdades
abrazando fuertemente
su pasión

Identidad, mi compañera y comadre, siempre cambiando, siempre abriendo sus puertas, expandiendo sus límites, estirando sus alas. Cuando uno vive y se mueve entre dos o más mundos, realidades y ambientes, negotiating and reassessing, renaming and redefining are daily acts of affirmation. Being labeled by those from within mi familia, my cultura, is painful and evokes feelings of rejection, injures self-esteem. Living entre culturas y realidades makes you stronger, teaches you daily that misconceptions abound, and that we need to unmask ignorance. For example, the term "hispanic" was coined in the 1980s and 1990s, during the Reagan-Bush demise, as a way of labeling a growing immigrant, Spanish-speaking, Latino population. As statistical and demographic data confirmed the reported population projections, the marketing and corporate world began gearing their campaigns to this new market. Thus, the term hispanic appeared officially in the census, was tossed about in all media outlets, and was subsequently imposed on myriad peoples representing twenty-two countries in the Américas and with distinct historical, cultural, and linguistic variations. There is, to be sure, a very definite divide in the use of this term as well. Along the East Coast, it appears that most Latinos use the term hispanic freely when referring to their ethnic identity, while on the West Coast, the term Latina/o is used to generalize Mestizo peoples. In fact, hissspaniccc appears to be rarely used in Califas (except when dealing with federal government representatives and entities). That is certainly the last term I would use to describe myself. Each one of us has to critically assess and define herself, understanding that self-definitions are fluid, that they will change as we grow and evolve too. Tenemos el derecho a nombrarnos a sí mismas/os, a definirnos, según nuestra experiencia vivida. No one ever asked me if I wanted to identify myself as a hisss paniccc!

Hisss Panicsss
hisss panicsss
your panic
her panic
their panic
our panic
whose panic
HISSS panic
so much raza
el patrón panicsss
he's in a tizzy
all this brown
makes him sooo dizzy
he needs to homogenize
a toda la gente
hisss panicsss
as in from Hissspania?
where's that?
non-existent country
non-existent people
no history or geography
no tongue to speak
of struggle
hisss panicsss
does it make me
more acceptable?
hisss panicsss
the ultimate white wash
it's hisss panic
to erase un MOVIMIENTO
hisss panicsss
with lots of mayo
in a big patty melt
y hasta con guaca moe lee
hisss panicsss
mcpanicsss

coorspanicsss
chale! not me!
no way!
that ain't mine baby
I continue to be
Sí, yo sigo siendo
simplemente
pura RAZA

Identity is an ever changing landscape. I am not the same as when I started out. The social and political contexts, the definitions and emotions attached to identity and other issues of my generation are not the same as those for my daughter's and son's generations. And yet, there are similarities. Como Mexicanos, Centroamericanos, Latinoamericanos en los Estados Unidos, todavía luchamos contra los estereotipos, la discriminación, la histeria anti-inmigrante que ya es parte de generación tras generación. To this racist and discriminatory system is added another disturbing trend: la criminalización de nuestra juventud. My son has been stopped by the police several times because of what he looks like, the clothes he is wearing, because of the color of his skin, because of who he is. Nowadays, young men of color with baggy pants are almost automatically suspect.

For the Middle-Aged Man
Who Sat at a Table in a Regular
Restaurant, in a Regular City, USA
this is for the middle-aged man
who sat at a regular restaurant
in a regular town (like mine) USA
this is for you mister
because I saw those daggers of disdain
you call your eyes
I saw your hatred your fear
as you sat at the head of that table
you see his brown skin
the glint of his obsidian eyes
the buzzed stubbles of dark hair
there is a gait about him
this budding coffee bean of youth
who looks straight ahead
mister, you see "messican"
maybe you think: "illegal"

you see baggy dark pants
hanging in folds
over hightop sneakers
the grey sweatshirt
splattered with paint
the raggedy sleeves and tattered hood
maybe you think "gang member"
I see your knuckles burst white
as you grip the table
and you don't even
know him
my son

The man in this poem, who aimed his hateful glare at my son, chilled, disturbed, angered, and moved me to respond. Racism and fear of our youth are alive and real. It is imperative that we respond to stop the destruction of our youth, our future.

The identity and other life issues of this mestiza Mexican immigrant in the United States have become more complex for the next generation. My son and daughter identify as Chicana/o and Jewish. Con ellos se agrega otro suelo, otro terreno para labrar. Future ground shiftings, redefinitions, and a reshaping of issues and identities are guaranteed for them. Identity, as in my continent dream, is a continuous progression of layer upon layer of soil, building land plates, washing these away to make room for new ones to be exposed. These plates mark, in cartohistographic time, the critical stages where we concientemente claim our identities at that point in life. It takes time to form these sólidas superficies, these solid surfaces that ground each stage and experience. Yet, the constant tension and friction of daily reality will lead inevitably to a quaking of land plates and then a resettling again. Identity remains an earth-moving experience.

Questions about discrimination, injustice, and poverty that I had asked thirty years ago are, unfortunately, still unanswered today. We continue fighting for justice and for positive change. However, there are new, more sinister forces in place: environmental urban racism, NAFTAlization's spread of destruction and poverty. In addition, while state and national politicians tout the decreasing crime rate, we have a menacing and grow- ing prison industrial complex, aiming to swallow up our disenfranchised brown and black men and women and youth.

Como cartohistógrafas, nuestro trabajo exige que tengamos conciencia, que analicemos y documentemos cuidadosamente nuestros relatos, cuentos, chistes, testimonios, nuestra visión, lo tierno y lo duro. Nuestra realidad demands that we work for more and immediate change, que nos concienticemos, que solidifiquemos esa energía y fuerza que nos lleve adelante.

I discovered worlds, my own and others, through reading. I discovered words, and through my own words, I have in the process discovered me. What I mean is that writing, whether poems, stories, or letters, has been a key to my own self-discovery. Like the physical evidence of life experience and change that we see on the pockmarked faces of ancient boulders or the neatly layered clay red and bark brown soils we see on rock formations, my writings have physically pockmarked the shared historical spaces of mine and others' worlds and the intimate nooks of my own experience.

Words and writing have been a way to deal with the powerful emotions that come with injustice. Mis escritos han sido una puerta a la expresión de lo que he sentido en carne propia. The anger I have felt has, in fact, collaborated many a time with my writing and propelled me to search for the strongest, most powerful words I can fuse together to name or question a harsh reality. In my experience, anger has potential to generate good; it has moved me enough to try to change some wrong, to speak about that wrong out loud; it has pushed me to do something. La cartohistógrafa se convierte en poeta, cantora, historiadora y activista a través de sus palabras y escritos.

La palabra has been a way to channel my reflections, to question myself, to give shape to the unknown, to honor my roots y mis lengualidades. Con las palabras puedo hacer y deshacer mundos, reclamar y definir mi humanidad, y hablar de mi ser de mujer.

Palabra de mujer
woman
her story
I sustain in my memory
the want you want
to erase
to domesticate
with your alphabet
you have wanted me mute
since childhood
once
my silence
carved the place
you call smile as
your frothing words

spilled out
your eyes sternly
warned
—don't think
you're prettier that way
once
I would hide
my forbidden voice
in the pleats of my conscience
entire cities trapped in my throat
now
my tongue
has birthed the words
challenging
what is
no longer accepted

NOTES

1. Though the author knows full well that mexicana, chicana, latina, and so on are adjectives en el español estándard, she purposefully chooses to capitalize them here.
2. Nahuatl: tepalcatl—fragmento de una pieza de barro.

Translating Herstory: A Reading of and

Responses to Elba Rosario Sánchez

RENATO ROSALDO

• • • • •

Dear Elba,

We've never met in person, but I heard you read your poetry at the Floricanto in San Jose in June 2000. I loved your work and bought the CD *When Skin Peels*, with twenty of your poems. So, when Pat Zavella asked if I would respond to your essay, I said yes.

Since you don't know me, I should say that I'm a cultural anthropologist—read *Culture and Truth* (1989), if you're curious. I've been writing poetry for over four years, not very long, but I've been working hard, and it has been a blessing in my life. A poem of mine, "El ángel de la guarda," is in the winter 2001 issue of *El Andar*.

I'd like to begin by trying to say what I hear you saying. If we were speaking in person, I'd end every paragraph by saying, "Is this what you mean?" When in what follows I try to say what you're saying, I'll do it in the third person: Elba, she, her. When I respond to your essay, I'll begin "Dear Elba," as if sending you a short note.

I found your essay insightful and inspiring. I love the mix of poetry, prose, and letters to your Aunt Inez. Thank you for your writing.

Saludos,

Renato

Elba Rosario Sánchez explores complex questions of identity through an extended reflection on the vicissitudes of her own life. Her identities include Mexican, immigrant, Chicana, and woman. Her method is auto-ethnographic, a self-reflection at once personal and collective. She writes simultaneously about the life of Elba Rosario Sánchez and about the historical contexts more widely shared by Chicanas and Chicanos.

"It began with a dream," she tells us in the beginning. "I was no longer body and flesh, eyes, hair, and teeth, but hills, valleys, orchards, forests." Her writing thus becomes a way of mapping her life, her development as a woman and a Chicana. It is an exploration of the growth of her political awareness.

The term she coins for this mapping is cartohistography, a notion that is both territorial and historical. Her concept delineates what is at once personal history and general history. Her landscape unfolds in history; her analysis is an archaeology—the stratigraphy—of her identities. Through her multiple identities, her consciousness is always developing, shifting, eroding, renewing. She inhabits a number of distinct communities: Chicana, working class, educator, woman, mother, and cultural worker.

Dear Elba,

I'm not enamored of cartohistography as an organizing concept for your essay. I know what you mean by the term and I know how much you like to hold opposites in tension (like hot/cold and death/birth), but mapping a landscape and grasping a history/herstory do not fit together very easily as activities or forms of understanding. I think your essay would be better served by presenting the notion of mapping a landscape as a metaphor, but not by making it into a conceit, as the Elizabethans called it, a metaphor or concept that runs through the whole essay.

Your concept of histocartography is more cerebral than your wonderful poem "Me siento continente/I Feel Myself a Continent," which is so sensuous and womanly. I recall "senos volcánicos/de lava candente/pezones que se hinchan/al besar el cielo/de mi vientre/he volcado/capas de sedimento/escombros/de quien fui."

My candidate for a concept running through the entire essay, if you feel you need one, would be lengualidades. This term emphasizes language and translation/untranslatability as well as your multiple (and shifting) identities and the various communities that guide and reflect your coming to political consciousness.

Saludos,

Renato

Perhaps the capacity to move between languages gives Sánchez the gift of poetry, a use of language that is about the music and rhythm of words, their lilt and flavor. Poetry makes present a phenomenon that otherwise might be observed and analyzed only from a distance. In this work of making present she moves into the most personal experiences and finds that the intensely personal reaches out to widely shared emotions and perceptions. One is reminded here of the feminist slogan "the personal is political," which is based in the practice of consciousness-raising, where one woman tells her private story and discovers that other women share similar stories. Thus, what at first appears idiosyncratic and private derives from the more general systemic or structural factors of patriarchal regimes. When working, as Sánchez is, in relatively unknown social and political terrain, the most personal can often be the surest path to the most general.

Like other women of color, Sánchez writes herself into existence. Through her writing she comes to know who she is and makes herself known to others. Language itself is a central theme of her writing. Spanish was her first language and the painful acquisition of English she recalls as an "aching of my jaw." Within six months of arriving as an immigrant to the United States, she took on the role of family translator, mediating between her native Spanish and her newly acquired English. In passing this demanding IQ test with flying colors she became the broker for complex transactions between adults, negotiating worlds that children often are not allowed to enter.

Her poem "A Gift of Tongues" says that her tongue "scorches the old/ announces the new." It "opens wounds/heals the hurt/with warm breath savors the other/the you that is also me/this tongue of mine." It burns the old and gives birth to the new; it is the gift of the creator/destroyer who bestows death and rebirth. It is both self-expression and collective expression. Her poem "Tepalcate a Tepalcate" makes present a set of perceptions about the experiences of an immigrant woman thrown into a hostile world. Speaking initially as an indigenous woman, she says her people were displaced from their ancestral lands and lifeways by greedy European men, by "esos hombres/de ojos pálidos/llegaron un dia/queriéndolo todo." She then addresses her arrival from Mexico to the Fillmore in San Francisco, when she was flung into the alien gray coldness: "nos arrojaron/a este frío hostil/pavimento gris/de mediocridad." Like her broken culture, shards of pottery fuse, through mutual recognition, into a whole community: "tepalcate a tepalcate/nos reconocemos/somos caras en relieve/de una misma pieza." She finds the word "tepalcate" untranslatable. The English "shard," for her, loses the smell of "barro" and the Nahuatl feel in the mouth. In moving between languages she cannot always translate herself.

Her story concerns living in the interstices between cultures, languages, and norms. Her poetry makes visceral the realizations that accompany the jolts of border crossings. Explored through letters, poems, and narrative, Sánchez's landscape shifts among lengualidades that interact, as she says, "like seasoned partners on the dance floor." Herstory thematizes coming to political consciousness in the manner of the Latin American genre of the testimonio—say, that of Rigoberta Menchú or Domitila.

She claims that at age 11, before immigrating to the United States, she was "pura mexicana." This period from birth to age 11 is her Garden of Eden, an epoch when she suffered no identity confusion because she knew exactly who she was and was proud of it.

Dear Elba,

I'm not convinced that you were in the Garden of Eden in Mexico. At some point in your life, perhaps around your fifteenth birthday, you would have noticed the racially tinged exclusions of class in Mexico. Or you'd have bumped into patriarchy. Or you'd have discovered urban prejudice toward rural people. Your prose and your poetry make a claim of stable membership in a community. In "Sowing Seeds" you say: "my ancestors knew their grains/like each of their offspring/once planted/ they watered and nurtured them/growing cycles/of sprouting sons and daughters/predicting harvests to come." This picture of a stable continuous life of repeated cycles does not square with your saying that in your family "as far back as three generations (that I know of), migration, physical distance, uprooting, immigration, and separation have been a constant." I know you mean that dislocation to the United States produced confusion about your identity. Had you remained in Mexico you might have been oppressed but not confused about who you were.

Saludos,

Renato

Sánchez's first jolt of awareness comes as her family, along with friends and relatives from La Experiencia and Atemajac, towns just north of Guadalajara, Mexico, settle in a predominantly African American neighborhood, the Fillmore in San Francisco. She is 11, the year is 1960. The climate in her new land is inhospitable because gringos think "los mexicanos somos unos cochinos, unos flojos." When she leaves the security of her five-family Mexican community she feels isolated because she does not speak English. At her predominantly African American school she quickly finds a friend, Krystal, but during recess she encounters another girl, wearing the disorienting face of hate. She says, "I didn't need a translation to read the anger on her face." The angry African American girl calls her a white patty, but Sánchez cannot find herself in this encounter because she regards herself as Mexican, not white.

Her second and more devastating jolt comes a couple of years after arriving in the Fillmore, when she returns home to Mexico and is rejected by her best friend, who tells her that she is a pocha, not a Mexican. As Sánchez says in a letter to her Aunt Inés, her best friend in Mexico "ya no piensa que yo soy de allá, que yo no soy mexicana, y acá me dicen que no soy de aquí." She finds herself belonging neither in the United States nor in Mexico. Wounded as she is, she agrees that "Mexican women don't sit on the floor," as she was doing. She no longer is the Mexicana she once was.

Dear Elba,

Your portrayal of being rejected both in the United States and in Mexico moves me. I, too, have found being called pocho more devastating than everyday racism in the United States. I think we are more prepared for the racism of Anglos than for rejection by Mexicans.

Saludos,

Renato

Sánchez's story of dislocations culminates in her sophomore year in high school, when she comes to political consciousness. When imagining her future, she does so through the United Farmworkers' movement. She identifies with the farmworkers in part by recalling the times her father was working away from the family. At this time she writes and publishes her first poem, "The Price of Color," in which she depicts the agony of finding her identity without help and in a hostile environment: "With no one to guide me or hold my hand/Why do they hate even my shadow." Her coming to consciousness is shaped by the marches and demonstrations of the civil rights movement. It is at the same time challenged by her family. Her sister calls her a communist. Her mother reprimands her, "no te andes metiendo con esos tales llamados chicanos. No son mas que puros troublemakers cochinos!" As Sánchez says, "Challenges posed by the restrictive walls and prohibitive borders of growing up in a traditional, Mexican immigrant family clashed with the reality of a changing world and a growing conciencia."

Dear Elba,

I am moved by your struggle to become yourself, to come to political awareness in the context of the civil rights movement and the difficulties of dealing with your traditional family. I like the way you privilege the bilingual reader, the one who moves easily from standard to slang, and the way you show the art involved in speaking the way we speak. Thank you.

Abrazos,

Renato

In the present, Sánchez's son and daughter identify as Chicana/o and Jewish. Alluding to a poem by Lorna Dee Cervantes, Sánchez's poem "For the Middle-Aged White Man Who Sat at a Table in a Regular Restaurant in a Regular City, USA" brings home the racism her son faces as he grows up. Her poem says, "maybe you think 'gang member'/I see your knuckles burst white/as you grip the table/and you don't even/know him/my son." She sees that the political issues that brought her to consciousness still persist, even if transformed: "Questions about discrimination, injustice, and poverty that I had asked thirty years ago are, unfortunately, still unanswered today. . . . However, there are new, more sinister forces in place: environmental urban racism . . . a menacing and growing prison industrial complex, aiming to swallow up our disenfranchised brown and black men and women and youth."

Dear Elba,

Your essay, as I now look back on it, works with five key words and is written in different lengualidades. *Geography* is your insistence on placing identities in space: near Guadalajara, the Fillmore, high school, and television images of the civil rights movement. It has been relatively rare for us Chicanas and Chicanos to locate ourselves in relation to Mexico, and I am grateful for the way you open this topic for discussion and analysis. *Herstory/history* is your way of underlining that identities are mutable and change through time in ways related to the historical context, such as the emergence of the United Farmworkers movement. *Language* is a term you use to depict what you move between, sometimes literally Spanish and English and other times different social contexts that operate with different grammars, like the Fillmore versus the Guadalajara area. Coming to *political consciousness* is the climax of the essay; it is where the stories of identity formation and loss lead. *Identities*—how they persist, drop away, and transform—are the central topic of your fine essay.

The lengualidades in your essay are wonderfully polyphonic (prose, poetry, letters) and polyglot (Spanish, English, standard speech, and slang). The essay embodies the very phenomena it analyzes. It is a tour de force that privileges the bilingual reader, making us feel at home as you write yourself into existence.

What a privilege to have spent this time with your words. Thank you.

Un abrazo,

Renato

CHAPTER TWO

Contested Histories: *Las Hijas de*

Cuauhtémoc, Chicana Feminisms, and Print

Culture in the Chicano Movement, 1968–1973

MAYLEI BLACKWELL

· · · · ·

The 1971 publication of the *Hijas de Cuauhtémoc* newspaper in its three editions marked a critical historical moment in the development of Chicana feminist theories and practices and a gendered shift in the print culture of the Chicano movement.[1] Despite the enduring legacy of the political interventions Chicana activists made during the 1960s and 1970s, the emergence of Chicana feminism within the Chicano movement has remained, until recently, largely an untold story.[2] The historiography or practice of telling the history of the Chicano movement often has not only erased women's early participation in the movement but has produced a masculine hegemony within those narratives, reinscribing dominant gender relations that were much more contested at the time. My oral history project with the members of the Hijas de Cuauhtémoc, an early Chicana feminist organization, has uncovered histories of the emergence of Chicana feminist resistance and challenges the mechanics of erasure that have produced these silences in the historiography of both the Chicano and the women's movements.[3] Focusing on how the Hijas de Cuauhtémoc engendered print media and built Chicana feminist print communities, this essay analyzes print culture as a strategic site of intervention and contestation for women in the Chicano movement.

The Chicano movement emerged from a multitude of community-based political and civil rights struggles, ranging from issues of agricultural and industrial labor to (im)migration, access to education, political representation, the Vietnam War, racism and discrimination, resistance to police and state repression, land grant claims, and local control of community institutions. Yet, Chicano movement historiography has been structured around a cosmology of male heroes, whereby the figures of Reies López Tijerina, Rodolfo "Corky" Gonzales, José Angel Gutiérrez, and César Chavez have come to stand in for fuller historical understanding of these social movements, especially women's participation in them.[4] Although these leaders' contributions are indeed important, the way they have been historicized has produced a monolithic portrayal of the Chicano movement, in which history is organized around hero narratives rather than the many participatory local struggles that coalesced into a national movement. This is a disservice to the historical memory of the majority of its participants.

Despite clear historical documentation of Chicana activism and the emergence of Chicana feminism as early as 1968, many Chicano movement histories have claimed that Chicanas did not begin to articulate their own agendas until the 1980s, thereby historicizing the emergence of Chicana feminism at the time of the decline of *el movimiento Chicano*.[5] Feminist historiography of the second wave women's movement is equally distorted, focusing almost exclusively on small East Coast, largely middle-class, white women's consciousness-raising groups, thereby erasing the participation of women of color in the women's movement and ignoring other diverse political formations that gave rise to women of color feminisms and theories outside of that movement.[6] These limitations have mistakenly led many to periodize the formation of women of color political identity as originating in the 1980s, marked by the publication of *This Bridge Called My Back: Writings by Radical Women of Color* (Moraga and Anzaldúa 1981).[7]

This essay analyzes Chicana feminist print cultures as social movement practices integral to creating the political context for such a vital women of color political project and publishing endeavor to emerge. Exploring the formation of Chicana print communities, I focus my analysis on the *Hijas de Cuauhtémoc* newspaper, its text, circulation, and function, as well as the first Chicana journal, *Encuentro Femenil*, which members of the organization helped to found in 1973. Although the newspaper was short-lived — all three issues were published in 1971 — it opened up spaces for Chicana dialogue across regions, social movement sectors, activist generations, and social differences. Print community modes of production are a crucial site of historical inquiry helping us to understand the development of Chicana feminist ideology, discourse, and political praxis in a way that accounts for how ideas traveled through local formations as well as larger cross-regional circulations. Weaving the history of this Chicana organization between 1968 and 1973 into a larger historical analysis of the emergence of Chicana feminisms, I illustrate the transformation of Chicana consciousness as their newspaper expanded its readership and imagined political community from local (campus) to regional and national audiences. Many negotiations over gender and sexuality occurred in the local power relationships and daily life politics of the Chicano movement. Movement print culture functioned as a mediating space where these debates circulated and where new ideas, theories, and political claims were forged.

In the late 1960s and early 1970s Chicana feminists circulated their political ideas in Raza magazines, feminist circulars, manifestos, organizational newsletters, and political pamphlets. As a form of political pedagogy (Bhabha 1990), these print-mediated dialogues among women from different movement sectors and social locations created a space not only to formulate Chicana demands but to constitute new political, racial, and gender identities. Community publications, newspapers, and magazines (such as *El Grito del Norte* and *Regeneración)* and feminist student newspapers (including *El Popo Femenil* and *Hijas de Cuauhtémoc)* were formative in producing a Chicana print community and furthered the development of scholarly Chicana publications and the field of Chicana Studies.

Chicana feminist historian Martha Cotera has chronicled the development of Chicana feminist print communities: "Chicanas also have expressed their feminism and their needs through their own journals like *Regeneración, Encuentro Femenil, Hijas de Cuauhtémoc, La Comadre, Fuego de Aztlán, Imágenes de la Chicana, Hembra, Tejidos, La Cosecha [De Colores]*, and *Hojas Poéticas.* Other popular journals like *La Luz, Nuestro, El Caracol,* and *El Grito* often feature feminist writings that are helping to raise the consciousness of Chicanas and women's development" (1980, 231). This rich genealogical site has facilitated an emerging countercanon of Chicana historiography that recuperates writings by Chicanas in the movement that have largely been ignored (A. García 1990; Alarcón 1990). Many newspaper articles and journal essays from this period testify to the unofficial history of women in the movement who played a crucial role in the formation of the "New Chicana" (Sosa-Riddell 1974; Cotera 1980).

For example, long-time labor activist Francisca Flores and Ramona Morín of the women's auxiliary of GI Forum founded *La Carta Editorial* in the mid-1960s to serve as a community-based publication that would report on political activities. Flores went on to found *Regeneración* in 1970 and made vital contributions through her magazine's singularly forthright analysis regarding women's issues. Besides two Chicana special issues published in 1971 and 1973, *Regeneración* was known for its news stories that reported on women's organizing, op-ed pieces that critiqued sexist practices in the Chicano movement, artwork featuring local Chicana artists, and articles analyzing political issues and legislation affecting the lives of Chicanas. The newsletters of the Comisión Femenil Mexicana and the Chicana Service Action Center were organizing tools that reported on Chicana community and employment issues in Los Angeles. Based in the New Mexican land grant movement, long-time civil rights activist and former SNCC member Elizabeth "Betita" Martinez edited the magazine *El Grito del Norte* along with Enriqueta Longeaux y Vásquez and several other activists. Under the leadership of Dorinda Moreno, the San Francisco–based Chicana feminist organization Concilio Mujeres began publishing *La Razón Mestiza* in 1974. Several university women's groups published campus newspapers or annual special issues on Chicanas, a tradition that continues today. These inventive forms of print intervention helped to constitute and document new forms of Chicana insurgency during this period.

HIJAS DE CUAUHTÉMOC: THE EMERGENCE OF CHICANA FEMINISM IN THE CHICANO STUDENT MOVEMENT

The Hijas de Cuauhtémoc was an early women's group that emerged out of the ranks of the Chicano student movement. They operated under such names as *las mujeres de Longo* (the caló term for Long Beach), *las hermanas,* and *las Chicanas de Aztlán* between 1968 and 1971. The group formed within United Mexican American Students (UMAS) at California State University, Long Beach, which later took up the call to Chicano political action under the name Movimiento Estudiantil Chicano de Aztlán (MEChA) after the 1969 Plan de Santa Barbara.

Because the leadership of UMAS, and later MEChA, held the attitude that new female recruits had less political knowledge than their male counterparts, the veteran women activists were charged with providing "political education" for the incoming women. One veteran Chicana activist, Corinne Sánchez (1997), noted that the Hijas de Cuauhtémoc was formed as an organizational mechanism for women's political education within the student movement and was "originally organized within MEChA or UMAS as a forum for educating and raising the awareness of the women."[8] Although ideological discussion and study groups were part of the student movement's consciousness-raising efforts, the women's group eventually became a vehicle through which to voice complaints about the contradictions between the civil rights discourse and the way women were treated in the organization. What the women "wanted, in essence, was some accountability from the men . . . that they be consistent with their ideology because the women weren't treated with respect" (NietoGomez 1991). The group became a way for women in the movement to organize collectively based on their own experiences as young, working-class Chicanas and to address issues that were ignored in the student movement.

One common depiction shared in the oral history interviews I conducted was the blockages to women's full participation and the dismissive attitudes they encountered in UMAS and MEChA. Several mentioned, for example, that when a woman brought up an idea in a meeting, it would go unrecognized until a guy brought up essentially the same idea; his resolution would then be discussed, engaged, and passed. The women's meetings operated as an informal support group and a place where they could discuss problems with the male leadership and openly articulate these contradictions (Castillo 1996). The group at California State University, Long Beach, along with other Chicana activists in the greater Los Angeles area, began to develop a critique of the sexual politics of the movement. Often, commitment to the revolution was measured by how "down" you were to a revolutionary man, and new female members complained that initiation into the movement included attempts by the men to "revolutionize" their pants off (Miranda 1994).[9] The women felt the gendered division of labor that relegated them to secretarial tasks and cooking for fundraisers limited their political development. They were frustrated by the lack of attention to the daily life issues Chicanas faced on campus.

Corinne Sánchez and Sylvia Castillo claim that one of the main factors in consolidating the women's group was the discrimination that arose when Anna NietoGomez was democratically elected president of MEChA for the academic year 1969–1970.[10] NietoGomez had wide support from the student body, who recognized her leadership capacity through her role as one of the first Chicana Equal Opportunity Program (EOP) peer counselors (C. Sánchez 1998). Although she had several male allies and was an effective student leader, her work as president was often disrupted by the old guard male leadership, who, seemingly threatened by the leadership of one of the first woman presidents of MEChA, attempted to hold shadow organizational control by holding meetings behind her back (C. Sánchez 1998; Castillo 1996). Although NietoGomez had already served as the vice president of UMAS in 1968–1969, some of the male leadership explicitly stated that they did not want to be represented by a woman at statewide conventions. As tensions mounted around the question of women's leadership, all of the women recalled how the silencing mechanisms used against them became more dramatic. For example, women leaders were hung in effigy outside of the MEChA trailer during this time, and later, after the publication of the newspaper, a mock burial for the Hijas de Cuauhtémoc was presided over by a MEChA "priest," with tombstones where several of the members' names were inscribed (NietoGomez 1991; L. Hernández 1992; C. Sánchez 1997).

Sonia López's study of Chicanas in the student movement found that women's organizations formed because of the "inconsistencies between the liberation rhetoric of the movement and the reality as it existed for Chicanas within the movement—that of being exploited by their own people for their labor and sexuality" (1977, 26). Several Chicana organizations and informal groups formed for similar reasons between 1970 and 1972 at universities across California, including San Diego State University, Fresno State College, California State University Los Angeles, and Stanford University. The women from California State University, Long Beach (CSULB) were extremely active in college recruitment, sponsoring some of the first Día de la Raza events that brought Chicana/o high school students to the university and helped to triple the Chicano enrollment in those early years. Yet, they found that despite the fact that only one third of new college recruits were women, over half of those women dropped out before their junior year in college. They investigated the high dropout rate among Chicanas and discovered that it had little to do with academic success as the majority of Chicanas had high grade-point averages overall. The reasons for the dropout rate ranged from a lack of academic, faculty, or peer support to guilt over leaving familial responsibilities and not being able to contribute to the household income of their families while in college, social pressures to get married, and economic difficulties. They also found that a silent factor was pregnancy and lack of access to birth control (NietoGomez 1991).[11]

The group's urgent need to focus on the survival of Chicanas in the university, as well as their commitment to increase their rapidly dropping retention rates, initiated their transformation from a support group to an advocacy group.[12] The women felt that internal politics were overshadowing the problems they were having and that conflicts around the presidency had polarized already existing tensions over labor, sexuality, and prescribed gender roles in the movement. Realizing that they were the main labor force of the movement, they began to assess their role in the organization. The group had been mobilized since 1968; by 1970 they were organizing themselves to address their common political needs in relation to women in the movement, the community, and the university. They began a dialogue with other Chicanas that facilitated a shift in consciousness and the articulation of an explicitly Chicana gendered political identity.

The group solidified around a shared interest in learning about Chicana history and identity and discussing the ways Chicanas could participate more fully in the national Chicano movement instead of being limited to cooking for the fundraisers on campus. But, because the women began to articulate their own political vision of what Chicano liberation should be—that it should include women—they were often told that their ideas were divisive or they were dismissed as sellouts, *vendidas,* or traitors, *Malinches.* Although their call for Chicana feminisms was grounded in their own lived daily experience and political insight gained in the movement, they were labeled *agringadas* or white-washed by those who claimed that feminism was antithetical to Chicano culture. Despite the ideological attacks against Chicana feminists and even those Chicanas who did not call themselves feminist at the time but actively worked against the gender discrimination in the movement, they overcame political intimidation like being hung in effigy and continued to organize. Members of the Hijas de Cuauhtémoc went on to publish their newspaper, founded the first Chicana feminist journal of scholarship in 1973, and made important contributions to the formulation of early Chicana feminist thought. Part of the backlash to women's organizing was tied to how Chicano cultural nationalism was not just an ideology of cultural pride and racial unity but a gendered construction that influenced how gender roles and expectations shaped the political practices of the Chicano student movement (Blackwell 2000b).

Much of the ideology of the student movement was articulated through concepts of gender mediated largely through masculinity, brotherhood, familialism, and carnalismo. This construction of masculinity shaped not only the discourse of nationalism but the social and cultural context of the Chicano youth movement as a whole, often authorizing asymmetrical gender relations, sexual politics, and the policing of women's sexuality (Blackwell 2000b). Moreover, when deployed within political organizations, it constituted a political practice that often informed a range of issues, from how meetings functioned to organizational styles and the question of women's leadership (Rendon 1971). This led to problems for the women who moved into the leadership of MEChA (and UMAS) in the late 1960s, because it was through acts of repudiation of women who were democratically elected to leadership that masculinist discourse became political practice. Although there have been various critiques of sexism and homophobia in the Chicano movement of the 1960s and 1970s,[13] it was not until the 1990s that scholars like Angie Chabram Dernersesian began to critically examine the ways that cultural nationalism was constructed through gender.[14]

Chicano nationalism also engendered constructions of idealized femininity largely through a conservative cultural construct of "tradition" within a patriarchal, heterosexual model of family. This view circumvented the daily culture of the movement and the lives of Chicana activists as *la familia* served both as an organizing model and a metaphor for the Chicano movement. The articulation of a Chicana/o political subjectivity through constructions of gender led early Chicano movement discourse to encounter problems building a coherent political space for women. For example, the discourse of nationalism created a contradictory position for women: they were seen as the bearers of tradition, culture, and family and simultaneously erased as the unspoken subjects of political rights. The construction of gender for women in the movement was based on what has been called the "Ideal Chicana," which "glorified Chicanas as strong, long-suffering women who had endured and kept Chicano culture and family intact" (A. García 1990, 420).

Many studies assume that Chicanas came from "traditional" backgrounds and then came to their forms of feminism through the movement. However, the oral histories of the Hijas de Cuauhtémoc reveal that many of the women drew their sense of political agency and gender identity from other community-based "traditions" of female strength and resistance. As descendants of female labor organizers, political party activists, railroad workers, and women who managed family survival on scarce resources, most often members of this organization said that it was their mother, abuela, or tia who served as their role model. These insights suggest that Chicana feminism emerged not only out of the gendered contradictions and sexism of the movement but from conflicts with movement discourses that constructed gender norms based on an idealized nationalist recovery of cultural "tradition" that did not resonate with their lived experience (Blackwell 2000a). More than mere recovery, nationalist discourse often produced traditions that also legitimized gender political identities (Hall 1988, 1989). Part of the political work of the *Hijas de Cuauhtémoc* newspaper was that it documented, explored, and honored a diversity of women's political and lived experiences by featuring Sor Juana Inés de la Cruz, local activists and family members, soldaderas fighting in the Mexican Revolution, and Chicana artists and theorists.

The first issue of *Hijas de Cuauhtémoc* was a watershed moment in the articulation of a Chicana feminist political, poetic, and historical vision that had been circulating beneath the surface of the movement. The newspaper theorized and editorialized new forms of *femenismo* and began to name the interconnections of class and race through an innovative mixed-genre format that was equal parts journalism, poetry, photography, art, social critique, recovered women's history, and political manifesto. It engaged economic and social issues, political consciousness, Mexicana/Chicana history, and campus and community struggles, reported on Chicana political developments, and created a space for many young activists to express their own political insights and visions.

Because the Hijas de Cuauhtémoc deployed strategic feminist reconfigurations of nationalist discourse in the newspaper they published, they played a vital role in the critique of the national subject as male and struggled to refigure the nation (Aztlán). By reworking notions of tradition, culture, and history that circumscribed racial, sexual, and gendered expectations of women, the work of the Hijas de Cuauhtémoc multiplied the critical dialogues between the constituencies of the imagined community of Aztlán (Mercer 1994). Their political and symbolic work broke down the unitary concept of the citizen-subject of Aztlán as male, thereby diversifying and multiplying the subjects of resistance enlisted in a Chicana/o project of liberation.

Benedict Anderson's (1991) influential conceptualization of the nation as imagined community has been effectively taken up to produce new insights about social movements and communities of resistance (Mohanty 1991; Fernández 1994).[15] Reconfiguring this formulation for the historical specificity of anticolonial nationalisms, Partha Chatterjee (1993), a historian involved in the Subaltern Studies Group, maintains that it is not through conflict with the state but within the cultural realm that prefigures this struggle that decolonizing nationalist imaginaries are constituted. He argues that anticolonial nationalism creates a domain of sovereignty within colonial society, and that this domain is produced through "an entire institutional network of printing presses, publishing houses, newspapers, [and] magazines . . . created . . . outside the purview of the state . . . through which the new language [of nationalist liberation] . . . is given shape" (7).

Whereas other Third World movements for national liberation aimed to overthrow the colonial state, the Chicano movement contested state power, its violence, discrimination, and lack of channels of representation.[16] Chicano cultural nationalism was a form of decolonizing nationalism in which the circulation of print media in the form of student and community newspapers, political pamphlets, and movement magazines played a formative role. While Anderson's contribution names the important role of print-mediated forms of communication in forming a national subject, Chatterjee illustrates how domains of cultural and social sovereignty were vital spaces for articulating an anticolonial political imaginary. Although questions of gender, race, and sexuality have historically been overlooked in theories of (anticolonial) nationalism, Emma Pérez's (1999) work on "sexing the decolonial imaginary" is a vital contribution that gives us tools to understand the complex ways questions of gender and sexuality are embedded in the processes of articulating political subjects and projects of decolonization.

For example, the Hijas de Cuauhtémoc created the space for Chicana political agency and cultural autonomy by refusing the confining masculinist codes of the Chicano nationalist imaginary. They shifted the terrain of nationalism from a precolonial imaginary of Aztlán (homeland of the Mexica located in what is now the Southwest of the United States) to a historical legacy of revolutionary women and Mexican feminism. Recasting their own political participation by reclaiming a tradition of female resistance, they adopted their name after a turn-of-the-century Mexican women's organization that ran an underground press and worked for women's right to education and political representation.[17] "Inspired and reassured that 'speaking out' was not alien to the Chicana's culture, las Mujeres de Longo named themselves after a Mexican feminist press organization, active in the Revolution of 1910, Hijas de Cuauhtémoc" (Introduction 1973, 5).

Taking on the name of Hijas de Cuauhtémoc unsettled the discursive terrain through which women were inscribed into movement scripts. The act of taking on the name performed a double function by subverting the silencing mechanism of the Malinche complex deployed by Chicano nationalists who felt that a women's agenda in the movement was divisive. By resignifying women's role in nationalist culture to take on the anticolonial struggle that Cuauhtémoc symbolized (as the last Aztec ruler who never surrendered power to the Spaniards), the Hijas de Cuauhtémoc simultaneously displaced the vendida logic of antifeminism and carved out a space for Chicana political subjectivity within the movement. They refigured gendered forms of representation in the movement through the production and circulation of new images in their newspaper.

Studying Mexican women's history was transformative and provided a sense of historical agency that infused the activism of the group, who began publishing the newspaper *Hijas de Cuauhtémoc* at California State University, Long Beach in March 1971. The stated goal of the newspaper was "to inform the Chicana about herself through history, by reporting Chicanas' political activities in the communities, and by educating her to the socioeconomic conditions that she must deal with as a woman in a minority culture of an oppressive society" (Introduction 1973, 4). Back on campus, the first issue of the paper was largely ignored by their male detractors in MEChA, who criticized the group for publishing something separate from their Chicano student newspaper, *El Alacrán*. Nevertheless, it was received with enthusiasm and support by others in both campus and community organizations. In fact, the women's group actually received the funding to publish their newspaper from a group of older men in a Norwalk Mutualista society (a tradition of Mexican migrant communities). It was their relationship to this group of older Mexicanos and Chicanos who supported their work that allowed the women to see that men on campus were construing a form of masculinity and gendered relations of power that was not consistent with the "community" so often evoked by those critiquing feminist ideas.

Reflecting on gender roles in the movement, Anna NietoGomez (1991) narrates the story of how they funded their newspaper: "Looking back, I see that these guys [on campus] were trying out idealized roles of manhood, so everything was exaggerated. Working in the community helped me out because I got to work with men that seemed more normal. . . . I saw their male identity as being comfortable and part of who they were. Back on campus it seemed the guys were role-playing the exaggerated stereotypical macho and forced women to play out their passive role, which was a very rigid thing, instead of being yourself. If these guys deviated from this hypermacho role they were criticized for being wimps or anglocized."

The publication of the newspaper galvanized the women's political activities on campus and out in the communities. Besides working on issues of incarceration, education, poverty, and social justice, members of the Hijas de Cuauhtémoc participated in community organizations and made links among the La Raza Community Center in Eastside Long Beach, the UFW's grape boycott, the women in the Orange County Brown Berets, Católicos por la Raza, Teatro Campesino, and community development projects in Hawaiian Gardens. Although these organizers were linked to community struggles before the publication of the newspaper, the paper gave them a vehicle to define and engage Chicana issues that were not being addressed adequately in the Chicano movement at that time. These issues included sterilization and reproductive health, welfare and labor rights, employment and gender discrimination, access to health care, Chicana incarceration, familial and cultural roles, as well as sexism, sexual politics, and women's role in the movement.

CHICANA FEMINIST PRINT CULTURES:
CONSTITUTING NEW COUNTERPUBLICS

Along with many other publications from California, New Mexico, and Texas, the gendered print community constituted through the circulation of the *Hijas de Cuauhtémoc* newspaper in 1971 was vital to the creation of Chicana feminist movement networks and alliances. Through print-mediated exchange, new identities, regional and ideological differences, strategies, theories, and practices were debated and discussed in campus and community meetings and local and national conferences. These ideas were then shared and transformed as they traveled through the process of republication of editorials, articles, conference proceedings, reports, movement debates, and political position papers. Moreover, the process of publication and circulation not only built new critical interpretive communities, it constituted a Chicana counterpublic or "parallel discursive arenas where members of subordinated social groups invent and circulate counter discourses so as to formulate oppositional interpretations of their identities, interests, and needs" (Fraser 1993, 14).

These publication practices and circuits of distribution formed part of a Chicana feminist strategy to rework modes of print communication already operating in the Chicano movement as well as to create new ones, thus multiplying the spaces of participation for women.[18] Through the late 1960s and early 1970s, new forms of print media and newspapers emerged out of the social justice struggles of the Chicano movement. It was common for each campus or community organization to have some form of publication and study group or political education sessions. Print-mediated dialogue and the exchange of reading materials allowed each group to know what the others were doing and thinking, because modes of communication were networked through movement print culture and the practice of circulating manifestos and theoretical treatises in mimeograph form. This was crucial to the ideological development of Chicana/o political community. Drawing on the experience that many of the women had working on *El Alacrán*, all of the women involved in the Hijas de Cuauhtémoc wrote for student or community newspapers such as *La Raza.* As part of a stated political agenda of linking campus to community, newspapers would ask college students to get involved and work on the newspaper at night by attending community meetings and then writing up a report.

Building Coalitions and Translocal Strategies

The translocal strategy and technology of republication helped to forge a new political subjectivity of la Nueva Chicana through critical dialogues that constructed the multiple meanings, locations, and practices of this emergent imagined political community. The *Hijas de Cuauhtémoc* newspaper, along with other publications, provided a forum for Chicanas to dialogue across regions and social movement sectors, which was crucial to the formation of Chicana feminism. The *Hijas de Cuauhtémoc* newspaper included articles by other Chicanas around the country. For example, Rosita Morales's "La Mujer Todavía Impotente," originally published in Spanish for Houston's *Papel Chicano,* appeared in the first issue of the newspaper and discussed the marginalization of women in the movement. The republication of articles circulated diverse Chicana political ideas in a multitude of places, formats, and modes of publication, which was crucial to communication across regions and regional political traditions and was an important translocal strategy to formulate shared political demands.

This mode of circulation and the emergence of a translocal Chicana feminist counterpublic is described by Tejana activist Martha Cotera who, reflecting back on the movement, acknowledged the impact of California Chicana feminist writings for Tejanas organizing within La Raza Unida Party. Speaking of Anna NietoGomez, Cotera (1994) states, "Well, you know, it was Anna's articles that always got us what we wanted from the men [in Texas]." Revealing a tactic used in local struggles to press for their demands, Cotera recalls that Tejana activists would draw on the most forthright feminist writings from California as a strategy to represent their call for women's leadership in keeping with other national developments. This tactic played on underlying regional tensions in the Chicano movement at a time when there were ideological differences over how to organize suitable strategies for different political contexts and regional variation (Zavella 1993). Not only was this tool used to press for women's demands in different regional contexts, but it served to spread ideas across geographic regions.

In fact, a primary mode of translocal dialogue happened when local community papers reprinted articles from across the regions and also published articles across different social movements, as exemplified by the republication of an *Hijas de Cuauhtémoc* article by a local women's movement paper in Eugene, Oregon, as well as in the newspaper of one of the Young Lords Party chapters, *El Young Lord.*[19] Discussion, discursive formations, and strategies traveled and were transformed by differing geographic communities and constituent audiences through the process of republication.

Conferences and Counterpublics

The *Hijas de Cuauhtémoc* newspaper and its outgrowth, the *Encuentro Femenil* journal, were important because they were among the first in the nation to publicly vocalize a Chicana feminist vision. This was crucial in the student movement because it gave women a place to move in and through and sometimes outside of nationalist discourse and created a space where sexism within the movement could be challenged. The students involved in the Hijas de Cuauhtémoc endured a great deal of harassment, scorn, and criticism, and all of the women I interviewed described the ostracism they encountered regardless of whether they defined themselves as feministas. Their detractors made a range of claims, including that they were on an "Anglo bourgeoisie trip," were *agringadas* (anglocized) or *Malinches.* In relation to these forms of silencing, Pesquera and Segura remark that "Chicanas who deviated from a nationalist political stance were subjected to negative sanctions" (1993, 102). Citing Martha Cotera's observation that "[Being called a feminist] was a good enough reason for not listening to some of the most active women in the community" (1977, 31), Pesquera and Segura argue that "such social and political sanctions discouraged women from articulating feminist issues" (1993, 102). It is important to note that feminist baiting was often articulated as lesbian baiting, which was another form of policing around issues of gender and sexuality (Moraga and Anzaldúa 1981; Moraga 1983).

As a means to subvert the silencing mechanisms deployed against them, Chicana feminists created a counterpublic by reconfiguring and engendering movement spaces in this era, not operating outside of it (del Castillo 1980). In the *Hijas de Cuauhtémoc* newspaper, the practice of publishing conference proceedings and continuing debates in print served not only as an important mode of circulation but as a mode of contestation. This is exemplified in the circulation of the infamous statement from the 1969 Denver Youth Liberation Conference, where it was declared on the floor of that historic conference that it was the consensus of the Chicana caucus that "the Chicana does not want to be liberated." As a defining moment of the Chicano movement where *El Plan Espiritual de Aztlán* (considered by many to be the movement manifesto) was adopted, this statement is in itself an interesting moment of contestation, when the rejection of the white women's liberation movement was clearly articulated (Cotera 1976). Some activists who were at the caucus meeting felt shocked to hear the proclamation at the final plenary because in the actual women's caucus meeting, strategies for gaining fuller participation for women within the movement were discussed (Pesquera 1995). This statement illustrates the contested and contestatory nature of Chicana feminism in the movement and the difficulty of articulating a new kind of Chicana political subject within the confines of masculinist nationalism. Yet, the declaration on the floor of the Denver Youth Liberation Conference also points to what I call hidden gender insurgencies, where subversive spaces were constituted in the movement's organizational structures largely through women's caucuses, which offered a continued focus on questions of gender and sexuality. When direct confrontation on women's issues was not tactically possible and not politically strategic, many demands were negotiated below the surface of public movement spaces.

The 1971 publication of the newspaper continued the dialogue on the role of women initiated at the Denver conference. A response was issued by Enriqueta Longeaux y Vásquez, which was printed in *El Grito del Norte* and reprinted in both Robin Morgan's *Sisterhood Is Powerful* and the first issue of *Hijas de Cuauhtémoc*. Another response was issued in *Hijas de Cuauhtémoc* by member Anna NietoGomez, entitled "Chicanas Identify!" The practice of publishing conference proceedings, debates, and conflicts through circulation and distribution in print community networks was crucial in crafting venues that promoted critically needed conversations regarding women's struggles. Chicana print culture constructed interpretive communities that served as spaces to build and discuss not only different political positions but the multiple political and regional meanings of Chicana identities. The fact that contending perspectives and controversial pieces were included in the publication of the newspaper illustrates that Chicana print communities were not unified discursive fields but sites of construction and contestation.

Regional Organizing and the Hijas de Cuauhtémoc
The publication strategy of the Hijas de Cuauhtémoc coincided with their long-term organizational goals and with a larger scope of regional organizing. For example, the first issue, published in March 1971, was primarily

concerned with Chicanas at CSULB in conversation with other groups, such as the women in the Orange County Brown Berets, but as new issues were published, the newspaper began to serve as a vehicle for Chicana regional communication (Miranda 1996). The second issue of *Hijas de Cuauhtémoc*, published as a regional organizing tool in April 1971, was designed to circulate ideas produced at the Los Angeles Chicana Educational Conference, which was organized in preparation for the first national Chicana Conference, La Conferenica de Mujeres por la Raza, to be held in Houston later that year.

In preparing to go to the first national conference, the Hijas membership realized there had been little sustained communication in California among Chicanas. As a remedy to this situation, they helped to organize the Chicana Educational Conference for May 8, 1971 with the host Chicana organization at CSU Los Angeles, inviting "Chicanas from the high schools, the community, the Pinta and the colleges." When 250 Chicanas attended, they realized that the newspaper needed to move beyond campus and become broader in scope to be effective at mobilizing statewide communication. The second issue marked a shift in the role of the newspaper as it became a regional forum for Chicanas, and the subsequent issue was planned to present the results from the Southern California conference to the National Conference. To develop the philosophical premise and ideological base of Chicana feminism, the Hijas de Cuauhtémoc began discussing and drafting their philosophy of Chicana sisterhood or "la Hermanidad" [*sic*].[20] The third issue that came out in June 1971 reported that the May Chicana Educational Conference was organized around five workshops and began with performances by las Adelitas and teatro de San Diego, a poetry reading of "Yo soy Chicana de Aztlán" by Sara Estrella, and an hour-long lecture on the "History of La Mexicana." The issue published proceedings of the conference and reports from the workshops.[21] The conference ended with a session that compiled all the ideas from the workshops into a platform for the National Conference in Houston and was followed by a dance where the "Fabulous Sounds" played.

Crossing the Desert and Ideological Divides (in a Station Wagon)
Modes of communication were crucial to building a political movement of Chicana feministas, and the newspaper aimed to fill an existing gap. "By 1971, the contact between Raza women had been sharply reduced out of pressures to close off the communication by the nationalist movement" (NietoGomez 1991). This closure of communication was probably most dramatically illustrated in the 1971 La Conferencia de Mujeres por la Raza in

Houston and its aftermath. The Hijas de Cuauhtémoc pooled their earnings to publish their third newspaper and held several fundraising activities to pay for their trip. Community members donated station wagons to transport the women from Los Angeles to Houston. They struggled to gather resources, and finally, some twelve women from CSU Long Beach, CSU Los Angeles, and Los Angeles City College piled into the station wagons and began their long journey across the desert. Ranging in age from 18 to 25, for many it was their first trip away from home alone.

What happened at the Houston conference would change the development of Chicana feminism in this era and reflected the contested terrain on which early Chicana feminist thought and practice emerged within an ideologically conflicted social movement field. The conference took place May 28–30, 1971 in Houston and was organized by community women, Elma Barrera, and the staff of the Magnolia Park Branch of the YWCA, which was located in a largely Mexican barrio (E. Barrera and NietoGomez 1975). The organizers included Chicana educators, community leaders, welfare women, and nuns. The group of community women planned and raised funds for two years to gather enough resources to organize the conference. Chicanas of all sectors were invited and the response was enormous. With more than six hundred Chicanas from more than twenty-three states in attendance, the conference brought together all of the prominent Chicana activists from around the country for the first time (Flores 1971; López 1977). The workshops included such groundbreaking topics as the role of the Church in the oppression of Chicanas, labor issues, Chicana feminism, women in the Raza Unida Party, health care, women's role in the movement, welfare rights, and women's history.

A rift began to develop on the first day of the conference when a small group began to criticize the conference as being bought out by the white women's movement because it was held at the YWCA, which they claimed had been historically a "white, racist institution." Critics claimed that the organizers were not based in the community, even though they were from the local Houston barrio and ran the predominantly Mexican YWCA. By the second day, a walkout was staged and nearly half of the conference participants left to meet in a local park and hold a counterconference. The Chicana activists from Long Beach who narrated these events all describe a factionalist group who spoke on the floor of the conference about how selfish it was for women to be sitting around talking about their problems when the real problems of la raza were going on outside. Many recall a charismatic woman who staged the walkout by getting control of the microphone and starting to "guilt-trip" women for being there at the conference when their men were dying in massive numbers in Vietnam and the real Chicano struggle was being waged in the farmworkers' march to Delano, where shots had been fired at marchers (Vidal 1971). She invited women who were committed to the liberation of Chicano people to join her and meet in the "community" at a nearby park to discuss the real issues facing Chicanos (C. Sánchez 1997; NietoGomez 1991; L. Hernández 1992; Miranda 1994; Martinez 1999).

Asserting that the division in the conference was no accident, several claim that the women who staged the walkout were sent there by a certain faction of Chicano nationalists based in Los Angeles with which the splinter group was affiliated. While all the women who attended from the Los Angeles area spent months fundraising enough money to travel by caravan and participate in the preparatory regional conference, the women who staged the walkout flew in on the first day of the conference and flew back to Los Angeles before the conference ended. Conference participants claim that they never planned to stay for the full meeting. Illustrating the importance of print in ideological debates, they point out that without staying to hear or debate the final resolutions, the splinter group reached all the local movement press and spread their perspective about the women who had "sold out" and remained at the conference (Racho, Meneses, Acosta, and Quijano 1971).

Despite feeling demoralized, the remaining participants continued the general conference by working together to debate issues, pass resolutions, and develop position papers.[22] Due to their regional preconference community organizing efforts, the Hijas de Cuauhtémoc and other representatives from the Los Angeles regional conference were fully prepared to participate in the national conference. They came armed with the newspaper, which contained the ideas and resolutions of the regional meeting in addition to the five-point plan of "Hermanidad." On the first day they met with Chicanas from all over the country and a resolution passed naming the *Hijas de Cuauhtémoc* newspaper the national print vehicle for Chicana communication that would be used to forge a national organization.

The newspaper never fulfilled the expectation to become a national paper. No further issues were published after the 1971 Houston conference. Although most accounts of the conference depict it as the height of early Chicana feminist activism, others point to the Houston incident as an example of how divided Chicana thinking was around women's politics and feminism, "vividly characteriz[ing] the polarization existing between feminists and nonfeminists" (del Castillo 1980, 13). Many of the Los Angeles–area women continued to work together, although the Houston experience shaded the field of political action and filtered the way activists understood the field of Chicana political positions. For example, NietoGomez (1974b) conceptualized a theory of Chicana feminism where she delineated the difference between "Feministas" and those movement women who, although they were "strong women" and good organizers, were "Loyalists" to the nationalist political line, an analysis echoed by other feminist scholars (Moraga 1983; Pesquera and Segura 1993; Córdova 1994). Despite these challenges, the political project of the Hijas was continued in community-based organizing, the development of early Chicana Studies, and the publication of the first journal of Chicana scholarship in 1973. Locally, the Hijas de Cuauhtémoc ceased to exist in its former configuration, and the kind of Chicana politics they engaged in moved off campus and into various community struggles. Many of the former members are still active today, serving in leadership capacities.

Building a Chicana Counterpublic:
Encuentro Femenil *and Community-Based Organizing*
Under a new political formation, leaders of Hijas de Cuauhtémoc went on to found *Encuentro Femenil* in the spring of 1973. The preface to the first volume marks the development of Chicana feminist consciousness: "Fully aware that feminism should not be viewed as any type of disadvantage, but rather as a means of recognizing one's full and total capabilities, the Hijas founded the *Encuentro Femenil* journal, which now has evolved into a totally independent publication. Realizing that our struggle is racial as well as sexual, we, as Raza women, could in no way fight for feminism without it being an effort on behalf of our people" (Preface 1973, n.p.).

The journal was edited by Anna NietoGomez in collaboration with other Los Angeles–area Chicana activists such as Adelaida del Castillo. Using print to create a counterpublic for education and dialogue on Chicana issues, the journal itself served as an important link and space for autonomous Chicana cultural autonomy outside of the restrictive forms of nationalism. For example, del Castillo's essay "Malintzin Tenépal: A Preliminary Look into a New Perspective" (1974), published in the second issue of the journal, was one of the first to demystify Malinche as a symbol of female betrayal.

The publication of *Encuentro Femenil* not only documented the political mobilization of Chicanas, but it fostered new forms of Chicana political solidarity and participation. In addition to a gendered print community, this period also witnessed the growth of Chicana community and political organizations. Organizations born in this period include the Chicana

Welfare Rights Organization, founded by Alicia Escalante in 1967, and the Comisión Femenil Mexicana Nacional, founded by Francisca Flores and Simmie Romero at a Women's Workshop of the Mexican American National Issues Conference in 1970. Campus and community alliances were forged the following year, when a Comisión Femenil Mexicana chapter was established on the campus of California State College, Los Angeles.[23] Chicanas were mobilizing across the country, and many new organizations began to form, including the National Chicana Political Caucus, MARA (a Chicana prison organization at the California Institute for Women), the formation of a Chicana Caucus at the 1970 Chicano Council in Higher Education (CCHE) meeting in San Diego, and the women's caucus of the Raza Unida Party in Texas.

Chicana public spheres were being forged and expanded not only through print culture but through political alliances. The founders of *Encuentro Femenil* formed alliances with Los Angeles Chicana leaders to document community issues and struggles and build greater political knowledge of these issues among a larger Chicana/o political community. For example, NietoGomez and Corinne Sánchez, who now runs a multiservice community center called Proyecto del Barrio, worked with Francisca Flores and the Comisión Femenil Mexicana to organize the Chicana Service Action Center (CSAC), the first employment training center for Chicanas in East L.A. NietoGomez's article "Chicanas in the Labor Force" (1974a), published in the second issue, records the employment issues and activities of the CSAC. In addition, *Encuentro Femenil* documented the struggle led by long-time welfare activist Alicia Escalante in her essay "A Letter from the Chicana Welfare Rights Organization" (1973b) and her testimony of welfare abuses in "Canto de Alicia" (1973a), which was recorded by NietoGomez and collaboratively published in the journal. The alliance between the two women resulted in NietoGomez's writing several pieces, such as "Madres por Justicia!" (1973b), and mobilizing opposition to the regressive welfare legislation through her article "What Is the Talmadge Amendment?" (1973c) in *Regeneración*.[24]

CONCLUSION: COLLECTIVE KNOWLEDGE
PRODUCTION AND CHICANA STUDIES

In the era I am describing, Chicana poetry and prose were a politicized strategy of self-representation and knowledge production. Chicana print culture formed out of the mandate not only to report and write but also to produce collective self-knowledge as an act of collective self-determination. Many contemporary Chicana intellectuals and writers got their training in the movement or through discursive traditions created by Chicana feminists who emerged out of it. As form and content are dialectically related, this period saw the growth of new, innovative forms of writing indicative of new forms of political subjectivities. Outside of the realist conventions of political journalism, the newsprint forms of the writing varied widely, from open letters to songs introducing a new Chicana poetics of free-form writing. This kind of mixed-genre format would come to form the basis of a pedagogy of liberation among Chicanas themselves as well as a coalitional strategy among women of color predating the profusion of women of color anthologizing in the 1970s and early 1980s. The diverse forms Chicanas invented to "speak themselves" into poetic and political discourse testifies to a new sense of creative agency of the time (Chabram Dernersesian 1993). Crucial in mapping these poetic and political traditions are the writings of Chicana lesbian feminists of the 1970s, who forged new forms of identity, community, and political consciousness.

Collective self-knowledge was often produced in a visual and narrative montage, a format common in the anthologizing practices used by women of color writers and political projects. Developed out of an early women's course in La Raza studies, Dorinda Gladden Moreno's 1973 collection of poetry, prose, and artwork, *La mujer en pie de lucha*, is an early example of these practices. Citing this collection as a way to locate their own project, the editors of the first issue of *Encuentro Femenil* created intertextual conversations across disparate regions, social locations, and ideological differences, which was a widespread practice and part of the exchange created by the Chicana print communities. These earlier forms of Chicana feminist print communities transformed both political discourse and the framework through which it was enunciated. Often portrayed as before their time, grassroots activist intellectuals such as Betita Martinez, Mirta Vidal, and Enriqueta Longeaux y Vásquez were very much women *of* their time who created a Chicana essayist tradition that chronicled how their feminist convictions emerged out of this historical context, often in dialogue with one another. This political essayist tradition was carried on throughout the 1970s through NietoGomez's (1974b) "La Femenista" [sic] and Cotera's two historical chronicles, *Diosa y Hembra* (1976) and *The Chicana Feminist* (1977).

New political communities of resistance nurtured the formation of Chicana print culture, and the production of knowledge was pivotal in building wider coalitions. Encouraged by the Third World Liberation Front strikes at San Francisco State and University of California, Berkeley, Hijas members

Anna NietoGomez and Corinne Sánchez played a critical role in the formation of early Chicana Studies. In 1971, the Chicana caucus of the CCHE demanded that both Chicana curriculum and affirmative action be developed (Castillo 1971; NietoGomez 1975). NietoGomez began teaching at California State University, Northridge in 1972, and in May of that year a Chicano Studies/MEChA conference was held at that campus where a resolution was passed that required all Chicano Studies majors to take at least one class on la Mujer. The resolution declared: "This proposal recognizes the need to lift the veil of the Virgin's face to show a real woman who is not exempt from the trials of life. In order to truly understand the needs and problems of La Raza, we must include the Chicana in our study" (NietoGomez 1973a, 59).

In 1973, a Chicana Curriculum Workshop at UCLA, which brought together leading Chicana thinkers, resulted in a groundbreaking program for the establishment of Chicana curriculum in universities and high schools, published as *New Directions in Education: Estudios femeniles de la chicana* (NietoGomez and Sánchez 1974). During July and August of that year, Sánchez headed an institute in Washington, D.C. to discuss issues of Chicanas in education and the Chicana Studies curriculum that had been previously developed at the UCLA workshop with people throughout the nation (Cotera 1980). Chicana print communities created the space of debate, ideological conflict, and knowledge production through the practice of publishing (and republishing in various translocal sites) conference proceedings, debates, and conflicts, providing the basis for Chicana scholarly production and later collaborative publication (R. Sánchez and Cruz 1977; National Association for Chicano Studies [NACS] 1990; Alarcón et al. 1993). An excellent example of this was the pivotal publication of *Unsettled Issues: Chicanas in the '80s*, the published proceedings of a landmark panel and debate at the NACS in 1982, organized by Berkeley-based Mujeres en Marcha (Córdova 1994).

These print communities were crucial sites of political struggle over meaning and provided a theoretical and historical basis for the formation of Chicana feminist scholarship. Movement print cultures were used to rework the discursive frames of social struggle to craft new spaces for women within masculinist registers of nationalism. These print interventions facilitated the construction of the political identity of the Nueva Chicana and also contributed to building solidarity with other women of color through print-mediated dialogues across communities and social locations.

While these histories give us insight into the new epistemologies, alternative feminist identities, and sites of knowledge production that operated throughout the 1960s and 1970s, they have not been adequately documented in the historical records of the Chicano and feminist movements. Historiography is a political practice, and social movement narratives function as a major site of identity production, often used to legitimate or police the boundaries of what is politically possible in our current context. Because these silences and erasures are taught in Women's Studies and Ethnic Studies departments, they have become institutionalized. Alternative modes of historical inquiry are urgently needed in our political context of retreat from the gains made in the 1960s and 1970s, such as the dismantling of affirmative action, because this retreat mentality is being mirrored in histories of the movements for social justice from this era.[25]

NOTES

I would like to thank the members of the Hijas de Cuauhtémoc and other Chicana feminists who shared their histories and archives with me as well as Angela Davis, Anna NietoGomez, Isabel Vélez, and Patricia Zavella for their feedback on earlier versions of this essay.

1. The spelling of Hijas de Cuauhtémoc varied (e.g., Cuahtemoc, Guatemoc, Cuauhtémoc); I employ the most common usage. All three editions of the newspaper came out in 1971 but were not dated. I refer to each issue in the order it was published and use volume and page numbers for easier reference. In 1991, when I began my project, there were no archived copies of the *Hijas de Cuauhtémoc* newspaper, to my knowledge. NietoGomez gave me permission to deposit her original set in the California State University, Long Beach archives, where numerous scholars have since accessed these materials.

2. Besides the early histories of Chicanas in the movement (López 1977; del Castillo 1980; and P. Hernández 1980) and A. García's (1990) important article, fuller histories are emerging, such as Ruiz (1998, 99–126), and a new generation of scholars has begun to uncover the important role of women in every sector of the Chicano movement (Bernal 1998; Espinoza 1996).

3. In addition to oral histories with the members of Hijas de Cuauhtémoc, Anna NietoGomez, Corrine Sánchez, Leticia Hernández, and Sylvia Castillo, I conducted interviews with activists involved in regional organizing with them, including Marie (Keta) Miranda, as well as several leading Chicanas from different regions active in the same era, Martha Cotera, Elizabeth "Betita" Martinez, and Beatriz Pesquera. Since I began this research, many of the documents discussed here have been published in a very important collection; see A. García (1997).

4. For example, see Acuña's (1988) chapter on the Chicano Movement, "The Day of the Heroes," which is organized by sections entitled José Angel Gutiérrez, Reies López Tijerina, and Rodolfo "Corky" Gonzales. In her study of Teatro Campesino, Broyles-González has critiqued Chicano historiography for using the great man conceptual framework, which, she argues, denies collective creative agency (1994, 135).

5. Examples of how this functions can be illustrated by Acuña's *Occupied America* (1988), which dedicates only a page and a half to women in the movement in a section called "La Chicana," and his section, "A Challenge to Male Domination," is located in the Hispanic (read sold-out) '80s chapter. The only book-length manuscript on the Chicano student movement, Muñoz's *Youth, Identity, Power*, dedicates two sentences to a discussion of sexism in the movement, concluding, "As a result, the various stances on sexism became another reason for division within MEChA, with many women deciding to spend their energy on the development of their own feminist organizations," which appears under the subtitle "The Decline of the Student Movement" (1989, 88). Instead of women's involvement in the movement being seen as a contribution, it is periodized as "decline." For other student movement histories, see Gómez-Quiñones (1978) and E. Chavez (1994).

6. For a discussion of the erasure of women of color as political subjects in social movement historiography and an alternative theory of "multiple insurgencies," see Blackwell (2000a). I began this research as part of an oral history collective aimed at rethinking the historiography of the second wave feminist movement collectively in our meetings and individually through each of our projects. Much of our thinking appears in "Whose Feminism, Whose History?" by Sherna Gluck in collaboration with Maylei Blackwell, Sharon Cotrell, and Karen S. harper (1997).

7. For example, Anna NietoGomez's 1974 article, "La Femenista" [sic], had already called attention to the concept of multiple oppressions and their simultaneous impact in shaping the lived conditions of Chicanas, insights that are often attributed to the women of color feminist theorizing of the 1980s.

8. The point that this was not a separate feminist group is crucial for historical accuracy because the emergence of Chicana feminisms is often narrated as occurring outside of and after the Chicano movement rather than emerging within it.

9. For a critique of movement sexual politics, see "Political Education Workshop" (1971), where women critiqued the practice of male members' "radicalizing (the pants off) of young recruits." Although the article appears with no author byline, Keta Miranda, who cofacilitated the workshop on which the article was based, wrote the piece to reflect the critique by Chicanas in the workshop (Miranda 1996).

10. Anna NietoGomez's name also appears as Nieto-Gómez in documents of the era, but she has clarified since that her last name is spelled NietoGomez.

11. Abortion and reproductive choice were difficult to discuss as a political issue at the time largely because of sterilization abuses. Along with other Latinas in the United States and Puerto Rico, Chicanas and Mexicanas in Los Angeles were the victims of forced sterilization ("Stop Forced Sterilization Now" 1975; Martinez 1998).

12. Eventually, when the group began publishing the paper, they included pieces on Chicana college survival strategies and printed student resources and services (Honesto 1971; M. Chavez 1971; L. Hernández 1971).

13. For critiques of sexism in Chicano Studies, see Orozco (1986) and Mujeres en Marcha (1983). The work of out Chicana lesbian scholars such as Emma Pérez, Deena Gonzalez, Carla Trujillo, Deborah Vargas, and Sandy Soto throughout the 1980s created Chicana lesbian spaces and introduced sexuality as an important category of social analysis within both the National Association of Chicana and Chicano Studies (NACCS) and Mujeres Activas en Letras y Cambio Social MALCS. Because there was so much lesbian baiting of Chicana feminists, critiques of homophobia have not always been forthcoming by all Chicana feminists. Despite these challenges, there is a rich history of Chicana lesbian social criticism, for example, Moraga and Anzaldúa (1981), Moraga (1983, 1993), Trujillo (1991), Pérez (1993), Anzaldúa (1987), and Leyva (1998).

14. Pivotal essays that shifted the debate include Chabram Dernersesian (1992), Alarcón (1990), Fregoso and Chabram Dernersesian (1990), and Gutiérrez (1993).

15. Fernández (1994) discusses Chicana writers' engagement with Chicano nationalism through textual sources, but without a larger contextual and historical analysis. While she deploys Anderson's theory to her reading of the 1973 women's issue of *El Grito*, my analysis differs in its focus on the function of print communities in the formation of new political subjectivities and as a space of Chicana political and cultural autonomy.

16. There was also a school of thought in the Chicano movement that saw Chicano communities in the United States as internal colonies; see Barrera, Muñoz, and Ornelas (1972) and Almaguer (1971).

17. NietoGomez found this tradition of Mexican feminism in Frederick Turner's *The Dynamic of Mexican Nationalism* (1968) and narrates how it was a pivotal turning point in the consciousness of the group. For further discussion of the original Mexican Hijas de Cuauhtémoc and Chicana feminist recuperation of Mexican feminism, see Blackwell (2000b).

18. For development of Chicana feminist discourse, see Alarcón (1990) and A. García (1990); for early Chicana literature, see Sweeny (1977); and for an expansive review of Chicana writings over two decades, see Córdova (1994).

19. Articles from *Hijas de Cuauhtémoc* by Jeanette Padilla and Leticia Hernández and a report on the Houston Conference appeared in *The Women's Press*, Eugene, Oregon (1971). The Puerto Rican Young Lords left the Denver Youth Liberation Conference due to the rhetoric of Chicano nationalism that excluded them; however, they followed Chicana activism through republication (Iris Morales, personal communication). For a history of the YLP and women's involvement, see Morales's film *¡Palante, Siempre Palante!* (1996).

20. Intensely debated, the correct spelling is Hermandad. Hermanidad was an attempt to theorize a Chicana feminist philosophy of sisterhood. Some thought that "correct" Spanish was important, whereas others felt that the "gender-neutral" term naturalized the centrality of male subjectivity into language and argued for refashioning the term to their own devices.

21. Philosophy of La Chicana Nueva (facilitated by Lola Marquez and Sandra Ugarte); Chicanas in Education (Carmen Delgado and Vicki Castro); La Chicana y La Comunidad covered welfare, child care, and community control of institutions (Linda Apodaca and Evy Alarcón); Chicana and Communication discussed the need for statewide newspaper and network (Anna NietoGomez and Gema Matsuda); Political Education of La Chicana discussed the Vietnam War, capitalism, and movement ideology (Keta Miranda and Blanca Olivares).

22. For pieces responding to the Houston conference that continued the dialogue, see Flores (1971), Guardiola (1971), L. Hernández (1971), R. M. Morales (1971), "National Chicana Conference" (1971), and Vidal (1971).

23. Chicana student organizing such as VELA, Chicana Forum, and Comisión Femenil is documented by Matsuda (1974), who describes the hostility Chicanas faced when trying to establish a Comisión chapter on campus by the leadership of MEChA at CSLA, who felt that a women's organization would be a distraction.

24. The Talmadge Amendment to the Social Security Act of 1973 would have required mothers on public assistance with children over 6 years of age to register with the state employment office and to report every two weeks until they found a job; it was short-sighted and had no child care provisions. While there is ample documentation of that, NietoGomez led opposition to the Talmadge Amendment with Escalante. The way her contributions to the Chicano movement have been erased in the historical record is evident in this debate. Acuña (1988, 395) omits her work on the issue and plugs in Francisca Flores, claiming that she led the opposition to the Talmadge Amendment. But Flores (1974) very publicly took the opposing position; because of her long history as a labor activist, her position centered on the dignity in work rather than on the claims being made by Chicana welfare rights activists. There was a major political battle in 1976 between Acuña and NietoGomez at Cal State Northridge when he was chair of the Chicano Studies program and she was terminated as a professor of Chicano Studies for not being "competent" (e.g., not speaking Spanish well enough or publishing enough). By 1976, she had published at least sixteen articles. See the special issue of *El Popo Femenil* (*Women Struggle* 1976) for the struggle by Chicanas on CSUN campus to support NietoGomez.

25. See Gitlin's (1995) retreat from difference into a unitary narrative of sameness through an articulation of a new left nationalism. For a retreat from the hard-won gains by Chicanas, see Ignacio García (1996).

WORKS CITED

Acuña, Rodolfo. 1988. *Occupied America: A History of Chicanos.* 3d ed. New York: HarperCollins.

Alarcón, Norma. 1990. "Chicana Feminism: In the Tracks of 'the' Native Woman." *Cultural Studies* 4(3): 248–56.

Alarcón, Norma, et al. 1993. *Chicana Critical Issues.* Berkeley: Third Woman Press.

Almaguer, Tomás. 1971. "Toward the Study of Chicano Colonialism." *Aztlán* 2 (spring): 137–42.

Anderson, Benedict. 1991. *Imagined Communities: Reflections on the Origin and Spread of Nationalism.* Rev. ed. London: Verso.

Anzaldúa, Gloria. 1987. *Borderlands/La Frontera: The New Mestiza.* San Francisco: Spinster/Aunt Lute.

Barrera, Elma, and Anna NietoGomez. 1975. "Chicana Encounter." *Regeneración* 2(4): 49–51.

Barrera, Mario, Carlos Muñoz, and Charles Ornelas. 1972. "The Barrio as Internal Colony." Pp. 465–98 in *People and Politics in Urban Society*, ed. Harlan Hahn. Urban Affairs Annual Review, vol. 6. Los Angeles: Sage Publications.

Bernal, Dolores Delgado. 1998. "Grassroots Leadership Reconceptualized: Chicana Oral Histories and the 1968 East Los Angeles School Blowouts." *Frontiers* 19(2): 113–42.

Bhabha, Homi K. 1990. "DisseminNation: Time, Narrative, and the Margins of the Modern Nation." Pp. 291–322 in *Nation and Narration,* ed. Homi K. Bhabha. New York: Routledge.

Blackwell, Maylei. 2000a. "Geographies of Difference: Mapping Multiple Insurgencies and Transnational Public Cultures in the Americas." Ph.D. diss, University of California, Santa Cruz.

Blackwell, Maylei. 2000b. "The Hijas de Cuauhtémoc: Chicana Feminist Historical Subjectivities between and beyond Nationalist Imaginaries." Pp. 783–818 in *Las nuevas fronteras del Siglo XXI,* ed. Norma Klahn, Pedro Castillo, Alejandro Alvarez, and Federico Manchón. México City: UNA.

Broyles-Gonzalez, Yolanda. 1994. *El Teatro Campesino: Theater in the Chicano Movement.* Austin: University of Texas Press.

Castillo, Sylvia. 1971. "CCHE Conference." *Hijas de Cuauhtémoc* 1: np.

———. 1996. Interview by author, 24 May, Long Beach, CA. Tape recording.

Chabram Dernersesian, Angie. 1992. "I Throw Punches for My Race, but I Don't Want to Be a Man: Writing Us—Chica-nos (Girl, Us)/Chicanas—into the Movement Script." Pp. 81–111 in *Cultural Studies,* ed. Lawrence Grossberg, Cary Nelson, and Paula A. Treichler. New York: Routledge.

———. 1993. "And, Yes . . . the Earth Did Part: On the Splitting of Chicana/o Subjectivity." Pp. 34–56 in *Building with Our Hands: New Directions in Chicana Studies,* ed. Adela de la Torre and Beatriz M. Pesquera. Los Angeles: University of California Press.

Chatterjee, Partha. 1993. *The Nation and Its Fragments: Colonial and Postcolonial Histories.* Princeton: Princeton University Press.

Chávez, Ernesto. 1994. "Creating Aztlán: The Chicano Student Movement in Los Angeles, 1966–1978." Ph.D. diss., University of California, Los Angeles.

Chavez, Marta. 1971. "Chicana on Campus." *Hijas de Cuauhtémoc,* 1: np.

Córdova, Teresa. 1994. "Roots and Resistance: The Emergent Writings of Twenty Years of Chicana Feminist Struggle." Pp. 175–202 in *Handbook of Hispanic Cultures in the United States: Sociology,* ed. Félix Padilla. Houston: Arte Público Press and Instituto de Cooperación Iberoamericana.

Cotera, Martha P. 1976. *Diosa y Hembra: The History and Heritage of Chicanas in the U.S.* Austin: Information Systems Development.

———. 1977. *The Chicana Feminist.* Austin: Information Systems Development.

———. 1980. "Feminism: The Chicana and Anglo Versions, a Historical Analysis." Pp. 217–34 in *Twice a Minority: Mexican American Women,* ed. Margarita Melville. St. Louis: C.V. Mosby.

———. 1994. Interview by author, 8 August, Santa Barbara, CA. Tape recording.

del Castillo, Adelaida R. 1974. "Malintzin Tenepal: A Preliminary Look into a New Perspective." *Encuentro Femenil* 1(2): 58–78.

———. 1980. "Mexican Women in Organization." Pp. 7–16 in *Mexican Women in the United States: Struggles Past and Present,* ed. Adelaida R. del Castillo and Magdalena Mora. Los Angeles: Chicano Studies Research Center Publications, UCLA.

Escalante, Alicia. 1973a. "Canto de Alicia." *Encuentro Femenil* 1(1):5–10.

———. 1973b. "A Letter from the Chicana Welfare Rights Organization." *Encuentro Femenil* 1(2):15–19.

Espinoza, Dionne. 1996. "Pedagogies of Nationalism and Gender: Cultural Resistance in Selected Representational Practices of Chicana/o Movement Activists, 1967–1972." Ph.D. diss., Cornell University.

Fernández, Roberta. 1994. "Abriendo Caminos in the Brotherland: Chicana Writers Respond to the Ideology of Literary Nationalism." *Frontiers: A Journal of Women's Studies* 14(2): 23–50.

Flores, Francisca. 1971. "Conference of Mexican Women: *Un Remolino.*" *Regeneración* 1(10): 1–5.

———. 1974. "A Reaction to Discussions on the Talmadge Amendment to the Social Security Act." *Encuentro Femenil* 1(2): 13–14.

Fraser, Nancy. 1993. "Rethinking the Public Sphere: A Contribution to the Critique of Actually Existing Democracy." Pp. 1–32 in *The Phantom Public Sphere*, ed. Bruce Robbins. Minneapolis: University of Minnesota Press.

Fregoso, Rosa Linda, and Angie Chabram Dernersesian. 1990. "Chicana/o Cultural Representations: Reframing Alternative Critical Discourses." *Cultural Studies*, special issue 4(3).

García, Alma M. 1990. "The Development of Chicana Feminist Discourse, 1970–1980." Pp. 418–31 in *Unequal Sisters: A Multicultural Reader in U.S. Women's History*, ed. Ellen Carol DuBois and Vicki L. Ruiz. New York: Routledge.

García, Ignacio. 1996. "Junctures in the Road: Chicano Studies since 'El Plan de Santa Barbara." Pp. 181–203 in *Chicanas/Chicanos at the Crossroads*, ed. David R. Maciel and Isidro D. Ortiz. Tucson: University of Arizona Press.

Gitlin, Todd. 1995. *The Twilight of Common Dreams: Why America Is Wracked by Culture Wars.* New York: Metropolitan Books.

Gluck, Sherna Berger, in collaboration with Maylei Blackwell, Sharon Cotrell, and Karen S. harper. 1997. "Whose Feminism, Whose History? Reflections on Excavating the History of (the) U.S. Women's Movement(s)." Pp. 31–56 in *Community Activism and Feminist Politics: Organizing across Race, Class, and Gender*, ed. Nancy A. Naples. New York: Routledge.

Gómez-Quiñones, Juan. 1978. *Mexican American Students por la Raza: The Chicano Student Movement in Southern California, 1966–1967.* Santa Barbara: Editorial La Causa.

Guardiola, Gloria. 1971. "*Conferencia de Mujeres por la Raza:* Point of View." *Papel Chicano* (June 12): 2.

Gutiérrez, Ramón. 1993. "Community, Patriarchy, and Individualism: The Politics of Chicano History and the Dream of Equality." *American Quarterly Journal* 45(1): 44–72.

Hall, Stuart. 1989. "Cultural Identity and Diaspora." In Jonathan Rutherford, ed. *Identities: Community, Culture, Difference.* London: Lawrence and Wishart, 222–37.

Hernández, Carmen. 1971. "*Conferencia de Mujeres:* Chicanas Speak Out." *Papel Chicano* (June 12): 1.

Hernández, Leticia. 1971. "A Letter from Leticia." *Hijas de Cuauhtémoc* 1: np.

———. 1992. Interview conducted by Maylei Blackwell, 28 July, 30 July, and 21 August, Long Beach, CA. Tape recording.

Hernández, Patricia. 1980. "Lives of Chicana Activists: The Chicano Student Movement

(A Case Study)." Pp. 17–25 in *Mexican Women in the United States: Struggles Past and Present*, ed. Magdelena Mora and Adelaida R. del Castillo, Occasional Paper No. 2. Los Angeles: Chicano Studies Research Center Publications, UCLA.

Honesto, Cindy. 1971. "Chicana on Campus." *Hijas de Cuauhtémoc* 2: 4.

"Introduction." 1973. *Encuentro Femenil* 1(2): 3–7.

Leyva, Yolanda. 1998. "Listening to the Silences in Latina/Chicana Lesbian History." Pp. 429–33 in *Living Chicana Theory*, ed. Carla Trujillo. Berkeley: Third Woman Press.

Longeaux y Vásquez, Enriqueta. 1969. "The Woman of La Raza." *El Grito del Norte* 2(9).

López, Sonia A. 1977. "The Role of the Chicana within the Student Movement." Pp. 16–29 in *Essays on la Mujer Anthology*, ed. Rosaura Sánchez and Rosa Martinez Cruz. Los Angeles: Chicano Studies Center Publications, University of California.

Martinez, Elizabeth. 1998. "Listen Up, Anglo Sisters." Pp. 182–89 in *De Colores Means All of Us: Latina Views for a Multi-Colored Century*. Cambridge, MA: South End Press.

———. 1999. Interview by author, 21 September, San Francisco. Tape recording.

Matsuda, Gema. 1974. "La Chicana Organizes: The Comisión Femenil Mexicana in Perspective." *Regeneración* 2(3): 25–27.

Mercer, Kobena. 1994. *Welcome to the Jungle: New Positions in Black Cultural Studies*. London: Routledge.

Miranda, Marie (Keta). 1994. Interview by author, 24 May, Santa Cruz, CA. Tape recording.

———. 1996. Interview by author, 22 May, Santa Cruz, CA. Tape recording.

Mohanty, Chandra Talpade. 1991. "Cartographies of Struggle: Third World Women and the Politics of Feminism." Pp. 1–47 in *Third World Women and the Politics of Feminism*, ed. Chandra Talpade Mohanty, Ann Russo, and Lourdes Torres. Indianapolis: Indiana University Press.

Moraga, Cherríe. 1983. *Loving in the War Years: Lo que nunca pasó por sus labios*. Boston: South End Press.

———. 1993. *The Last Generation: Prose and Poetry*. Boston: South End Press.

Moraga, Cherríe, and Gloria Anzaldúa. 1981. *This Bridge Called My Back: Writings by Radical Women of Color*. Watertown, MA: Persephone Press.

Morales, Rosa Marta. 1971. "Conferencia de Mujeres por la Raza: Rosa en Español." *Papel Chicano* (June 12): 1–2.

Morales, Rosita. 1971. "La Mujer Todavía Impotente." *Hijas de Cuauhtémoc* 1: 2.

Moreno, Dorinda Gladden, ed. 1973. *La mujer en pie de lucha*. San Francisco: Espina del Norte Publications.

Mujeres en Marcha. 1983. *Unsettled Issues: Chicanas in the '80s*. Berkeley: Chicano Studies Library Publications Unit.

Muñoz, Carlos, Jr. 1989. *Youth, Identity, Power: The Chicano Movement*. London: Verso.

National Association for Chicano Studies (NACS). 1990. *Chicana Voices: Intersections of Class, Race and Gender*. Colorado Springs: NACS, Chicano Studies, Department of Sociology, Colorado College.

"National Chicana Conference." 1971. *La Verdad* (July–August): 15–17.

NietoGomez, Anna. 1971. "Chicanas Identify!" *Hijas de Cuauhtémoc* 1(1): 2.

———. 1973a. "Chicanas: Perspective for Education." *Encuentro Femenil* 1(1): 34–61.

———. 1973b. "Madres por Justicia!" *Encuentro Femenil* 1(2): 12–18.

———. 1973c. "What Is the Talmadge Amendment?" *Regeneración* 2(3): 14–16.

———. 1974a. "Chicanas in the Labor Force." *Encuentro Femenil* 1(2): 28–33.

———. 1974b. "La Femenista [*sic*]." *Encuentro Femenil* 1(2): 28–33.

———. 1975. "Un Proposito para Estudios Femeniles de la Chicana." *Regeneración* 2(4): 30–32.

———. 1991. Interviews by author, 7, 18, 22, 29 April, Norwalk, CA. Tape recordings. Los Angeles Women's Movements Oral History Collection, California State University, Long Beach.

NietoGomez, Anna, and Corinne Sánchez, eds. 1974. *New Directions in Education: Estudios femeniles de la chicana.* Los Angeles: University of California Press.

Orozco, Cynthia. 1986. "Sexism in Chicano Studies and the Community." Pp. 11–18 in *Chicana Voices: Intersections of Class, Race, and Gender,* ed. Teresa Córdova et al. Austin: Center for Mexican American Studies Publications.

Pérez, Emma. 1993. "Speaking from the Margin: Uninvited Discourse on Sexuality and Power." Pp. 51–71 in *Building with Our Hands: New Directions in Chicana Studies,* ed. Adela de la Torre and Beatriz Pesquera. Berkeley: University of California Press.

———. 1999. *The Decolonial Imaginary: Writing Chicanas into History.* Indianapolis: Indiana University Press.

Pérez-Torres, Rafael. 1995. *Movements in Chicano Poetry: Against Myths, against Margins.* Cambridge, England: Cambridge University Press.

Pesquera, Beatriz. 1995. Interview by author, 23 March, Long Beach, CA. 16mm film.

Pesquera, Beatriz, and Denise Segura. 1993. "There Is No Going Back: Chicanas and Feminism." Pp. 95–116 in *Chicana Critical Issues,* ed. The editorial board of Mujeres Activas en Letras y Cambio Social. Berkeley: Third Women Press.

"Political Education Workshop." 1971. *Hijas de Cuauhtémoc* 3: np.

Preface. 1974. *Encuentro Femenil* 1(2): n.p.

Racho, Susan, Gloria Meneses, Socorro Acosta, and Chicki Quijano. 1971. "Houston Chicana Conference." *La Gente* (May 31).

Rendon, Armando B. 1971. *Chicano manifesto.* New York: Macmillian.

Ruiz, Vicki R. 1998. *From Out of the Shadows: Mexican Women in Twentieth-Century America.* New York: Oxford University Press.

Sánchez, Corrine. 1997. Interview by author, 3 September, San Fernando Valley, CA. Tape recording. Los Angeles Women's Movements Oral History Collection, California State University, Long Beach.

———. 1998. Interview by author, 2 January, San Fernando Valley, CA. Tape recording. Los Angeles Women's Movements Oral History Collection, California State University, Long Beach.

Sánchez, Rosaura, and Rosa Martinez Cruz, eds. 1977. *Essays on La Mujer.* Los Angeles: Chicano Studies Center Publications, UCLA.

Sosa-Riddell, Adaljiza. 1974. "Chicanas and El Movimiento." *Aztlán* 5(1): 155–65.

"Stop Forced Sterilization Now!" 1975. *La Raza* 2(4): 12–15.

Sweeny, Judith. 1977. "Chicana History: A Review of the Literature." Pp. 99–123 in *Essays on La Mujer,* ed. Rosaura Sánchez and Rosa Martinez Cruz. Los Angeles: Chicano Studies Center Publications, UCLA.

Trujillo, Carla. 1991. "Chicana Lesbians: Fear and Loathing in the Chicano Community." Pp. 186–94 in *Chicana Lesbians: The Girls Our Mothers Warned Us About,* ed. Carla Trujillo. Berkeley: Third Women Press.

Turner, Frederick. 1968. *The Dynamic of Mexican Nationalism.* Chapel Hill: University of North Carolina Press.

Vidal, Mirta. 1971. *Women, New Voice of La Raza.* New York: Pathfinder Press.

Zavella, Patricia. 1993. "Feminist Insider Dilemmas: Constructing Ethnic Identity with 'Chicana' Informants." *Frontiers* 13(3): 53–76.

Chicana Print Culture and

Chicana Studies: A Testimony to the

Development of Chicana Feminist Culture

ANNA NIETOGOMEZ

• • • • •

In her essay, "Contested Histories: *Las Hijas de Cuauhtémoc*," Maylei Blackwell aptly describes how print media was used to build a cultural challenge. The development of Chicana print culture became a pedagogical tool to identify, discuss, and develop Chicana feminist values, Chicana feminist issues, and Chicana studies.

In the beginning, the Chicana feminist print culture of the 1970s began by reporting the ideas presented at Chicana forums. In time, Chicana feminist print culture also became a forum for the articulation of Chicana ideas. The forum became an opportunity for Chicanas to discuss their political, social, economic, and cultural conditions. They raised feminist questions that challenged the institutions predetermining their conditions. Most important, they shared ideas as to what Chicanas had done or could do to make their situations better and developed critiques of Chicano civil rights organizations. Feminist proposals were presented to civil rights leaders rejecting discrimination against Chicanas and promoting a political platform for equal rights and equal opportunities for Chicanas. The Chicana print culture reported these activities and produced a collective knowledge that created a sense of collective feminist leadership for cultural social change. Blackwell identifies this process as the building of a counterpublic. I define this counterpublic as Chicana Thought.

The development of a Chicana studies curriculum at the California State University campus parallels the construction of the Chicana feminist counterculture in the nation.

I was hired to teach Chicana studies at California State University at Northridge in September 1971. I taught four classes a semester. For the first year, two of these classes were "The Mexican Family" and "La Chicana." The first collection of readings for the first classes was composed of articles from books, magazines, and newspapers. The first English books I encountered were about women of Mexico. They included Ward Morton's *Women's Suffrage in Mexico* and Gerald Flynn's *Sor Juana Inés de la Cruz.* There was some research on the Chicana experience in social science journals but it was often redundant, overgeneralized, and superficial. Therefore, the ideas and information coming from the Chicana print culture were a critical resource of the Chicana experience.

Articles from Chicana print media and the development and publication of oral histories played a vital role in the development of the Chicana studies curriculum. The Chicana press included Francesca Flores's *Regeneración,* a magazine published in Los Angeles; Chicana newspapers such as *Hijas de Cuauhtémoc* and Pepita Martinez's *El Grito del Norte* from New Mexico; and journals such as *Encuentro Femenil,* a Chicana feminist journal from Long Beach, and San Francisco's Dorinda Moreno's *La Mestiza.* In addition, there were special edition community newspapers from all parts of the nation. Community and student newspapers from New York, Texas, and Kansas periodically devoted an issue to *La Mujer.* These special editions would be distributed throughout the nation by the Chicano/Chicana press network. Blackwell refers to these publications as major cultural sites of identity production. This identity production documented the emergence of Chicana feminism and played an integral part in the Chicana studies curriculum.

CREATING A KNOWLEDGE BASE FROM THE COMMUNITY

I concur with Blackwell's concept that oral history foregrounded a discourse of the Chicana feminist experience. Oral history was an important method because it created a body of knowledge about different types of Chicanas. Oral histories of Chicana leaders and their organizations illustrated the diverse political ideas Chicanas had about social change. Access to these women was essential to the development of an accurate and relevant Chicana studies curriculum. Participation in different Chicana organizations provided access to the people whose oral history reflected the Chicana feminist contemporary experience.

Participation in Comisión Femenil, the Chicana Service Action Center, and the East Los Angeles Chicana Welfare Rights Organization provided access to two oral histories. I was able to document the political ideas of two significant Chicana leaders in Los Angeles in the 1960s and the 1970s, Francisca Flores and Alicia Escalante. The *Encuentro Femenil* journal published these oral histories and became a critical Chicana press publication. At that time, Los Angeles was bustling with organizing around Chicana issues. Escalante organized a national but unsuccessful effort to prevent the passage of the Talmadge "Right to Work" welfare/workfare legislation. She also started Channel 34's annual telethon, the Christmas toy drive for the poor, that continues to this day. Flores organized the first Chicana employment training center, the Chicana Service Center, and Comisión Femenil, one of the first political Chicana organizations. She organized Chicanas to lobby the legislature to fund child care centers, arguing that they raised the family's socioeconomic status by freeing women to work. Flores also edited and published *Regeneración*, a Los Angeles Chicano magazine, making visible the work of artists and writers.

Participation in other community organizations provided a pedagogical environment that included the exploration of Chicana feminist issues. Carmen and Ramona Duran, a mother-and-daughter team from San Fernando, organized Mujeres Unidas. One of the many accomplishments of Mujeres Unidas was to organize a child care center to create opportunities for mothers to finish their high school education and to continue on to college. Chicana teenagers organized a support group at the Van Nuys Community Center. These young women came together to deal with the obstacles that interfered with their ability to have a normal childhood and prepare for a successful future. Education was their goal, but adult responsibilities in the family, family and gang violence, and unwanted pregnancies diverted their energies away from a better life. These young women taught me what the educational issues of their Chicana experience were. My participation in these organizations provided me with the necessary education to teach Chicana studies. The publication of *Encuentro Femenil* provided the necessary vehicle to document the product of this learning and create a space for Chicana Thought and Chicana studies.

Developing Chicana studies also played a major role in producing a collective knowledge that sustained and expanded Chicana print culture. Chicanas organized annual Chicana conferences and used print culture to document Chicana Thought. Chicana student newspapers created a supportive environment to generate the development of Chicana Thought and a Chicana studies curriculum. Each year Chicanas would agree to organize an annual conference as a special project one semester, and then they would document the collective ideas, interview the speakers, and report the events of the conference in a special edition of the newspaper the next semester.

For example, in 1971, students organized a Chicana workshop for a Cinco de Mayo celebration as part of a Chicana studies class project. The students dedicated one day to celebrate and recognize Chicana leaders and to discuss Chicana issues. The students reported the events in a special Chicana edition of the CSUN MEChA student newspaper, *El Popo.* In 1972, the Chicana student leaders organized La Semana de la Mujer (The Week of the Woman) as a class project. Linda Arrequin, president of CSUN Associated Women's Students, Audrey Camarillo of the EPIC Program, and the students of the Chicana independent studies class brought together their resources to produce the first week-long forum devoted to the Chicana. Again the students documented and published the Chicana feminist experience in *El Popo Femenil,* a special edition of the MEChA student newspaper. Following the example of other Chicana student newspapers, this special edition adopted its own identity and called itself *Hermandad.*

The annual Chicana conferences were forums to discuss Chicana issues. These issues included (1) the right to adequate women's health care; (2) education about women's bodies and reproduction; (3) child care issues in higher education; (4) sexism in the Chicano movement; (5) the Chicana feminist movement; (6) stereotypes of Mexican women in literature; and (7) history of the Mexican woman. Following are examples of three of the issues.

Chicana Health

At the 1971 CSUN Dia de la Mujer (Women's Day), Chicana students proposed that a Chicana health education program be developed at the student health center. The goal of this program would be to provide health information to help Chicanas gain control of their future by gaining control of their body in the present. Health information would address issues of menstruation, contraceptives, pregnancy, abortion, breast cancer, and diabetes.

The discussion about Chicana health issues continued at the 1972 Semana de la Mujer Conference. Enriqueta V. Chavez and Maria Garcia led a discussion on the health delivery system's failure to meet the needs of the Chicana. Sylvia Delgado, a birth control counselor at the Northeast Health Center in East Los Angeles, described the psychosocial issues of reproduction. She gave an account of the ambivalent attitudes, contradictory behaviors, and consequences that occurred when Chicanas made or avoided decisions about premarital sex, sex in marriage, contraceptives, pregnancy, and abortions.

Child Care in Higher Education

One of the 1972 workshops addressed an obstacle students confronted when they were also parents: the lack of adequate child care on campus and in the community. The campus child care center had a long waiting list, and the Chicanas felt that additional child care programs should be developed. A student organizing committee grew out of this workshop, and in 1973 they established a campus student/parent child care co-op. Parents volunteered to work at the center in exchange for child care.

The Chicana Feminist Movement

At the 1972 conference, Marianna Hernandez spoke about the Chicana movement. She reassured Chicanas that they were doing the right thing. She asked Chicanas not to be taken aback at name-calling strategies, acknowledging that efforts to label the Chicana movement a "white women's movement" were attempts to discredit and stop the people who were organizing a new movement. She offered that one of the tasks of a new movement is to explain itself and that organizing Chicana conferences and publishing new ideas was an important way for the Chicana movement to do this.

DEVELOPMENT OF A CHICANA STUDIES CURRICULUM

The issues and ideas heard at the Chicana conferences provided direction and readings for the development of the Chicana studies classes. A course entitled "Contemporary Issues of the Chicana" evolved a section on women's health, reproductive rights, child care, education, and identity. Students in the "Mexican American Family" class collected oral histories from parents and grandparents and found out how their families dealt with feminist issues.

The Chicana students successfully negotiated with the Chicano Studies Department to require all majors to take at least one Chicana studies class. In 1975, the department identified "Contemporary Issues of La Chicana" as a class that could be used to meet graduate requirements for its major.

In the summer of 1976, I came to realize that discourse and the Chicana print culture lacked the visual reinforcement that Maylei Blackwell calls the collective remembrances that could fortify the public histories of the Chicana experience. The production of identity needed to incorporate a multitude of images into the culture of Chicana Feminist Thought. This understanding motivated me to research and develop a "History of La Chicana" slide show. The slide show presented images of leadership outside of the family, including pre-Columbian women and historical figures of the Mexican independence and revolution. Images showed women fighting for democratic rights in the Mexican women's suffrage movement, the labor movement, and civil rights movements in the United States. I never got to present the slide show at CSUN. But Cyn D. Honesto, a photographer, poet, and former member of Hijas, introduced me to Sylvia Morales, a UCLA film student. Morales obtained funding from the American Film Institute to do a film on the Chicana. She asked me to write the film script and Honesto to be the cameraperson. In 1980, the film, *Chicana,* was completed. It fell short of my expectation, but it did contribute to the collective remembrances of the Chicana experience.

The leadership of Chicano studies at CSUN came to view my perspectives in the Chicana studies classes as a threat to its pedagogy, and I was denied tenure my last year of teaching. In reaction to this decision, the students organized a conference on sexism in Chicano studies. Workshops were held on the lawns, and the issues were depicted in the student newspaper, *Women's Struggle.* Again, through Chicana print culture, this experience became a part of the larger Chicana feminist culture.

Chicana print culture and Chicana studies reinforced each other. They created new pedagogical, political, and historical learning. They nurtured the production of collective identity and the formation of the Chicana public cultures.

This short story is an example of Maylei Blackwell's premise that print media were used to build a cultural challenge and helped create a community of feminist values. It is women's work to define what these feminist values are. What are these values? They are democratic values. Women and men are equally valued. Respect is not dependent on gender. Women are the decision makers of their individual lives. Women and children have the right to live in a violence-free environment.

The Chicana feminist culture is still in development. There are stories of "men's work" yet to tell: of men creating a cultural forum to challenge male roles. It is the story of the democratic challenge to the authoritarian values that depend on the sexual inequality of women and violence.

WORKS CITED

Flynn, Gerard C. 1971. *Sor Juana Inés de la Cruz.* New York: Twayne Publishers.
Morton, Ward M. 1962. *Women's Suffrage in Mexico.* Gainesville: University Press of Florida.

CHAPTER THREE

The Writing of *Canícula:*

Breaking Boundaries, Finding Forms

NORMA E. CANTÚ

• • • • •

I have always written—I may not have always shared what I was writing, and I may not have let others know—but, ever since I learned the magic that gives letters sound and meaning, I have written. I have always written. And I have always read, at least as long as I can remember from about age 5 or 6, when I learned to read and to write in Spanish. Both reading and writing have become a need for me. In this brief piece, I want to dwell on this need of mine but focus on one particular project, my first published novel, *Canícula: Snapshots of a Girlhood en la Frontera,* for its publication has wrought significant changes in my life. I'd like to trace the major aspect of its production in an act of self-reflection; I'd like to cite the various influences, literary and not, that led me to write it; and, finally, I explore my feelings as a critic vis-à-vis my newfound role of writer. In a way, all that I write here is self-revealing and disturbing. The recursive manner in which the topics come up shows that they are nudging each other for attention even as I think about what and how I am going to write. As I think about this thing that I do—this need of mine called writing—I agonize seeking to establish a semblance of order to my thoughts, trying to address each of these inextricably bound activities and my many roles: feminist, Chicana, professor, student, writer, cultural and literary critic.

In the 1990s a "new" genre that merges fiction and autobiography came to the forefront. It is at this *fin de siècle* when the "creative nonfiction" genre finally established itself in the way that most literary genres have in the past, with authors who claim to write in that genre, with a literary publication devoted to the genre, and with university classes on the subject. *Faction* or *creative nonfiction,* it is the same: personal narratives turned tales. The roman à clef of an earlier era has found an audience in contemporary U.S. society. In the past, writers published personal *testimonios* or autobiographical essays and even what could be called creative nonfiction, but it has really only been in the past ten years or so that the strict boundaries of fiction and nonfiction have blurred in particular ways. Audre Lorde (1982), Gloria Anzaldúa (1987), Sandra Cisneros (1983), and Cherríe Moraga (1983) were among the first in the 1980s to publish works that defied classification in terms of traditional genres. It was in the 1990s when the strictly autobiographical *Hoyt Street* by Mary Helen Ponce (1993), *Red Camp* by Debra Diaz (1996), and the more recent *Barefoot Heart: Stories of a Migrant Child* by Elva Treviño Hart (1999) were published. Of course, Richard Rodríguez (1981) and others, such as Ernesto Galarza, had published personal autobiographical narratives even before; and much earlier, as Rebolledo and Rivera (1993) have noted, women had written and published personal ethnographic works. Unbeknownst to me, this new genre, creative nonfiction, was coming into being just as I was planning and writing *Canícula* in the spring and summer of 1993.

But how does one become a writer of creative nonfiction? That summer, when I made time to write, I was not quite sure what kind of narrative I would produce. Perhaps here I need to go back and trace my memories of reading and writing. I have been hooked from the time in the early 1950s when my maternal grandmother, Celia Becerra Ramón, taught me to read in Spanish from *El Diario,* the newspaper from Nuevo Laredo. I have memories of lying sprawled on the linoleum-covered floor of our kitchen on Santa Maria Street. While Bueli ironed or cleaned beans or engaged in some other household task, I sounded out letters and made sense or, more often, read and did not make sense. I read to her words I did not comprehend and that she sometimes explained and other times just glossed over with some vague remark.

I read. I have always read. Ever since I can remember, I have read. I can and often do read two or three books a week, reading a 200-page novel in one sitting. This skill comes, I believe, from practice. In high school my appetite for fiction grew exponentially after Ms. Gutiérrez, my sophomore English teacher, fed my hunger for novels and allowed me to do nothing but read for a whole semester. I loved it, and although I read mostly classics by British authors for school, at home I read Spanish-language romance novels by Corin Tellado and the magazines my parents read: Mami read *Confidencias;* Papi read *Siempre* and *novelas,* those tiny paperback westerns sold in newsstands all over Mexico.[1] I was also very aware of what my teachers were reading. The same Ms. Gutiérrez read works by Faulkner and Steinbeck, and of course I was intrigued and went looking for *Winter of Our Discontent* after she mentioned the book in class. Reading definitely influenced my love of writing, and I don't believe I would have ever dared write anything for publication if I had not had the early models at home and in the various communities I inhabited. I have kept a journal since 1963, when my friend Berta Lucila Gómez gave me a red fake leather-bound diary with a lock and a tiny key for Christmas. We had agreed to give each other the diaries, but when I finally had the money and had convinced my mother to go with me to buy it, the diaries had sold out, so Berta didn't get the gift but I did. I was distraught but joyous, because I now had a real book where I could keep my secret writings. I still have this and other journals filled with the musings of a high school Chicana in Laredo, Texas, full of lists. I listed my favorite songs—"Sad Movies Make Me Cry," "Angelito," "la cama de piedra"—whose lyrics spoke to me in poetry, songs I heard on the radio from Nuevo Laredo and San Antonio.[2] I listed favorite foods and recipes, mostly foods I dreamed about and rarely ate: shrimp cocktail, lemon meringue pie, as well as the foods I was learning to cook, *calabacita con pollo, migas* (a squash with chicken dish, corn tortilla strips cooked with fried eggs or with a spicy sauce known as *chilaquiles* in other places). I listed movies and celebrities I loved and of course poetry, some copied from the Chilean poet Neruda, the Mexican sixteenth-century feminist poet Sor Juana, and the romantic Amado Nervo. My early journals are full of my own poetry, which I never dared show anyone. I even drafted short stories in those early journals. The pattern was set. The journal was and is where I record dreams and musings, where I plan creative pieces and let off steam. It functions as a prayer book of sorts as well as a log of activities. Most of my writing happens in the journal, but *Canícula* wasn't born in the journal, at least not directly. Only a couple of pieces appear as early entries in the journal: *Mase* is one of them. I came home from my mom's cousin's funeral and wrote and wrote to expiate the pain. Some of those thoughts are in *Canícula.* Alongside the writing, there has always been the reading.

I could say that my literary influences for *Canícula* have been all the reading I've done in forty years or so, readings that of course include all the canonical texts an English major and professor must be familiar with, but, more significant perhaps, all the Chicano/a literary production I could lay my hands on from the early Quinto Sol publications, the journal *El Grito,* and the novels from Rivera (1972) and Anaya (1972) to Castillo (1979) and Cisneros (1983) and most of what had been published up to 1993. But the more conscious influences, I believe, are two particular works whose influence can more clearly be noted in the genre I chose to shape my narrative. I read *Six of One* by Rita Mae Brown (1983) while I was in Spain in 1985, and I had read Maxine Hong Kingston's (1989 [1976]) *Woman Warrior: Memoirs of a Girlhood Amongst Ghosts* when it first came out. I can honestly say that these two creative nonfiction works, the former a novel that the author calls creative autobiography and the latter a novel the author was encouraged to categorize as autobiography, started me thinking about a narrative set on the border that used an autobiographical strategy. In 1980, I had begun writing the historical novel that remains unpublished, *Papeles de mujer* (Women's Papers/Women's Roles), where I relied on real and fictionalized documents, a diary, immigration papers, and letters to tell a story. I often think up exercises for my writing classes, and in the early 1980s I began using a photo for a guided imagery exercise. The students loved it and so did I. Both of these, the unpublished work and the photo exercise, provided experiences that led me to focus on a vehicle to frame the narrative that was to be *Canícula*, the idea of the photos as the starting points for the stories. But not only did the photos work well as springboards for memory and consequently for writing, they also framed my notions of memory and narrative well. I had read Sontag (1990) and Barthes (1981), and as an amateur photographer I had been considering how visual literacy and visual images shape our memories and indeed communicate stories. I am still fascinated by the way one can "read" images and the epistemological frameworks one develops through early visual literacy.

But all this sounds terribly planned; I can't honestly say that I set out to write *Canícula* the way that I did. I had submitted a proposal to the University of New Mexico Press in 1992 for a collection of ethnographic personal essays, a project born, in large part, from my research on the fiestas in Laredo, one of which was the Matachines dance drama I had been studying since 1975.[3] It was in fact these books, one on Matachines and the other an ethnography of fiestas in Laredo, that I had in mind when I drove out of Laredo right after completing all teaching duties for the first summer session of 1993. I was so anxious that I forgot to gas up and ended up in west Texas during a summer rainstorm praying that I could reach a gas station. When I saw a desolate service station appear out of nowhere, I offered a prayer of thanksgiving and sighed with relief. I stopped for the night in El Paso and finally arrived in Albuquerque.

In July, during the dog days of summer, the *canícula*, I became a "nun" and cloistered myself at Ana Castillo's home in Old Town and wrote and wrote and wrote on a rented PC in a room the size of a small walk-in closet behind the kitchen. It was in the middle of the hottest days of the year. As I had planned, I began writing the Matachines book. However, I found myself consistently straying into the other project, the pieces for the ethnography of Laredo fiestas. Soon I realized that what I was writing didn't really fit the proposal and that I was spending much more time on this project and neglecting the Matachines project. Having published a few of the pieces I was already calling "Snapshots of a Girlhood *en la Frontera*" in *The Texas Humanist*, I had already decided on the photographs as the objective correlative, borrowing Eliot's term, to include visual allusions. The ideas of Barthes and Sontag kept coming to my mind—of how photography is truth, yet it is unreliable. So I went from there. The stories emerged, merged, flowed, and bled on the page. Once I let go of the Matachines and the ethnography projects, I couldn't stop. Wounds I'd kept hidden began to bleed and old scars to hurt. I was writing from ten to fifteen hours a day. My fear of electrical storms helped. Afternoon thunderstorms would often force me to quit and go sit out on the patio waiting for rain that never came; only the thunderclouds, ominous *culebras* (bolts, literally "snakes") of light across the gray firmament visited me. After the storm passed, I'd sit at the tiny kitchen table turned desk and write, the smell of wet earth whetting my wish for rain. I would write after having thought and rethought what I had written earlier. I wish I could say it was easy. It was not. It's probably one of the hardest things I've ever done. I expiated long forgotten demons that would suddenly creep up as I recalled an incident, a word, a slight, an innuendo. But along with pain came joy, as I remembered family celebrations and triumphs. I resurrected family and friends long gone, and the spirits of both those who have passed on and those who have only been absent from me visited in that tiny room as I wrote and wrote.

At night, dream-filled sleep would find me awake at odd hours, 3 A.M., 6 A.M. I who love to sleep late was up by 7 every morning and eating a *mariachi* (elsewhere known as a breakfast taco and in New Mexico as a burrito) at a restaurant off the plaza in Old Town, reading the local newspaper. The Pope was visiting Denver; a priest was being tried for sexual crimes; the local politicians went on with their back-and-forth banter. I worked the crossword puzzle and read the paper cover to cover—even the want ads and the Sunday travel section. It was the only outside reading I allowed myself. I remember the frenzy of finishing up in the allotted time, aware that I had to return to Laredo to my heavy teaching load at the end of the summer. I was feeling a rush as well as panic; I knew I must finish. I also felt dangerously alone, yet I loved it—loved the solitude, the quiet, the total immersion in the text.

With conscious effort, I worked on the text. Intent on not writing a long sustained narrative, I was also bent on not writing a purely autobiographical book either. Chronological order had to go; after all, we don't think in clean, clear chronological order; life doesn't happen in neat little packages. I wanted a narrative that, like my memory, worked in a recursive and overlapping fashion. Even when orally telling a story, I tell multiple stories and sequence things according to the effect I desire. So in the narrative, I would force order on all my memories and even invent photos and memories. But what was I trying to do in these stories that would not let me be? The stories that were driving me to write? I finally figured out that one of the ways of telling the overarching story about growing up on the border and about memory and photography was to use the haphazard order of the shoebox full of photos. I wanted to focus on the "what" as much as the "why" and "how" of the stories. I recall feeling triumphant when I finished the piece that would become the last piece, "Martin High," for although I wrote it about a third of the way into the book, I immediately realized it was to be the last piece. And almost as a catharsis, I suddenly saw that what I was writing was a novel. I didn't go back and "fill in" what was missing in this piece, even after I had finished the other pieces. I chose instead to let the gaps remain wide open for readers to fill in themselves. But this was later, when I was conscious of a reader; I didn't start with that awareness. I wrote because I had to write. The "why" was clear; I had no choice. And the "how" had become an organic process. *Canícula* practically wrote itself. I felt as if I were merely sifting through memories, translating them into English; in fact, some of the pieces I wrote in Spanish.

Late in the summer, just as I was about to finish my manuscript, I was offered a position in Washington, D.C. to work in the folk and traditional arts program at the National Endowment for the Arts. The pressure of going back to the heavy teaching load was off, and I knew that I could work on the manuscript through the fall. But I wasn't sure I could continue writing. Indeed, it was in D.C. that I really worked on structuring the manuscript into a novel, where with full consciousness I titled the pieces and added the photographs and documents. It was then that I came up with the "autobioethnography" genre, as suggested by a close friend back in Laredo with whom I shared the dilemma of having to write an introduction and a prologue that explained the title and added the narrative frame.

What was I accomplishing with the fictionalized autobioethnography? As a consequence of choices made as I wrote, the narrative evolved into this genre, breaking the restraints placed on traditional narrative structures. I wanted to tell my story of growing up on the *Tejas*-Mexico geographical border, but I wanted to do this in a way that, with my literary critic's eye, I could layer the narrative so that the text would speak to many—my family, my friends, Chicanas/os, readers at large—about many things: relationships (grandparents, parents and children, men and women, women and women, among children, among women, among men, etc.). I also wanted to write about the way childhood and coming-of-age constitute sites where multiple identities develop: the little girl dressed as a China Poblana who also wears a cowgirl costume and first communion white; the teenager wearing hand-me-downs whose shoes signify different things. Being familiar with studies on costume and on dress made me especially aware of such details, but I would venture that having learned to sew and being the daughter of a seamstress also added to my knowledge of how dress plays out in identity formation. My work in semiotic literary analysis, principally in my dissertation, probably shaped the way I explored meaning. This discussion of theory brings me to how I was very aware in the process of putting the pieces together that there would be order but an order that appeared to be haphazard. At this point, I found that I needed to title the pieces, which I had written and numbered but never titled. Yet, I found myself referring to them by descriptive titles: "China Poblana 1" and "Tino."[4] Because I did not have the photos with me as I wrote, I was able to confirm the theory of how memory actually frees the past and photos freeze the moment. When I went back to Laredo to look for the photos and complete the text, I found that the narrative proved the tenuous nature of memory and the apparent rigidity of a photograph. The making of theory through narrative became a subtext for the novel as I worked in the themes presented in the epigraphs—childhood, border, photography, and memory.

The physical act of writing has always been for me a mixed blessing; it can mean aching joints, wrists, elbows, shoulders, and even migraine headaches. Real and physical pain. Of course, there is also the emotional toil that doesn't lag far behind. But then, it's such a joy, this writing, this putting down on paper feelings, observations, and thoughts and making sense of reality. Writing the pain, the anger, the joy, there's nothing comparable. Then, once it's done, the heart-wrenching self-doubts begin. Virginia Woolf's diaries are full of it and so are mine—the "what ifs" and the "I should'ves," never ending. Then I'm the critic. How do I divorce the sharp critical eye, the mind, from the soul that's writing? Again it's not easy. And I'm not so sure I've ever fully achieved the detachment I strive for and that more recently I have not even pretended to achieve.

A while back, I read at UC Davis, and literary critic Angie Chabram interviewed me for her wonderful project on writers writing. I was exhausted after the session and again reflexive. I questioned my state of being. There were a few gems in my journal and much "shoulding"—I should've told her this or that, or I shouldn't have said this or that. *En fin,* the questions Angie asked probed deeper than I'd done on my own. And as a critic I was not quite sure I wanted to reveal so much. The mystery was gone. All it boiled down to was hard work and decisions that led to other decisions. Choices in life that took me up or down a path I had not known existed. I took Machado's wise words, *"caminante no hay camino se hace camino al andar"* (one makes one's path as one walks it), as my own. Yes, I am a critic. I interpret literature, write book reviews and critical articles on fiction and poetry by fellow writers, and I now find myself bridging even these borders that have those who police, who dictate what's what and who's a legal or proper critic or novelist. The impact on my own sense of my work has been positive beyond my expectations. I finally feel free to write as I want. My current projects, like the ethnography of the Matachines de la Santa Cruz and my novel *Hair Matters,* are less bound by the border restrictions of genre specification. Yet I struggle with some questions. Jokingly, a critic asks, "Come on, Norma, why don't the photos match the stories?" And of course my harshest critics, my sisters, read *Canícula* and say "That's not how it happened" and struggle to find the "real" person I'm depicting in a fictitious character who is an amalgam of many. I have faced a community that refuses to engage in an intellectual discussion that explores who we are on the border, refuses to see beyond stereotypes. I still wonder at how the mind works, how memory is elusive, and how past life is shaped by present conditions. In my current projects, I still grapple with the difficult yet necessary work of portraying reality along my beloved borderlands.

All in all, the critic had to write *Canícula,* and the novelist had to be the soul for the mind. *Canícula* is a critical work of fiction and an ethnography. I am after all an ethnographer, if not by training, then through practice. My first publication was a collection of children's folklore back in 1973. My literary precursors, my foremothers, include Cleofas Jaramillo, Jovita González, and Aurora Lucero White as well as Josefina Niggli and Sara Estela Ramírez (Rebolledo and Rivera 1993, 35–39). How can someone who writes in all these genres—literary criticism, folklore, ethnography, and fiction— separate them into neat little boxes labeled and set aside? Maybe it can be done, but I can't do it. Others can write criticism devoid of ethnographic insight, I can't. Others may write novels without cultural trappings, I can't;

others may write ethnography without lyrical linguistic expression, I can't. My choices at this point in my academic career are free because I have stayed true to a commitment I made almost twenty-five years ago to be a teacher who writes. I now face a new challenge and a new identity: I am a writer who teaches. I have morphed into a new role. I like it.

I have heard the charge that *Canícula* is a woman's story. "Where are the boy stories?" a friend in Laredo asks. All I can answer is that they are there but told from a female perspective. Besides, as I told this person, I wasn't going to *la zona* across the river at 15 or feeling that I had to support the family when I was 12. I didn't play football in high school or feel what it was like to not play when that was all that mattered in the world. These stories remain to be told. Someday. I am not sure, though, that I am the person to tell them. I did delete some stories, mostly stories that I felt were extraneous to the project at hand. The feminist in me consciously included the strong women—the mothers, grandmothers, aunts, *comadres.* But it was not a difficult task, for they were there in my life and in my childhood. I wanted to tell the stories of women who survived, who struggled, who worked as schoolteachers, who sold Avon and Stanley products door to door, as well as the mothers who went to work in the fields alongside the men. The women who peopled my childhood belonged to various social classes and survived in the world through different means, but all of them influenced me.

There is another question that scholars have asked me: why it is that, when other writers refuse to engage in an analysis of their own work, I seem to relish jumping into the fray. I don't know if I relish analyzing it, but I do know that it is natural for me to speak of the writing as if someone else had written it. And yes, I explore how the photographs work in *Canícula* to disrupt notions of a reliable narrator. And yes, I love to work through with others the problems that I had in ordering the pieces to give the semblance of haphazard development and why often the photo described is not the one that is on the page in front of the reader, as is the case in "Tino." I will not claim to have the definitive answer to what *Canícula* is saying or doing, but I can tell those who ask what it is I wanted to communicate. Why, for example, "Tino" is one of the shortest pieces and how it took hours, if not days, of sifting through almost twenty pages of prose to arrive at the published piece. Or whether the epigraph I agonized over does indeed presage what the narrative discloses about life on the border, about childhood, and about photography and memory. Photography is not just the structural component for the text, it is a complementary text whereby the reader can "read" in a postmodern fashion much more than the words tell.

The teddy bear on the running board of grandfather's car, the refrigerator on the porch of the frame house, the words on the immigration document—none of these are written about or explained, yet the reader confronted with these details completes the story told in words with a story told through the photo; the icons and symbols that appear in the photos contest or affirm the narrative text. Semiotics holds that all images have meaning; in *Canícula* all images hold stories.

I come back to my first point: I write because I cannot not write. It took many years before I dared publish my work, and many more before I dared write something called a novel. I do not write fast; it takes time and energy, both of which I tend to spend on my teaching, giving to my writing what is left over. But because it is so rare, I value it that much more. And yes, I have been known to clean the kitchen—I mean really clean, from the oven to the refrigerator, scrub not just the floors but the walls and cabinets, rearrange all my cookbooks, and line the shelves with contact paper—when I am avoiding a writing assignment like this one. But, as I tell my students, writing doesn't just occur when one is sitting at the computer or putting pencil to paper. It is an ongoing process that is with the writer in dreams and, yes, while doing household chores or taking a walk. I wrote *Canícula* in an unusually short period of time, four weeks, but it took me over forty years of life to get there, and months of revision and polishing. The writing marathon that summer of 1993 was a necessity; I do not advocate that writers always do it that way. In fact, it is perhaps better to work consistently on a project over a long period of time, immersing oneself in the work and coming up for air. I like to write while I bake bread or do laundry. That way I force myself to get up, take care of an ordinary task, and allow myself to ponder what I am writing. I love to have long periods of uninterrupted time to mentally chew on an image, to daydream a scenario, to mull over a thought. But, for me, such luxury doesn't exist. I have to find time, make time, steal time from my community work, from my students; I have to carve out time to indulge my need to write.

I have been working on my current project for over a year: writing late at night, exhausted from a long day at the office; writing during long airplane trips, pulling out a yellow pad and a pen right after takeoff; writing in the middle of a boring meeting. Whenever I can, I steal away mentally and physically to surreptitiously write a story, a scene, a dialogue, a poem. I love travel metaphors, so I often talk of the task of writing as taking a trip. Writing *Canícula* was not at all like getting in your car and taking a thirty-hour trip across the country, where you plan to stop every three hours or so to stretch, eat, and go to the bathroom and stay with friends each night along the way. No, it was more like getting on a bus where you only get off every six or eight hours to eat something, snack as you read, and sleep in your seat for the thirty-hour trip. You are not driving, you have no control, and you see no one you know. You are not there until you get there, whenever that is. It is a way of traveling, but it is exhausting and not always advisable. There are many ways to travel. One can hike along the Inca trail in Peru, take a cab in New York City, drive cross-country, take a train in Mexico, bicycle in Ireland, fly across an ocean. There are many ways to write. I have traveled in many ways and I have written in many ways, and I can tell you all paths are worthwhile, and ultimately you get there anyway. And I can tell you that for me, the writing—the traveling—is just as significant, if not more so, as arriving.

NOTES

1. *Confidencias* is a woman's magazine that includes recipes, stories, and a column titled "Cartas que se extraviaron" (Lost Letters); *Siempre* is a Mexican publication that has traditionally focused on politics.

2. As teenagers in Laredo in the 1960s, we listened to the one Spanish-language radio program, *Serenata nocturna,* on KVOZ in Laredo and to KTSA in San Antonio for rock and roll music in English. The Spanish radio stations in Nuevo Laredo played mostly romantic ballads and ranchera music.

3. I am still working on this ethnography of the group Matachines de la Santa Cruz. The book, *Soldiers of the Cross: Los Matachines de la Santa Cruz,* is on contract with Texas A&M University Press.

4. Both "China Poblana" and "Tino" ended up with these titles in the published work. The first refers to the traditional costume of Mexico that the little girl Nena wears to the George Washington's birthday celebration parade; there is also a "China Poblana Two" where the mother wears the costume in another photo.

WORKS CITED

Anaya, Rudolfo. 1972. *Bless Me, Ultima.* Berkeley: Quinto Sol Publications.

Anzaldúa, Gloria. 1987. *Borderlands/La Frontera: The New Mestiza.* San Francisco: Aunt Lute.

Barthes, Roland. 1981. *Camera Lucida: Reflections on Photography.* Trans. Richard Howard. New York: Hill and Wang.

Brown, Rita Mae. 1983. *Six of One.* New York: Bantam.

Castillo, Ana. 1979. *The Invitation.* Chicago: Author.

Cisneros, Sandra. 1983. *The House on Mango Street.* Houston: Arte Público Press.

Diaz, Debra. 1996. *The Red Camp.* Houston: Arte Público Press.

Kingston, Maxine Hong. 1989 [1976]. *Woman Warrior: Memoirs of a Girlhood Amongst Ghosts.* New York: Vintage Books.

Lorde, Audre. 1982. *Zami, a New Spelling of My Name*. Watertown, MA: Persephone Press.

Moraga, Cherríe. 1983. *Loving in the War Years: Lo que nunca pasó por sus labios*. Boston: South End Press.

Ponce, Mary Helen. 1993. *Hoyt Street: An Autobiography*. Albuquerque: University of New Mexico Press.

Rebolledo, Tey Diana, and Eliana Rivero. 1993. *Infinite Divisions: An Anthology of Chicana Literature*. Tucson: University of Arizona Press.

Rivera, Tomas. 1972. *Y no se lo trago la tierra*. Berkeley: Quinto Sol Publications.

Rodríguez, Richard. 1981. *Hunger of Memory: An Autobiography. The Education of Richard Rodríguez*. Boston: Godine.

Sontag, Susan. 1990. *On Photography*. New York: Doubleday.

Treviño Hart, Elva. 1999. *Barefoot Heart: Stories of a Migrant Child*. Tempe, AZ: Bilingual Review Press.

Sad Movies Make Me Cry

RUTH BEHAR

· · · · ·

Norma Cantú's essay is about how she comes to writing, and especially how she comes to the writing she is doing now, when she has freed herself to write across genres, memories, languages, and the facts and fictions of her own life story. If she must classify her writing somehow, she chooses to call it "fictionalized autobioethnography." She finds that she can't separate the various forms of writing she does, which include literary criticism, folklore, ethnography, and fiction. She wants to write criticism that is illuminated by ethnography. She wants to write ethnography that respects and remembers poetry. She wants to write novels that are informed by precise and profound knowledge of the cultural nexus in which they are spun. But most of all, she wants to mix it all up, mix all of these desires up, to write in a way that weaves together the groundedness of ethnography in people and place with the personal compulsion of memoir, and, finally, and most challenging, with the enormous risk of taking the imaginative journey of fiction. In *Canícula*, she further adds the counterpoint of photographs to her lucid, subtle, and graceful text, adding the desire for visual pleasure and visual rootedness to her quest for new forms of storytelling.

What can I say? I wholeheartedly support Norma Cantú's agenda. I've been pursuing a very similar agenda myself during the past few years as an anthropologist who comes to the discipline of scripting otherness out of a love for reading and literature that was born, like Cantú's, in an immigrant Latina girlhood and nurtured by supportive high school teachers who put books in our hands or whispered the names of book titles in our always receptive young ears. So I am thrilled, but also a touch *asustada,* to see Cantú articulate a position with which I feel completely at home. I too have been calling for texts that can seamlessly blend personal reflections, ethnographic rigor, and poetic forms of speaking. There is nothing I disagree with in Cantú's essay, and that is why I am asustada. I have a fear of growing complacent, a fear of losing our critical edge as Latina feminist writers if our response to one another's work is only celebratory, only an occasion for praise of one another.

Even so, I want to begin and must begin by *felicitando a la* Norma Cantú, whose integrity, depth, grace, and kindness define both who she is as a person and who she is as a writer. In her, the two are inseparable, the person and the writer, and if, as in my case, you know both, you can count yourself very fortunate, as I do. What draws me to Cantú, the person and the writer, is how she can propose big agendas with such sincerity and humility and thereby make it possible for them to be *realizados,* to become really real.

Cantú brings a sublime tenderness to her autobioethnography. One of the pieces I most appreciate in *Canícula* is "The Wedding," which takes off from a wedding picture of her parents. With care, Cantú chooses the details she wants to emphasize. We learn that her mother's dress had "fifty tiny satin-covered buttons down the back and seven more on each sleeve down to the wrist" and that her father "waited till he was twenty-nine to be sure he'd found the right woman to be the mother of his children." Everything appeared to be perfect, but the couple was plagued by fears and doubts. Not only had the groom's mother expressed her disapproval of the marriage, but it was November, "not a good month for a wedding. Could rain and ruin everything. Could turn cold." Gently, Cantú brings the tensions in the story to a reassuring close: "Stars shine in the clear, crisp night, and it's a good wedding, a good marriage." There is a deceptive simplicity to this story. Free of jargon, deeply feeling, and yet quietly maintaining an observer's tough consciousness, it achieves Cantú's goal of blending ethnography, memoir, fiction, and photographic evocativeness to portray reality in what she describes as her "beloved borderlands."

But I have promised to say not only what is wonderful but also what is maybe problematic about the agenda that Cantú proposes and that other Chicanas and Latinas, myself included, have enthusiastically embraced in recent years. I want to think of these critical remarks as questions that I'm posing to myself as well as to all of us who are seeking to break down the borders between the various forms of expression that we have learned, on the one hand, through our hard-earned academic training and, on the other, through our independent reading and writing, often begun in girlhood, when we dared to dream ambitiously of what we might one day produce as creative thinkers, even though we lacked any sense of entitlement.

This writing that feels so liberating, that blurs and blends genres, that reads so very prettily, poses unique challenges. It is writing that sits uneasily in the academy and that seeks a wider readership beyond its walls. It is writing that, like sad movies, sometimes makes us cry. It is writing that, reminiscent of the journals we kept in our girlhood and continue to keep as grown women, is a source of comfort, affirmation, necessary self-doubt, and dreams. It is writing that we enjoy writing, that gives us great pleasure as writers. It is writing that we've always wanted to do, but that we kept postponing until we had a Ph.D., a teaching job, a decent salary, a roof over our head, and maybe even tenure, or even better, a literary agent. It is writing that takes risks, that *can* take risks, because we're no longer floating in a sea of uncertainty but are safely ashore, either as writers in the academy or writers who are accepted by the academy.

But I worry: As genre outlaws, does our writing become so unclassifiable that it gets lost in the cracks of all those forms we are meshing together? Does its *ni aquí ni allá* quality render it too amorphous to make a mark in the very fields of anthropology, criticism, and fiction writing that we wish both to be accepted by and, at the same time, transform? Will our writing be "too soft" for the academy and "too hard" for our readers outside, most especially for members of our own Latino communities? By doing this writing, do we express our doubleness as Latinas, finding our place in the academy by writing our way home, or are we expressing our profound ambivalence about our own position as uncertain travelers both within the academy and in our various Latino communities that we have had to abandon, intellectually if not emotionally, in order to move forward in our lives? For it seems that what is most poignant about this blended-genre writing among Latinas is that it expresses the desire for a map that will take us back home. Yet ultimately, it is not to our real communities that we return but to imaginative worlds built by the languages we have learned in school and then willfully unlearned to be able to do the writing that is closest to our hearts.

Although I have raised these critical questions for discussion, I don't pretend to have any ready answers. There is no turning back from the kind of writing that Norma Cantú and other Latinas like her, with one foot in the academy and one foot outside, are doing. We will simply have to face the consequences of our writing as they unfold. We don't need to explain ourselves or justify what we're doing. But we must rush to do our own self-critiques, before the critics who don't understand why we're doing what we're doing arrive on the scene and attempt to dismiss our work with claims about its "self-indulgence."

When, in presentations of my own work, I've been asked why I choose to do the kind of writing I do, what I have called an "anthropology that breaks your heart," I say that for many of us it is not a matter of choice but rather a matter of necessity. I cannot, any longer, write in a way that alienates me. I did, for several years, work hard at mastering academic writing forms and, what at first I found virtually impossible, learning to make a logical and cohesive argument. Although I don't regret this training, for it did teach me how to get my often unruly thoughts in order, I'm now moving, like Cantú, more and more into the realm of fiction, building from everything I know and everything I wish I knew but will never know through the use of strictly ethnographic, historiographic, folkloric, and critical forms of elicitation and research.

As I now try to write the story of my Jewish Cuban family's life in Cuba in the three decades before the Cuban revolution of 1959, I am drawing on what I have seen and heard and felt on my thirty trips to Cuba over the past nine years, on family memories and stories, on my reading of modern Cuban literature, and on historical research. But, like Cantú, I reached a point where I had to invent and imagine what I would never otherwise know. I too have stared and stared at photographs of my parents at their wedding and needed to imagine who they were before I knew them. No amount of anthropology will answer that question, or others like it, to my full satisfaction. So I am now working on a novel in which my family's story is told from the perspective of the Afro-Cuban woman who cared for me as a child. She and I have become close again in the course of my trips to Cuba and I have come to realize that she observed my family very closely, immersing herself in the lives of the various members with whom she crossed paths, as anthropologists and domestic workers typically do.

Me está costando trabajo, this writing, because I haven't been able to cloister myself, as Cantú so wisely did, and concentrate all my energies on my writing. But something unexpected and wonderful has happened to me in the course of my willingness to explore the meshing of fact and fiction. I have taken up dancing, especially cha-cha and tango, which together allow me to express both what is light and playful in my spirit and what is deep and melancholy in my soul. When I'm not writing now, I'm dancing, finding my way to as yet unspoken truths as I allow myself to be led around the dance floor, held, in turn, in the embrace of men of all different ages and sizes and skill.

As I dance these days, as I write these days, I am happier than I have ever been. I recognize that, having started in the middle of my life both to write fiction and to dance, I will probably never be very good at either art. Yet I am immensely grateful to have at least begun. *Más vale tarde que nunca.* I will try to learn patience from Norma Cantú. And faith. And during those times when neither the dancing nor the writing go well, I will remember to see a sad movie, so I can cry.

CHAPTER FOUR

Literary (Re)Mappings: Autobiographical (Dis)Placements by Chicana Writers

NORMA KLAHN

•   •   •   •   •

Let us pay attention now, we said, to women: let men and women make a conscious
act of attention when women speak; let us insist on kinds of process which allow
more women to speak; let us get back to earth—not as paradigm for "women," but
as place of location.—Adrienne Rich, "Notes toward a Politics of Location"

DECOLONIZING LITERARY SPACE

From its initial struggle for interpretive power, Chicano literature in the
late 1960s and early 1970s constituted an alternative space from which to
construct an identity, a culture, and an imaginary. In retrospect, we can
now situate the urban Zoot Suit riots in the 1940s as a proto-ethnic moment when a community defiantly opened an "other" place from which to
construct a new identity. Marked by the spirit of vanguard poetics and politics, the Zoot Suiters/the Pachucos, in their search for generating a new
look and a new language (Caló), were implicitly rejecting the colonizing
language taught (English), which did not contain their experiences and the
language violently erased (Spanish), from which they had been estranged.
A decade later, Américo Paredes spoke to the effects of colonization and
subsequent marginalization of a people that took effect after the 1848 war.
Paredes (1958) effectively re-members a community by remapping a territory and retrieving a memory of lost, unheard stories that had been erased,

denied, or made invisible. His decolonizing work represents that of the previously settled Spanish/Mexican communities whose long history has been defaced, absent from history textbooks and from the discourses of Anglo-Euro nationalist ideologies.[1]

In fact, since the 1848 war, Mexican Americans had voiced persistent critiques of their treatment as second-class citizens. These works marked in lived experience a space of resistance and a collective memory bank. The work of Paredes in the 1950s was a direct affront to traditional Texas historians and opened the way for a critique of internal colonialism, addressing the racism not only against the "colonial subject" but against those of the diasporic Mexicans who indefatigably continue to migrate to the United States for political or economic reasons. It is the struggles through an overt political position in the 1960s, however, that confronted the legacy of colonialism head on and that made possible the emergence of a body of works that, taken together, constituted a significant talking back to discourses that either excluded or objectified peoples of Mexican origin in the United States.

Tomás Rivera's (1983) writings identified Chicano literature as representing the implicit desire of a people for a sense of community, particularly the centrality of memory and language. He traced the ways the Chicano movement located a place from which to anchor a project of decolonization that would lead to the intellectual emancipation of a people. Historically and politically marginalized by the practices and discourses of a nation-state whose imperialist project of Anglo hegemony looked to deface the cultures of lands usurped, the underrepresented struggled for interpretive and representative power in the political climate of the 1960s and 1970s, opening a space for itself to regain and redefine its historical ethos.

In this essay, I am interested in mapping the literary production of Chicanos/Mexicanos in the United States and particularly the self-writing practices by Chicanas that emerged at the end of the twentieth century. As counterhegemonic activities, they mark both a commitment to and continuity of the decolonizing practices emerging with the civil rights movements and a rupture and discontinuity that insists on the inscription of gender and sexuality as the missing elements of the initial male nationalist propositions. I (re)trace these shifts and the ways these histories of literary and cultural interventions mark a particular relationship to the discourse of modernity and to the nation-state.

This remapping of cultural and literary territories defies the arbitrariness of colonial enterprises and the violence that accompanied the imposition of a dominant culture, its language, and its ideology. The redrawing of sociocultural and symbolic boundaries has memory as its organizing element. This act of re-membering of a people acquired and opened important sites for contestation after the civil rights movements, when the disenfranchised sought to recuperate their sense of history and community.[2] One of the sites for rememorating was literature, where questions of cultural and national identity became both centrally present and critically problematized.

The Chicano literature that emerged out of the post–civil rights movement now counts several generations of writers and a significant literary production that engages, from distinct genres, the experiences of a people who identify as belonging to a particular imagined community. Given the contestatory nature of this writing, which narrates the untold stories of silenced peoples, it is not unusual, as is the case with other minority writing, to see a proliferation of autobiographies. These permit the construction of first-person narratives, which, as Nancy Harsock points out, allow minority voices to write "an account of the world as seen from the margins, an account which can expose the falseness of the view from the top . . . which treats our perspectives not as subjugated or disruptive knowledges, but as primary and constitutive of a different world" (1990, 171).

Several decades of autobiographical literature by different generations of Chicanas have created a varied and impressive corpus of works. These constitute possible new ways of reading and mapping continuities and ruptures and demonstrate the distinct contributions these writers are making to literary and lived representations. Although writing the self by Chicanas has taken many forms, I am especially interested in theorizing a body of writing that I call "autobiographical fictions" and the ways this narration of self constitutes a genre that takes on specific characteristics as practiced by Sandra Cisneros in *House on Mango Street* (1984), Norma Cantú in *Canícula* (1995), Mary Helen Ponce in *Hoyt Street* (1933), and Pat Mora in *House of Houses* (1997). I read these texts as representative of self-writing where emplotments are explicitly marked by spatial configurations in which the writers are engaged in the construction of identities in the present by reactivating memories situated in social and symbolic geographies. These narratives of place recognize the ways space and location are important in the processes of identity formation, for they are necessarily implicated in history, language, and community.

Arguing against essentialist renderings of Chicana identity, my study looks at the way the texts, even though caught in familial (and familiar) resemblances, offer distinct stories through differentiated emplotments. They take into account what Betty Bergland proposes is "the complex relationships between cultures and discourses that produce the speaking subject," which also "avoids viewing language as a transparent representation of the imagined real" (1994, 130). These particularly structured narratives speak to the multiple positionalities and experiences of a population whose differences are still marked by a legacy of colonization, diasporic displacements, and continued racism.

If earlier autobiographical writings produced after the Chicano movement of the 1960s were written mainly by male writers such as Tomás Rivera (*Y no se lo tragó la tierra*, 1971), Ernesto Galarza (*Barrio Boy*, 1971), and Richard Rodríguez (*Hunger of Memory*, 1981), by the 1980s and especially the 1990s a large body of women's self-writing appeared, constituting a visible genre worthy of attention.[3] The different forms that autobiographical writings took, including poetry, essays, fictions, chronicles, and *testimonios*, have been recognized as constituting a radical feminist cultural practice. I am thinking of the work of, among others, Gloria Anzaldúa, Cherríe Moraga, Ana Castillo, Sandra Cisneros, Pat Mora, Mary Helen Ponce, and Alma Villanueva. Chicanas' distinct contribution to the genre of self-writing has elicited a rich critical corpus, which studies their work as innovative and experimental. This is captured in the generic classifications under which they are analyzed. But whether studied as "outlaw genres"(Kaplan 1992, 119), "ethnic autobiographies" (Bergland 1994), "autographies" (Perreault 1995), "cultural autobiographies and biomythographies" (Blake 1997), or "autoethnographies" (Pratt 1994), there is no doubt that their work is being recognized nationally and internationally as initiating verbal constructs indicative of a new poetics and politics. This literature has opened a symbolic space for talking back and a feminist practice of intervention that seeks to speak from the experience of marginalization.

Gaining agency through the act of writing, Chicanas/Mexicanas had the added burden of necessarily engaging the discourses of a racist Anglo society and the patriarchal structures present in both Anglo and Chicano cultures. If the struggle for Chicano civil rights in the 1960s was depicted as a male-oriented praxis, the concept of feminism that emerged during this same period was taken up by the Chicanas, who asserted their right within the radicalized struggles for democracy and social justice to voice their experiences outside the "laws of the fathers." They contested being called *Malinchistas* by redefining the historical notions of betrayal inherent in the sexist terminology. Resignifying the figure of Malintzin, Chicanas decided to be true to themselves in an act of rebirth outside the narrow parameters of male-defined nationalisms (Castillo 1977; Alarcón 1981; Moraga 1983).

As creative writers and critics, the Chicana feminists contested Aztlán as a male-privileged territory and insisted on a self-critical politics, historically and politically grounded. Gloria Anzaldúa in *Borderlands/ La Frontera: The New Mestiza* (1987) established a geographical location and space of colonization: South Texas—that is, the borderlands—a space from which a new consciousness could emerge. In a strategic multilayered move, Anzaldúa breaks away from the initial nationalist male constructions of Aztlán (an imaginative and no less powerful referent than Anzaldúa's mythical origin, which located a territory and a culture previous to Columbus's discovery or English settlement) by feminizing and lesbianizing the foundational terrain through her elaboration of the "Coatlicue State," a privileging of the female pantheon. An empowering myth, it re-turns to the origins, inscribing a fe-male re-membering of the community intent on retrieving a cultural sense of self erased through colonization. This return to the scene of the crime reinscribes colonization as the site of past and present conflict but also of future possibilities. From this plurilingual, multicultural space built by the layering of histories of conquest, imperialism, and diaspora, a "new mestiza consciousness" is born, one that contests the patriarchal hierarchies deeply entrenched in the imagined community. The shift to a specific spatial mapping marks the displacement from the margins, which centers and makes concrete a geography of colonization, exclusivity, sexism, and homophobia out of which a poetics and politics emerges.

I argue that in the process of authoring, these writers gained authority and inserted themselves into a history that had excluded them, their people, culture, and language. Life writing is a tie to the past in relation to a contested present, and the ways authors situate themselves in historical and political terms becomes crucial. The genre, in the case of Chicanas, thus possesses ideological power; it serves a political function because the speaking subject is positioned outside the dominant symbolic order. This positionality of "becoming minor," say Abdul JanMohamed and David Lloyd, "is not a question of essence (as the stereotypes of minorities in dominant ideology would want us to believe), but a question of position: a subject position that in the final analysis can be defined only in 'political' terms—that is, in terms of the effects of economic exploitation, political disenfranchisement, social manipulation, and ideological domination on the cultural formation of minority subjects and discourses" (1990, 7). This ideological power, I would insist, cannot be separated from its aesthetic imaginings. In fact, Chicano/a literature, as Renato Rosaldo (1990) has argued, cannot be read as "minor literature," following Deleuze and Guattari's Eurocentric model: rather, it must be read in the contexts of Chicano/a struggles and the text's own rhetorical strategies.[4]

The autobiographical fictions by Cisneros, Ponce, Cantú, and Mora contest ethnic and gender discrimination from the particularities of a culture, making possible a comparative study of the ways gender, ethnicity, and class have altered a genre with a long tradition in Western literary production. The positionality taken from an ethnic gendered paradigm recognizes the place of history, language, and culture in the construction of subjectivity and identity and acknowledges the situatedness of knowledge (Haraway 1991, 111). Thus, culture and identity, outside modernist premises that would define them as fixed, are transformative, continuously redefined and recontextualized. Their work thus contributes to cultural critique, feminist thought, and literary form.

I would like to emphasize the importance of their contribution to the literary form of autobiographical fiction. Their long narrative fictions are different from other self-writings by Chicanas that engage, contest, and redefine poetic, essay, and short narrative forms. They invite, I argue, a certain kind of attention and way of reading that renders a particular kind of textual meaning and understanding of the world represented. I define autobiographical fictions as constituting a mixed genre that takes verifiable events and characters for their inspiration but insists on their fictional (imaginative rendering) delivery. The genre, that is, has to establish a delicate balance to engage the reader. Even if the writer establishes an imaginative rendering of events, he or she is committed to a project of constructing a recognizable self who participates in a story credible to the readers and who is caught in a narrative that appears to point to an outside of the text (the referent) while it insists on keeping you inside the text (the emplotment).

These autobiographical fictions could best be called "testimonial autobiographical fictions," linking them to the function of *testimonio* literature as it emerged in Latin America. Even as John Beverley privileges the genre of testimonio over other first-person genres such as the picaresque and the autobiography, he recognizes similarities when asserting: "What *testimonio* does have in common with the picaresque novel and with autobiography is the powerful textual affirmation of the speaking subject itself. The dominant formal aspect of the *testimonio* is that voice which speaks to the reader in the form of an 'I' that demands to be recognized, that wants or needs to stake a claim on our attention. This presence of the voice, which we are meant to experience as the voice of a real rather than fictional person, is the mark of a desire not to be silenced or defeated, to impose oneself on an institution of power like literature from the position of the excluded or the marginal" (1993, 75–77). I argue that Chicana autobiographical fictions complicate autobiography as it is understood in traditional Western literatures, the individual will for personal agency, and the genre of testimonio, which relies on the role of a mediator whose class position is distinct from that of the voice being recorded and transmitted in writing. These Chicana writers bear witness from a particular space gained through struggle that permits them to act as the interlocutors/mediators of marginalized voices lacking access to the printed word. They also refuse to give up the privileges of authorship and use it to select and create a text that constructs an "I" as that of the narrator whose personal awareness and individual growth is fundamental to the story but who cannot be seen outside the group or class situation that has historically marked her as marginal. It is from this culturally or politically rooted position that the narrator becomes the voice, her own, of a self who recollects her memories and those of other members of her community.

"The narrator in *testimonio*," writes Beverley, "is a real person who continues living and acting in a real social history, which also continues. *Testimonio* can never, in this sense, create the illusion of that textual in-itselfness, set against and above the everyday life and struggle, that is the basis of literary formalism" (1993, 84). Testimonial autobiographical fictions refuse simple classifications and remind us, as Derrida (1980) points out in the "Law of Genre," of the difficulties of differentiating specific genres because of the inherent contradictions contained within the texts and hence the project of defining a corpus. "Every text," affirms Derrida, "participates in one or several genres, there is no genreless text, yet such participation never amounts to a belonging" (203–204). Regardless of that admonition, many Chicanas are involved in what Caren Kaplan (1992) calls "the genre of choice" at this historical moment. She reminds us that "Autobiographical writing surrounds us, but the more it surrounds us, the more it defies generic stabilization, the more its laws are broken, the more it drifts toward other practices, the more formerly 'out-law' practices drift into its domain. While popular practitioners carry on the old autobiographical tradition, other practitioners play with forms that challenge us to recognize their experiments in subjectivity and account for their exclusion from 'high literature'" (xviii).

The genre of self-writing, as Derrida points out, has both limits and possibilities. The possibilities outside traditional modes are what Chicanas are exploring productively. Theirs is a politics that cannot be divorced from their poetics; that is, their innovative literary forms are inextricable from the stories they tell, stories that fall outside the discourses of dominant Western autobiographies. They are plotting a different itinerary. Their texts acknowledge a correspondence to a lived reality but ask that the reader participate in the truth of fiction. Narrativizing the events of their lives, they impose on them the form of a story. This emplotment, which Hayden White defines as "the way by which a sequence of events fashioned into a story is gradually revealed to be a story of a particular kind," will "provide the 'meaning' of a story by identifying the kind of story told" (1973, 7). In a later essay, White explains further that "the production of meaning in this case can be regarded as a performance, because any given set of real events can be emplotted in a number of ways, can bear the weight of being told as any number of different kinds of stories. Since no given set or sequence of real events is intrinsically tragic, comic, farcical, and so on, but can be constructed as such only by the imposition of the structure of a given story type on the events, it is the choice of the story type and its imposition upon the events that endow them with meaning" (1987, 4).

White is speaking about the emplotment of historical accounts, but his observations are especially applicable to life-telling accounts as well. He attests to the substantial truth value of explanation by emplotment, affirming that "in the historical narrative, experiences distilled into fiction as typifications are subjected to the test of their capacity to endow 'real' events with meaning. And it would take a *Kulturephilistinismus*[5] of a very high order to deny to the results of this testing procedure the status of genuine knowledge" (1987, 45).

THE LOCATION OF IDENTITY

If autobiographical fictions by women in general have been seen to disrupt the lifelines of male *Bildungsromane* in the European tradition,[6] these Chicana stories do double duty, contesting both traditional European models and male Chicano models of lifetelling. Taken as a whole, their narratives contest unified or essentialist concepts of Chicana identity as they construct what Norma Alarcón calls "subjects-in-process" through the textual narrative (1996, 135). Their individual stories delineate a complex map of an ever-changing imagined community, no less real in fiction, that is differentiated by gender, generation, sexual preference, class, race, and regional distinctions.

Their located stories privilege a spatial categorization that rejects stories whose organizing principle seems to be grounded primarily in temporal configurations. Memory matters as the self constructs an identity in relation to place. Explicit in their privileging of spatial categories, the texts redirect the perspective of the protagonist from an "I in time" as the privileged locus of enunciation to an "I in location." This locational poetics of self-writing is constitutive of the ways these writers ground their stories in the complex interactions of language, history, and place, marking a difference from narratives of temporality.

In narratives of temporality in Chicano literature at least two types of narrative emplotments seem prevalent. There are those that establish linear time and posit a narrative of integration/assimilation, such as that of Richard Rodríguez in *Hunger of Memory*, a documentary Bildungsroman, which trace the narrator's entrance into the dominant order, and those that configure a mythical structure, which posit a search in time past for origins (Aztlán) to ground a genealogy, such as *Peregrinos de Aztlán* by Miguel Méndez (1974) and *Heart of Aztlán* by Rodolfo Anaya (1976). The narrative of assimilation would accept colonization; the other proposes an alternate decolonizing project. The return to Aztlán, in fact, contested modernity's linear progressive time and teleology. It constituted an empowering moment to re-member a community and thus a fundamental move for self-affirmation, constructing, albeit an identity located in myth, a temporal inscription in the past. Whereas Rodríguez's narrative posits a move forward, toward a future time where/when memory is lost as the condition of arrival to modernity, the mythical narratives by Anaya and Méndez are engaged in a backward move, a retrieval of memory that will make possible an "other" future, where the self enters "modernity" culturally whole but essentialized, that is, from a fixed notion of cultural nationalist identity.

In privileging a spatial category, the narratives by Cisneros, Mora, Cantú, and Ponce contest teleological conceptions of progress, that is, narratives of assimilation, beside nationalist mythical essentialist paradigms and space conceived from patriarchal perspectives. In this sense they can be read as opening an alternative space that considers the temporal through place. They open a space where time is located in a specific represented and representable site, elaborating an identity constructed and located differentially in history that transcends the also contestatory but essentialized identities located in myth.

The four narratives chosen construct a self in space using different narrative strategies. The narrating subject of enunciation is constructed in a present of narration (moment of [re]writing the past) different from the time of narration (when events in the story took place). This construction of identity through writing represents a synchronic moment fixed through the text itself. In their retellings, the authors escape the plots and portrayals of male texts as they rewrite homes and habitats in barrios or borders, (re)drawing geographies and genealogies. In these autobiographical/testimonial fictions, the authors, chroniclers of their time, put on different masks. As historians, they unearth the past; as ethnographers, they describe and interpret cultural patterns; as linguists, they capture the language of their time/space, the work that writers/narrators/novelists have always done. They change their name to Esperanza or Azucena, a narrative strategy that establishes a critical distance between the person in the past that is being constructed and the narrator who is speaking from the present of narration and insists on the truth of fiction over the truth of correspondence to reality.

Refusing to write a straightforward testimonial that might be read as a transparent window onto their lives, they engage the complexities of literary form. In these Chicana narratives the individual story, which treasures choice details of the personal life, is merged with the collective memory that the writer records as witness or historian (*memorista*). The narratives implicitly deconstruct notions of essentialized identities as well as cohesive senses of cultural community. The return to community and tradition is not nostalgic but a feminist political positioning, fundamental to the regrouping of a community dis-(re)membered. It is the struggle for a rewriting of history, in the words of David Kazanjian and Anahid Kassabian, "a [textual] quest for truth, for truth in historical discourse" (Kazanjian and Kassabian 1993, 34). As Erica Carter, James Donald, and Judith Squares state in their introduction, commenting on the article on Armenian narratives by David Kazanjian and Anahid Kassabian, "the search for a homeland is not an innocent utopia for them. The recognition these quests seek to gain involves a certain narrative position of historical truth, which corresponds to specific political issues that recognition will allow—for example, reparations (perhaps material—a 'homeland'—yet certainly emotional, a space to feel, and feel justified)" (1993, xiv–xv).

The spatial configurations in the texts by Cisneros, Ponce, Cantú, and Mora point to the spaces of colonization, the borders and geographies of exclusions such as urban barrios and rural communities. These writers' counterhegemonic narratives contest the marginalization of a people and also the space of domesticity, which can be seen as either containment or the basis for a new thinking about community and family. Both become the sites for writing the self, new cartographies where space implicates a physical, social, and political territory. In this next section, I trace the ways these stories are mapped and the ways gender and culture are inscribed onto the space of the text to analyze how the figuration of facts and the choice of emplotment affects the nature of the story told and the constitution of the subject constructed in the process.

An awareness of marginality is central in Sandra Cisneros's *House on Mango Street* (1984). There is no nostalgia in her recounting, no past illusions, no celebration of community. The act of remembering becomes a painful recollection and naming of the marginality, the inequality, the injustice, and the poverty suffered in the barrio. The desire and dreams of the protagonist are charted to escape but not to forget her origins as she retraces her steps to return to the site of her childhood, a point of origin and destination. The protagonist/narrator does not engage in any idealization of home or barrio. Critical of women's subordination, Esperanza deconstructs male narratives that would celebrate barrio camaraderie.[7] She vividly recreates scenes portraying how neither streets nor homes are safe spaces/places for women under patriarchy and also refuses to accept the "place by the window" that the great-grandmother occupied. Concerns of space in Cisneros are linked both to the ways women have been restricted under patriarchy to assume "a place" in the home (private sphere) and in society (subservient) and to the houses occupied by the marginalized classes in these "out of place" settings.

The iconoclastic narrator critiques the living conditions in which most disenfranchised families survive. She sees family values, rituals, and celebrations with an outsider/insider eye that affirms her cultural roots yet refuses to accept the marginality. The protagonist remains critical of oppression, no matter its source. Home here is unhomely, crowded, and dirty: "But the house on Mango Street is not the way they told it at all. It's small and red with little steps in front and windows so small you'd think they were holding their breath. Bricks are crumbling in places, and the front door is so swollen you have to push hard to get in. There is no front yard. Our back is a small garage for the car we don't own yet. There are stairs in our house, but they're ordinary hallway stairs, the house has only one washroom, very small. Everybody has to share a bedroom . . . the third floor, the paint peeling, wooden bars Papa had nailed on the windows so we wouldn't fall out" (8–9). Cisneros's description is responding to lived realities and to the literary tradition of authors reconstructing the grand houses, desired or dwelled in, of their childhood, from Manderley to Tara, Thornfield, and the House of Seven Gables. Paradoxically and most intentionally, the unliterary house on Mango Street serves, as in the Anglo-European tradition, as the repository of memories and has become a powerful literary image.

A home can either be a place of origin or a place of destination, and the circularly structured narrative of *House on Mango Street* breaks linearity and the idea of progression or progressive journey out of the barrio and culture into dominant society. A narrative of progressive assimilation and integration into the dominant order would be better represented by Richard Rodríguez's (1982) *Hunger of Memory* or Esmeralda Santiago's (1993) *When I Was Puerto Rican.* In those autobiographical fictions the linear structure does belie a liberal ideology whereby education and English literacy, to the detriment of native culture, permit the protagonist to assimilate into sameness. These are Bildungsromans, novels of personal development, albeit, as in Rodriguez, of a disenfranchised person, who in the novel (but not necessarily in life, as the authors have their books to mark them as marginal) demonstrates the power of the individual will to self-fulfillment.

Cisneros refuses that emplotment. Her stories do not pretend a realist (documentary) aesthetic even as they insist on verisimilitude.[8] The characters are placed in specific situations, but the lack of realist detail and her poetic sense of language direct our attention away from any verifiable referent. We are not asked as readers to identify this or that city, person, or event as factual entities. By naming the childhood protagonist Esperanza, Cisneros both creates a distance for remembering the child she was and assigns herself the role of a self who is more intent on rendering true the conditions of oppression she witnessed than in constructing a self who might be read as a transparent and "true" correspondence to a lived reality. This strategy redirects our gaze inwardly to the site of the textual production which elaborates what appears to be a timeless scene, an ever present geography of exclusion[9] narrating the daily and ongoing encounters of a people struggling for survival.

The distanced and critical narrator does not equate victimization with goodness but with a system that is unjust. The circular structure gives the reader a feeling of desperation and entrapment, which underlines the fact that even if Esperanza escaped, others did not. They have stayed behind and are still there, like Sally, who got married and whose husband "doesn't (even) let her look out the window" and so she "sits at home because she is afraid to go outside without his permission" (95). Transformation in this geography of exclusion is not about possible escapes through individuated ambition. This emplotment marks a difference from the narrative of individual triumph traced by Rodríguez and Santiago, where the will to self-fulfillment is the message. The protagonist's remembering is painful. It constitutes the return itself because, in the process of writing, Esperanza constructs a subject in the present, one with agency that makes evident her intervention, through writing, for social change. In the chronological disposition (story line), Cisneros's protagonist succeeds, but the artistic disposition (circular structure) emphasizes that attention be paid to the dynamics at play in the barrio, that is, of the barrios that stay behind. The focus of the autobiographical fiction shifts from the person who left to those who remain trapped because of exclusionary racist, classist, and sexist practices from the outside or from within. The protagonist continues, nevertheless, to identify, even if critically, with her cultural community. The conflicting pattern of allegiance to community and allegiance to self is symbolically resolved. The theme both defies and affirms the saying "Home is where the heart is." This is an unhomely place that remains fixed in the affective space of the writing subject's memory and, by extension, the reader.

Her intense yearning for another place is to be interpreted not as a desire to move and join the dominant order but rather as a move for emancipation, an escape from the private domains assigned by patriarchy and an entrance into the public space of writing. To publish becomes a defiant act in a culture where a *mujer que publica* is admonished as *una mujer pública,* a wicked woman who contests the positions sanctioned by a still male-dominated society. A quote from Aída Hurtado explicating the poem "Letting Go" by Gloria Anzaldúa speaks directly to this independent act of self-birth: "To love oneself as a woman is a revolutionary act. The reclaiming of self has come for Chicana feminists through self love—not narcissistic, selfish involvement but as a political act of valuing what patriarchy has devalued. Chicana feminists proclaim that redemption does not come through men but, rather, comes from giving up the illusion of security and safety that results from being chosen by a man" (1996, 89).

Sandra Cisneros's early narrative, written in 1984, anticipated, energized, and could be said to have opened the way for both postmodern and post-Western autobiographical fictions. Cisneros writes her life as fiction, that is, by her strategy of self-conscious writing, portraying the child she was and the writer she was becoming. She foregrounds the fictional and always textual nature of the autobiographical enterprise or any attempt at constructing the autonomous identity. When she wrote, women's raised consciousness and access to formal education created the spaces from where an important body of writing emerged that has now found an equally broadened international public.

At that time, such writers could not foresee the falling of the Berlin wall, the disintegration of the Soviet Union, or the enormous changes being brought about by the policies of neoliberalism and the politics of globalization. The 1990s were marked by tremendous fluidity, mobility, displacements, and repositionings. With the continuous diasporas from the South forming communities in the United States with cultures that maintain strong ties to their original homelands and that establish regular circuits of communication, the original and arbitrary lines of demarcation become less clear. This movement has always occurred, but at the turn of the twentieth century it is accelerating the linkages between nations and between diasporic communities and their places of origin. The growth of other Latino populations and the use of the Spanish language are bringing about a renewed energy that continues to generate a rich literature. These changes in linguistic and writing practices are decentering Western (Euro-Anglo) hegemony as Latinos continue to speak ever more clearly from these contestatory spaces.[10]

BORDER REGIONS

Canícula by Norma Cantú (1995) maps a territory that defies nationalist political boundaries. It redraws a cultural geography, which, like the borderlands described by Anzaldúa, literally and metaphorically speak directly to the effects that the displacement of conquest and colonization brought about during and prior to 1848. Even if people there stayed in what is now a shared "space," it is through the imposition of the colonizing language and its accompanying cultural literacy that the sense of place held by peoples of Mexican descent and embedded in cultural history, legend, and language was (and continues to be) disrupted. The displacement in situ transforms the former "homeland" into a contested site of struggle. The literal and literary description of the depressed "borderlands," where dwellers have survived lynchings, burnings, rapes, and other aggressions, blocks any celebratory reading of border spaces. The border zone, however, can be read metaphorically as a place that emblematizes the social relations embedded in its geopolitics.

Cisneros's unsentimental and unnostalgic story, located in an unnamed space (even as we read "Chicago"), posits from the perspective of a nomadic subject the search for a place she can call home, outside patriarchy and poverty. Cantú's text locates an identity that is recovering her sense of place/in place through memory. Both texts are counterdiscursive acts as they speak to the exclusivist nature of the nation-state discourse that forces "the other" to a marginality configured as an off-space, that is, a place outside the centers of power. Even if the protagonist Esperanza finds her way to writing, it is a writing that takes her back again and again to the place of disenfranchisement. The desire for a home and fulfillment is not a transformative act in the text because the writer seems to be in a bind, always anticipating a house/homely abode in the future, always returning to the house on Mango Street. Caught between memory and desire, the poetic protagonist/writer dwells in an eternal and interiorized present time that contains both the past and the future.

Norma Cantú's *Canícula* recenters the marginal area of the border to speak from its heterogeneous nature, defies the monolithic and officialist discourses of both nation-states, and chooses a realist aesthetic that is far from traditional. Cantú's narrative locates a contained transnational border space, thus documenting a region and its people. It is no less experimental in its autography than Cisneros. Under the guise or behind the mask of an invented name, Azucena, she makes sense of her bilingual, bicultural life on the border. The protagonist/narrator thus distances her self as author from her self as protagonist to re-member and recreate an area on both sides of the Rio Grande/Rio Bravo called Laredo and Nuevo Laredo and to re-locate her self. This repositioning symbolically reclaims a territory lost and retrieves its silenced voices and images. She speaks from a differentiated persona—Azucena—not only to underscore the mediated nature of autobiography, but because Cantú, like Cisneros, is participating in what Walter Mignolo calls, in reference to the writings of Rigoberta Menchú, "the belief in the truth of enactment rather than the truth of representation, a belief which distinguishes between hegemonic epistemologies with emphasis on denotation and truth, and subaltern epistemologies with emphasis on performance and transformation" and "which shows the intentions and the struggle for power" (2000, 26). Cantú warns us that "what may appear to be autobiographical is not always so," as "many of the events are completely fictional, although others may be true in an historical context. Although it may appear that these stories are my family's, they are not precisely, and yet they are. But then again, as Pat Mora claims, life *en la frontera* is raw truth, and stories of such life, fictitious as they may be, are even truer than true" (1997, xi).

In *Canícula*, memory is triggered by looking at family photographs. This act of re-membering a community is implicitly connected to the moment when in Madrid the narrator learns about the death of Roland Barthes and reads his book on photography, *Camera Lucida*. Theory is not the only motor that triggers her imagination; there is another complementary and competing act. As the protagonist is looking through her lover's album and listening to his voice narrate and recall the stories that the photographs inspire, her imagination is awakened to a different way of self-writing in community. Sylvia Molloy points out that even autobiographies plunder other texts and not just lives for their staging, and certainly these texts invite an intertextual reading:

> Travelogues, first-person accounts of various types, *testimonios*, diaries, autobiographies, all "genres" or hybrid modes of representation that would have the reader believe he is dealing with direct, unmediated accounts of real life narrated by real individuals, are no exception: these modes of structuring reality through writing that claim not to obey preconceived structures are also dependent upon a textual (if sometimes unwritten) prefiguration. Dependency does not mean, here, the strict observance of a model or a slavish form of imitation but reference to an often incongruous conflation of possible texts that the writer uses as a literary springboard, a way of projecting himself (herself) into the void of writing, even when that writing directly concerns the self. (1991, 16–17)

Within the spatial reconfiguration of the border, the narrator organizes and recreates voice/orality (a speaking), produces script (a writing), and presents photographs (a seeing) to record her people and her language. These become the necessary media through which a community outside representation can be remembered. From the distance, Spain, the "Old World," she directs her vision to a space in the "New World." Spain remains connected through language and culture, and this new border space has yet to be narrated and represented. It cannot be left unsaid. The use of photography can be subversive, says Barthes, "since photographs speak, make us reflect, suggest a meaning different to the literal one . . . not when it frightens, repels, or even stigmatizes, but when it is pensive, when it thinks" (1983, 38). Cantú thinks from the photographs. Her purpose is evident: to narrate a geography and a people within a specific historical space-time, her space-time, and to fix in time their forgotten images, their untold stories and knowledges. Not photographed because they were famous, the previously unknown people are now immortalized and endowed with status, circulating in the public sphere of cultural production. The words of Barthes are illuminating in this respect: "The photograph does not necessarily say what is no longer, but only and for certain what has been. This distinction is decisive. In front of a photograph, our consciousness does not necessarily take the nostalgic path of memory, but for every photograph existing in the world, the path of certainty: The photograph's essence is to ratify what I represent. The important thing is that the photograph possesses an eviden-tial force, and that its testimony bears not on the object but on time. From a phenomenological viewpoint, in the photograph, the power of authenti-cation exceeds the power of representation" (1983, 87–89). Cantú plays with both the representational and fictional aspects of narrating a self from the present, naming herself Azucena, and yet in displaying her passport picture she insists on authenticating Azucena as herself. The picture is her "real" self even if it is forged with another name. As Barthes says, "the photograph [in general] is not metaphoric; it carries its referent with itself" (5).

In its emplotment, *Canícula* constitutes a different undertaking from the excellent autobiographical fictions of Julia Alvarez's (1991) *How the García Girls Lost Their Accents* or Cristina Garcia's (1992) *Dreaming in Cuban*. Their narratives demonstrate a tension in the traveling between the Caribbean Islands and the Mainland. In *Canícula*, there is no conflict in the going back and forth between cultures because the territory drawn is a geocultural area arbitrarily separated but containing a rooted and settled people whose linguistic practices disrupt notions of purity as the language of the cultural imaginary. Spanish, its legend, traditions, and worldviews, seeps through to disrupt the imposed language and its legacies, creating what Mignolo, following Anzaldúa, calls bilanguaging, "as the moment in which 'a living language' (as Anzaldúa puts it) describes itself as a way of life (*'un modo de vivir'*), at the intersection of two (or more) languages, . . . a dialogical, ethic, aesthetic, and political process of social transformation rather than *ergeia* emanating from an isolated speaker" (2000, 264–65).

This is clear in the following passage by Cantú: "Panchita came around weekly with her bags full of 'encargos' and to collect money owed on mer-chandise bought on time. She was our Avon Lady, instead of the 'ding-dong' of the doorbell, we heard 'Ave Maria Purísima,' and Mami or Bueli or who-ever was closest would answer, *'Sin pecado concebida'*" (52). In this case, the bilanguaging mind is a product of the colonial experience but has, in the process, acquired what Cherríe Moraga (1993) calls a "bicultural mind," a genealogy built on dual memories, articulated in two languages. In speak-ing about her songs, Cantú makes evident how she constructs her memo-ries from realities and discourses lived in two languages: "Then at home, *declamando* for New Year's and for parties. Tino and I testing our memo-rization skills, competing to see who could *declamar* the longest poems and remember the most lyrics from songs—*en* English and Spanish: '*El brindis del bohemio,*' 'The Raven,' '*Porque me dejé del vicio,*' 'Anabelle Lee,' '*El Seminarista de los ojos negros,*' and on and on through high school when we would write down the lyrics to our favorite songs: '*La cama de piedra,' 'México lindo y querido,'* 'Sad Movies Made Me Cry,' 'Go Away Little Girl'" (62).

Because Cisneros's lived space in childhood is reconfigured as unlivable, one with which she cannot identify and wishes to transcend, she constructs a self outside the space of enunciation. Cantú constructs a self in a felicitous space—she is her space. This is not to say that she does not critique the racisms lived or the sexisms fought on a daily basis. In what appears to be a much different project, she participates in narrativizing the lives of peoples in a geopolitical space that was colonized, but whose culture and daily practices she sees as life affirming. This new remapping of regionalism contests discourses of homogeneity of the nation-state and Anglo-Western history—the melting pot assimilative narrative—to privilege bilingual, biliterate, and bicultural practices that point to multicultural and linguistic ones.

This geographical/genealogical story through photographs becomes the story of all those left out of history, the heroes and heroines of a space-time location. Neither migrants nor immigrants, the characters represent the settled and rooted communities whose stories and presence disrupts the nation-state discourses of a monolithic culture and implicitly proposes a redefinition that posits a new concept of nation and community from a politics of inclusion. Unlike migrant stories where spaces become reterritorialized representation, the multilayered stories by a rooted people indicate a process of de/re/territorialization that is implicitly pointing to a community (symbolically and materially) becoming aware of its own power as it recovers memory and history.

Cantú's text constitutes a new regional writing that transcends the old definitions of regionalism as "local colour" (Jordan 1994). Ideologically, this "new regionalism" posits a complex regional and transregional history where legacies of empire have left their mark. The text makes evident the global consequences of industrial capitalism, the disruptive effects on the region from economic restructuring and the policing and maintaining of an inside/outside mindset. It also offers lessons in perspective as it posits questions from both sides—from the Rio Grande and from the Rio Bravo—engaging questions of purity and authenticity, property and propriety, legality and illegitimacy. In the process, the narrative disrupts traditional categories of self and other, sameness and difference, national and foreign culture. It deconstructs the teleology of assimilation and constitutes a radical questioning of the very concept of distinction between identity and alterity.

Cantú's cartography draws an unofficial geography of exclusion that has its own center. There is no idealization by the protagonist but certainly no wish to escape or be outside it. Her story self-consciously shows the mechanisms writing exploits, illustrating the chaotic and erratic ways memory works to recover the past. Moving back and forth from the present moment of enunciation to the story time of the past, the narrator shifts personas as she gathers and presents her memories from childhood to the adult she is at the end of the story. The story, necessarily in chronicle fashion, remains inconclusive, that is, without closure, open to the future. The "I" becomes a "we" as she collapses individual self and community. "And some of us never leave, and some of us never come back. Some of us keep coming back. Some of us love, and some of us hate, some of us both love and hate our borderlands. Some of us remember, some of us forget" (132).

RURAL TERRAINS

In *Hoyt Street: An Autobiography*, Mary Helen Ponce (1993) seemingly assumes a more traditional strategy, as the text links protagonist, narrator, and author and calls itself purely and simply an autobiography. Her story, however, is the antithesis of an individuated self in search of self-definition or liberation. In her project of recreating the 1940s and 1950s in Pacoima, California, she constructs an "I" in the Mexican American community of immigrant and migrant agricultural workers where space becomes reterritorialized place. Although she sees her writing as a "social history of sorts," she says in a brief introduction to the text that it was "written *de memoria.* I thought of researching Pacoima history, the founding of the town. Often my siblings corrected a fact or two, but for the most part, I wrote what I remember. The end result is an autobiography, or life story, but also a communal history" (x).

The space is remembered through the liturgical calendar of Catholicism, a space the narrator presents as offering dignity and hope to the displaced populations. The territorialization of the workers in places with Spanish names speaks to an origin that culturally contains them and makes the foreignness of the new land less ominous. The narrator begins the recollection of stories heard, remembered, or imagined, changing names, characteristics, and physical descriptions of people "to avoid embarrassing or hurting anyone" (x). She recreates the stories of a community marginalized from the dominant Anglo society of the time that is Pacoima or, as she says, "my Macondo," alluding to the work and literary place created in Latin America by Gabriel García Márquez.

The story is chronologically narrated but sequenced through the ritual calendar of Catholicism, that is, through the eternal recurrence of rituals and acts. This configures and contains the community recreated in a tightly organized spatial form in which the child remembers a happy childhood lived within this social and moral order. It is a geography of community. The story symbolically resignifies the rural regions whose stories have been misrepresented in or absent from the literary imaginary. "For those who wonder why I feel my life story merits discussion, let alone publication, let me say that Mexican-Americans need to tell their side of the story in order to put to rest negative stereotypes. The majority of Mejicanos who lived in Pacoima during the 1920s to the 1950s (when some homes were torn down to build the 'projects') were hard-working, decent, and honorable. It is for them that I write"(x). It is a talking-back to the stereotypical images in *Tortilla Flat* (1935) by John Steinbeck for sure and a female rewriting of *Y no se lo tragó la tierra* (1971) by Tomás Rivera.

The narrator maps a community whose internal spatial ordering is regulated by the Church and patriarchy. Although at times she idealizes the community, the liturgical calendar that structures the stories marks a geography of dynamic immobility. Movement occurs but is manifested as recurring cycles, whether secular or sacred. Memory constructs the harvesting rhythms that mark how the time passes for the farmworkers and migrants in rural agricultural areas. "In the summer many Mexican families in Pacoima harvested crops. Picking fruit *entre familia* was what folks did come June, July, and August; it was the only way we had to add to the income earned by a parent" (169). Memory also constructs Mary Helen's religious space: "Catechism was where we went on Saturdays. *Cada sábado* before ten o'clock, Concha, Mundo, Virgie and I would trot up the street, across the lane that bordered Doña Chonita's yard, and on to the church yard, where we waited for the black-robed nuns who taught *el catecismo* at Guardian Angel Church" (188).

There is no transformation of the social conditions of poverty, isolation, and gender inequality. The autobiographical novel ends with the narrator's menstruation and at the point of entry into the "adult" world. Ponce refuses to continue her story into the present as a success narrative, which could showcase her achievements and the ways she escaped from poverty. Instead, she constructs a specific space-time in the past, which is not textually brought into the present. It is the story of a loss of innocence, the loss of a sacred and communal space. There seems to be a nostalgia for a community, for a sense of belonging to an organic and holistic space that would once again secure a stable identity.

Her ordering, however, and the lack of intervention of the adult narrator in the telling of the story from the child's point of view, is more complicated than it appears. There are only two photographs, both outside the narrative text: a picture of herself as a child on the front cover and a picture of herself at the time of publication on the back flap. The lack of a postmodern self-reflexive protagonist, which announces the constructedness of her fictional "I," does not erase the critical eye of the ethnic decolonizing and adult author. Even as she speaks about her happy childhood, a careful reading reveals the marginalization suffered by the adult population. Ponce's spatial ordering implicitly posits a community impeded by its economic and ethnic marginalization from a life of bettered social conditions. "Mostly we were poor folks who welcomed the extra money in summer. Working *entre familia* was trying for some. Whole families were forced to share a tent or tiny hut. As the summer temperatures rose, tempers flared and children became irritable. Still most families did become accustomed to sleeping 3 to a bed" (170).

A time suspended in a marginalized space, whether secular or sacred, is telling of a hierarchical society where patriarchy reigned and a racist society kept the community outside the centers of power. In fact, the lack of irony and the spatial-temporal ordering becomes a self-critical representation of a time when the child could not see what the adult in retrospect could interpret but leaves outside the text. The sense of a cultural community and the importance of memory and language is not abandoned, yet there is an implicit critique of the structures of power that impeded the group's transformation into legitimacy, equality, and futurity.

If Cisneros recreated an urban geography of exclusion, Ponce reconfigures the rural geographies of exclusion that the displaced migrants occupied, but her Hoyt Street is not the unhomely Mango Street. "Mejicanos in our town took pride in their homes and, when money allowed, repaired dilapidated roofs or painted their casitas a bright color. They took special pride in having a yard full of plants and flowers, and these grew well in the rich California soil. . . . Our house was built by my father when he and my mother and their three older children moved from Ventura to the San Fernando Valley, sometime in the 1920s" (5, 7). Home and community are remembered warmly and generously, and their inhabitants become idealized in their practices of everyday life. This works because all is seen from the eyes of a child who feels nurtured and protected.

Ponce, who acts as both narrator and protagonist, has the information and manipulates the events. In presenting the "I" of narration as herself, she seemingly refuses to escape from establishing what might appear as unmediated representation, as she decides not to hide behind a guise allowing the reader to forget her real existence. This, of course, can be read as yet another Barthesian strategy to create "the effect of the real." The text in its 338 pages is rich in dialogue and detail of the experiences of the child. These are structured in three sections, from "Innocence" to "Knowledge" and conforming to the traditional novel of formation, the Bildungsroman. But, as is true of all autobiography, especially read by postmodern readers, this is a reconstructed self. The following by William Cronon points to the manipulative nature of writing, including autobiography, or perhaps particularly autobiography, because the author is the authority on the subject: "It is a commonplace of modern literary theory that the very authority with which narrative presents its vision of reality is achieved by obscuring large portions of that reality. Narrative succeeds to the extent that it hides the discontinuities, ellipses, and contradictory experiences that would undermine the intended meanings of its story. Whatever its overt purpose, it cannot avoid a covert exercise of power: it inevitably sanctions some voices while silencing others" (1992, 1349–50).

Ponce's narrative structuring chooses to hide the adult voice and persona in the present of enunciation, thus sanctioning the voice of the adult and with it the knowledge that experience and hindsight bring to the past. This is a virtuoso rendering that eliminates any interference from the future. It ironically moves us in the opposite direction that designs her text, that is, a move from "knowledge to innocence." She insists that we "willingly suspend disbelief" to relive with her the moment of childhood, unhampered by the future. This makes the recreated past come to life, a historical moment in which we, like the child, live for the duration of the writing.

PRIVATE PROVINCES

Pat Mora (1997) in *House of Houses* constructs a self in the literal and metaphoric space of her home. Mora might have had the home Cisneros desired. A marked symbolic class difference from the other protagonist is noticeable in this text: this family is not suffering from conditions of economic displacement but from cognitive dissonance and cultural discontinuities. This is a border story not of rootedness, as in the case of Norma Cantú, but of uprootings and reroutings that construct a different and equally powerful story. Trapped in the house of memories, the narrator becomes a prisoner of a time-space paradigm from which she brings back the dead to tell the stories of a family displaced from Mexico during the Mexican Revolution of 1910 who resettled in El Paso, Texas. Mora structures a time captive in the space of the family house. Her narration is triggered not by Roland Barthes, as in Cantú, but by Gaston Bachelard (1969), who sees the home as the space of protected intimacy. A self-reflexive narrator like Cantú and Cisneros, Mora theorizes as she narrates. She speaks from the physical and metaphoric house that grounds and contains her past identity. From her memories, she constructs an "I" as she maps a geographic genealogy.

Memory through writing is reactivated from a here and now to a there and before. She recognizes, as David Morley and Kevin Robbins do in their article on identity and memory, that the stories we tell ourselves about our past construct our identities in the present (1993, 9). The stories are remembered through the yearly calendar. The chapters proceed from January to December, establishing again a circular time contained in the space of the house. The reader becomes a captive audience as the stories of several generations are told. The house contains a garden, which is described according to the seasons and becomes the only space of respite from the house of memories past. It offers a temporary escape from the enclosed and, at times, stifling atmosphere of yesteryear, but in its design as an inner and circular patio integrated into an overall architectural plan (textual and contextual), it makes unavoidable the reentry into the rooms that house memory and from which the narrator cannot escape until the last spirit/ghost is exorcised through rememorialization.

Even though the text begins with a series of family photographs emphasizing the autobiographical pact of correspondence to lived experiences, the photographs and reproduced genealogical tree become the documentation that serve as a textual strategy to verify identities. As Barthes affirms in his study of photography:

> First of all I had to conceive, and therefore if possible express properly (even if it is a simple thing) how Photography's Referent is not the same as the referent of other systems of representation. I call "photographic referent" not the *optionally* real thing to which an image or a sign refers but the *necessarily* real thing which has been placed before the lens, without which there would be no photograph. Painting can feign reality without having seen it. Discourse combines signs which have referents, of course, but these referents can be and are most often "chimeras." Contrary to these imitations, in Photography I can never deny *that the thing has been there*. There is a superimposition here: of reality and of the past. . . . what I see has been here, in this place which extends between infinity and the subject (*operator* or *spectator*); it has been here, and yet

immediately separated; it has been absolutely, irrefutably present, and yet already deferred. (1983, 76–77)

The photographs included as preface to the narrative serve as "circumstantial evidence" to more fundamentally foreground the haunting voices that come back from the past to narrate their untold tales. Voices and dialogues are recreated, as in *Hoyt Street*, signaling the strategic use of mimesis (representation), but the narrating self remains ubiquitously present through self-reflexive diegesis (narration). Mora's narrator roams the rooms of the private abode dialoguing with the dead brought back to inhabit the house-text:

> How can you still be hungry if you're dead? Aunt Chole sing-songs her question in the high pitch she reserves for birds, children, spirits. "*Ay, mi Raúl, querido,* what do you want?" "I'll get him something, Tía," I say. In my dreamhouse father returns, dark-skinned, balding, filling the room. "What do you want, Daddy? Coffee?" . . ."Get her some honey, Patsy," he says using my childhood name, seeing me both in the past and in the present. . . . My father chuckles, munches his cookies and sips his coffee, smiles at me. "How are you doing, honey? Everything all right?" I want to say: how can it be all right if you're dead? How can it be that I will never again lean on your chest, feel your arms encircling, protecting, like the house? (1–2)

The home is not unhomely, as in Cisneros, but affects the narrator in contradictory ways, making her feel secure at times and helpless at others. Her search for self becomes the search for origins, a symbolic entrance into the house-womb, a ritual endeavor from which she will be reborn. Registering the passage of time as the sure marker of the passage of peoples, her text speaks to the irretrievability of the past and the transmutations it brings about:

> Why in my fifties did I decide to explore this house and its garden? Indeed a place to put the stories and the voices before they vanished like blooms and leaves will vanish on the wind outside, voices which, perceived as ordinary, would be unprotected, blown into oblivion. Since the family isn't together geographically, using the tools I know, I created a place welcoming to our spirits, a place for communion and reunion, no invitation necessary; a space, like all spaces, as real as we choose to make it, ample enough for the family spirits who will refer to us in the past tense can turn to us and create with us what they need, the cycle continuing, as they have inhabited one of our bodies, inhabit the body of

the house, a complex earth dwelling as we are dwellings and dwellers; the past, our present in the house and garden with its water song, daily wind-swept, transformed by light. (272–73)

Mora's circularly structured narrative and lyrical language create the space for inwardness and self-reflection in a tribute, recasting Proust's *Remembrance of Things Past* and Elena Garro's (1963) *Los Recuerdos del Porvenir.* Cisneros projects an escape from an unhomely place. Mora looks to inhabit a haunted one. Ponce imagines a happy home from a distanced present. For Cantú, it's just a place called home. All finally construct an "I" at home in writing, for writing is, finally, their true home and final destination.

The genealogies traced in Cantú all belonged to an already hybrid, mixed border culture whose territory during colonization changed the terms of their inhabiting it. In Mora, the stories narrate a space of before (Mexico) and after (United States), a politics of displacement and cultural dislocation, a once Mexican and indigenous space now under Anglo domination: "The house knows the sound of el Río Grande, river that for centuries wandered through this Chihuahua desert, the largest desert in North America, old ocean bed where millions of years ago, land emerged from water, mountains rose. Brown women and men knew this river, washed in it, planted with it, played in it, slept with its voice, long before conquistadores, historians, and politicians divided the land into countries and states, directed the river to become a border" (3). Allowing the language of the cultural imaginary to seep through, she refuses to translate the Spanish as she bilanguages to join other Chicanas/Latinas in a process of creating an "other tongue" that comes from living between languages. This cannot be read as just a bilingual aesthetic exercise but a "way of life" (Mignolo 2000, 264).

The use of Spanish in Chicana writings of self, I would add, implicitly validates the language of the cultural imaginary, establishing its value as a public language equal to English. The use of English is also subversive, for the Chicanas appropriated the language of the colonizer to indict the long history of oppression and defacement of a language and culture. Spanish is close to English in a hierarchy of languages, says Alfred Arteaga, and the presence of an alternative and literate linguistic tradition causes a crisis for Anglo America because "it precludes the status for English as sole, unchallenged mode for civilized American discourse, but it also underlines several myths that are at the very heart of the self-image propagated by Anglo America" (1994, 22).

In her book of essays, *Nepantla: Essays from the Land in the Middle,*[11] Pat Mora states, "These old arguments that citizens must shed their language to 'melt in' simply no longer apply. Many of us are not immigrants. This country has both the opportunity and the responsibility to demonstrate to this world of emerging representative governments that nurturing variety is central, not marginal, to democracy" (1993, 19).

ROUTES FOR READING/PLOTS FOR WRITING

At the turn of the twentieth century, Latin American writers initiated the literary movement called modernismo, a new aesthetic that liberated writing from Spanish literary models. Seen as a final decolonizing move against Spanish cultural dominance and U.S. imperialist imaginings, it opened the way for the Golden Age of Latin American writing in the twentieth century. Now, in the twenty-first century, it is Latinos/as, as previously colonized settlers, migrants, exiles, or citizens of semicolonies, who continue through their writings this long process of decolonization against both Hispanism's distancing gestures and Anglo assimilative politics.

In the United States, the 1980s prompted the so-called Decade of the Hispanic and recognized the arrival on the literary scene of Latino Americans at the same time that Latin American literature had established an international reputation. This conflation of Latin American and Latino literatures is both problematic and liberating. On the one hand it tends to essentialize and/or neutralize the particularisms out of which the different literatures and texts emerge, while on the other it proposes a strategic and powerful alliance against hegemonic conceptions of "Third World" peoples and their cultures. "At times," says Latin American cultural and literary critic Roman de la Campa, "one can sense the potential for a clash between the British and Hispanic literary traditions, jockeying to see which will constitute the true precursor for a new global literary order" (1999, 14). Latino literature complicates that purposefully dichotomized and provocative statement.

As I have traced in this essay, at the beginning of this century it is necessary not only to consider Latina/o literary production as cultural political intervention but also to distinguish among the different histories of a heterogeneous people of about 37 million. The different literary productions of Latinos/as in the United States are in many ways a collective project of peoples linked through similar histories, cultures, language, and imaginary. Their literature is constitutive of an alternative canon, one in the process of remapping cultural and literary terrains, which defy a monolithic conceptualization of the nation-state by marking the porous nature of literal and imaginative borders.

The Chicana writers I studied, no longer a silenced society, are in search of attentive outside readers that should, according to Doris Sommer (1999), "proceed with caution" when reading "minority literature," take care not to read the other as same but in fact to recognize the differences inscribed in the text (whether cultural, linguistic, or ideological). Sommer proposes a "particularist" reading instead of a "universalist" one that would neither maintain the "other" as an essentialized exotic other nor assimilate the "other" to self, finally neutralizing or deafening the texts' intervention in lived realities:

> Particularist literature would logically vie for central importance while holding off universalists who would claim co-authorship. But our [Anglo-European] tradition of criticism takes the underdeveloped practices of "reader response" theory as basic and unobjectional [*sic*]. The "strategies of containment" that claim our attention here would defend cultural difference as a value in itself. It is what Jean Francois Lyotard calls the differend, the stubborn residue that survives on the margins of normalizing discourse. Acknowledging that residue is the precondition for democratic negotiations. Difference safeguards particularist identities against seamless assimilation, a word that rhymes with neutralization and sometimes also with physical annihilation. (xiii)

I suggest that the texts by the Chicanas I have examined want to be read in their difference, by insiders and outsiders, as both products and producers of a collective imaginary, selectively retrieving from a cultural heritage as well as constructing new rituals, patterns, and memories for future sharing. Books are made from and make societies and, in that sense, this literature is clearing itself a space from which to think and be, a space Mignolo calls "border knowing." He cites Gloria Anzaldúa's *Borderlands* as "articulating a powerful alternative aesthetic and political hermeneutic by placing herself at the cross-road of three traditions (Spanish-American, Nahuatl, and Anglo-American) and by creating a locus of enunciation where different ways of knowing and individual and collective expressions mingle" (2000, 5). Modeled on the Chicano experience and owing to the idea of "African *gnosis*," he says, "border knowing is unthinkable without understanding the colonial difference. Furthermore, it is the recognition of the colonial difference from subaltern perspectives that demands border thinking" (6). bell hooks (1990) calls this "a space of radical openness," and Homi Bhabha defines it as "a context from which to build communities of resistance and renewal that cross the boundaries and double-cross the binaries of race, gender, class and all oppressively Othering categories" (1994, 84). Bhabha calls it a "third space of enunciation," the transitional space between colonization and its erasure and which Emma Pérez refers to as the "decolonizing imaginary" where "the silent gain their agency" (1999, 33).

In the autobiographical testimonial fictions I discuss, there is a radical break with rhetorical patterns traditionally found in autobiographical literature. As Nellie Y. McKay (1988) points out in reference to the literature of Zora Neale Hurston, life and autobiography are not the same. Strategies rather than truths are used to construct realities lived and to deconstruct racism (and, I would add, sexism). She reminds us that Hurston was not the first writer to create an image that did not offer a wholly accurate reading of the self. The discrepancies in Frederick Douglass's three narratives of self, she says, were "less interested in documenting facts than in employing rhetorical strategies that enabled him to replace the erroneous identity that dominant culture had bestowed on him with an equally fictitious soiled black self"(180–181). For Emma Pérez, women's voices are creating a "third space feminism," a "practice that implements the decolonial imaginary"(1999, 33), and it is here that I place the self-writing counterhegemonic practices of these Chicanas.

NOTES

I would like to thank the Chicano/Latino Research Center of the University of California, Santa Cruz for providing support for this research. For valuable comments and suggestions on earlier drafts of this paper, I am grateful to Guillermo Delgado, Elizabeth Corsun, and the members of the Chicana Feminisms Research Cluster: Pat Zavella, Aída Hurtado, Olga Nájera-Ramírez, and Gabriela Arredondo. For stimulating discussions on space and identity, I thank the members of the Borders, Nations and Regions Research Cluster.
1. The Hispanic Recovery Project, directed by Nicholas Kanellos, is a project engaged in the recuperation and publication of primary literary sources written by Hispanics in the geographic area that is now the United States from the colonial period to 1960. In the enormous endeavor of recovering historical and literary texts, the Project has contributed to making visible alternative literary and cultural practices in the Southwest, among other regions of the United States. These have been crucial in affirming and reinscribing the presence of local/border resistance by an ethnic and linguistic community vis-à-vis an Anglo national/nationalist center.
2. This statement should not be read as attributing any foundational status to that historical moment, but as one that recognizes a particular watershed period when a people's political intervention directly contested colonization, racism, sexism, homophobia, etc.
3. For analysis of comparative male autobiography, see Ramón Saldívar (1985), Antonio C. Márquez (1990), and Lauro Flores (1990).
4. Renato Rosaldo (1990) argues against the theories set forth by Gilles Deleuze and Felix Guattari (1983) in asserting that minority discourse can be distinguished from great lit-

erature by three features: deterritorialization, an emphasis on politics, and a collective value. He asserts that these theories are not applicable to Chicano literature or history because, like "the experiences of blacks and Native Americans," they "cannot readily be assimilated to a tale of immigration and displacement" (127).

5. The notion implied in this term refers to those whose attitude makes them smugly narrow and conventional, indifferent to cultural and aesthetic values, and, in this particular case, to the power of fiction to endow meaning.

6. Bildungsromane, or novels of formation, have, with few exceptions, followed the personal growth and development of a protagonist from childhood or adolescence into adulthood. The representations of female and minority protagonists have more recently questioned the assumed universality of the traditional form, offering, from the perspective of gender and ethnicity, variations on the coming-of-age story.

7. Cisneros says about Esperanza:

> Yes, she wants to get out, she sees the barrio as something very threatening, and rightfully so. I wrote it as a reaction against those people who want to make our barrios look like Sesame Street, or someplace really warm and beautiful. Poor neighborhoods lose their charm after dark, they really do. It's nice to go visit a poor neighborhood, but if you've got to live there every day, and deal with garbage that doesn't get picked up, and kids getting shot in your backyard, and people running through your doorway at night, and rats, and poor housing. It loses its charm real quick. I was writing about it in the most real sense that I knew, as a person walking those neighborhoods with a vagina. I saw it a lot differently than all those "machos" that are writing all those bullshit pieces about their barrios. (quoted in Rodríguez Aranda 1990, 69)

8. In an interview Cisneros says: "What I'm doing is writing true stories. They're all stories I lived or witnessed or heard of, stories that were told to me. . . . In Iowa City I decided to write about something far removed from here which was my childhood. . . . Some of these stories happened to my mother, and I combined them with something that happened to me. . . . Some of the stories were my students' when I was a counselor; women would confide in me and I was so overwhelmed with my inability to connect their lives that I wrote about them" (quoted in Rodríguez Aranda 1990, 64).

9. David Sibley writes in the introduction to *Geographies of Exclusion:* "Because power is expressed in the monopolization of space and the relegation of weaker groups in society to less desirable environments, any text on the social geography of advanced capitalism should be concerned with the question of exclusion. . . . Human geography, in particular, should be concerned with raising consciousness of the domination of space in its critique of the hegemonic culture. . . . To get beyond the myths which secure capitalist hegemony, to expose oppressive practices, it is necessary to examine the assumptions about inclusion and exclusion which are implicit in the design of spaces and places" (1995, ix–x).

10. See Rosaura Sánchez for the role the Spanish language is playing in the Latino communities, which she sees as "a heterogeneous population, politically fragmented, but united by a history of conquest and colonialism, a history of proletarianization and disempowerment in this country and, to a large extent, by a common language" (1998, 111).

11. *Nepantla* is a Nahuatl preposition meaning "in the middle," which can be used either as in *Tlalnepantla* (in the middle of the earth) or as in *Nepantla Tonatiuh* (in the middle of the day). It was used in the sixteenth century by Nahuatl people to describe their situation in relation to the Spanish colonizer. "*Estamos nepantla*," they would say in response to their situation. Rubén Bonifaz Nuño, renowned Mexican poet and Nahuatl scholar, translates the sentence as meaning "We are in a state of waiting. It is no longer the place we knew, but we don't know yet what it will become" (conversation, Mexico City, 1990).

WORKS CITED

Alarcón, Norma. 1981. "Chicana's Feminist Literature: A Re-Vision through Malint-zin/or Malintzin: Putting Flesh Back on the Object." Pp. 182–90 in *This Bridge Called My Back: Writings by Radical Women of Color,* ed. Cherríe Moraga and Gloria Anzaldúa. New York: Kitchen Table.

———. 1996. "Conjugating Subjects in the Age of Multiculturalism." Pp. 127–48 in *Mapping Multiculturalism,* ed. Avery F. Gordon and Christopher Newfield. Minneapolis: University of Minnesota Press.

Alvarez, Julia. 1991. *How the García Girls Lost Their Accents.* Chapel Hill, NC: Algonquin Books.

Anaya, Rodolfo. 1976. *Heart of Aztlán.* Berkeley: Editorial Justa.

Anzaldúa, Gloria. 1987. *Borderlands/La Frontera: The New Mestiza.* San Francisco: Aunt Lute.

Arteaga, Alfred. 1994. *An Other Tongue: Nation and Ethnicity in the Linguistic Borderlands.* Durham, NC: Duke University Press.

Bachelard, Gaston. 1969. *The Poetics of Space.* Boston: Beacon Press.

Barthes, Roland. 1983. *Camera Lucida: Reflections on Photography.* Trans. Richard Howard. New York: Hill and Wang.

Bergland, Betty. 1994. "Postmodernism and the Autobiographical Subject: Reconstructing the 'Other.'" Pp. 130–66 in *Autobiography and Postmodernism,* ed. K. Ashley, Leigh Gilmore, and Gerald Peters. Amherst: University of Massachusetts Press.

Beverley, John. 1993. *Against Literature.* Minneapolis: University of Minnesota Press.

Bhabha, Homi K. 1994. *The Location of Culture.* New York: Routledge.

Blake, Debra J. 1997. "Unsettling Identities: Transitive Subjectivity in Cherríe Moraga's *Loving in the War Years.*" *a/b: Auto: Biography Studies* 12(1): 72–89.

Cantú, Norma Elia. 1995. *Canícula.* Albuquerque: University of New Mexico Press.

Carter, Erica, James Donald, and Judith Squires, eds. 1993. Introduction. Pp. vii–xv in *Space and Place: Theories of Identity and Location.* London: Lawrence and Wishart.

Castillo, Adela del. 1974. "Malintzin Tenépal: A Preliminary Look into a New Perspective." *Encuentro Femenil* 1(2): 58–78. Reprinted in *Essays on La Mujer,* ed. Rosaura Sánchez and Rosa Martínez Cruz, 124–49. Los Angeles: Chicano Studies Center Publications, University of California, 1977.

Cisneros, Sandra. 1984. *The House on Mango Street.* Houston: Arte Publico Press.

Cronon, William. 1992. "A Place of Stories: Nature, History and Narrative." *Journal of American History* 78 (March): 1347–76.

de la Campa, Román. 1999. *Latin Americanism.* Minneapolis: University of Minnesota Press.

Deleuze, Gilles, and Felix Guattari. 1983. "What Is Minor Literature?" *Mississippi Review* 11(3): 13–33.

Derrida, Jacques. 1980. "The Law of Genre." *Glyph* 7: 203–4.

Flores, Lauro. 1990. "Chicano Autobiography: Culture, Ideology and the Self." *The Americas Review* 18(2): 80–91.

Galarza, Ernesto. 1971. *Barrio Boy.* Notre Dame: University of Notre Dame Press.

García, Cristina. 1992. *Dreaming in Cuban.* New York: Knopf.

Garro, Elena. 1963. *Los recuerdos del porvenir.* Mexico City: Joaquín Mortiz.

Haraway, Donna J. 1991. *Simians, Cyborgs, and Women: The Reinvention of Nature.* New York: Routledge.

Harsock, Nancy. 1990. "Foucault on Power: A Theory for Women?" Pp. 157–75 in *Feminism/Postmodernism,* ed. L. J. Nicholson. New York: Routledge.

hooks, bell. 1990. "Choosing the Margin as a Space of Radical Openness," in *Yearning: Race, Gender and Cultural Politics.* Boston: South End Press.

Hurtado, Aída. 1996. *The Color of Privilege: Three Blasphemies on Race and Feminism.* Ann Arbor: University of Michigan Press.

JanMohamed, Abdul R., and David Lloyd, eds. 1990. *The Nature and Context of Minority Discourse.* Oxford: Oxford University Press.

Jordan, David M. 1994. *New World Regionalism: Literature in the Americas.* Toronto: University of Toronto Press.

Kaplan, Caren. 1992. "Resisting Autobiography: Out-Law Genres and Transnational Feminist Subjects." Pp. 115–38 in *De/Colonizing the Subject: The Politics of Gender in Women's Autobiography,* ed. Sidoni Smith and Julia Watson. Minneapolis: University of Minnesota Press.

Kazanjian, David, and Anahid Kassabian. 1993. "Naming the Armenian Genocide: The Quest for 'Truth' and a Search for Possibilities." Pp. 33–55 in *Space and Place: Theories of Identity and Location,* ed. Erica Carter, James Donald, and Judith Squires. London: Lawrence and Wishart.

Márquez, Antonio C. 1990. "Self and Culture: Autobiography as Cultural Narrative." *Discurso* 7(1): 51–66.

McKay, Nellie Y. 1988. "Race, Gender and Cultural Context in Zora Neale Hurston's *Dust Tracks on a Road.*" Pp. 175–88 in *Life Lines: Theorizing Women's Autobiography,* ed. Bella Brodzki and Celeste Schenck. Ithaca: Cornell University Press.

Méndez, Miguel. 1974. *Peregrinos de Aztlán.* Tucson: Editorial Peregrinos.

Mignolo, Walter D. 2000. *Local Histories/Global Designs: Coloniality, Subaltern Knowledges, and Border Thinking.* Princeton: Princeton University Press.

Molloy, Sylvia. 1991. *At Face Value: Autobiographical Writing in Spanish America.* Cambridge, England: Cambridge University Press.

Mora, Pat. 1993. *Nepantla: Essays from the Land in the Middle.* Albuquerque: University of New Mexico Press.

———. 1997. *House of Houses.* Boston: Beacon Press.

Moraga, Cherríe. 1983. "A Long Line of Vendidas." Pp. 90–145 in *Loving in the War Years: Lo que nunca pasó por sus labios.* Boston: South End Press.

———. 1993. "The Breakdown of the Bi-Cultural Mind." Pp. 112–31 in *The Last Generation: Prose and Poetry*. Boston: South End Press.

Morley, David, and Kevin Robbins. 1993. "No Place Like Heimat: Images of Home(land) in European Culture." Pp. 3–31 in *Space and Place: Theories of Identity and Location*, ed. Erica Carter, James Donald, and Judith Squires. London: Lawrence and Wishart.

Paredes, Américo. 1958. *With His Pistol in His Hand: A Border Ballad and Its Hero*. Austin: University of Texas Press.

Pérez, Emma. 1999. *The Decolonial Imaginary: Writing Chicanas into History*. Bloomington: Indiana University Press.

Perreault, Jeanne. 1995. *Writing Selves: Contemporary Feminist Autography*. Minneapolis: University of Minnesota Press.

Ponce, Mary Helen. 1993. *Hoyt Street: An Autobiography*. Albuquerque: University of New Mexico Press.

Pratt, Mary Louise. 1994. "Transculturation and Autoethnography: Perú, 1615/1980." Pp. 24–46 in *Colonial Discourse/Postcolonial Theory*, ed. F. Barker, Peter Hulme, and Margaret Iversen. New York: Manchester University Press.

Rivera, Tomás. 1983. "Mexican-American Literature: The Establishment of Community." Pp. 124–30 in *The Texas Literary Tradition: Fiction, Folklore, History*, ed. Don Graham et al. Austin: College of Liberal Arts, University of Texas, Texas State Historical Association.

———. 1971. *Y no se lo tragó la tierra*. Berkeley: Quinto Sol.

Rodríguez Aranda, Pilar E. 1990. "On the Solitary Fate of Being Mexican, Female, Wicked and Thirty-Three: An Interview with Writer Sandra Cisneros." *The Americas Review* 18(1): 64–80.

Rodríguez, Richard. 1982. *Hunger of Memory: The Education of Richard Rodríguez*. New York: Bantam.

Rosaldo, Renato. 1990. "Politics, Patriarchs, and Laughter." Pp. 124–45 in *The Nature and Context of Minority Discourse*, ed. Abdul R. JanMohamed and David Lloyd. New York: Oxford University Press.

Saldivar, Ramón. 1985. "Ideologies of the Self: Chicano Autobiography." *Diacritics* (fall): 25–33. Reprinted in Ramón Saldivar, *Chicano Narrative: The Dialectics of Difference*. Madison: University of Wisconsin Press, 1990.

Sánchez, Rosaura. 1998. "Mapping the Spanish Language along a Multiethnic and Multilingual Border." Pp. 101–25 in *The Latino Studies Reader: Culture, Economy and Society*, ed. Antonia Darder and Rodolfo D. Torres. Malden, MA: Blackwell Press.

Santiago, Esmeralda. 1993. *When I Was Puerto Rican*. New York: Addison-Wesley.

Sibley, David. 1995. *Geographies of Exclusion: Society and Difference in the West*. New York: Routledge.

Sommer, Doris. 1999. *Proceed with Caution, When Engaged by Minority Writing in the Americas*. Cambridge, MA: Harvard University Press.

White, Hayden. 1973. *Metahistory: The Historical Imagination in Nineteenth-Century Europe*. Baltimore: John Hopkins University Press.

———. 1987. *The Content of the Form: Narrative Discourse and Historical Representation*. Baltimore: Johns Hopkins University Press.

(Re)Mapping *mexicanidades:* (Re)Locating
Chicana Writings and Translation Politics

CLAIRE JOYSMITH

• • • • •

In (re)mapping the transformative and transgressional nature of the politics
and poetics inherent in Chicana autobiographical fiction, Norma Klahn's
discursive positionality becomes itself transgressive. This would seem to
set a mood for responding through resonance, by counterpointing positionalities and addressing other implications of (re)mapping, (dis)placement,
and (re)location.

The key positioning of Chicana autobiographical fiction within the en-
visioned impact of Chicana/o literature in broader cultural (re)mappings,
such as Klahn proposes, has resonance in gendered cultural politics outside
U.S. cultural locations. In the closing section of her essay, she mentions
that Chicana writers are "in search of attentive outside readers." This allu-
sion to non-Chicana/o readers within yet also outside of U.S. cultural locations is significant, because, by extension, there emerges an associative link
to the umbrella concept of *mexicanidades,* whereby issues of difference
and inclusion/exclusion dynamics are problematized, further complicating
(re)location and positionality. Along these same lines, the (re)mappings and
(dis)placement Klahn addresses would seem to resonate in the (re)location
of politics and poetics vis-à-vis a potential all-Spanish-speaking readership
in Mexico as a cultural location.

In (re)mapping what Klahn calls "the situatedness of knowledge" within
the nature of culture and identity that, as she points out, is "transformative,

continuously redefined and recontextualized," her work opens up opportunities for charting a cartography of complexities contained in the concept of *mexicanidades*. It also offers new routes and further "reroutings" for cultural, linguistic, and aesthetic translational politics, discussed briefly in the following annotations.

(RE)LOCATIONS AND (DIS)LOCATIONS: CHICANA WRITERS READ(ING) IN MEXICO

As a respondent to Norma Klahn's text, in which positionality and (dis)-placement are core issues, I have a corresponding need to position myself from the outset as born and raised bilingually/biculturally in Mexico, a critic of Mexicana and Chicana literature, and a translator of Chicana writings. I also speak/write from Mexico (central Mexico, to be positionally specific) as a site of reception and discursivity, where Chicana/o literature is indeed barely known/read and where I find myself situated as a minority in reading, writing about, responding to, and translating this particular literature.

Klahn reminds us that self-writing practices at the heart of Chicana writings and poetics "want to be read in their difference, by insiders and outsiders, as both products and producers of a collective imaginary, selectively retrieving from a cultural heritage as well as constructing new rituals, patterns, and memories for future sharing." I would like to suggest, in taking this statement a step further, that this is complicated when Chicana auto-biographicality—in which, as Klahn points out, "memory matters as the self constructs an identity in relation to place" and in which the "situated-ness of knowledge" is a crucial expression of Chicana counterhegemonic writing practices—is read to/by "outsiders," particularly if the specificity of these "outsiders" is a Spanish-speaking audience/readership in Mexico as a cultural location. This can be exemplified in the concrete context of a colloquium on Chicana writing that took place in Mexico City,[1] in which the reactions to Chicana writings (many of them autobiographical fictions, in fact) and their relation to Mexicana writings were textualized and, for the first time in central Mexico, opened up extra/intratextually to discussion.[2]

In this case, the status of the audience as "outsiders" yet within those very *mexicanidades* that Chicana writers/writings lay claim to as constituting a signifier of difference in a U.S. cultural site exemplified a (dis)location problematizing issues of inclusion/exclusion, among several others. Because the concept of mexicanidad has remained monolithic and singular in Mexico as a cultural location until very recently (neozapatista discursivity, for instance, has contributed toward pluralizing it), the participation and positionality of *chicanidad(es)* within *mexicanidad(es)* is an issue scarcely addressed textually, academically, and theoretically from the specificity of Mexico as a cultural location.

For readers—or an audience, in the case of this colloquium—unfamiliar with Chicana/o practices and politics, the very fact of using English (even if nonstandard) and code-switching/interlingual practices for self-expression and autobiographicality as a means of implementing "counterhegemonic activities," while *simultaneously* making a claim to *mexicanidades*, necessarily provokes disruption as well as reaction. This "resistant reaction,"[3] as we might call it, is a linguistically and culturally determined response to an immediate referent: the counterpointing umbrella term *gringo*, a signifier of (mostly English-speaking) foreignness, of outsiderness and otherness, of American imperialism representing a threat to *mexicanidad(es)*. This reaction through opposition is, in a certain sense and generally speaking, counterhegemonic, although it is, needless to say, at odds with the resistances associated with Chicana/o writings.

A conscious transformative approach to the problematization of *mexicanidades*, however, can only be taken beyond scattered discursive misunderstandings (such as those that occurred, for instance, in the above-mentioned colloquium)[4] and enter transformative dynamics once an interdependent double translational task is undertaken. The first would be the actual linguistic translation and the second would imply additional (dis)placement and (re)location of identity and culture that are in any case, as Klahn points out, "transformative, continuously redefined and recontextualized." This would promote a receptive context for these very translations and literature, and further (re)mapping discursive grounds textually, pragmatically, and theoretically.

I would like to suggest that the function of translation itself, from a perspective that transcends mere linguistic considerations, may be (re)located and transmuted as a mediating and transculturing agency in a context of broader transformative textual and critical practices. This also implies the (re)creation of another kind of readership, a task that would expand Gloria Anzaldúa's claim about Chicana writings: "In addition to the task of writing, or perhaps included in the task of writing, we've had to create a readership and teach it how to 'read' our work" (1990, xviii).

In her essay, Klahn makes an interesting point in identifying the use of English in Chicana writing as "subversive because the Chicanas appropriated the language of the colonizer to accuse the long history of oppression and defacement of a language and culture." In this way the language of cultural expression (English) is not only appropriated but problematized and reconfigured from within a linguistic and cultural stronghold such as literature.

Another subversive factor is that, as Klahn mentions, quoting Arteaga, the presence of Spanish in Chicana texts provokes a crisis because "it precludes the status of English as sole, unchallenged mode for civilized American discourse."[5] It would seem that the deliberate presence/permanence of Spanish in Chicana "life-telling accounts" written in English—what Pérez-Torres calls the "mestizaje of linguistic form"(1995, 213)—may well provoke a textual rupture for a non-Spanish-speaking reader unfamiliar with the language and culture. In this case, these identity markings or markers of chicanidad function as reminders that demand acknowledgment. Anzaldúa defiantly states in her preface to *Borderlands/La Frontera: The New Mestiza* that "this bastard language, Chicano Spanish, is not approved by any society. But we Chicanos no longer feel that we need . . . to translate to Anglos, Mexicans and Latinos, apology blurting out of our mouths with every step. Today we ask to be met halfway" (1987, n.p.). She then proceeds to implement this textually by using both bilingual and interlingual strategies.[6]

In Chicana autobiographical fiction there are visible attempts to write "attentive outside readers" into the text by using what could be called "intratextual translational strategies." These are integrated in Chicana/o politics of (non)translation and are closely related to the particularities of Chicana/o poetics as there is an intentional "bilanguaging" (as Walter Mignolo, following Anzaldúa, terms it) that aesthetizes and "privilege[s] bilingual, biliterate, and bicultural practices," as Klahn points out.

An example of (non)translation byways, as well as subversive poetic singularities of Chicano writings in general and of Chicana autobiographical fiction in particular, is visible in this fragment from *Canícula: Snapshots of a Girlhood en la Frontera* by Norma Elia Cantú, in which interlingualism becomes an aesthetic strategy implementing the creation of singular poetic devices and rhythmicity: "Strange insects—frailesillos, chinches, garrapatas, hormigas—some or all of these pests—ticks, fleas, tiny spiders the color of sand—some or all of these bichos—find their way to exposed ankles, arms, necks and suck life-blood, leaving welts, ronchas—red and itchy—and even pus-filled ampulas that burst and burn with the sun" (1995, 113).

We could say that (English-speaking) "attentive outside readers" are, in a sense, acknowledged through the use of intratextual translational strategies. These are deliberately complicated here, it is worth noting, by means of "dislocated" intratextual translation and nontranslation.[7]

TRANSLATING CHICANA/O TEXTS INTO SPANISH

If translation of Chicana/o texts is regarded not merely as a process of transcribing a text into another language and culture but as an active means of (dis)placing, (dis)locating, and (re)locating its textuality, of rewriting it, as well as problematizing *mexicanidades* and concepts such as "culture of origin" / "culture of destination" (to use translation theory terms; see Carbonell i Cortés 1997), the translational act can be seen as a means of furthering the participation of Chicana/o poetics within the transformative dynamics and flux of culture / identity that Klahn underscores in the concluding section of her essay.

(Re)mapping and (re)location are further problematized if we consider that once Chicana/o texts written in English are translated into Spanish they begin to "speak," as it were, in an "other" tongue, in a language inextricable from the very *mexicanidades* Chicana poetics lay claim to as a signifier of difference. Yet because the Spanish language becomes the "dominant" code in a translation, the encoded subtextual signifiers, the visible markers of *chicanidad(es)*—particularly in texts that integrate interlingualism—are (re)located, (dis)located, and consequently subjected to probable erasure and to a particular kind of (linguistic) assimilation.

One response to this is the creation and implementation of pragmatic translational strategies that would (re)locate chicanidad by rewriting a Spanish-speaking readership with the specificity of Mexico as a cultural location into these rewritten/translated texts. As a translator concerned and fascinated with such issues, I have had the opportunity to explore possible translation strategies in a recent anthology of Chicana literature to be published in Mexico City (Joysmith, in press).[8]

The poetic and political devices of interlingualism risk invisibility in a Spanish translation, for which alternative strategies can be implemented, such as the use of distinct typographical markers. Another translation strategy is to create equivalent visible markings of disruption (and identity) through inverted mirroring and the "appropriation" of the choice *not* to translate the original, selectively allowing it to remain unaltered linguistically in the terminal text, even though it is altered in cultural terms. By allowing certain words/expressions to remain in English (that is, through a deliberate use of nontranslation, a strategy not to be confused with issues of linguistic untranslatability) the presence and effect of visible markers in Chicana/o textuality are rewritten into the terminal text. Moreover, elements at variance with standard Spanish usage (for instance, grammatical "anomalies" and misspellings, archaic and oral expressions) that may problematize the Spanish language itself are reproduced unaltered in the "terminal" translated text, a deliberate positioning that has activated resistance reactions among editors and readers in Mexico.[9] It should be added that underlying syntactical variants in English are also acknowledged in these translational strategies.

BY WAY OF CONCLUSION

Given the conspicuous unavailability of Chicana/o texts in Mexico (whether written originally in Spanish, translated from English, or in bilingual versions), in addition to the quasi-absence of discursivity related to Chicana/o politics and poetics (whether in mass media, literary, or academic circles), there seems to be a need to undertake the above-mentioned double translational task.[10] That is, on the one hand, the linguistic translation of Chicana/o textuality and, on the other, facilitating an increase in consciousness of its implications in general and of the groundbreaking impact of Chicana autobiographical fiction in particular.

Such a task demands a positionality (and a necessary corresponding implementation) that problematizes and explores mexicanidades—in which "attentive outside readers" become key figures—as part of an ongoing project, a continued dialogue, both pragmatic and theoretical, through orality and textuality, offered in opportunities such as discussion meetings, seminars, colloquiums, conference presentations, and conference panels both in and outside U.S. (cultural) locations, as well as, for instance, interinstitutional and binational exchanges.[11]

This task of discursive and dialogic exchange and openness is one Klahn acknowledges and inscribes herself into by participating in such exchange dynamics and by proposing Chicana autobiographical fictions as intrinsic in (re)mapping gendered cultural awareness into a broader context of cultural production.

1. This event took place at the Universidad Nacional Autónoma de México (UNAM) in Mexico City, organized by the Centro de Investigaciones Sobre América del Norte (CISAN) and held in the auditorium of the Facultad de Filosofía y Letras of the UNAM (June 24–25, 1993).

Participating Chicana writers included Norma Cantú, Ana Castillo, Sandra Cisneros, Lucha Corpi, Mary Helen Ponce, and Helena María Viramontes, as well as Chicana critics such as Norma Alarcón. The Mexicana writers included Margo Glantz, Ethel Krauze, Guadalupe Loaeza, Aline Petterson, Elena Poniatowska, and María Luisa Puga.

Prior to this colloquium, three others that centered on Chicana and Mexicana writers took place in Tijuana with very different dynamics and ended in an impasse; these were sponsored by the Colegio de la Frontera Norte and the Women's Studies Program (PIEM) of the Colegio de México. See López González, Malagamba, and Urrutia (1988, 1990).

2. The texts that were originated in this event were collected in a book; see Joysmith (1995). It includes essays on Chicana writings, the contents of an "*encuentro*," that is, an attempted dialogue between Chicana and Mexicana writers, as well as thirteen postcolloquium interviews with the participating writers and an extensive bibliography.

3. See Joysmith (2000). In the present text I have substituted "reactive resistance" for "resistance reactions."

4. To give a concrete example, during the *encuentro* or meeting between Chicana and Mexicana writers, the self-narrating practices of Chicana Mary Helen Ponce and Mexicana Guadalupe Loaeza in recounting childhood delousing experiences (the first in a Mexican immigrant setting; the second at a private boarding school in Montreal) were (dis)located and (re)located through positioning. The awareness of Ponce's autobiographical I as "a self who recollects her memories and those of other members of her community" (as Klahn states in her essay) differed from Loaeza's autobiographical I that assumed mexicanidad to be an exclusive mode of identity formation, thereby precluding race, class, and ethnicity awareness (see Joysmith 1995, 223–24). In Norma Alarcón's view, "what each writer said became a monologue. As each writer spoke about her work and the modes and styles of inscription of the subject, she did not create a discursive space of relationality to others. Indeed, twelve monologues do not make for dialogue. The sense of difference is magnified rather than mapped" (quoted in Joysmith 1995, 274).

5. It is interesting to note the emergence of texts that challenge this, such as the recently published Shell and Sollers (2000).

6. " 'Bilingualism' implies moving from one language code to another; 'interlingualism' implies the constant tension of the two at once" (Bruce-Novoa 1982, 226). Also see Sánchez (1985, 21).

7. Such (dis)locations are exemplified in the insect listing, where the actual order of the translations is altered (despite the apparently symmetrical syntactical structure), and only two out of the four are actually translated, "ticks" and "fleas," whereas "frailesillos" and "hormigas" remain untranslated.

8. The research for this project was partly funded by the Mexico-U.S. Cultural Fund/ Fundación Cultural México-Estados Unidos.

9. See Joysmith (2000). Interestingly, a letter from the publisher granting permission for Gloria Anzaldúa's poems insisted that "no change in spelling or accents (or lack thereof) is acceptable if it originally appears as Spanish in the poem." This would seem to indicate that some "tampering" may have occurred previously, in either English- or Spanish-language editions.

10. There are only a handful of novels, short story collections, and anthologies published in Spanish and in Spanish-language translations by Mexican publishing houses and very little distribution. A case in point is Sandra Cisneros's best-selling *The House on Mango Street* (1984), translated as *La casa en Mango Street* (1995) by Elena Poniatowska and Juan Antonio Ascencio and published in Mexico several years after it was first published in the United States, even though a translation (not distributed in Mexico) appeared in Spain several years before.

The scarcity of Chicana/o texts available in Mexico is partly due to economic reasons, such as overpriced reprinting and translation rights by U.S. publishers and literary agents as well as a severe generalized publishing crisis in Mexico; it is also due to the belief that there is no readership for this kind of publication, as some publishers have voiced it, which I believe to be gradually changing.

11. An example is the Latin American Studies Association (LASA) 2000 panel entitled "Transcultural Textualities and Translation: Chicana and Mexicana (Re)Writings in Transit," among other efforts of its kind.

WORKS CITED

Alarcón, Norma. 1995. "Interlocutions: An Afterword to the Coloquio on Mexicana and Chicana Writers." Pp. 273–77 in *Las formas de nuestras voces: Chicana and Mexicana Writers in Mexico*, ed. Claire Joysmith. Berkeley: Third Woman Press; Mexico City: CISAN/UNAM.

Anzaldúa, Gloria. 1987. *Borderlands/La Frontera: The New Mestiza.* San Francisco: Aunt Lute.

———. 1990. Introduction Pp. xv–xviii in *Making Face/Making Soul: Haciendo Caras. Creative and Critical Perspectives by Women of Color*, ed. Gloria Anzaldúa. San Francisco: Aunt Lute.

Bruce-Novoa, Juan. 1982. *Chicano Poetry: A Response to Chaos.* Austin: University of Texas Press.

Cantú, Norma Elia. 1995. *Canícula: Snapshots of a Girlhood en la Frontera.* Albuquerque: University of New Mexico Press.

Carbonell i Cortés, Ovidi. 1997. *Traducir al otro: Traducción, exotismo, poscolonialismo.* Cuenca, Spain: Ediciones de la Universidad de Castilla-La Mancha, Colección Escuela de Traductores de Toledo.

Cisneros, Sandra. 1995. *La casa en Mango Street* [The House on Mango Street]. Trans. Elena Poniatowska and Juan Antonio Ascencio. Mexico City: Alfaguara Literaturas.

Joysmith, Claire. 2000. "(Re)Writings in Transit: *Apuntes a colores.*" *A Quien Corresponda* 101 (July): 8–12.

———, ed. 1995. *Las formas de nuestras voces: Chicana and Mexicana Writers in Mexico.* Berkeley: Third Woman Press; Mexico City: CISAN/UNAM.

———, ed. In press. *Cantar de espejos/Singing Mirrors: Antología bilingüe de literatura contemporánea escrita por chicanas/Bilingual Anthology of Contemporary Chicana Literature.* Vol. 1, *Poesía/Poetry.* Mexico City: La Casa de las Imágenes.

López González, Aralia, Amelia Malagamba, and Elena Urrutia, eds. 1988. *Mujer y literatura mexicana y chicana: Culturas en contacto. Primer coloquio fronterizo.* Tijuana, México: El Colegio de la Frontera Norte; México City: El Colegio de México/PIEM.

———, eds. 1990. *Mujer y literatura mexicana y chicana: Culturas en contacto,* vol. 2. México City: El Colegio de México/PIEM; Tijuana, México: El Colegio de la Frontera Norte.

Pérez-Torres, Rafael. 1995. *Movements in Chicano Poetry: Against Myths, Against Margins.* New York: Cambridge University Press.

Sánchez, Marta E. 1985. *Contemporary Chicana Poetry: A Critical Approach to an Emerging Literature.* Berkeley: University of California Press.

Shell, Marc, and Werner Sollors, eds. 2000. *The Multilingual Anthology of American Literature: A Reader of Original Texts with English Translations.* New York: New York University Press.

CHAPTER FIVE

Chronotope of Desire:

Emma Pérez's *Gulf Dreams*

ELLIE HERNÁNDEZ

• • • • •

Emma Pérez's *Gulf Dreams* (1996) makes the unusual aesthetic claim that
the dislocated histories of Chicanas can be traced to contemporary discourses of sexuality. In signifying historical memory as desire, her claim
reveals how Chicana sexuality is formed and suppressed in historical discourse (Lacan 1977, esp. 211–27). In *The Decolonial Imaginary: Writing
Chicanas into History*, Pérez explains that "desire, its historical construction, its discourse, has been repressive, even fascist, in its colonial forms"
(1999, 125). Like Pérez's theorizations of Chicana subjectivity in history,
this same notion of desire assumes an aesthetic expression in *Gulf Dreams*.
By centralizing the concept of desire with Chicana lesbian sexuality and
history, she establishes a connection among the social, political, psychological, and historical processes that have shaped Chicana feminist criticisms in colonial and postcolonial contexts. The novel itself seems to embody a different historical account of the cultural representation of Chicana
lesbian sexuality by making visible the traumatic psychological ruptures
of colonial memory in Chicana/o discourse. By framing historical memory
as desire, Pérez makes the aesthetic claim that representing Chicana lesbians in history is next to impossible without summoning the violent tropes
embedded in a Chicana/o colonial and nationalistic history. She suggests
that Chicana/o gays and lesbians are caught up in the violent ruptures of

the colonial experience. This effect becomes visible in the aesthetic terms of Chicana/o national history and culture. The specific colonial/national experience renders the sexuality of gays and lesbians as a central mediating ideological factor that exposes the gender power dynamics in Chicana/o history.

Pérez suggests that Chicana/o gays and lesbians are caught up in the violent ruptures of the colonial experience. This effect becomes visible in the aesthetic terms of Chicana/o national history and culture. Pérez, I argue, seeks to account for the terms of articulation for gays and lesbians that often render silent the voices of Chicana/o gays and lesbians. *Gulf Dreams* must be seen, then, as an attempt to create aesthetic terms of articulation for Chicana/o gays and lesbians in sexuality and history. This understanding of Chicanas/os in history makes it necessary for us to consider how sexuality serves as a valid, even powerful, pedagogical method for studying gender power relations in Chicana/o and feminist studies.

A few words may be necessary to explain my engagement with some of these terms. "History" and "desire" are critical concepts that Pérez frames in her own feminist theorization of Lacan and Foucault. Her critical essay "Sexuality and Discourse: Notes from a Chicana Survivor" (1991) describes how the colonial history implied in discourse of sexuality actually erases Chicanas from history. Pérez describes this effect as follows: "If discourse reveals the history of sexuality, then women of color face an obstacle. We have not had our own language and voice in history. We have been spoken about, written about, spoken at but never spoken with or listened to" (62). She stresses the way in which historical discourses deny or suppress Chicana self-production and furthermore demonstrates how "history" serves the interest of the empowered individual already formed in existing power relations. Pérez's attempt to formulate a theory of historical memory as a resistance in Chicanas' discourse becomes apparent in the novel as the fragmentation of the Chicana colonial psyche that is represented in the term "desire."

"Desire" is an especially slippery term. Pérez argues in *The Decolonial Imaginary* that the symbolic terms for inscribing Chicanas into history are already determined by the history of colonization. According to Pérez, the subject/object mirroring found in Western psychoanalytic theory cannot thus be said to pertain to the inscriptions of Chicanas in the "imaginary." "The imaginary is the mirrored identity where coloniality overshadows the image in the mirror. Ever present, it is that which is between the subject and the object being reflected, splintering the object in a shattered mirror, where kaleidoscopic identities are burst open and where the colonial self and the colonized other become elements of multiple, mobile categoric identities" (7).

By evoking a discussion of the deeper unconscious aspects of language in the construction of historical subjects, Pérez engages a critical analysis of Chicana lesbian subjectivity as the site of resistance from the terms of history making. Her understanding of Chicana lesbian sexuality in discourse intends to reclaim the terms of articulation by returning to the unconscious structures of the colonial imaginary. In this, she has been able to look at Chicana lesbian subjectivity as it exists outside of history. In a sense, this marginal and liminal existence creates the possibility of disrupting the dialectics of history we have thus far experienced under colonialism and national revolutionary paradigms.

One of the ambitions of this reading serves as a critical discussion that reconvenes Chicana sexuality in the aesthetic and cultural analysis of Chicana/o gay and lesbian representation.[1] In the course of this essay, I delineate the various ways Pérez uses desire in constructing a lesbian countermemory. In the most basic sense, her claim of desire must be understood as a prelingual state of consciousness. The claim of desire in the most literal reading of *Gulf Dreams* represents the "lack" of historical representation for Chicanas. As such, the novel can be seen as a self-conscious attempt by Pérez to blur the distinction between what is "real" and what is actually representable. This voicing of desire in this sense sets the tone for the primary political challenge about the validity of a representational history for inscribing the Chicana voice in aesthetic literary terms. It would appear remarkable enough to acquaint something as obtuse and loaded with psychoanalytic currency as desire with something so palpable as lived reality. Both history and desire are critical terms that Pérez associates in order to question the role of knowledge in the production of the Chicana lesbian voice. Historical representations at the cultural national level have precluded the individualized political and aesthetic interests of Chicana lesbians in creating a terminology for self-production. There is also the desire for self-representation in language, for self-fulfillment in sexuality itself, and, finally, for legitimacy as historical subjectivity, all of which emanate from the different sexual dynamics she sets up in the story.

One must come to understand this model of desire that Pérez has constructed as a demystification of the colonial female sexual subjectivity. Her own critical remarks reflect the extent to which "the female subject" is the "subject of violence" based on the dialectics of a colonial and national cultural history. For example, Pérez creates an aesthetic of fragmentation that is directed at the failure of cultural nationalism to recuperate from the colonial violence an actualization of Chicana female autonomy as sexual subjects. This effect is no less obvious in Pérez's own essay on the subject of history, "Sexuality and Discourse: Notes from a Chicana Survivor," where she discusses at length the problem of lesbian sexuality within the framework of an American cultural national minority paradigm.

Desire makes it possible to examine the problem of representation for Chicana lesbians, who are inscribed in discourse as historical and sexual subjects. But this framing also leads us to a fundamental contradiction in Chicana feminist criticism: How can one seek to inscribe oneself into a historical (narrative) process that has long been viewed as prohibitive, tainted by exclusion and silence, especially when the terms of history making itself appear suspect? This question becomes relevant as we begin to question the implications of our national identity and how this drive for reinscription in feminist practices would lead to some apprehension over the way history renders particular agents invisible and mute. Given the possible claims to historical legitimacy as an accessible and legitimized form of identity formation, this drive for history in our own quest to reconnect with the past cannot be so easily reclaimed without some problematic result.

Pérez identifies this dilemma as female sexual desire in narration and in the desire for completion, for unity, for history and a place in discourse.[2] But if we accept the notion that "completion" is necessary to produce a lesbian historical subject, do we also remove the critical edge Pérez introduces as the disassembled colonial female voice? For this reason, there appears to be an unexamined reluctance among some Chicana writers, scholars, and artists to remove from the "conventional" tracking of history the traditional role women serve in inscribing into history an aesthetic function. Those who do, I think, soon realize that a performance or deconstruction of history becomes the only real theoretical consequence.[3] To consider this situation as a postmodern anomaly or a way of rethinking feminist practice would be correct in both instances, but it is a consideration that should remain ancillary to any discussion of the historical legitimacy of our marginal subjectivity. Much of what we do understand about Chicana representation, at this point, is that this preoccupation with history becomes an entry point into many critical discussions for the way our disrupted narratives have come to represent the Chicana lesbian experience in various literary situations.

The goal of this reading is to establish a connection between Chicana lesbian representation and a new readership for the procurement of alternative interpretive strategies, which move beyond the assumption that women share mutual goals in their historical self-production.[4] Even though the novel suggests that desire for history may be an illusory quest for an impossible ideal, a vacillation among quixotic, romantic elements, the harsh psychological realism becomes apparent as a major aesthetic tension. The major critical point that should be drawn from this is that Pérez rejects the typical form of narration found in more reality-based Chicana narratives, because, more often than not, these narratives unwittingly instill a traditional view of female subjects.[5] We can see this in the way Pérez rejects the conventional coming-of-age narrative as the source of development for female sexuality because the desire for history capitulates in a relentless pursuit of subject/sexual reconciliations through national recodification found in the virgin, mother, goddess figures or even in feminist revisionary practices such as recent feminist resurrections of women of color, U.S. Third World feminism, and lesbian feminist criticisms (Bejarano 1991).

Gulf Dreams, I argue, attempts to address the false idealizations of our history by disrupting the traditional Mexican and Chicana/o female cultural representations at the deepest level of meaning and to embark on a different aesthetic process (Pérez 1991; Trujillo 1991). To varying degrees, these disruptive feminine representations range in presentation from the unruly and sexually autonomous woman, to the muted lesbian bound by unspoken words, to the piety of the señoras hiding behind the all-assuming sanctity of the culture. The effect of some of these traditional assumptions about Chicana sexuality appears so deeply embedded in the Chicana/o culture that any derivation ultimately leads to a violent end both symbolically and in actuality (Ricatelli 1974). This is part of the subject matter Pérez thoughtfully considers when she uses female sexuality as a case for the disruption of the historical representation of Chicanas/os as national subjects, because she intends to rewrite the female narrative altogether a feminist critical analysis of discourse. Using a female continuum, she rewrites the cultural national narrative of *la familia sagrada* by structuring the dysfunctions of the community to represent the allegories of the colonial trauma in the spaces of the narrative scripts that are already laid out (Lomeli 1980). These dysfunctions are heavily coded in larger metadiscourses on colonialism, nationalism, masculinity, and female subjugation, all of which entwine the complexity of colonialism, its entropy and chaos into the microcosm of a small-town mindset. The most obvious result is the disembodied voice as the emblem of psychic fragmentation. Pérez suggests that "fragmentation" represents the state of mind of the Chicana, and this state of mind is the basis for desire. The lesbian narrative thus serves as a representation of Chicana consciousness, a consciousness that cannot be understood within a typical developmental format with all the properties of the conventional story line. One might even remark that it is conceivable to regard this form of narration as a type of historical dysphoria that challenges the value of the historical meaning as a cogent and transparent reflection of the lived reality.

Written in a style that is closer to "self-revelation" than a conventional autobiographical form of disclosure, the novel makes use of autobiographical tracing to bring to life a nameless protagonist, whose experiences we follow throughout her years growing up in a small Texas town.[6] But unlike a conventional autobiographical narrative that builds on the author's experience to secure the narrator's emotional growth, *Gulf Dreams* undermines the developmental presentation altogether by depicting the troubled circumstances of a Chicana lesbian trying to come to terms with the violence in the small town of El Pueblo.[7] This engagement of subject matter is necessary to enlist yet another dimension of the novel. By forming the subjective consciousness as the primary voice in the narrative, Pérez makes an uncanny association between the subjective lesbian voice and the violent circumstances that surround the protagonist's life. The subjective lesbian voice is an important critical choice to distinguish the reading of the novel as an uncomplicated coming-of-age narrative from one that focuses on the crisis of legitimacy as its foremost concern.

The lack of a physical presence in this subjective voice, represented by the protagonist's fluid state of mind, stages the first problem of self-representation. This problem of articulation occurs first and foremost as the main protagonist engages in understanding her own position in the community when she tries to reconcile her lesbian desires by forming an obsessive relationship with a young girl she meets at a friend's house (an ironic choice of therapy, as the community itself figures as a wasteland of detachment and social pathology that makes lesbianism look like a healthy alternative in contrast to the violence that permeates the predominantly heterosexual community). The second problem of articulation originates in the framing of the story as subaltern narrative, where the protagonist assumes several subjective locations to establish an analogy between the sexual dynamics of the female characters and the absence of representational form in the lived reality. In this sense, the subjective voice must be seen as the type of "desire" that implies the lack of historical representation and works primarily through an unconsciousness of Chicana female sexuality.

I have titled my essay "Chronotope of Desire" to illustrate the narrative technique Pérez raises in coming to terms with the historical problem of articulation and to demonstrate how the problem of female reinscription is already complicated by various historical assumptions about Chicana sexuality.[8] The chronotope of desire points to both the rise of the subjective voice in the novel and the disintegration of historical time as the plausible recourse to the dilemma Pérez has raised in her feminist critical analysis, expressed in the aesthetics of the historical memory as "desire" in the novel. The subjective voice as desire, as chronotope of Chicana lesbian expression, also comes to represent "the lack" of an authoritative position one would associate with the absence of historical presence and legitimacy (Swindell 1989).

Desire takes effect in *Gulf Dreams* as the subjective voice of a Chicana lesbian who remains faceless and nameless throughout the story. It is crucial, then, to understand that this same desire, or rather, the "lack of historical legitimacy" is a choice of articulation that allows the Chicana lesbian protagonist to remain outside of the rules that govern reality and intelligibility while maintaining a sense of agency and voice. The fact that the protagonist resolves the question of agency, despite the obvious lack of a larger historical narrative, is part of the novel's critical allure.[9] This is vividly demonstrated by the lack of sequential order in the novel's presentation but also in the choice of subject matter. The protagonist rejects the rules that govern sequential purpose, causality, and genre distinction by using dreams and memories as a counterhistory that can be read against the trapping of a realistic narrative expression (Halbwach 1992). This effect is accomplished primarily by the subjective voice that allows for freedom from the rules of sequential reality. However, this lack of sequential purpose does not necessarily reveal a lack of realistic expression. In fact, the lack of order, characteristic of the protagonist's worldview and sensibilities, symbolizes Chicanas' latent colonial consciousness in more modern terms (Durand 1983). This aspect of the novel tends to reveal an allegory of colonized female subjects as modern women who are unable to access the codes of democratic freedom because of the cultural constraints they experience in the terms of discourse.

This crisis of meaning works primarily off the disenchanted world of Chicana female narration with the reinscription of a more self-determined narrative process of history making as traumatic recovery. Pérez thus transforms the female victim script to one of active agency by using fragmentary narrative form to represent the encoding of Chicana history as fragmented. I also look at desire in the most obvious of all interpretations, that is, as an unrequited courtship between the two main Chicana female characters. The overarching claim to this is that desire occurs as a frustration with language and what appears to be an insatiable relationship between the two women in real life. I do not distinguish between the term desire as part of the lesbian story and the matter of historical representation Chicanas encounter as female subjects, because Pérez inscribes the lesbian love story as a way of creating a social context for the legitimacy of Chicana subjectivity in discourse and in sexual expression.

The story itself takes shape when a young woman begins to recount a series of memories, events, and recollections about her childhood. The fluid style makes it difficult to understand the story in a conventional reading with a definite plot or sequence. Many times we find that actual time and setting play a secondary role to commentary on the state of mind of the protagonist. The fragmentation inherent in the story line forces the reader to engage in a different interpretative approach, where plot and sequence of events are mired by the lack of a clear teleology of development, a device that disintegrates the presumed logic of history. Most of the events appear situated in the small coastal Texas town of El Pueblo, where we see the psychic impression of a young girl finding her sexuality. But the fragmentary nature of the narration makes it difficult to map according to conventional spatial time and locations. By so doing, *Gulf Dreams* is able to form a critique of particular authoritative currents, of male dominance, of physical threat and violence based on the history of colonization and the possible sites of resistance expressed by some of the Chicanas.

The novel is organized into four chapters: "The Confession," "The Trial," "Desire," and "The Epilogue." The first chapter, "The Confession," can also be read as the coming-out stage of the story line within the larger novel that also serves as an exposition of the events that follow. The first chapter alone constitutes a great part of the novel, where the protagonist reveals a crush on a young girl she meets while visiting her sister's friend. The protagonist develops an infatuation for this young girl that develops into a romantic obsession. The story moves from a sentimental coming-of-age story, suggested by the protagonist's youthful naïveté, to a matter of female legitimacy when she confronts the problems of growing up in this provincial and oppressive environment.

By the middle of the first chapter, we get the sense that the protagonist's relationship with the young woman leads her to remember several disturbing events. These recurring dreams and memories lead us into the second chapter, "The Trial," where a shift in narration and tone changes the entire delivery. These changes in narration, which take place primarily when the protagonist returns to El Pueblo as a mature version of the younger voice found in "The Confession," signal a confrontation "before the law." The protagonist chronicles Ermila's rape in this second chapter in order to transform the protagonist into a feminist critical voice. The introduction of Ermila, a beautiful but brash woman whose audacious behavior as a sexually autonomous woman becomes the subject of the protagonist's commentary in "The Trial," allows the protagonist to transform her subjective voice into a more critical feminist voice in the remaining chapters. Both of the last two chapters, "Desire" and "The Epilogue," attempt to put closure on the novel by completing the events in "The Trial." However, it is not certain whether the protagonist resolves her relationship with the women. For the same young woman the protagonist opens the novel with in "The Confession" is found later throughout the novel in the form of a persistent but contentious engagement with heterosexuality as a mirror of legal and cultural laws. It is also this same young woman who, despite being married to the defense attorney for the rapists in "The Trial," seduces the protagonist into witnessing her sordid relationship with her husband.

The romance opens the first chapter. The protagonist confesses to the reader her affection for the young girl. This first encounter with this girl marks her consciousness in relationship to love and sexual awakening. It is important to note that the protagonist's own physical sensibilities remain obscured by her feelings for the girl. "I met her in the summer of my restless dreams. It was a time when infatuation emerges erotic and pure in a young girl's dreams. She was a small girl, a young woman. Her eyes revealed secrets, mysteries I yearned to know long after that summer ended" (1).

The first line engages the reader into thinking that a romantic story is about to be revealed by virtue of her disclosure. But as love is quite capable of deceiving, her infatuation for the young girl leads us to think that she has dissolved her own physical sensibilities for the image of the girl. We assume that the act of meeting her "in the summer of my restless dreams" implies that she is confessing to the reader, as audience, the taboo of her attraction for another woman. It is her later description that compels a deeper reading of that initial moment. She says, "Her eyes revealed secrets, mysteries I yearned to know long after that summer ended." This first encounter is suggestive of the earliest impressions of her obsession with the young girl, which lead her into a series of obsessive refrains.

Upon first encounter with the protagonist, we get the sense that dislocation is determined by her youthful naïveté and disaffection for the external world. The mood intensifies and a repetitive scheme develops when the protagonist replays the memory of the girl. The nature of her obsession, I think, demonstrates a disaffection from social reality. By reliving over and over her desire for this woman, the protagonist can only dream of being with her in fantasy. While one can make the determination that the protagonist simply has expressed a selfless kind of love, one often attributed to youthful folly, her disaffection for things external to her own narrative appears related to something else.

It is not just a sense of self-erasure that appears to conceal the protagonist's physical sense of being; her surroundings also appear detached from any sensual representation. This erasure manifests itself in other ways. The name El Pueblo, for example, gives the impression of a nonspecific town. Its generic name emphasizes both the perfunctory and putative functions of naming one's location. It is a location devoid of historical specificity. El Pueblo represents anytown, making it appear as if the location is merely incidental to the protagonist's ulterior task in the narrative, which is to dissolve, not to situate, space.

The story reveals very little by way of a real or plausible setting. The reference to the Texas coastal town may be the most specific of any of the details; otherwise, the deeply subjective elements of her voice project vague impressions with little to offer outside of her subjective view. I do not believe all meaning is lost to this effect. The generic naming of the town creates a collective presence. As the subjective voice obscures the location, the generic naming of the town also enlarges the view into a collective image that indicates these events could take place anywhere. Coupled with the youthful naïveté, the sense of anonymity adds to the protagonist's lack of self-awareness. It is here the protagonist undertakes a profound entry into the latent materiality of colonial consciousness by speaking from a position of complete and utter dissolution about events in her own story. Although the protagonist remains steadfast in her pursuit of the woman, she does so at the expense of her own personal development as a character. An example of this dissolution takes place in her description of the young woman when Pérez uses highly poetic language to depict her love: "How can I explain she was the core of me? I repeat this over and over, to you, to myself. We merged before birth, entwined in each other's souls, wrapped together like a bubble of mist, floating freely, reflecting rainbows. This was a time before flesh, before bones crushed each other foolishly trying to join mortal bodies, before the outline of skin shielded us from one another. We both knew this, that we came from the same place, that we were joined in a place so uncommon that this world, which bound and confined us, could not understand—the bond that flesh frustrated" (15). I am especially drawn to the line "a time before flesh." Signaling all the psychoanalytic claims of desire as a prelingual state of consciousness, this line reveals her profound frustration with discourse. It is as if the primal connection with this woman has transcended the discourse that binds them as female subjects. She attempts to capture the tension between language and body. What "a time before flesh" also means is the time before we are inscribed culturally into genders. Lines such as "the bond that flesh frustrated" and "we merged before birth" likewise discourage a gendered body, a historical body. If this interaction suggests a prehistoric, a prelingual and pregendered body, is Pérez really qualifying a lesbian body? Of significance here is the transcendence of the primal love scene that signals the impossibility of a love connection outside of heterosexuality. But just as the protagonist completes one passage, the scene shifts suddenly to another instance that compels the protagonist to recall one excruciating event after another. This sudden shift is characteristic of the fragmented narrative technique Pérez uses to characterize racial memory, a memory that links colonization with her sexual identity. It cannot be denied that a great part of the protagonist's response to her own physical body is dually processed as erasure and reinscription. In a perverse twist, the protagonist is able to pass for white and is traumatized by her inability to identify with her family because of her lighter skin color: "As a young woman of fifteen in a rural Texas coastal town, I didn't recognize love. In a town where humidity bred hostility, I memorized hate. Bronze in the summer with hair and eyes so light that I could pass through doors that shut out my sisters and brother. Their color and brown eyes, I envied. I grew to resent the color that set me apart from my family. At four, my sisters convinced me I was adopted. Eyes so green, this was not my family. At five, I took a butcher knife, sat calmly, sadly, on the pink chenille bedspread, threatening to slice away at tanned skin, I remember the scene like a dream. Always the sad child, burdened" (6). As a consequence of this figurative racialization, the protagonist claims not "to recognize love," a thought that reflects her family situation and reveals a subtle dissonance about her sexual identity. Her racial identity appears as a deep-seated aversion to herself, noted in the way she sees herself differently from her family. Because she feels estranged from her family for being *la güera*, the light one, the primary basis of her sexuality appears to be this "disidentification." It is not as if she benefits from her fair skin and green eyes. Her realization about her racial identity releases a negative response. What does it mean "to not recognize love"? Is it that she is not able to see her reflection in her family because they are darker? Or does she wittingly recognize this contradictory view of race, which then leads her to disavow her ambivalent attraction to Anglo boys? To be "fair"-skinned and with "green eyes" appeals to the colonial metaphors of racial miscegenation found in slave and colonial narratives, where masters violated their female servants.

This demonstrates how she is unable to locate herself racially and, presumably because of this, is unable to form a self-reflective perspective about her own sexual autonomy. As she describes this childhood memory, she realizes that her light skin may have led her to repudiate her white identification when she takes the knife to her skin, threatening to slice away her body. Moments such as this one point to her uneasiness with Anglo culture as well as the racial tensions between the Chicana and Anglo cultures, and only later do we realize that "race" is symptomatically related to other forms of epistemic violence.

Whereas the matter of race allows the reader to understand the protagonist's attitudes about her ambivalent racial identity, it is gender that allows us to truly comprehend the deep meaning of the social dimensions of the community's trauma. Race is determined as a subjective and psychoanalytic experience, whereas gender symbolizes another social trauma associated with actions and events. This occurs in the second chapter, when a discussion over race and gender progresses into a discussion about the psychic traumas. In my view, the most important commentary in the novel develops when Pérez makes a connection between racial trauma and the socialization of gender as an allegory for history. She arrives at this through a discussion of the role of the women in El Pueblo: "The town stifled loud irreverent women, women expected to stay in their place, to spoil men, to listen to their troubles, and if wives or sisters disputed husbands or brothers, they were called *putas* or *jotas*. A woman's strength was judged by how she accepted her husband, no matter what kind of life he dealt her, drunkenness, womanizing, a slap or a firm word. This was the bargain of marriage" (92).

This attitude forms the two primary types of epistemic violence that lead the women in the community to conform to an established view of female sexual behavior. Common among these cultural transgressions is the *puta* (whore) and *jota* (dyke) designations. The puta and jota occupy the same transgressive location, because these two designations also resist the conforming ways of the community. But it is arguably the lesbian, la jota, who is able to transform female sexuality. This becomes evident in the way the narrative shifts in "The Trial." The protagonist's sexual liminality as lesbian and Ermila's rape at first seem unrelated. But as becomes evident later on, the protagonist's own narrative mirrors some aspect of Ermila's sexual transgression.

Pérez enlarges the metaphor of colonization by suggesting that Ermila's sexuality is tied to the Malinche figure, the symbolic rape of Mexico's colonial past. Pérez makes this association with female sexual transgression when she describes Ermila as "la malinchista, la chingada, a betrayer, her own people called her" (93). Because of her independent-mindedness, Ermila is figured as a Malinche-type character whose sexual proclivities lead her astray from the traditional female role. Because of Ermila's own transgressive behavior as a sexual nonconformist, she, like the protagonist, is expected to accommodate sexual violence as a fact of femaleness in the community. This situation sheds light on Ermila's rape as a "social death," a deterrent against female autonomy played out publicly, which serves as a symbolic reminder of male power over women.[10] The scene of the rape symbolizes the "social death" of all the female agents of the community through the censorship of their sexual being (Patterson 1982). It is at this point that the romantic love story intersects with the trial.

The policing of female desire thus extends beyond the sexual act as a form of violation. Nowhere is this more evident than in Ermila's story as the sexually transgressive cultural figure who at the same time defies cultural conformity in the way the protagonist does: "At home Ermila gave her brothers orders; at school, she defied her teachers, on the play ground she winced at Anglos, especially girls who wore crisp white blouses with loosely pleated cotton skirts" (94). Her defiance signals all aspects of rebellion. One must consider how this rebellion affects the protagonist's life. Arguably, through Ermila's character, Pérez energizes the unvoiced protagonist to achieve greater meaning in the narrative. What this situation means to the protagonist, as a lesbian, is that she finds an alter ego in Ermila. Because of this, she is able to develop an alternate narrative voice that appears omniscient and observant of Ermila's own life. This sense of omniscience, as a form of mirroring, is exemplified by the protagonist's interest in the rape trial and her subsequent rejuvenation as a feminist voice. The return to El Pueblo thus evokes a larger commentary on the female narrative contained within the historical consciousness of the women: "They tried to censor her anger. The compassion some offered was not compassion at all, but instead words meant to stifle her, to say, 'Don't do this, Ermila, don't talk to strangers. Why do you say these things? You make your life harder.' These words came from women, *tias y vecinas,* only her *güelita* listened and repaired her broken flesh the night she stumbled in wailing at her abductors: 'Desgraciados,' Ermila shrieked" (89–90).

The urging of the female relatives and neighbors to remain silent about the rape in this scene adds to the sense that their "silence" will secure male hegemony. The "social death" occurs once again when the sexual violation functions at the symbolic level against all the women. The don't-say-anything attitude expressed by the women implies that their reluctance to publicize their outrage originates out of fear of violence. Except for Ermila's grandmother's sympathetic response, everyone else wishes to keep silent.

Pérez emphasizes here a common feminist claim that women's interests are divided among their roles in a heterosexual economy. So it is quite possible that the denial, so pervasive among the community members during the trial, serves as a rationalization for cultural "patrimony."[11] This psychic wounding expressed by the male characters leads the protagonist to respond sympathetically to the men as they experience their own "social death" as a form of castration. Through less public displays of that wounding, Pérez captures this issue when she describes Ermila's brother. Pérez illustrates how the Chicano male psychic wounding originates in colonial racism:

> Pepito, driven by math and science, would have graduated high school with honors and a scholarship to junior college, but something happened that year. He started coming home late, drugged, and disinterested when he crashed his shiny, nineteen fifty four, two-tone Chevy sedan. A mechanically perfect, white and peach-colored car was parked in the middle of the front yard with the back end smashed, the passenger side was wrinkled metal. Something has disillusioned her older brother. Ermila wanted to ask him for help with her math homework, hoping he would gain interest in what had once excited him, but her brother just lay in an unlit bedroom listening to deadening music on his headphones. She couldn't understand how or why he'd given up. Neighbors rumored about a white girl whose father shut the door on Pepito. (95–96)

This indicates that Pepito's intellectual development is stifled through an episode in his youth involving an Anglo girl whom he wishes to date. This episode further appears to dramatize the psychosocial dynamics of race relations between the Anglo and Mexican American cultures and relates the sexual dynamics of the community as a whole. The Anglo father's rejection of Pepito's dating his daughter is once again an occasion for the anxiety of miscegenation between the cultures and the sexual violence. As a result, however, Pepito appears to be devastated by this experience. This psychic devastation is transferred onto the car as the locus for his own wounding. Pérez narrates the demise of Pepito's ambition: "He started coming home late, drugged, and disinterested when he crashed his shiny, nineteen fifty four, two-tone Chevy sedan. A mechanically perfect, white and peach-colored car was parked in the middle of the front yard with the back end smashed, the passenger side was wrinkled metal." While the nature of the violence is at best symbolic, the disfiguring aspect of epistemic wounding is particular to the sexual dynamics between the Anglo and Mexican cultures.

None of the characters displays a healthy sexual demeanor. Like the protagonist who is unable to actualize her lesbian desire except in fantasy, Ermila relies on sexual play as a way of stepping outside the rules of sexual hegemony. The male figures are unable to participate productively in the family because of the violence that permeates their lives. The romantic aspects of the story naturally fall apart because the entire Oedipal structure of the community collapses when violence against women is sanctioned in such a way as to uphold the archaic structure of the cultural over the moral and ethical course of sexual autonomy. What concerns me here, then, is the way women's sexuality impacts the entire sexual history of the community. The successful acquisition of female sexuality has been one of the arguments against a Chicana feminism all along because of the social roles women play in their respective communities. Is there a way to conceive of a community, real or imagined, outside of the phallocentric structure? *Gulf Dreams* establishes a valid critique of masculinity in culture as the demise of Oedipal structure. As it stands, the demoralization of the macho male figure leads the community to break apart, because the male ego seems to be central to the community's structure through the excessive valorization of the family's reputation over and above the autonomous development of the female characters.

As it is dealt with in Ermila's family, her dating practices bring in yet another element of the family romance—that is, the chastity and reputation of the female in the family: "Her older brothers didn't like the rich *bolillo* Ermila allowed into their house. He was a blond, a football player who drove a bright red, Ford Mustang and called them spics, sneering jokingly. Ermila's brother believed *el bolillo* used their little sister the way the white boys used the girls in their *pueblito* branding them easy girls with reputations. Her younger brother observed the *bolillo* jealously" (99). Her brothers express more concern about their own reputation than their sister's well-being.

This dynamic between Ermila and her brothers implies that Ermila's sexual autonomy threatens the social standing of the male figures through her promiscuous behavior. The brothers' "defense" of Ermila, which is really a coded defense of the family's reputation and their position in the patrilinear narrative, also creates a different racial dialogue about sexuality. Ermila's reputation is of greater concern to her brothers because they believe she may be compromising their own integrity as male figures. Her rape is therefore seen as retribution for having dated white boys and for her detachment from the protection of the Chicano family. The circulation of the colonization myth assumes an even stranger relationship to offset Ermila's sexual autonomy. It is not so much that her sexual promiscuity seems to be in question here, but the fact that she dates white boys makes her seem even more despicable in the eyes of her brothers. Once again the image of the Malinche figure is seen as betrayer of the family's integrity and defiance of the culture: "To escape El Pueblo, Ermila would trade herself to a white boy hoping he'd leave and take her with him. She ignored racist words that inferred he couldn't appreciate her world. But after she heard him, repeatedly, make the same stupid remarks about 'greasers' or announce loudly, 'the wetbacks are back,' pointing at her brothers who entered their own house, she'd berate him calling him a *gringo pendejo* who didn't know anything about anybody. She had no patience or tolerance for his ignorance, incapable of easing him into awareness; she was born impatient and intolerant" (100).

Ermila wishes to escape the world that subjects her to the misogyny of the Chicano culture. By contrast, she thinks the Anglo world is racist and derisive toward her own family. None of these circumstances can fully liberate her from her situation, and her circumstances appear to frustrate her even more. Pérez uses the rape spectacle to conceive of a colonial mirroring of the Mexican myth about Malinztin—*la chingada*. Another view of the rape scene can be viewed as a case of "masculine panic": the Anglo boys exerting their virility through their sexual prowess; the Mexican boys exercising their masculinity over the Anglo girls, only to be symbolically castrated by the Anglo male, which in turn leads to a tension between the male figures on either side. It is revealed just a few pages from this sequence that Chencho, the primary rapist in the trial, is himself alleged to be a closeted homosexual whose rape of Ermila arises from masculine panic:

An older brother showed Chenchito things about sex, things not for a little boy, not yet. As he grew older, an uncle, his mother's brother, would frequent their house. The nephews liked him, played with him, but the youngest one, the one who was so pretty, the uncle liked him the best. Twenty years between them did not keep the uncle and the nephew from being inseparable. When the boy became a teenager, they went to baseball games, to cock fights, things he would have done with a father. But the uncle became too familiar. He raped the boy, kept raping him until the boy was strong enough to beat up the old man and spit in his face.

More and more, when he drove to the city, he snuck into men's bars, fooling himself, convincing himself he was there to spy on men from El Pueblo, "to check on queers," he'd lie. Men would straddle a bar stool beside him. The regular customers saw him every few weeks. They recognized his type, confused yet eager to prove he wasn't weak or soft. Most of the men avoided him. . . . Once drunk, he'd slip outside to the parking lot. A stocky man with thin hair combed forward to cover a bald spot would drive up. He'd jump in the car, go to the stranger's apartment, have sex and pass out from the alcohol, smelling like poppers. (103–4)

If at this point we conclude that Chencho's motivation for the rape is somehow tied to his repressed homosexuality, we must therefore question to what extent homosexuality is implicated in the violence of colonization or ask how it is that homosexuality figures so violently in the transgression of normative culture. Pérez makes this point in order for us to conclude that lesbian subjectivity is still a condition within heterosexuality. Chencho's inability to actualize a gay male identity is attributed to his own sexual abuse, his own social as well as figurative violation.

Whereas this precondition leads us to inquire further into the motivating current, his masculine panic, which in turn leads to the policing of others, is about returning to the Law as a signifying force that is there to recuperate what has been lost under the terms of colonial violation. Is it not part of the fantasy of heterosexuality to preserve some sense of order once the myth of heterosexuality faces its own dissolution?[12] There is the sense that the genealogy of violent aggression in this scenario originates from the collapse of phallic order due, in part, to the homosexual act as "desire" and "violation." I'm not sure if this was the best way for Pérez to arrive at an explanation for the rape, as heterosexuality can no longer be seen as the source of the repression but instead reappears as a problem of homosexuality; the dispersal of heterosexual ideology can no longer be seen at all. Instead, Pérez returns the problem of masculine panic to a perverse form of machismo. Here, the matter of repressed male homosexuality seems to be the scapegoat for a perverse heterosexual hysteria.

Chencho's "repressed homosexuality" appears to be encoding a form of displaced homosocial behavior. But his masquerade as a straight man appears as a silly façade that confounds even the customers at the bar he frequents. We should really return to the act of violation to arrive at a better reading. The violation itself is intended as a heterosexual form of aggression. What I think Chencho symbolizes more than anything else is the complications of masculine desire in a nationalist culture. The product of this begins with the supposition that sexuality must be regulated if it is to make sense. This form of policing others provides Chencho with a distorted symbolic identity. His unwillingness to accept a gay male identity is part of the dilemma for Chicano gay men.

But if "masculine panic" is to be one of the primary reasons the community is experiencing its demise, not only because of Chencho but because it appears to be symptomatic of the entire community's pathos, then what type of criticism can be assumed from this situation? From another standpoint, one can make the determination that in this 1990s scenario, the location of Chicana and Chicano sexuality is complicated by an elaborate discussion of power and sexuality. Whereas Chencho's initiation of sexual violence is ascribed to a case of homosexual panic, the appearance of weakness and the collapse of his virility seem related to the absence of a phallic order altogether. By way of conclusion, one of the later scenes confirms this very point when the concerns of castration and penis envy converge in one of the final segments of the novel.

In the closing moments of the novel, Pelón, Chencho's lawyer in the rape trial (and the husband of the woman the protagonist developed a crush on in the first chapter), initiates another case of masculine panic. He has a dream about the protagonist that captures his sense of guilt over the trial:

> Pelón had visions that night. In terror he awoke, cold from sweat, grabbing a floppy penis, frightened by the same grisly nightmare since the trial began. In the darkness he argues with me. I scream at him, "You believe those *desgraciados*!"
> "They're young boys, they just need help, some guidance."
> "Yeah, sure, young *pendejos* who treat women like a bunch of *putas*."
> "What do you want from me. *Mira ten esto. Póntelo tu.*"
> He holds a sharp six inch blade in his right hand, the wooden handle indented. He clutches the shining knife. In a swift gesture he slashes his penis, holding it in his left hand. I refuse it, gazing blankly at him as he grips a bleeding, puny genital. Pelón awoke with a moan, shaking. The bed sheets were soaked throughout. Urgently, he looked for his wife. She slept peacefully. (118)

Pelón's apparent preoccupation with his own castration in the dream suggests that the protagonist's presence in the trial and her regard for his wife manifest themselves as forms of revenge for his having defended the assailants. In his frustration with the protagonist, Pelón cuts his own penis and offers it to her as a symbolic castration: Ten póntelo/Here, you wear it. The symbolic value of his nightmare marks his own castration as the final abdication of the male power that he, in effect, relinquishes and hands over to the protagonist to wear. It is also symbolic of the way her lesbian autonomy somehow becomes associated with the castration anxieties. Underlying this castration dream, the protagonist is able to form into the subject. It releases her from her wandering and allows her to achieve closure.[13]

I, too, shall close this reading by citing the last line, where we see the protagonist regain that poetic voice, the one voice she had reserved for the romantic story. She says, "This part of the story has to be over, even though I don't believe in endings. I believe in the imagination, its pleasure indelible, transgressive, a dream" (157). The inconclusive nature of this commentary at the end of the story leads us to speculate that the story line has some larger imaginative, fictive quality to it, a narration that is subjective in nature.

The fact that *Gulf Dreams* does not takes place in the exterior world means that the possibility of narrating female sexual subjectivity is overwrought with narrative tensions. The events that we do read occur primarily in the mind of the protagonist and raise the question of the reliability of the narrative. This aspect of the novel is familiar to feminism in that many arguments against women's literature or history, especially lesbian arguments, have been assailed for the subjective voice as a naïve representation of individual grievances in lieu of more literary ones. The argument is that by conventional standards, the dissolution of omniscience in the narrative gives the impression of an autobiographical disclosure, as a subjective experience, that would cast on the author a type of bias that is useless for understanding history. But is it? It is important for framing the double current of desire that traces the life of a young girl coming into her own sexual agency, which results in a mature woman's intention to gain a sense of legitimacy, in spite of her community's restrictions. This dual effect of desire intertwines the basis of sexuality and literature to the same goal of personal fulfillment through acts of (self-)representation. What is being desired is a sense of orientation in the absence of corporeal meaning—that is what constitutes our modern situation as colonized female subjects.

NOTES

I would like to thank Alfred Arteaga for his friendship and support of my ideas during the initial writing of this essay. His intellectual freedom allowed me to write on the subject of Chicana lesbian desire for a seminar on Bakhtin. Thanks also to Norma Alarcón for her comments and readings of a chapter from my dissertation, which is a larger version of this essay, and for insisting that the question of female sexuality is central to any significant social change. And finally, thanks to Carolyn Dinshaw, whose support and comments at the earliest phase of this essay pushed me to yet another level of inquiry. It is important to acknowledge these wonderful and brilliant people as they gave of themselves generously in support of my work and development here at Berkeley.

1. Rosalinda Fregoso's "Introduction: The Bronze Screen Looking at Us" (1993) explains the rise of Chicano and Chicana cinema as an oppositional enterprise. Chicana/o film is one instance where reworkings of hypersexualized stereotypical images of Mexicanas, Chicanas, and Latinas has been successful (xii–xxiii).

2. Michel Foucault's discussion of power as a "discursive field" of exchange in *Power/Knowledge: Selected Interviews* (1972) supplants the notion that absolute power is what determines power relations. Foucault states clearly that "power is no longer substantially identified with an individual who possesses or exercises it by right of birth; it becomes a machinery that no one owns. Certainly, everyone doesn't occupy the same position; certain positions preponderate and permit an effect of supremacy to be produced. This is so much the case that class domination can be exercised just to the extent that power is disassociated from individual might" (156). This added condition may be a bit problematic for women of color who regard patriarchal power to be a source of absolute hegemony. Such oppression manifests itself discretely in the normalized structure of everyday life rather than in dispersed ways. One of the challenges of Chicana feminism today can be found in Foucault's theory of power. Pérez exposes the view that there is an individualized subject informed in Chicana/o subjectivity. If anything, she sees that the signs of recognizing and exercising Western notions of power are rendered opaque by the shadowing of colonialism.

3. Paula Moya's "Postmodernism, Realism, and the Politics of Identity: Cherríe Moraga and Chicana Feminism" (1997) argues the issue of self-representation of Chicana lesbian subjectivity. In a section titled "Towards a Realist Theory of Chicana Identity" Moya attempts to reconstitute an ethical argument for reading against postmodern interventions in criticizing gender and specifically "heterosexual privilege" in Chicana/o queer theory. It seems a bit ironic that Moya wishes to return to a "realist" identity theory because of what appears to be certain misgivings about the question of gender and queer analysis in refuting the illusory gender game. It is my understanding that she wishes to return to a foundationalist grounding of identity to make accountable racial grievances at the expense of gender and sexuality (155).

4. Tey Diana Rebolledo's essay "Mujeres Andariegas: Good Girls and Bad" (1995) describes the very problem Pérez's novel deals with in lesbian narrative production: "Thus lesbian writers not only have had to forge their own identity, but they also had to try to come to terms with their past (and to forge a sexual meaning to the past). This forging of sexual meaning to the past is relatively new to Chicana literature because it means giving meaning to a body that has been seen as culturally meaningless (or considered *atravesada*)" (199).

5. The need to associate oneself with other related discourses such as sexuality elicits a much deeper understanding of self-determination within the social sphere. In many respects, this change can also be seen in Arif Dirlik's (1997) thinking of the "postcolonial aura" in the formation of the Third World intellectual.

6. It is not certain which aspects of the novel are intended to be attributed to the author. By most accounts, Pérez moves in and out of a first-person narrative, making it difficult to determine the autobiographical intent. My argument suggests that the sub-

jective voice in the narrative precludes an autobiographical function—the way the voice works here; however, it creates the effect of social rather than personal dimensions. The subjective voicing of the events in the novel suggests a fictional intervention, one that is not necessarily attributable to an autobiographical voice but that has, by virtue of its being the first novel, a small element of personal disclosure.

7. *Push,* a novel by Sapphire, became a sleeper success in 1996. It depicts the story of a young black woman whose life is transformed from illiteracy to self-awareness. The profound sexual and psychological abuse she endures at the hands of her wretched parents plays out the African American pathology in relationship to American liberalism. The chronicle of her life story traces this woman's transformation from one of absolute abjection to one of semi–self-fulfillment through reinscription in the narrative function vis-à-vis disclosure. I remain suspicious of its reception, especially by the *New York Times* for heralding this new voice as "courageous." Its positive reception by the liberal media suggests that the novel is acceptable to the U.S. palate for its salacious import of race exploitation. The fact that the novel was promoted in such a flashy and glitzy manner invites ire and skepticism and adds further testament to the sanctimonious and self-righteous gaze of the American public's willingness to consume racial pathologies as reality-based fiction.

8. Mikhail Bakhtin's (1990) notion of the chronotope in *The Dialogic Imagination* literally refers to the time-space relations in literature that distinguish genre formations across history. I believe the time-space of subjects who remain outside of a historical context is a form of desire. As I argue in this essay, female narration, by a Chicana lesbian, occurs as a process of desire. It is not just the sense of longing expressed by the term but the condition of not being actualized in real time that is being suggested in the chronotope of desire.

9. Lisa Lowe's essay "Unfaithful to the Original: The Subject of *Dictee*" (1994) on Teresa Hak Kyung Cha's *Dictee* offers an astute reading of the aesthetics of counterhegemony as well as a feminist critique of the problem of the nation with respect to subject formation.

10. Orlando Patterson's *Slavery and Social Death: A Comparative Study* (1982) offers a useful analysis of the symbolic function of violence. A "social death" occurs as a symbolic destruction of the slave. This occurs primarily as the act of violence not solely as punishment but as a means of maintaining order. Social death means that symbolic destruction underlies the threat of violence.

11. Nestor Garcia Canclini (1995) describes "cultural patrimony" as the disintegration of hierarchical structures in modern Latin American culture. Canclini speaks of this cultural patrimony as the response for securing symbolic power in the wake of heterogeneity in the modernization of Latin America—authenticity, fundamentalism, traditionalism, and regenerated forms of power once thought to be antiquated vestiges of emergence.

12. Tomás Almaguer (1991) touches on the issue of Mexican/Chicano sexuality in a way similar to Pérez's characterization of her scene. But whereas Almaguer believes that homosexual practices cannot be assumed under a sexual identity, Pérez suggests that this same homosocial behavior without an identity leads to a masculine panic. This recuperation of Chencho's masculine identity seems to be the reason he rapes Ermila.

13. In the opening segment of *Hegemony and Social Strategy: Toward a Radical Democratic Politics,* Laclau and Mouffe (1993) describe hegemony as an "absent totality." I use their notion of the absent totality to describe the collapse of the male figures in the story. It is important to note that this collapse does not necessarily translate into female autonomy, because male dominance has achieved a level of hegemony whereby the rule of order is explicitly and implicitly drawn symbolically from the social death of the female characters.

WORKS CITED

Almaguer, Tomás. 1991. "Chicano Men: A Cartography of Homosexual Identity and Behavior." *Differences: A Journal of Feminist Cultural Studies* 3(2): 75-100.

Bakhtin, Mikhail. 1990. *Dialogic Imagination.* Austin: University of Texas Press.

Bejarano, Yvonne Yarbro. 1991. "Deconstructing the Lesbian Body: Cherríe Moraga's Loving in the War Years." Pp. 143-55 in *Chicana Lesbians: The Girls Our Mothers Warned Us About,* ed. Carla Trujillo. Berkeley: Third Woman Press.

Canclini, Nestor Garcia. 1995. *Hybrid Cultures: Strategies for Entering and Leaving Modernity.* Minneapolis: University of Minnesota Press.

Dirlik, Arif. 1997. *The Postcolonial Aura: Third World Criticism in the Age of Global Capital.* Boulder, CO: Westview Press.

Durand, Regis. 1983. "Aphanasis: A Note on the Dramaturgy of the Subject in Narrative Analysis." Pp. 860-70 in *Lacan and Narration: The Psychoanalytic Difference in Narrative Theory,* ed. Robert Con Davis. Baltimore: Johns Hopkins University Press.

Fregoso, Rosa Linda. 1993. "Introduction: The Bronze Screen Looking at Us." Pp. xiii-xxiii in *The Bronze Screen: Chicana and Chicano Film Culture.* Minneapolis: University of Minnesota Press.

Halbwach, Maurice. 1992. "Dreams and Memory Images." Pp. 41-42 in *On Collective Memory* Trans. Lewis A. Coser. Chicago: University of Chicago Press.

Lacan, Jacques. 1977. *Ecrits: A Selection.* Trans. A. Sherridan. New York: Norton.

Laclau, Ernesto, and Chantal Mouffe. 1993. *Hegemony and Social Strategy: Toward a Radical Democratic Politics.* New York: Verso Press.

Lomeli, Francisco A. 1980. "The Family Crisis in Three Chicano Novels: Disintegration vs. Continuity." Pp. 141-55 in *Work, Family, Sex Roles, Language: The NACS Selected Papers 1979,* ed. Mario Barrera, Alberto Camarillo, and Francisco Hernández. Berkeley: Tonatiuh-Quinto Sol.

Lowe, Lisa. 1994. "Unfaithful to the Original: The Subject of *Dictee.*" Pp. 35-69 in *Writing Self/Writing Nation,* ed. Norma Alarcón and Elaine Kim. Berkeley: Third Woman Press.

Moya, Paula. 1997. "Postmodernism, Realism and the Politics of Identity: Cherríe Moraga and Chicana Feminism." Pp. 125-50 in *Feminist Genealogies, Colonial Legacies, Democratic Futures,* ed. M. Jacqui Alexander and Chandra Talpade Mohanty. New York: Routledge.

Patterson, Orlando. 1982. *Slavery and Social Death: A Comparative Study.* Cambridge, MA: Harvard University Press.

Pérez, Emma. 1991. "Sexuality and Discourse: Notes from a Chicana Survivor." Pp. 159-

84 in *Chicana Lesbians: The Girls Our Mothers Warned Us About,* ed. Carla Trujillo. Berkeley: Third Woman Press.

———. 1999. *The Decolonial Imaginary: Writing Chicanas into History.* Bloomington: Indiana University Press.

Rebolledo, Tey Diana. 1995. "Mujeres Andariegas: Good Girls and Bad." Pp. 183–210 in *Women Singing in the Snow: A Cultural Analysis of Chicana Literature.* Tucson: University of Arizona Press.

Ricatelli, Ralph. 1974. "The Sexual Stereotypes of the Chicana in Literature." *Encuentro Femenil* 2: 48–56.

Sapphire. 1996. *Push: A Novel.* New York: Knopf.

Swindell, Julia. 1989. "Liberating the Subject? Autobiography and 'Women's History': A Reading of *The Diaries of Hannah Cullwick.*" Pp. 24–38 in *Interpreting Women's Lives: Feminist Theory and Personal Narratives,* ed. The Personal Narratives Group. Bloomington: University of Indiana Press.

Trujillo, Carla, ed. 1991. *Chicana Lesbians: The Girls Our Mothers Warned Us About.* Berkeley: Third Women Press.

RESPONSE TO CHAPTER FIVE

The Lessons of Chicana Lesbian Fictions and Theories

SERGIO DE LA MORA

• • • • •

Chicana lesbian theory and literature has circulated for well over three decades, yet only since the late 1990s has scholarship begun to focus on writers other than Gloria Anzaldúa and Cherríe Moraga, whose importance has overshadowed the work of their contemporaries. The exceptionalism and tokenism conferred on the latter figures is finally shifting as scholarship by and about other Chicana lesbians is slowly gaining wider currency (Esquibel 1999).

The critical interventions of Chicana lesbians on sexuality transformed Chicana/o studies, as can be gauged by a recent anthology on Chicana feminist writing (A. García 1997). Heterosexual Chicanas and gay male Chicanos are indebted to our lesbian sisters for putting themselves on the line to map out the terrain of sexuality and power, which we have all learned from. Notwithstanding the spurious anti-Chicana lesbian backlash blamed for alienating Chicano scholars and for purportedly being instrumental in causing divisions within our intellectual community symbolized by the National Association for Chicana and Chicano Studies (I. García 1996), Chicano scholarship can no longer ignore the differences and tensions that have destabilized the patriarchal heteronormativity inscribed into the Chicano national body politic (González 1998). Be it fiction, poetry, theory, drama, or hybrid literary forms spanning disciplines and theoretical approaches, the introduction of sexuality as a primary category of analysis in assessing the study of power relations addressed the blind spots of previous intellectual production written by Chicanas and Chicanos. Chicana feminists in particular owe a great deal to the debates introduced by Chicana lesbians who broke ground by articulating how sexuality, in all its multiple forms, shapes all social formations and informs the grand narratives espoused by the Chicano civil rights movement.

Texas Chicana feminist lesbian intellectuals such as Gloria Anzaldúa and Emma Pérez have been on the cutting edge of Chicana feminist theory and literature for over two decades. The Tejana Ellie Hernández, representative of the second generation of postnationalist queer scholars, has been jockeying for a position in that circle of leading Tejana intellectuals since at least 1991 when her poetry and critical prose appeared in Carla Trujillo's (1991) groundbreaking anthology, *Chicana Lesbians: The Girls Our Mothers Warned Us About*.[1] Hernández's rich and suggestive analysis of her *compatriota* Emma Pérez's *Gulf Dreams* (1996) is a welcome contribution to Chicana/o literary scholarship and to the growing print-based critical reception of Pérez's novel (de Lauretis 1996; Esquibel 1998). Her theoretically challenging essay engages a variety of critical discourses, including Lacanian psychoanalysis, Foucauldian discourse analysis, Bakhtinian formalism, postcolonial subaltern studies, historiography, and textual analysis. Her argument is structured around the psychoanalytic concept of desire but reinflected with dimensions of M. M. Bakhtin's equally complex concept of the chronotope. At this particular historical moment, Hernández's privileged sign of the times is lesbian desire, and discourses on Chicana sexuality as these are linked to narratology. She identifies three levels of desire in the novel: "representation in language," "self-fulfillment through the sexual encounter," and "legitimacy as a historical subject." Her analysis of the first two levels of desire clearly articulates the multiple interpretive angles encouraged by Pérez's highly experimental and poetic prose. The third level proves to be more problematic. She argues at length for the legitimacy of historical knowledge and representation of Chicana sexuality through literary forms but seems to be conflating history and fiction. Hernández acknowledges that Pérez's novel is fiction, not autobiography, and that the novel self-consciously lacks a referential historical context. However, she continually pushes the envelope on blurring the boundary between reality and fantasy, a strategy consistent with her psychoanalytic hermeneutics. I appreciate the political gesture of interrogating and expanding what constitutes accepted understandings of history, truth, and valid forms of knowledge. It is beyond question that history does indeed use fictional strategies to emplot its story and that historians pick and choose "facts" and fictionalize them to suit their "truths" and political agendas (White 1978). Hernández's essay thus poses a methodological and epistemic challenge: how to go outside the margins of accepted definitions of disciplines of knowledge to redefine the boundaries.

Given the imposed silence and the unspoken stories surrounding Chicana sexual experiences, Hernández proposes a narrative paradigm that addresses the politics of representation for Chicana lesbians, a paradigm that addresses the specificities of Chicana lesbian subjectivities. She argues that the experimental form and the use of the subjective voice allow for the construction of an internal reality that does not depend on nineteenth-century notions of realism. She argues further that Pérez's novel, in displaying the failure of male-centered Chicano nationalism to empower Chicanas, thus poses a critique of the liberation politics of the movement, which was modeled after the heterosexual family. Chicana lesbian literary forms represent what is not allowed in nationalist narratives, namely, lesbian sexuality. She goes to great lengths to argue for the legitimacy of Chicana lesbian sexuality as a "source of self-production." This issue seems to be a mute point because previous Chicana lesbian scholarship from Yvonne Yarboro-Bejarano to Alicia Gaspar de Alba to Mary Patricia Brady, to name but a few, have already established the legitimacy of Chicana lesbian sexuality and subjectivity. Hernández, however, goes on to posit an alternative politics of liberation rooted in Chicana lesbian subjectivity, one that refuses to occupy the space of the other so as to gain access to "the possibilities afforded by the fluidity of power."

One of Hernández's most illuminating avenues of research is her analysis of the relationship between language and women's experiences, which in turn echoes Pérez's (1999) often cited concept of *sitios y lenguas* (sites and discourses): a Chicana space for the construction of language and theory rooted in the daily lived experiences of colonization, oppression, marginalization, and exploitation (130; see also Pérez 1991, 1998). In more ways than one, Hernández seems to be reading Pérez's fiction through Pérez's theories about Chicana history.

This struggle with silence and Western patriarchal language leads Hernández to claim that the novel's fragmented narrative is a symptom of the historical limitations placed on the self-representation of Chicana lesbians' sexuality. This crisis in meaning and frustration with inherited language finds a model in the work of French feminists and their *escriture féminine*. The scholars that come to mind include not only Luce Irigaray and Monique Wittig but also Marguerite Duras, whose elliptical, cinematic narrative prose style, particularly that fashioned in *The Lover* ([1985] 1992), seems clearly to have shaped the expressive contours of Pérez's equally elusive and poetic fiction.

Sexual violence has long been one of the most effective strategies for colonizing peoples and for constructing social identities and relations (Trexler 1995). Rape and other forms of sexual violence mobilize patriarchal property rights and are a central component in exerting and maintaining domination. In the European colonization of the Americas, and specifically in the case of Mexico, rape has been the foundational act of violence, which has engendered mestizaje and nationhood. This narrative of origins has been mythologized in the figure of Malinche, aka *la chingada*, the violated symbolic mother of the mestizo (Paz 1950). Very little, however, has been said about sexual violence against men. In Chicano cultural production, the rape of men and women has been uniquely broached in Edward James Olmos's *American Me* (1992).[2] With the exception of Floyd Salas's *Tattoo the Wicked Cross* (1967), Chicana/o literature has avoided addressing how gendered sexual violence against men and children impacts not only the individual but also the community. With the publication of Pérez's *Gulf Dreams*, the specter of this utterly taboo subject is raised once and for all.

Although the consequences of sexual abuse against male and female children shape the entire narrative, they are largely left underexamined by Hernández. Inocencio, aka Chencho, a victim of child abuse and one of the men involved in Ermila's rape, is a classic study of victim turned victimizer. He is both object of scorn for instigating and perpetrating the rape of Ermila, the narrator's object of desire, and also a source of ambivalent empathy and pity not only on the part of this reader but also for the novel's narrator. Both were sexually abused as children. Both live troubled lives as scarred adults with damaged minds and bodies. Possibly a repressed homosexual but certainly a closeted bisexual, Chencho is absolved of his responsibility for partaking in Ermila's rape, but "justice" strikes him in the form of an antihomosexual hate crime. His mutilated body is found outside a gay bar he frequented. The violence directed at him is shocking: "A shapeless face with shocked eyes had a gaping mouth stuffed with something. . . . Flattened, pale testicles with dried cakes of blood were jammed into Inocencio's mouth" (Pérez 1996, 154). This frightening and bloody image brands the reader's mind somewhat like a lynching. Chencho's murder and lynching function primarily as a deterrent against defying heterosexual norms.[3]

This hate crime functions as an intimidation tactic aimed at maintaining complete subservience to heterosexual patriarchal power. Only by linking all forms of sexual violence can the terrorism re-enacted daily against our minds, bodies, and pleasures be effectively challenged.

NOTES

1. See especially her autobiographical essay, "Discussion, Discourse and Direction: The Dilemmas of a Chicana Lesbian" (in Trujillo 1991).

2. For a discussion on the terror tactics inscribed in the trope of male rape, see de la Mora (1995).

3. For analysis of the relationship between rape and lynching, see Hall (1983).

WORKS CITED

de la Mora, Sergio. 1995. " 'Giving It Away': *American Me* and the Defilement of Chicano Manhood." *Cine Estudiantil 1995 Catalogue*, 14. San Diego: Centro Cultural de la Raza.

de Lauretis, Teresa. 1996. "Closing the Gulf between Us." *Lesbian Review of Books* 2(4): 3–4.

Duras, Marguerite. (1985) 1992. *The Lover.* Trans. Barbara Bray. New York: Harper.

Esquibel, Catriona Rueda. 1998. "Memories of Girlhood: Chicana Lesbian Fictions." *Signs: A Feminist Journal* 23(3): 59–98. Reprinted in *Chicano/Latino Homoerotic Identities*, ed. David William Foster. New York: Garland, 1999, 59–98.

———. 1999. "Chicana Lesbian Fictions: Ambivalence, Erotics, and Authenticity." Ph.D. diss., University of California, Santa Cruz.

Garcia, Alma M., ed. 1997. *Chicana Feminist Thought: The Basic Historical Writings.* New York: Routledge.

García, Ignacio M. 1996. "Juncture in the Road: Chicano Studies since 'El Plan de Santa Barbara.' " Pp. 181–203 in *Chicanas/Chicanos at the Crossroads: Social, Economic, and Political Change*, ed. David R. Maciel and Isidro D. Ortiz. Tucson: University of Arizona Press.

González, Deena J. 1998. "Speaking Secrets: Living Chicana Theory." Pp. 46–77 in *Living Chicana Theory*, ed. Carla Trujillo. Berkeley: Third Woman Press.

Hall, Jacquelyn Dowd. 1983. " 'The Mind That Burns in Each Body': Women, Rape, and Sexual Violence." Pp. 328–49 in *Powers of Desire: The Politics of Sexuality*, ed. Ann Snitow, Christine Stansell, and Sharon Thompson. New York: Monthly Review Press.

Hernández, Ellie. 1991. "Discussion, Discourse and Direction: The Dilemmas of a Chicana Lesbian." Pp. 138–40 in *Chicana Lesbians: The Girls Our Mothers Warned Us About*, ed. Carla Trujillo. Berkeley: Third Woman Press.

Paz, Octavio. 1950. *El laberinto de la soledad.* México City: Fondo de Cultura Económica.

Pérez, Emma. 1991. "Sexuality and Discourse: Notes from a Chicana Survivor." Pp. 159–84 in *Chicana Lesbians: The Girls Our Mothers Warned Us About*, ed. Carla Trujillo. Berkeley: Third Woman Press.

———. 1996. *Gulf Dreams.* Berkeley: Third Woman Press.

———. 1998. "Irigaray's Female Symbolic in the Making of Chicana Lesbian *Sitios y Lenguas* (Sites and Discourses)." Pp. 87–101 in *Living Chicana Theory*, ed. Carla Trujillo. Berkeley: Third Woman Press.

———. 1999. *The Decolonial Imaginary: Writing Chicanas into History.* Bloomington: Indiana University Press.

Salas, Floyd. 1967. *Tattoo the Wicked Cross.* New York: Grove.

Trexler, Richard C. 1995. *Sex and Conquest: Gendered Violence, Political Order, and the European Conquest of the Americas.* Ithaca: Cornell University Press.

Trujillo, Carla, ed. 1991. *Chicana Lesbians: The Girls Our Mothers Warned Us About.* Berkeley: Third Woman Press.

White, Hayden. 1978. "The Historical Text as Literary Artifact." Pp. 81–100 in *Tropics of Discourse: Essays in Cultural Criticism.* Baltimore: Johns Hopkins University Press.

CHAPTER SIX

Unruly Passions: Poetics, Performance,

and Gender in the Ranchera Song

OLGA NÁJERA-RAMÍREZ

• • • • •

I am convinced that a fruitful study of the *canción ranchera* would be one that interprets the cruel, fickle woman, so bitterly denounced in many of these songs, and alcohol, so ready at hand, as symbols that scapegoat for social and economic oppression. — Manuel Peña, *The Texas-Mexican Conjunto*

Since the mid–nineteenth century a country's music has become a political ideology by stressing national characteristics, appearing as a representative of a nation, and everywhere confirming the national principle. . . . Yet music, more than any other artistic medium, expresses the national principle's antinomies as well.
— Theodor W. Adorno, *The Sociology of Music*

The Mexican ranchera is an expressive musical form intimately associated with Mexican cultural identity on both sides of the U.S.-Mexico border.[1] As an anthropologist concerned with the ways Mexican culture is perceived, constructed, and represented, I am intrigued by the ranchera as a critical site for exploring issues of *lo mexicano* or Mexicanness. Although the ranchera has occasionally been taken up as a topic of serious scholarly inquiry, detailed analyses of it are limited.[2] Moreover, most of these studies have failed to adequately theorize, and in some cases have even failed to acknowledge, women's participation as performers, composers, and consumers of the ranchera.[3] Hence, the goal of this paper is to contribute to the scholarship of the ranchera in two ways. First, by drawing on recent scholarship on melodrama and performance studies, I argue that the ranchera embodies a poetics that resists facile and essentialist interpretations. In particular, I show how the ranchera may be considered a form of melodrama—a discursive space characterized by the intensity of emotion in which issues of profound social concern may be addressed. Second, I explore several ways women have employed the ranchera as a site through which they may make feminist interventions. The following discussion is intended to provide a theoretical synthesis and direction for future empirically based research. Although my own ethnographic research is preliminary, based on formal interviews with Lydia Mendoza and a working-class woman, some participant observation, and numerous informal conversations, it illustrates that the ranchera is a rich site for feminist investigation.[4]

LA RANCHERA AS A FORM OF MELODRAMA

Briefly, the ranchera is a type of Mexican popular music characterized by theme (lyrical content), performance style, and, to some extent, musical structure. Generally, the themes revolve around fervent sentiments toward particular people and specific places (i.e., town, state, region, or country). Punctuated with *gritos* (soulful cries of emotion), the ranchera is characterized by the intense expression of emotions, and in this respect may be favorably compared to the blues and country western music.[5] Although the musical structure of the ranchera is not rigid, scholars generally agree that, particularly in commercially recorded versions, it is strophic, often including an instrumental introduction, a verse, a refrain, and an instrumental interlude (Mendoza 1988 [1961]). The number and structure of the verses vary from song to song.

The term *canción ranchera* (literally, country song) first emerged in the early twentieth century during the post-Revolutionary period when Mexico experienced a surge in urban migration. Evoking a rural sensibility, the ranchera expressed nostalgia for a provincial lifestyle and projected a romanticized idyllic vision of the past.[6] As cultural critic Carlos Monsiváis observes:

> El estruendo y la melodía implorante y la letra sacrificial bosquejan una actitud distante de lo "urbano" y lo "contemporáneo." En su adjetivo, la canción ranchera elije el estilo y la calidad de las emociones al alcance de su auditorio y opta por aquellas inscritas en la idea de "rancho," de

epoca anterior a lo industrial y lo tecnológico. [The cries and imploring melody and the sacrificial lyrics delineate an attitude distant from the "urban" and the "contemporary." As an adjective, the ranchera song chooses a style and quality of emotions at the reach of its audience and opts for those inscribed in the idea of the "ranch" of the era before the industrial and the technological.] (1994b [1977], 90)

Considered an ideal expression of lo mexicano (Mexicanness) by romantic nationalists of the 1930s, the ranchera attained widespread popularity through radio and film, especially the *comedia ranchera* (western comedy).[7] According to ethnomusicologist Manuel Peña, "People respond, instinctively, to a ranchero sound, whether it be interpreted for them by a *conjunto*, an *orquesta* or a *mariachi*. And inevitably, by virtue of its symbolic association, it gives rise to vaguely articulated feelings of *mexicanismo*— momentary recreations of a simpler and romanticized folk heritage, tempered nonetheless by the realization that it is an ineffable existence, lost forever like the elusive lover of most ranchera song lyrics" (1985, 11). Particularly important in Peña's commentary is his suggestion that the nostalgic longing for another time or place becomes expressed metaphorically as the longing for an elusive lover. His insight anticipates my own argument that the ranchera has to be understood in poetic, rather than literal, terms. Peña's observation that the canción ranchera evokes a sentimental response among its (Mexican) audiences on both sides of the border is also noteworthy.

Other scholars also associate passionate sentimentalism with the ranchera song, yet few have considered it a distinctive stylistic attribute of the song form. Instead, in the most extreme cases, sentimentality and emotion are read as uniquely Mexican cultural attributes. Geijerstam, for example, claims, "The performance of the ranchera songs exhibits an inimitable sentimentality, even tearfulness, which seems to be characteristically Mexican" (1976, 125). Injecting a class and gendered dimension, Fogelquist goes even further, stating that "the underlying sense of desperation of the lower-class Mexican male, the fatalism, and the view that *la vida no vale nada* (life is worth nothing) and of course large quantities of alcohol, give rise to the total rejection of reason and the indulgence of passion" (1975, 60).

Without espousing Fogelquist's negative stereotypes of the lower-class Mexican male as desperate, fatalistic, and alcoholic, Gradante also attributes the popular appeal of ranchera to the fact that the experiences embodied in the text resonate with those of the everyday working-class individual: "The brevity, simplicity and straightforwardness of the poetic structure of the *canción ranchera* served as the most appropriate vehicle for the expression of the sentiments of the lower classes without pretense or unnecessary elaboration" (1983, 112).

In addition to assuming that indulgence in passion is a unique Mexican trait, such readings assume that the ranchera, like the people to whom it speaks, is simple, unsophisticated, and therefore transparent in meaning.[8] However, as Paredes skillfully demonstrated years ago, the failure to recognize the artistic dimension of Greater Mexican expressive behavior has resulted in gross interpretative inaccuracies by scholars who "proceed as if language had only one level of meaning or as if informants were incapable of any kind of language use but that of minimum communication" (1977, 8). Paredes's work on proverbs is particularly instructive, for he clearly illustrates that brevity and apparent simplicity of an expressive form are not accurate indicators of the sophistication of the speaker or meaning of the message. Consequently, he warns, "If explanations can be so far off the mark with proverbs—which seem to be all 'message'—this is even truer of the more complex forms of folklore, such as legends, *corridos*, customs, or beliefs. We must know the situation in which this folklore is performed; and we must know the language and the people well" (1982, 11). Paredes provides a compelling argument for attending to both the poetics and the performative dimensions of an expressive form. That is, rather than assume that the expression of passion in the lyrics or in the performance is a "naive expression of a simple people" (Stewart 1993, 221), we must recognize emotional excess as a deliberate aesthetic quality of the ranchera.[9]

The emphasis on the "emotional excess" of the ranchera points to its affinity with melodramatic forms. Indeed, melodramatic forms are by definition a roller coaster of emotions. As film theorist Marcia Landy observes, "Seduction, betrayal, abandonment, extortion, murder, suicide, revenge, jealousy, incurable illness, obsession, and compulsion—these are part of the familiar terrain of melodrama" (1991, 14). Significantly, just as in the case of the ranchera, the emotional excess in melodrama previously provided scholars with sufficient grounds on which to regard melodrama as vulgar and insignificant. In recent years, however, cultural critics from a number of theoretical perspectives—feminism, psychoanalysis, Marxism, and semiotics—have reevaluated melodrama as an aesthetic practice with its own set of strategies of communication. These critics now affirm that melodrama offers far more important insights into culture than had been previously considered (Brooks 1976; Landy 1991; Williams 1991; Gledhill 1987).

Emotional excess is not only expressed in the narrative content (i.e., the lyrics); the performance of melodrama calls for a style intended to induce emotional responses from the audience as well (Landy 1991, 15). The emotions exhibited—and, one may assume, induced—in the performance style of the ranchera include sadness, despair, contempt, love, and pride. Typically, the ranchera performance style includes not only a vocal display of emotions but *ademanes* (facial, hand, and body gestures) and even tears. Such displays of emotion render the performance one in which the singer, in the words of many ranchera performers, "vive lo que canta" (lives what he or she sings). In contrast to the aforementioned claims that rancheras transparently express what the singers (and their audiences) live, the ranchera singers claim they live what they sing as they perform, thus emphasizing the fact that it is a performance. For instance, in an interview I conducted with Lydia Mendoza, she explained, "Yo vivo lo que canto. Cuando estoy cantando siento como si estuviera viviendo aquellos sentimientos. [I live what I sing. When I am singing, I feel as if I were living those sentiments.]"[10] According to Mendoza, and judging by the audience's reactions to her live performances, her ability to sing as if she is experiencing the narrative is precisely what makes her music touch others. Similarly, 9-year-old singing sensation Tatiana Bolaños, who belts out ranchera songs with the emotion and sentimentalism of some of the greatest ranchera singers, clearly illustrates that the ability to exhibit a range of emotions is indeed a performance style that can be (and should be) acquired and manipulated by an accomplished ranchera singer.

Indeed, how well ranchera singers render a performance is a subject of great attention. The singer's ability to engage the audience depends on his or her ability to invoke a broad range of emotions rather than to limit the performance to one emotion. Singers who merely sob through an entire song lose the emotional tension that a skilled ranchera performer manages and prompt such criticism as "Es muy llorona. [She's just a whiner.]"

In addition to an emphasis on sensibility and emotion, other characteristics of melodrama include the "dichotomizing of the world, its Manicheanism, and its inflation of personal conflicts and its internalization of external social conflicts" (Landy 1991, 16). This latter point has been especially evident in the recent research on Mexican melodramatic films by scholars who cogently assert that melodramatic films serve as fictional spaces in which issues of Mexican identity and social change are explored and represented (Monsiváis 1992; López 1991; Podalsky 1993). In particular, Podalsky and López persuasively argue for a more nuanced reading of Mexican melodramas that acknowledges their contestative potential even as they reinforce the dominant ideology. For instance, Podalsky claims that "melodrama is formally and practically linked with the specific trajectory of Mexican national identity and the significance of the Revolution for the nation-building project." Yet, she argues, "the ability of melodrama to incorporate contradictory messages about the nation made it a viable formula for political as well as cinematic texts" (1993, 63). Similarly, López concludes that "to dismiss melodrama as a simple 'tool of domination' is to ignore the complex intersections of strategies of representation and particular social relations of difference" (1991, 47). These insights on Mexican film are particularly noteworthy because, as I noted earlier, the Mexican movie industry served as a critical site for the dissemination and popularization of the ranchera song.[11]

Understood as a form of melodrama, rancheras may productively be approached as a discursive space in which topics of emotional weight may be addressed in culturally appropriate ways. That is, rancheras may be considered culturally sanctioned sites in which the ideas and values of a community are not merely displayed but, more important, are transmitted, produced, reproduced, and contested. Hence, far from being transparent expressions of a simple people, rancheras are complex forms rife with contradictions. Moreover, rancheras, like other melodramatic forms, are "inextricable from social conflict, revealing, obliquely or directly, class, gender, and generational conflicts" (Landy 1991, 18). Because the ranchera relies heavily on the use of metaphor, the meanings are much more open-ended and situationally sensitive than scholars have heretofore suggested. Songs about abandonment, loss, and desire, for example, take on new meanings when examined in the context of the increased globalization that has intensified domestic as well as transnational migrations within Greater Mexico. Such displacements often rupture families (at least temporarily, sometimes permanently), threaten partnerships, and complicate preexisting notions of national identity. The nostalgia, longing, and despair that Mexicanos experience in all aspects of their lives, not just their love lives, is given expression through the ranchera.

Below, I provide the excerpts of one ranchera to illustrate how the text allows listeners to bring to bear their own experiences to interpret the song:

Cruz de olvido
Con el atardecer me iré de ti
me iré sin ti
me alejaré de ti
con un dolor dentro de mi

Te juro corazón
que no es falta de amor
pero es mejor así
un día comprenderás
que lo hice por tu bien
que todo fue por ti

The Burden of Forgetting
At sunset I will leave you
I will leave without you
I will distance myself from you
With a pain deep within me
I swear to you, sweetheart
It's not for lack of love
But it's better this way
One day you'll understand
That I did it for your own good
That everything was for you

Clearly, the song speaks about the emotional turmoil experienced by a person who must leave a loved one. Although composer Juan Zaizar most likely wrote this song about an adult love relationship, the text is sufficiently fluid to apply to various situations. Engaged listeners can read the song according to their own experiences, filling in the specific details regarding exactly why the departure has to occur and what the nature of the relationship is between the subject and the object. Considering the long history of labor migration within Greater Mexico, which has caused the fragmentation of families, I argue that for many listeners such songs may apply as much to parent-child separations as to separations experienced by two lovers.[12]

The notion of multiple, and even contested, meanings in melodrama also lays the groundwork for exploring issues of gender. Indeed, Gledhill observes:

The figure of woman, which has served so long as a powerful and ambivalent patriarchal symbol, is also a generator of female discourses drawn from the social realities of women's lives—discourses which negotiate a space within and sometimes resist patriarchal domination. In order to command the recognition of its female audiences, melodrama must draw on such discourses. Thus in twentieth-century melodrama the dual role of woman as symbol for a whole culture and as representative of a historical, gendered point of view produces a struggle between male and female voices: the symbol cannot be owned but is contested. (1987, 37)

Similarly, as Ana López has argued, Mexican melodrama "always addresses questions of individual (gendered) identity within patriarchal culture" (1991, 33).

Extending their insights into my analysis of the ranchera, I now turn to examine the question of how we might consider women's participation in the performance, production, and consumption of the ranchera as a feminist intervention. I argue that by participating actively in what was predominantly a male genre, women have been able to employ the ranchera for their own purposes, sometimes highlighting their subordination, sometimes talking back to that subordination, but always calling attention to their concerns, desires, experiences, and needs. In particular, I show that through the manipulation of text, costume, and performance style, women may use the ranchera to challenge, transgress, and even ameliorate gender constraints prevalent in Mexican society.

ENGENDERING PERFORMANCES

The lyrics of the ranchera provide one opportunity for women to make important interventions. In a short but provocative study, Mexican anthropologist Marta Lamas (1978) provides a feminist interpretation of some ranchera lyrics, noting the use of metaphor as a strategy for objectifying women and for discussing sexual themes that would otherwise be considered taboo. For example, women are often spoken of as flowers to be cared for, plucked, or stolen by their lovers, while their father, brother, or husband is the protective gardener. Below I provide two brief examples to illustrate this point.

Rosa de castilla
Rosa de castilla
Que buena te estas poniendo
para cortarte en una fresca mañana

Rose of the Castle
Rose of the castle
You are getting so ripe
that I can cut you on a fresh morning

Rosita amarilla
Ah qué aroma de esa flor

de esa rosita amarilla
el trabajo que me dió
para verle la semilla
pero no se me escapó
le corte hasta la ramilla

Yellow Rose
Oh what an aroma that flower has
that yellow rose
the trouble it caused me
to see her seed
but she didn't escape me
I even cut her limbs

Lamas's attention to the use of metaphor is instructive, for even this limited treatment of the poetic dimension challenges Gradante's claim and Fogelquist's assumption that the ranchera is simple and straightforward. Together with Paredes's observations discussed above, Lamas's insights call attention to the need to take a fuller account of the poetic and performative dimensions of a ranchera.

Consider, for example, what happens to the traditional ranchera text when a woman performs it: the poetics of the ranchera become reconfigured from a male to either a female or a gender-neutral point of view. Indeed, the same text may assume a very different meaning when the subjective "I" is a female and the "you" is a male. For example, a sexist double standard is blatantly revealed when a woman sings a "male song" such as "Ni en defensa propia" (Not Even in My Own Defense). In this song, the male protagonist decides to leave his girlfriend when he discovers that she is not a virgin. When the lyrics are sung by a woman, however, the protagonist may be interpreted as a female. That a woman would leave her male partner simply because he is not a virgin seems absurd in Mexican cultural conventions. Thus, the changes produced by transposing the gender roles in this case are monumental because they powerfully expose male privilege. Furthermore, by making very small but critical changes, women (and for that matter, men) can decenter the male perspective embedded in the narrative. For example, in the song "Tú sólo tú," women singers such as Selena have changed the opening line from "Mira como ando mujer [Look at the state I'm in, woman]" to "Mira como ando mi amor [Look at the state I'm in, my love]."[13] Such changes are significant because they open the text to a wider range of possible meanings.

A famous potpourri performed by José Alfredo Jímenez and Alicia Juárez entitled "Las coplas" (The Couplets, or Verses) nicely illustrates how performers can manipulate the meaning of the ranchera text. "Las coplas" consists of a series of excerpts from various well-known rancheras. By singing the verses in a call-response fashion, these two singers create an intertextual dialogue between the rancheras and between a man and a woman. Accordingly, the "I" and "you" shift depending on who is singing. Further, the singer may take the liberty of changing the words to alter the meaning even more profoundly. Note, for example, how the second verse taken from the song "Cuando viva conmigo" has been radically changed from the original text.[14] Hence, the performance becomes a sort of contest in which the singers try to outdo each other by engaging a range of sentiments, including desperation, control, pride, self-pity, submission, and reconciliation. Because of the length of this potpourri, I provide only exemplary excerpts below. José Alfredo Jímenez initiates the dialogue by singing the following excerpt of "No me amenaces":

No me amenaces, no me amenaces
cuando estés decidida a buscar otra vida
pos, agarra tu rumbo y vete
Pero no me amenaces, no me amenaces
ya estas grandecita, ya entiendes la vida
y ya sabes lo que haces
porque estás que te vas y te vas
y te vas y te vas y te vas, y no te has ido
y yo estoy esperando tu amor,
esperando tu amor, esperando tu amor
o esperando tu olvido

Don't threaten me, don't threaten
when you decide to search for another life
well hit the road and go, but
don't threaten me, don't threaten me
you're grown, you understand life
and you know what you're doing.
Because you say that you're leaving,
leaving, leaving, but you haven't gone
and I'm waiting for your love,
waiting for your love, waiting for your
love or waiting to be forgotten.

Alicia Juárez responds with excerpts of "Cuando vivas conmigo":

De tus ojos está brotando llanto
a tus años estás enamorado
traes el pelo completamente blanco
ya no vas a sacar juventud de tu pasado
¿qué me vas a enseñar a querer
si tu nunca has querido?
Díme ¿qué es lo que voy a aprender
cuando viva contigo?

From your eyes a cry is erupting.
At your age, you're in love.
Your hair is completely white.
You can't get youth from your past.
What are you going to teach me
about love if you've never loved?
Tell me, what am I going to learn
when I live with you?

(José responds with excerpts of "La media vuelta"):

Te vas porque yo quiero que te vayas
a la hora que yo quiero te detengo
yo se que mi cariño te hace falta
porque quieras o no yo soy tu dueño
yo quiero que te vayas por el mundo
y quiero que conozcas mucha gente
yo quiero que te besen otros labios
para que me compares hoy como siempre

You're leaving because I want you to.
I can keep you any time I want to.
I know that you need my love
because like it or not I own you.
I want you to travel around the world.
I want you to meet lots of people.
I want other lips to kiss you
so you can compare me as always.

Alicia sings excerpts of "Me equivoqué contigo":

Me equivoqué contigo
como si no supiera
que las más grandes penas

las debo a mis amores
pero que triste realidad me has ofrecido
que decepción tan grande
haberte conocido
yo no sé Dios por que
te puso en mi camino

I made a mistake with you
as if I didn't know
that my biggest regrets in life
are due to my loves.
But what a sad reality you offer me.
What a big deception
it's been knowing you.
I don't know why God
put you in my path.

José sings excerpts of "La mano de Dios":

Porque solamente la mano de Dios
podrá separarnos
nuestro amor es más grande
que todas las cosas del mundo
yo sé bien que nacimos los dos
para siempre adorarnos
nuestro amor es lo mismo
que el mar cristalino y profundo

Because only God's hand
can separate us.
Our love is much bigger
than anything in the world.
I know well that we were born
to always adore each other.
Our love is like the sea,
crystal clear and deep.

Alicia sings excerpts of "Amanecí entre tus brazos":

Amanecí otra vez entre tus brazos
y desperté llorando de alegría
me cobijé la cara con tus manos
para seguirte amando todavía

te despertaste tú casi dormido
y me querías decir no sé qué cosa
pero callé tu boca con mis besos
y así pasaron muchas muchas horas

I woke up again in your arms
and I woke up crying for joy.
I covered my face with your hands
to continue loving you still.
You awoke almost asleep
and you wanted to say something
but I hushed your mouth with my kisses
and we spent many hours that way.

Together, José and Alicia sing excerpts of "Si nos dejan":

Si nos dejan nos vamos
a querer toda la vida
si nos dejan nos vamos
a vivir a un mundo nuevo
yo creo podemos ver el nuevo
amanecer de un nuevo día
yo pienso que tú y yo podemos
ser felices todavía

If they let us, we're going to love
each other all life long.
If they let us, we're going to live
in a brand new world.
I think we can see a new world
a new sunrise of a new day.
I think that you and I can
still be happy.

The shifting of subjects in the performance of the ranchera clearly underscores the fact that the text cannot be adequately interpreted outside of its socially situated use. As the above example demonstrates, singers may manipulate the meaning of the texts in subtle yet powerful ways. Indeed, by participating as performers of the ranchera, women, by virtue of singing in their "female" voice, recontextualize a text even when they do not change a single word.[15] As Bauman and Briggs have argued, "to decontextualize and recontextualize a text is an act of control" (1990, 76). Hence, each performance presents women with the opportunity to take control of the text to convey their own, subversive, message.

In recent years women have pushed further to expand the scope of the ranchera by composing and performing songs that speak more openly about premarital sex, that "talk back" to the sexist tenets, and that project women as taking a more reflective and active stance in selecting and shaping a relationship. In her study, Lamas briefly mentions two specific examples of ranchera songs composed and performed by women: "La leona" (The Lioness), in which the protagonist defiantly asserts her right to seek a relationship on her own terms, "que sea feo pero sincero [it doesn't matter if he's ugly as long as he's sincere]," and "La arrepentida" (The Repented One), in which the protagonist refuses marriage altogether (1978, 27). More recent examples could be added to her list. For instance, "Es demasiado tarde" (It's Too Late) and "Tu lo decidiste" (You Made the Decision), composed and sung by Ana Gabriel, both feature a protagonist who refuses to take back her lover after their breakup. To illustrate, I provide the full text and translation of "Es demasiado tarde" below:

Tu quisiste estar allá
dijiste que quizá ése era tu destino
después que todo te falló
hoy quieres regresar
y ser felíz conmigo
pero tú no piensas que mi amor
por siempre te olvidó
y exiges mi cariño
de veras lo siento no podré
volverme a enamorar
de ti ya no es lo mismo

(coro)
sólo espero que entiendas que un amor
se debe de cuidar y no jugar con nadie
porque yo te daba mi querer
y aun si merecer no te dolió dejarme
ahora vuelves buscando mi calor
diciendo que jamás lograste olvidarme
pero yo te aclaro de una vez
lo debes entender es demasiado tarde
yo no te guardo rencor
pero tampoco amor

de ti ya nada queda
no niego fue mucho mi dolor
pero eso ya pasó
mejor ya nunca vuelvas
(se repite el coro)
porque tú quisiste estar allá

You wanted to be there
You said that perhaps that was your destiny
After everything failed you
Now you want to return
and be happy with me
But you don't think that my love
has forgotten you forever
and you demand my affection
I am truly sorry that I can't
fall in love with you again
it's just not the same anymore

(chorus)
I just hope that you understand that love
should be cared for and never played with
because I gave you my love and though I
didn't deserve it, it didn't hurt you to leave me
Now you return, looking for my warmth
telling me you never managed to forget me
but I want to be perfectly clear
you should understand that it's too late
I don't resent you
but I don't love you either
there's nothing left of you (for me)
I don't deny that it was very painful
but that's over now
it's best that you never return
(repeat chorus)
because you wanted to be there

Such songs are powerful because they do not assume a heterosexual relationship and because they portray women with agency staunchly refusing to become victims. As such, they broaden the notion of womanhood.

The implicit and explicit gendering of a text is only one example of how paralinguistic communication is accomplished in a ranchera performance. Just as important as the texts are the dynamics of performance, that is, the singing style, costuming, gestures, and other theatrical devices, as well as the sites of performance.[16] Together these elements provide the ranchera singer the means through which she can express that which is otherwise unspeakable.

The singing style constitutes a particularly important aspect of performance. As noted earlier, in general, the ranchera singing style may be characterized as encompassing a whole range of emotions, including "feminine" qualities such as tenderness, softness, and sweetness, and "masculine" qualities of assertiveness, toughness, and bravado. Yet, whereas men who sang softly or tenderly in their performances were read as "romantic" rather than feminine (see Nájera-Ramírez 1994, 9), "masculine" qualities were regarded as vulgar and therefore not appropriate for a lady until the appearance of Lucha Reyes, a famous ranchera singer in the early part of this century who popularized a defiant assertive attitude:

> La aparición de Lucha Reyes marcó el surgimiento del estilo de interpretación femenina de la canción ranchera. En 1927, después de una gira en Europa con la típica del maestro Torreblanca, la cantante había quedado afónica durante más de un año. Al recuperar la voz pudo entonar con un color de contralto y un matiz enronquecido y bronco la naciente canción ranchera-citadina. La personalidad y la neurosis hicieron el resto. Prodigaba su voz hasta desgarrarla, gemía, lloraba, reía e imprecaba. Nunca antes se habían escuchado interpretaciones de ese estilo. Sobreponiendose a las críticas que no aceptaban su falta de refinamiento, pronto Lucha Reyes simbolizaba y personificaba a la mujer bravia y temperamental a la mexicana. [The appearance of Lucha Reyes marked the emergence of a female style of singing the ranchera. In 1927, after a tour in Europe with the regional orchestra directed by Torreblanca, the singer lost her voice for almost a year. Upon recovery, she gained the ability to sing the nascent urban ranchera song in a contralto voice with a hoarse and rough quality. Her personality and neurosis did the rest. She exhausted her voice to the breaking point, she grunted, she cried, she laughed, and she cursed. Never before had this kind of interpretation been heard. Overcoming the critics who did not accept her lack of refinement, Lucha Reyes came to symbolize and personify the Mexican version of the fierce and temperamental woman.] (Moreno Rivas 1989, 190)

By incorporating a range of qualities culturally regarded as masculine, Reyes challenged the sexist division of emotions, making it possible for women to access both male and female qualities. In so doing, she also challenged the idea that women were confined to being sweet, proper, and innocent. As music critic Yolanda Moreno Rivas observes, "Había quedado atrás la dulce e ingenua rancherita encargada de confeccionar los 'calzones de cuero del ranchero.' Ahora, 'la flor más bella del ejido' gritaría, se emborracharía y experimentaría terribles pasiones y abandonos dignos de una verdadera citadina. [The idea of the sweet and innocent country girl in charge of 'making the leather pants for the cowboy'[17] was left behind. Now, the 'most beautiful woman of the village' would scream, get drunk, and experience terrible passions and wild abandon worthy of the true urban woman]" (1989, 191). Reyes's style has since been emulated by many of the great ranchera singers, including Lola Beltrán, Lucha Villa, Irma Serrano, Alicia Juaréz, and Beatriz Adriana, to name but a few. Significantly, as performers of the ranchera, women portray variegated images of the Mexican woman: she is mean and tough, sweet, loving, forgiving or vengeful. By offering multiple ways of being a woman, the women ranchera singers help expand the idea of what constitutes womanhood.

Costume choices for performing ranchera songs provide women another opportunity to break out of a strictly gendered code. The classic female ranchera singer offers at least two options. Either she exaggerates her femininity by wearing some version of the Adelita outfit—a long, lacy, and often, in this performance context, low-cut dress—or she wears a female version of the charro outfit, where long skirts (and, more recently, sometimes a short skirt or short shorts) substitute for pants. In contrast to female participants of the *charreada* (Mexican rodeo), whose use of the Adelita outfit and the charro costume is strictly regulated to ensure a wholesome appearance,[18] the ranchera singer enjoys much more flexibility concerning what kind of image she wishes to display. Indeed, some women singers have opted to break out of the traditional folkloric image altogether by wearing modern apparel such as evening gowns and pant suits.[19] Through costuming, ranchera singers manipulate a range of images that expand the dualistic category of male/female to recuperate sexuality, agency, and independence as qualities available to women, not just men.

The sites of performance also suggest another domain in which female ranchera singers are transgressive of gender conventions. Although some performances occur at family-oriented spaces—such as charreadas, fairs, restaurants, and theaters—most are held in adult-oriented sites, including nightclubs, bars, cockfights, large concert halls, and dance halls. For women to sing outside of domestic spaces is already a transgression of traditional gender roles, but to sing in adult-oriented sites is especially challeng-

Nydia Rojas in ranchera dress. Photograph provided
by Gilbert Martinez, personal collection.

ing. In an interview, Lydia Mendoza openly disclosed to me that her husband disapproved of her performances in nightclubs and bars. Valdez and
Halley cite a club owner who makes a similar observation about Mendoza's
husband:

> I remember when she used to come to the salon and perform. She was
> excellent. She would give a command performance. Her only setback
> was her husband, I can't quite remember his name. Anyway, he would
> drink a lot. This would affect her because many times he would cause
> scenes there at the dance hall. She would get extremely embarrassed and
> ashamed of what he would do. In addition to that, he would get very jeal-
> ous with her and he would take it out on her. There were times that they
> would argue out in the back and I had to calm him down. It would take
> a while to explain to him that everything was going to be all right and
> that Lydia was doing this for him as well. It's very hard to explain things
> to a drunk! If she would have had a better husband or would have been
> single, things would have been so much better. (1996, 157)

Lucero in white charro outfit. Photograph provided by Gilbert Martinez, personal collection.

Rosenda Bernal in hotpants-style charro outfit. Jacket cover of 1980 album entitled *Rosenda Bernal con Mariachi Mexico de Pepe Villa,* courtesy of EMI-Capitol of Mexico.

Noting that *los vicios* (literally, the vices, i.e., drugs, alcohol, and sex) pose serious occupational hazards for anyone in show business, Mendoza emphasized that these dangers, along with scandalous cases of women who succumbed to them, have made it especially difficult for women to pursue a singing career and remain respectable.

Fully aware of the risks, real and exaggerated, that a public singing career poses for women, experienced ranchera singers negotiate performance spaces by skillfully weaving a narrative in between each song in which they explain the special meaning that a particular song holds for them.[20] Some have opted to strategically exploit the power of "scandal" and "spectacle." Ranchera singer Irma Serrano, "La tigresa" (the Tigress), provides a fascinating case in point, as Mexican critic Carlos Monsiváis (1977a [1994]) has observed.[21] Working in several genres, including books, films, theater, and politics, Serrano takes full advantage of the power of performance. Using sarcasm and tongue-in-cheek humor, she powerfully questions many social conventions regarding women, sexuality, pleasure, and authority. Whether on stage, in the courtroom, or in a political campaign, Serrano purposefully wears the most scandalous sexy outfits, thereby calling attention to herself as an object of beauty and desire and at the same time confirming the powerful hold she has on the public. Regarding Serrano's subversive style, literary critic Deborah Castillo remarks:

> Her rhetorical strategy is to keep this parodic character constantly in motion, to amuse and to ironize, taking nothing seriously: not her sometimes disturbing revelations, not even her own ironic and amused commentaries on severe social problems. From her first exposure to the Mexican film industry, Serrano learned the lesson of accommodation: "[Y]o quería llevar una carrera limpia, digna, honesta, pero era inútil" [I wanted to have a clean, dignified, honest career but it was useless] (Serrano and Robledo 1978, 21). Of the three writers studied here, Serrano is the most consistently and consciously aware of the value of a hardheaded exploitation of apparent frivolity for extremely businesslike ends. (1998, 197)

Alert to the power of spectacle, Serrano has cultivated a flamboyant image to fascinate, shock, disgust, or mock. By so doing, she remains in the public eye, assured of captivating an audience for personal gain as well as for political ends. Ironically, she ran unsuccessfully for senator in the state of Chiapas in 1991, but in 1994 she was elected to the national congress as a state representative.

Having explored the role of women as performers and composers of ranchera songs, let me now briefly take up the issue of women as consumers of rancheras. Obviously, a detailed ethnographic investigation focusing on how women experience and interpret the ranchera is beyond the scope of this essay. However, I offer a few initial observations based on an extensive interview I conducted with an elderly Mexican woman who has been an avid consumer of ranchera music for most of her life. My informant told me that her earliest recollection of hearing rancheras performed by women dated back to the 1930s in her family home when, at the request of her father, two teenage female cousins sang for the family (this was before radio was available in her hometown in Mexico). At public community dances, she explained, only men were allowed to perform as singers, and women could not even attend a dance except under the careful supervision of a chaperone (usually their father).

By the 1940s, as radio—and later films and record players—became more accessible (especially when her family moved to the city), ranchera music took on greater meaning in my informant's life. Surrounded by it, she came to associate certain songs with specific events in her life. She recalled, for instance, how, after the breakup of a romance between her brother and his girlfriend, her brother played a particular ranchera, evoking tears from their mother, who grieved for, and along with, her son. Rancheras have also served to chronicle many significant moments in my informant's own personal life. Even today, her eyes fill with tears when she listens to particular songs. "El amor de la paloma" (The Love of the Dove), popularized by Irma Serrano in 1964, powerfully evokes memories of the tragic death of her husband that same year. Interestingly, "El amor de la paloma" speaks about how a female dove struggles to survive after her male partner abandons her, but what my informant appreciated most about the song was that Serrano sang it with so much passion and sadness. By articulating her own sense of grief, this ranchera song provided a means through which my informant could give expression to, and even wallow in, her own sadness. Faced with the daunting task of raising a large family by herself, my informant had to focus on the practical matters of securing employment and maintaining a strong front for her children. She continuously struggled to keep her emotions in check. By listening to the ranchera she could, at least momentarily, release her pent-up emotions. Similarly, the song "Una lágrima" (A Teardrop) reminds her of when her eldest son joined the armed forces. Again, it was the emotional response to abandonment expressed in the song, rather than the literal narrative, that engaged her. She confided, "¡Cómo lloraba con esa canción! [How I cried with that song!]"

Listening to ranchera music on a transistor radio also helped reduce the monotony of working in the fields. She laughed, recalling how one of her coworkers, tired of the numerous commercial advertisements, would turn off the radio to "cantar más a gusto [sing more comfortably]." Even though the Spanish-language radio stations remain the most important vehicle for disseminating ranchera music internationally, televised musical variety programs such as *Al fin de la semana* and *Sabado gigante* and special musical shows on the Spanish-language television networks also reach a broad audience.[22] According to one report, female artists—including ranchera singers Ana Gabriel, Aida Cuevas, and, more recently, Nydia Rojas and Graciela Beltrán—currently contribute significantly to the Mexican music industry (Burr 1996).

Although my informant does not frequent bars, nightclubs, dance halls, or even restaurants, she remains an avid consumer of ranchera music via Spanish-language radio stations, Spanish-language television programs, compact discs, and occasionally a concert.[23] Having spent most of her adult life in the United States, she finds the ranchera is one way she stays connected to her Mexican roots.

This brief profile suggests some of the ways women engage the ranchera as consumers: to give expression to and help them cope with, confront, and even remember their concerns, desires, losses, disappointments, and joys. Further study would surely expand our understanding of the strategies women employ as consumers of the ranchera and, in turn, show how women consumers affect the marketing strategies of ranchera music.

CONCLUSION

Clearly, the ranchera is a sophisticated art form that requires equally sophisticated analytical tools to avoid essentialist explications. Its use of emotional excess is evidence of its melodramatic form rather than, as some have claimed, of an essential, and in some cases negative, attribute of Mexican culture and identity. Further, as a melodramatic form, the ranchera provides a discursive space for contemplating personal, national, and global crises or anxieties in culturally appropriate ways. An examination of the situated use of the ranchera—that is, the performance context—enables more specificity regarding issues of class, gender, ethnicity, and nationality.

As this brief discussion of women as performers, producers, and consumers of the ranchera suggests, women have increasingly taken what was once a predominantly male expressive form to give expression to their own desires, needs, and experiences. Indeed, women have employed the ranchera to expand that which is deemed culturally appropriate for both women and men. Therefore, the ranchera may speak to women's quotidian struggles in contemporary Greater Mexico even as it retains its nationalist, pastoral sensibility. The point is that only in and through situated renderings can we see displayed, and therefore understand, certain cultural preoccupations expressed in the rancheras.

NOTES

1. An earlier version of this essay was presented at the 1998 NACCS conference in Mexico City. I wish to thank Pat Zavella, Aída Hurtado, Norma Klahn, Russell Rodríguez, and Gabriela Arredondo for their thoughtful critiques and suggestions on earlier drafts of this essay. Although I alone am responsible for all claims made in this paper, I recognize that my understanding of the ranchera has been significantly enriched by the numerous conversations I had with close friends and family members over the years, in particular, Mrs. E. Nájera, Alicia, Elena, and John Nájera, Becky Silva, Rosita Ruíz, and Josie Méndez Negrete, and my two mariachi friends, Laura Sobrino and Russell Rodríguez. Unless otherwise noted, all translations are mine.

2. The majority of the studies focus on the historical roots of the ranchera, offering various definitions and trajectories (Grial 1973; Geijerstam 1976; Mayer-Serra 1941; Reuter 1983; Saldivar 1934). Among the most complete studies are those offered by Mendoza (1988 [1961]), Garrido (1974), and Moreno Rivas (1989). Interpretative studies of the ranchera are provided by Fogelquist (1975), Gradante (1982, 1983), Lamas (1978), and Monsiváis (1977a, 1977b). Peña (1985) also offers important insights on the ranchera in his work on conjunto music.

3. However, see also Broyles-Gonzalez (2002).

4. I had the opportunity to interview Lydia Mendoza in 1984 in Houston when I was conducting fieldwork for the Folk Art and Texas Agricultural Heritage Project sponsored by the Texas Department of Agriculture.

5. Indeed, claiming that "country music, if you listen, is filled with the sounds of Mexico," Lewis notes the influences of the ranchera song on country music (1993, 94).

6. For a good discussion of the concept of lo ranchero in English, see Peña (1985, 10–12).

7. Mexican musiciologist Garrido (1974, 70) explains that the term canción ranchera did not emerge until the twentieth century, when this type of music became associated with Mexican sound film.

8. In her insightful work on the blues and feminism, Angela Davis makes a similar claim, stating, "The realism of the blues does not confine us to literal interpretations. On the contrary, blues contain many layers of meanings and are often astounding in their complexity and profundity" (1998, 24).

9. For a similar argument regarding country music, see Kathleen Stewart (1993).

10. Personal interview conducted by author, July 30, 1984, Houston.

11. For discussions of the Mexican movie industry, see Reyes (1988) and Mora (1982). For a gender analysis of the charro in Mexican films, see Nájera-Ramírez (1994).

12. Many laborers migrate without their children and spouse to reduce the expense of re-

location and to reduce the risk to the family. Typically, the laborer will send remittances to the family until they have accumulated sufficient resources to reunite. Studies indicate, however, that instead of permanent reunification, families are increasingly constructing binational relations (see, for example, Zavella 1997 and Rouse 1992).

13. Juan Gabriel's songs commonly avoid the use of gendered pronouns, making them subject to a range of uses and interpretations; that is, he doesn't privilege a heterosexual male point of view. Yarbo-Bejarano (1997) makes a similar point in her discussion of Chabela Vargas.

14. The original verse reads as follows:

De mis ojos está brotando llanto
a mis años estoy enamorado
tengo el pelo completamente blanco
pero voy a sacar juventud de mi pasado
Y te voy a enseñar a querer
porque tu no has querido
ya verás lo que vas a aprender
cuando vivas conmigo

From my eyes a cry is erupting
At my (old) age, I am in love
My hair is completely white
But I'm going to extract youth from my past
And I'm going to teach you to love
because you have not yet loved
you'll see how much you'll learn
when you live with me

15. Even when women possess very deep, low voices, as does Lucha Villa, the singers are recognized as female.

16. The importance of the dynamics of performance has been taken up by scholars in numerous fields, including anthropology, folklore, ethnomusicology, and cultural studies. I have been particularly influenced by the "performance-oriented" approach to folkloristics as developed by Américo Paredes and Richard Bauman. Paredes's work on the subversive uses of performance by minorities in ethnographic encounters has been especially important in my own work.

17. This line makes reference to the classic ranchera song "Alla en el rancho grande," which portrays the *rancherita* (little country gal) as one who gladly offers to sew clothing for her cowboy.

18. The charro rule book dictates the appropriate costume for all charreada participants.

19. According to mariachi musician Russell Rodriguez, ranchera singers often change costumes several times during a performance.

20. I thank Russell Rodriguez for reminding me of this point.

21. For two provocative discussions of Irma Serrano, please see Monsiváis (1977a [1994]) and Castillo (1998).

22. Onda Max features interviews with and musical videos of Latin singers, including ranchera singers. Ranchera singers are also sometimes featured on talk shows such as *Cristina* and morning shows like *Despierta América*.

23. Personal interview conducted by author, November and December 1998, Santa Cruz, CA.

WORKS CITED

Adorno, Theodor. 1976. *Introduction to the Sociology of Music.* New York: Seabury Press.

Bauman, Richard, and Charles Briggs. 1990. "Poetics and Performance as Critical Perspectives on Language and Social Life." *Annual Review of Anthropology* 19: 59–88.

Brooks, Peter. 1976. *The Melodramatic Imagination: Balzac, Henry James, Melodrama, and the Mode of Excess.* New Haven: Yale University Press.

Broyles-Gonzalez, Yolanda. 2002. "Ranchera Music(s) and the Legendary Lydia Mendoza: Performing Social Location and Relations." In *Chicana Traditions: Continuity and Change,* ed. Norma Cantú and Olga Nájera-Ramírez. Champagne: University of Illinois Press.

Burr, Ramiro. 1996. "Women Helping Drive Thriving Mexican Market." *Billboard* 108(33): 1 (3 pages).

Castillo, Debra A. 1998. *Easy Women: Sex and Gender in Modern Mexican Fiction.* Minneapolis: University of Minnesota Press.

Davis, Angela Y. 1998. *Blues Legacies and Black Feminism.* New York: Pantheon Books.

Fogelquist, Mark. 1975. "Rhythm and Form in the Contemporary Son Jalisciense." Master's thesis, UCLA.

Garrido, Juan S. 1974. *Historia de la música popular de México.* México City: Editorial Extemporaneos.

Geijerstam, Claes. 1976. *Popular Music in México.* Albuquerque: University of New México Press.

Gledhill, Christine. 1987. Introduction. Pp. 1–39 in *Home Is Where the Heart Is: Studies in Melodrama and the Woman's Film,* ed. Christine Gledhill. London: BFI.

Gradante, William. 1982. "El Hijo del Pueblo: José Alfredo Jimenez and the Mexican Canción Ranchera." *Latin American Music Review* 3(1): 36–59.

———. 1983. "Mexican Popular Music at Mid-Century: The Role of José Alfredo Jimenez and the Canción Ranchera." *Studies in Latin American Popular Culture* 2: 99–114.

Grial, Hugo de. 1973. *Músicos mexicanos.* México City: Editorial Diana.

Guillermoprieto, Alma. 1992. "Serenading the Future." *New Yorker Magazine* (November 9): 96–104.

Kaplan, E. Ann. 1992. *Motherhood and Representation: The Mother in Popular Culture and Melodrama.* New York: Routledge.

Lamas, Marta. 1978. "De abandonada a leona: La imagen de la mujer en la canción ranchera." *Fem* 2(6): 20–28.

Landy, Marcia. 1991. Introduction. Pp. 13–30 in *Imitations of Life: A Reader on Film and Television Melodrama,* ed. Marcia Landy. Detroit: Wayne State University Press.

Lewis, George H. 1993. "Mexican Musical Influences on Country Songs and Styles." Pp.

94–101 in *All That Glitters: Country Music in America,* ed. George Lewis. Bowling
Green, OH: Bowling Green University Popular Press.

López, Ana. 1991. "Celluloid Tears: Melodrama in the 'Old' Mexican Cinema." *Iris* 13:
29–51.

Mayer-Serra, Otto. 1941. *Panorama de la música Mexicana desde la independencia hasta
la actualidad.* México City: El Colegio de México.

Mendoza, Vicente T. 1988 [1961]. *La canción mexicana.* México City: Fondo de Cultura
Económica.

Monsiváis, Carlos. 1992. "Las mitologias del cine mexicano." *Intermedios* 2 (June–July):
12–23.

———. 1994. "Se sufre, pero se aprende (el melodrama y las reglas de la falta de limites)."
Pp. 99–224 in *A través del espejo: El cine mexicano y su público,* ed. Carlos Monsi-
váis and Carlos Bonfil. México City: Ediciones el Milagro, Instituto Mexicano de
Cinematografia.

———. 1977a [1994]. "Irma Serrano: Entre apariciones de la venus de fuego." Pp. 297–318
in *Amor perdido.* México City: Ediciones Era.

———. 1977b [1994]. "José Alfredo Jiménez: No vengo a pedir lectores (Se repite el disco
por mi puritita gana)." Pp. 87–97 in *Amor perdido.* México City: Ediciones Era.

Mora, Carlos. 1982. *Mexican Cinema.* Berkeley: University of California Press.

Moreno Rivas, Yolanda. 1989. *Historia de la música popular mexicana.* México City:
Alianza Editorial Mexicana, Consejo Nacional para la Cultura y las Artes.

Nájera-Ramírez, Olga. 1994. "Engendering Nationalism: Identity, Discourse, and the
Mexican Charro." *Anthropological Quarterly* 67(1): 1–14.

Paredes, Américo. 1977. "On Ethnographic Work among Minorities: A Folklorist's Perspective." *New Scholar* 6: 1–32.

———. 1982. "Folklore, Lo Mexicano and Proverbs." *Aztlán* 13: 1–11.

Peña, Manuel. 1985. *The Texas-Mexican Conjunto: History of a Working-class Music.*
Austin: University of Texas.

Podalsky, Laura. 1993. "Disjointed Frames: Melodrama, Nationalism and Representation
in 1940s México." *Studies in Latin American Popular Culture* 12: 57–73.

Reuter, Jas. 1983. *La música popular de México: Origen e historia de la música que canta
y toca el pueblo mexicano.* México City: Panorama Editorial.

Reyes, Aurelio de los. 1988. *Medio siglo de cine mexicano (1896–1947).* México City:
Editorial Trillas.

Rouse, Roger. 1992. "Making Sense of Settlement: Class Transformation, Cultural Struggle, and Transnationalism among Mexican Migrants in the United States." *Annals
of the New York Academy of Sciences* 645:25–82.

Saldivar, Gabriel. 1934. *Historia de la música en México.* México City: Secretaría de Edu-
cación Pública.

Stewart, Kathleen. 1993. "Engendering Narratives of Lament in Country Music." Pp.
221–25 in *All That Glitters: Country Music in America,* ed. George Lewis. Bowling
Green, OH: Bowling Green University Popular Press.

Valdez, Avelardo, and Jeffrey A. Halley. 1996. "Gender in the Culture of Mexican American Conjunto Music." *Gender and Society* 10(2): 148–67.

Williams, Linda. 1991. "Film Bodies: Gender, Genre and Excess." *Film Quarterly* 44 (4): 3–13.

Yarbo-Bejarano, Yvonne. 1997. "Crossing the Border with Chabela Vargas: A Chicana Femme's Tribute." Pp. 33–43 in *Sex and Sexuality in Latin America*, ed. Daniel Balderston and Donna J. Guy. New York: New York University Press.

Zavella, Patricia. 1997. "The Tables Are Turned: Immigration, Poverty, and Social Conflict in California Communities." Pp. 136–61 in *Immigrants Out! The New Nativism and the Anti-Immigrant Impulse in the United States*, ed. Juan F. Perea. New York: New York University Press.

. . . Y volver a sufrir: Nuevos acercamientos al melodrama

JOSÉ MANUEL VALENZUELA ARCE

• • • • •

Qué triste agonía

Tener que olvidarte,

Queriéndote así.

Qué suerte la mía,

Después de una pena

Volver a sufrir.

Qué triste agonía

Después de caído, volver a caer.

Qué suerte la mía,

Estar tan perdido y volver a perder.

—José Alfredo Jiménez

El artículo de Olga Nájera-Ramírez, "Unruly Passions: Poetics, Performance, and Gender in the Ranchera Song," ofrece una sugerente reflexión sobre la necesidad de construir nuevos acercamientos a la interpretación de la canción popular. La autora analiza a la canción ranchera como forma musical expresiva íntimamente asociada con la identidad cultural mexicana en ambos lados de la frontera México-Estados Unidos. Nájera analiza lo mexicano y a la mexicanidad a partir de la canción ranchera como recurso interpretativo de las formas en que la cultura mexicana es percibida, construída y representada. Pero Nájera va más allá e incursiona en el campo de escenificación de las pasiones desbordadas, indómitas y desenfrenadas que dan vida a la canción ranchera. Pasiones que al cantarse demarcan auto-definiciones y fortalecen identificaciones que son formas de explorar nuestros "piensos" y "sentires."

Para ello, Nájera construye dos ejes analíticos. En el primero de ellos recupera los estudios recientes del melodrama y el "performance" para sostener que la canción ranchera *encuerpa* una poética que resiste y se niega a las interpretaciones facilistas o esencialistas. Nájera, al igual que otros autores y autoras, define a la canción ranchera como una forma expresiva inscrita en el melodrama, y a éste como un espacio discursivo caracterizado por la intensidad de emociones, donde se pueden presentar aspectos de profundo interés social. En segundo término explora diferentes formas desde las cuales las mujeres han utilizado a las rancheras como espacios dentro de los cuales pueden realizar intervenciones feministas. De esta manera, Nájera logra una interpretación de género y feminista de las canciones rancheras, presentando algunas ideas concluyentes y abriendo preguntas que podrían aclararse en trabajos más amplios que continúen esta línea analítica.

DESPUÉS DE UNA PENA VOLVER A SUFRIR

Algunos de los aspectos centrales definidos por Nájera hacen explícita la posibilidad de analizar a la canción ranchera como forma de melodrama. Debido a la intensa expresión de emociones que conlleva, y destaca, puede ser favorablemente comparada con "el blues" y la música country-western. A Nájera no le interesa el regodeo en los excesos del melodrama sino su integración en la conformación de significados sociales y en la delimitación de relaciones de resistencia. Siguiendo a Landy, dice que adicionalmente al énfasis en la sensibilidad y el sentimiento, destacan otras características del melodrama incluida la dicotomización del mundo, sus mecanismos, exaltación de los conflictos personales y la internalización de los conflictos sociales.

La autora no sucumbe a la tentación de sobreponderar los elementos que definen formas de resistencia en la canción ranchera, sino que interpreta sus diversos usos sociales, entre los cuales también se encuentran importantes elementos que participan en el reforzamiento de la ideología política y patriarcal dominante. Por ello, Nájera sostiene la importancia de considerar a las canciones rancheras como melodramas, pues podría resultar productivo aproximarse a ellas como espacios discursivos en los cuales tópicos que poseen un fuerte peso emocional pueden ser expresados a través de formas culturales apropiadas.

Otro de los elementos destacados por la antropóloga de UC Santa Cruz, es que las rancheras pueden ser consideradas como sitios culturalmente sancionados en los cuales las ideas y valores de una comunidad no son meramente desplegadas, sino, más importante aún, transmitidas, producidas, reproducidas y contestadas. Las canciones rancheras lejos der ser expresiones transparentes de la gente simple, son formas complejas plagadas de contradicciones. Como otras formas melodramáticas, la canción ranchera se relaciona de forma abigarrada con los conflictos sociales, revelando, de manera directa o indirecta, conflictos de clase, de género y generacionales.

Nájera incursiona en la exploración de formas interpretativas que permitan considerar la participación de la mujer en la escenificación, producción y consumo de la canción ranchera como una intervención feminista. Por ello destaca que, participando activamente en lo que fue predominantemente un género masculino, la mujer ha sido capaz de emplear a la canción ranchera para sus propios propósitos, algunas veces destacando su subordinación, algunas veces como respuesta o confrontación a esa subordinación, pero siempre llamando la atención a sus intereses, deseos, experiencias y necesidades. A partir de los elementos señalados, la autora considera que mediante la manipulación del estilo del texto, su consumo y su performance la mujer utiliza a la canción ranchera para cambiar, transgredir o cuestionar aspectos importantes constitutivos de la reproducción de la desigualdad de género que prevalecen en la sociedad mexicana.

Y A LLORAR POR LOS MISMOS ERRORES

El melodrama en México se construye en los intersticios de la ruralidad urbanizada y su recreación en los medios masivos de comunicación, especialmente el cine y luego la televisión. Las masas campesinas expulsadas del campo con la Revolución de principios del Siglo XX y los éxodos subsiguientes asociados a la miseria y el despojo, conformaron importantes adaptaciones, reterritorializaciones y recreaciones culturales de formas expresivas y de sentido de la vida campesina en los nuevos contextos urbanos no menos plagados de abusos e injusticias. Los cantos eran ámbitos evocativos que magnificaban la pérdida, el dolor, la desgracia, al mismo tiempo que registraban estallidos de júbilo y dolor que quedaban como constancia estruendosa del aferramiento a identidades individuales y colectivas gritadas con el pecho abierto, o como registro desgarrado que consigna el valor de una palabra empeñada avalada por las fuerzas divinas: "verdad de dios."

La canción ranchera se deplegó en los años veinte, una vez concluido el levantamiento revolucionario, cuando México experimentaba fuertes procesos de migración del campo a las ciudades. Evocando una sensibilidad rural, la canción ranchera expresaba la tirisia por el terruño, la nostalgia provinciana, la evocación del pasado evanescente y amenazado por un presente que desestructuraba las redes sociales, los afectos entrañables y las certezas cotidianas. De esta manera, la canción ranchera participó en los campos simbólicos desde donde se conformaron anclajes entre la nueva realidad urbana y los mundos bucólicos que migraron a las ciudades.

En este escenario límite marcado por la desestructuración social y la irrupción de los sectores populares urbanos, cobró fuerza el melodrama que escenifica los afectos, teatraliza las emociones, y caricaturiza los sentimientos. El melodrama es un recurso popular contrastante con el cuidado de las formas aprendidas en manuales de urbanidad y buenas maneras por las clases altas, idea destacada por Jesús Martín Barbero (1991).

El melodrama había surgido en las postrimerías del siglo XVIII en Europa como espectáculo popular que era más y menos que un teatro, como refiere Martín Barbero, quien añade que éste tomó la forma de espectáculos de ferias, así como temas y relatos de la literatura oral, permitiendo la entrada del pueblo y sus emociones en la escenografía donde el melodrama es el "espejo de una conciencia colectiva." En México, el melodrama irrumpió con una carga plagada de imágenes bucólicas y de símbolos que expresaban los intentos fallidos por mantener costumbres y relaciones que se desdibujaban en los nuevos escenarios urbanos. Por ello, para confrontar estas realidades evanescentes e inaprehensibles, los sectores populares tuvieron que atribuirles rasgos magnificados.

Al igual que otras formas de expresión popular como los corridos, en el melodrama se dicotomizan los campos morales y los criterios que separan a los buenos de los malos. De la misma manera, los actores se conforman desde ámbitos desbordados de pasión, de amores y odios definidos, de admiración o desdén, de lealtad o traición. En el melodrama los mundos afectivos traspasan los ámbitos domésticos para escenificarse en los espacios públicos y exponerse sin ambajes a las miradas de los otros. Frente a esos públicos difusos, se exhibe sin pudor el alma herida, el corazón destrozado o las trizas del proyecto personal. También se señala a los responsables y a las responsables del dolor, el traidor o la traidora que sin compasión han propinado el golpe o la cuchillada trapera. De igual forma, en el canto se construyen los rasgos sublimados de la mujer (o el hombre) productoras del exceso amoroso.

Hemos destacado que la canción ranchera cobra significado en los ámbitos donde se definen las culturas populares de nuestro país. Es dentro del campo de producción de sentidos populares donde se posibilita una forma de expresión reiteradamente definida desde el campo expresivo de los de abajo, de los pobres, de los que están afuera, de los carentes de tronos y reinas, de los detractores vergonzantes del *dinero maldito que nada vale,* de los que asumen con orgullo el haber nacido *en el barrio más humilde* y de quienes encuentran en la dignificación de la pobreza una ética que deviene refrendo lúdico frente a las carencias: *voy camino de la vida, muy feliz con mi pobreza.* En pocas palabras, la cultura popular y la canción ranchera permiten identificar las fronteras entre *los hijos del pueblo* y aquellos que pertenecen a la *falsa sociedad.*

Sin embargo, componentes centrales de las culturas populares del México postrevolucionario, se recrean en las articulaciones de los medios masivos de comunicación y la nueva experiencia social, por ello Martín Barbero sitúa al melodrama "en el vértice mismo del proceso que lleva de lo popular a lo masivo: lugar de llegada de una memoria narrativa y gestual populares y lugar de emergencia de una escena de masa, esto es, donde lo popular comienza a ser objeto de una operación de borradura de las fronteras que arranca con la constitución de un discurso homogéneo y una imagen unificada de lo popular, primera figura de la masa" (1991, 125).[1]

En México, el melodrama, como vértice de lo popular y lo masivo, encontró en la canción ranchera una de sus formas expresivas privilegiadas, y Pedro Infante, Jorge Negrete, Lucha Reyes, Lola Beltrán, Javier Solis, Lucha Villa, Cuco Sánchez y José Alfredo Jiménez, son algunos de sus intérpretes consagrados.

En su análisis de la canción ranchera, Olga Nájera se centra en la obra del cantante y compositor guanajuatense José Alfredo Jiménez, sin duda una de las figuras imprescindibles entre aquellos y aquellas que le dieron relieve. José Alfredo Jiménez, llamado por Carlos Monsiváis (1998) "el vocero de la lírica cantinera," "criatura de la tradición" y "poeta de la desolación marginal." La lluvia de imágenes que Monsiváis ofrece sobre José Alfredo definen el conjunto de anclajes que el cantor conforma con "el pueblo." Para Monsiváis, José Alfredo "no es estrictamente 'producto de una época,' así lo haga posible la industria del nacionalismo cultural y así dependa de lo que una época dicta: la invensión de un pueblo y de un estilo nacional. Pero José Alfredo trasciende su ámbito formativo y su 'Mexicanidad,' aunque lo constituya, es la más de las veces elemento decorativo, y no es obstáculo ni para la fuerza de sus canciones ni para su éxito en el mundo de habla hispana" (13).

Coincido con Monsiváis en que José Alfredo no cuestiona valores fundamentales de su medio. Su filosofía popular y sus canciones son elementos de mediación con las experiencias cotidianas de millones de mexicanos a quienes les permite convertirse en protagonistas de las canciones, participar en sus historias, dolerse de sus tragedias y descalabros emocionales, festinar sus victorias amorosas pensando en la propia biografía sentimental, irrumpir con gritos que certifican que cantamos nuestra propia historia y le añadimos los complementos que la hacen aún más nuestra.

Desde la perspectiva monsivaisiana, José Alfredo es un antihéroe marginal que "vive en la mitología del sedentarismo y el vértigo": "borracheras, destino implacable, adoración sin límites a la pérfida, autocompasión asumida con el placer del triunfo . . ." uno es más verdadero en la derrota: "Es mi orgullo haber nacido en el barrio más humilde, alejado del bullicio de la falsa sociedad," por ello, afirma Monsiváis que en la antiheroicidad marginal de José Alfredo: "la pobreza es la cima de los valores morales," con sus cantores populares imprescindibles: Tomás Méndez, Cuco Sánchez, José Alfredo Jiménez, Rubén Fuentes, continuadores de la tradición de Tata Nacho, Manuel Esperón y Chucho Monge. De esta manera, las canciones rancheras, son la continuación temática del melodrama de "La época de oro" del cine mexicano (Monsiváis 1998).[2]

PORQUE QUIERAS O NO, YO SOY TU DUEÑO

No obstante la fuerte misoginia que atraviesa a la canción ranchera, como a casi todos los géneros producidos por sociedades patriarcales, la ausencia de espacios propios posibilita que las mujeres se apropien de las canciones dotándolas de componentes híbridos desde los cuales se diluyen las fronteras donde se atrincheraba la exclusividad de la experiencia masculina. Las mujeres cantan las mismas canciones deconstruyendo los significados originales, pero manteniendo su carga emotiva, sus escenarios sórdidos, sus ayes dolorosos y sus arrebatos de júbilo.

La irrupción de la mujer en el discurso masculino conculca los sentidos originales posibilitando la transgresión de las atmósferas donde ella era sólo el objeto de la rabia, la pasión, el desdén o el amor del hombre. Esta condición también es destacada por Monsiváis: "Por costumbre, las cantantes de ranchero son por así decirlo impersonales, y se apoderan del espíritu masculino para cantarle a la mancornadora, a la prófuga, al amor de la vida. Nadie piensa siquiera en otras inclinaciones sexuales, el machismo no lo permitiría. Y por eso, las cantantes integran la perspectiva del hombre y las destrezas de la mujer" (1998, 36).

Dentro de este campo transgresor destacan las mujeres bravías, mujeres temperamentales que se atreven a cantar sin inhibiciones sus deseos, pesares y pasiones. También pregonan cantos de amor y desamor, donde el hombre deviene sujeto-objeto de amor y del deseo femenino. Los papeles se invierten, las mujeres ganan la voz. Algunas de las cantantes de rancheras y embajadoras del dolor, el gozo y el deseo femenino son Lucha Reyes, Lola Beltrán, Lucha Villa, Amalia Mendoza, Chavela Vargas. Ellas son pioneras de nuevos campos expresivos donde las mujeres toman la palabra y a quienes se unirán nuevas voces y propuestas que presentarán sin ambages propuestas disruptoras a las perspectivas que se han desplegado al amparo del machismo. Entre ellas podemos mencionar a Irma Serrano, Paquita la del Barrio, Guadalupe D'alessio, Beatriz Adriana, Aida Cuevas, Eugenia León o Guadalupe Pineda.

PORQUE ESTAMOS UNIDOS DEL ALMA, QUIÉN SABE HASTA CUANDO

A partir de los elementos considerados, podemos recuperar el trabajo de Nájera para otorgarle la importancia que posee. La perspectiva que la autora ofrece cobra relevancia al desarrollar una línea interpretativa que busca decodificar la lógica desde la cual los discursos masculinos homogeneizantes y excluyentes reproducen formas de relación conformadas desde la desigualdad. Esta condición, sin embargo, no es exclusiva de la canción ranchera sino que atraviesa el conjunto de discursos sobre los que se apoyan los poderes patriarcales. En otro trabajo hemos mostrado cómo se ha construido la invisibilización de las mujeres en los discursos sobre la nación mexicana (Valenzuela Arce 1999).

La representación subordinada de las mujeres también se encuentra en otras narrativas populares como el corrido, donde la lógica de los y las participantes mantiene una fuerte diferenciación de género y lo común es que la mujer quede adscrita en las imágenes de madre abnegada, mujer sublimada, fatal, coqueta o traidora. En ellos se destaca la ausencia de protagonismo femenino. La otra dimensión que se acentúa en los corridos es la imagen femenina como contravalor o parámetro de contraste donde cobran fuerza las cualidades masculinas, mientras que la condición femenina sólo adquiere centralidad en el dolor, el sufrimiento o en la abnegación; condiciones que definen una posición social que le expropia el *ser para sí misma* o para delimitar su valor en la condición del *ser para otro*.

Sin embargo, en la nueva producción corridística también encontramos diversos corridos donde las mujeres adquieren papeles protagónicos, especialmente desde los campos ilegítimos del narcotráfico, o desde la constancia que registra la participación femenina en los movimientos sociales (Valenzuela Arce 1998, 2000; Herrera Sobek 1990).

La participación protagónica de las mujeres en los escenarios dominados por los hombres, y la deconstrucción de los textos masculinos como elementos que permitan la presencia activa de las mujeres es uno de los ejes presentes en trabajos como el que realiza Olga Nájera. En ellos interesa no sólo comprender las transgresiones a las sintaxis narrativa, sino trabajar las articulaciones entre texto y contexto, redefinir la performatividad de los discursos y decodificar los campos discursivos que reproducen y fortalecen la desigualdad. Por ello, siguiendo a Bauman y Briggs, Nájera analiza las posibilidades de apropiación de la canción ranchera por parte de las mujeres; sus posibilidades de descontextualizarla y recontextualizarla, como recurso de control mediante el cual se reposicionan frente a la perspectiva patriarcal que les subyace. Al apropiárselas, las mujeres recrean las canciones rancheras y las cargan con nuevos significados transgrediendo su dimensión masculinizada, excluyente y machista. Es a partir de estos elementos que Nájera sostiene que estas apropiaciones y recreaciones (performances) le permiten a la mujer la oportunidad de tomar el control del texto para convertirlo en su propio mensaje subversivo.

NOTAS

1. Barbero afirma que, "como en las plazas de mercado, en el melodrama está todo revuelto, las estructuras sociales con las del sentimiento, mucho de lo que somos—machistas, fatalistas, supersticiosos—y de lo que soñamos ser, el robo de la identidad, la nostalgia y la rabia. En forma de tango o de telenovela, de cine mexicano o de crónica roja el melodrama trabaja en estas tierras una veta profunda de nuestro imaginario colectivo, y no hay acceso a la memoria histórica ni proyección posible del futuro que no pase por el imaginario" (243).

2. El desarrollo de esta idea corresponde a Carlos Monsiváis.

OBRAS CITADAS

Herrera Sobek, María. 1990. *The Mexican Corrido: A Feminist Analysis.* Bloomington: Indiana University Press.

Martín Barbero, Jesús. 1991. *De los medios a las mediaciones: Comunicación, cultura y hegemonía.* México City: Editorial Gustavo Gili.

Monsiváis, Carlos. 1998. "José Alfredo Jiménez: Les diré que llegué de un mundo raro."

Pp. 13–38 en *Y sigue siendo el rey: Homenaje a José Alfredo Jiménez,* ed. Carlos Monsiváis y Emiliano Gironella Parra. México City: Fundación Cultural Artención.

Valenzuela Arce, José Manuel. 1998. *Nuestros piensos: Culturas populares en la frontera México-Estados Unidos.* México City: CONACULTA.

———. 1999. *Impecable y diamantina, la deconstrucción del discurso nacional.* Guadalajara, México: ITESO, El Colegio de la Frontera Norte.

———. 2000. *Jefe de jefes: Corridos y narcocultura en México.* México City: Raya en el Agua y Plaza y Janés.

TRANSLATION OF RESPONSE TO CHAPTER SIX

. . . And to Suffer Again: New Approaches to Melodrama

JOSÉ MANUEL VALENZUELA ARCE

Translated by Rebecca M. Gámez

• • • • •

> What sad agony
> To have to forget you,
> Loving you this way.
> What luck I have,
> After such pain
> To suffer again.
> What sad agony
> Having fallen,
> To fall again.
> What luck I have,
> To be so lost
> And to lose again.
> —José Alfredo Jiménez

Olga Nájera-Ramírez's essay "Unruly Passions: Poetics, Performance, and Gender in the Ranchera Song" offers a suggestive reflection about the need to construct new approaches to the interpretation of popular music. The author analyzes the *ranchera* song as an expressive musical form intimately associated with Mexican cultural identity on both sides of the Mexican-U.S. border. Nájera interprets what is "Mexican" and "Mexicanness" beginning with the ranchera song as an interpretive resource for the forms in which Mexican culture is perceived, constructed, and represented. But she goes beyond that and enters into the field of performance of the overflowing, untamable, and unbridled passions that give life to the ranchera song. Passions that, on being sung, demarcate self-definitions and fortify identifications, which are ways to explore our "thoughts" and "feelings."

For that reason, Nájera constructs two crucial analytical points. First, she recovers recent studies of melodrama and performance to assert that the ranchera song *embodies* a poetic that resists and denies facile and essentialist interpretations. Like other authors, she defines the ranchera song as an expressive form inscribed in melodrama, and the latter as a discursive space characterized by intense emotions where aspects of profound social interest can be presented. Second, she explores different ways women have utilized rancheras as spaces within which they can realize feminist interventions. In this way, Nájera produces a gendered and feminist interpretation of rancheras, presenting some conclusive ideas and putting forth questions that could be clarified in more substantial works that continue this line of analysis.

AFTER SUCH PAIN TO SUFFER AGAIN

Some of the central aspects defined by Nájera make explicit the possibility of analyzing the ranchera song as a form of melodrama. She notes that due to the ranchera's intense expression of emotions, it can be favorably compared with blues and country western music. She is not interested in pleasure in the excesses of melodrama but its integration into the construction of social meanings and in the delimitation of relationships of resistance. Following Landy, she says that in addition to the emphasis on sensitivity and feeling, rancheras highlight other characteristics of melodrama, including the dichotomization of the world, its mechanisms, the exaltation of personal conflicts, and the internalization of social conflicts.

The author does not succumb to the temptation to overexamine the elements that define forms of resistance in rancheras; rather, she interprets their diverse social uses, among which can also be found important elements that reinforce the dominant political and patriarchal ideology. For that reason, Nájera maintains the importance of considering rancheras as melodramas, because it can be productive to approach them as discursive spaces in which topics that possess strong emotional weight can be expressed through appropriated cultural forms.

Another of the elements highlighted by the University of California at Santa Cruz anthropologist is that rancheras can be considered culturally sanctioned sites in which the ideas and values of a community are not merely shown but, even more important, transmitted, produced, reproduced, and contested. Rancheras, far from being transparent expressions of a simple people, are complex forms plagued by contradictions. Like other melodramatic forms, the ranchera song is related in a variegated manner to social conflicts, revealing, direct and indirectly, conflicts of class, gender, and generations.

Nájera enters into the exploration of interpretive forms that allows one to consider the participation of women in the performance, composing, and consumption of rancheras as a feminist intervention. To do so she notes that by participating actively in what was predominantly a masculine genre, women have been able to employ the ranchera song for their own purposes, sometimes emphasizing their subordination, but always calling attention to their interests, desires, experiences, and needs. Taking into consideration the indicated elements, the author believes that through the manipulation of the style of the text, its consumption, and performance, women utilize rancheras to change, transgress, or question important aspects constitutive of the reproduction of the gender inequality that prevails in Mexican society.

AND TO CRY OVER THE SAME MISTAKES

Melodrama in Mexico is constructed in the interstices of urbanized rurality and its recreation in mass communication, especially cinema and later television. The *campesino* masses expelled from the countryside with the Revolution at the beginning of the twentieth century, and the subsequent exoduses associated with misery and dispossession, formed important cultural adaptations, reterritorializations, and recreations of expressive forms and of campesino ways of life in new urban contexts no less plagued by abuses and injustices.[1] The songs were evocative spaces that magnified loss, pain, and misfortune. At the same time, they registered bursts of jubilation and pain that remained as thunderous proof, characterized by open-hearted shouts, of people's insistence on clinging to individual and collective identities, or as a brazen chronicle that assigns value to a compelling word endorsed by divine forces: "God's truth."

The ranchera song spread in the 1920s, once the revolutionary uprising was concluded, when Mexico experienced strong patterns of migration from the country to the cities. Evoking a rural sensibility, rancheras expressed the hostility of the land, provincial nostalgia, and the evocation of a vanishing and threatened past by a present that dismantled social networks, beloved attachments, and quotidian truths. In this way, rancheras participated in the symbolic fields that anchored the new urban reality to the bucolic worlds that migrated to the cities.

On this limited stage marked by social fragmentation and the eruption of popular urban sectors, melodrama gained strength as it performed affections, dramatized emotions, and caricatured feelings. Melodrama is a popular resource compared with the attention of forms learned by the upper classes in manuals of urbanity and good manners, an idea put forward by Jesús Martín Barbero (1993).

Melodrama had emerged in the final stages of the eighteenth century in Europe as a popular spectacle that was more or less theater, according to Martín Barbero, who adds that it took the form of such spectacles as fairs, as well as the themes and tales of oral literature, which allowed people and their emotions to enter onto the stage where melodrama is "the mirror of a collective conscience" (1993). In Mexico, melodrama burst in charged with bucolic images and with symbols that expressed the failed attempts to maintain customs and relationships that became blurred in new urban settings. Because of this, and to confront these vanishing and unattainable realities, popular sectors had to attribute exaggerated traits to them.

Just as in other forms of popular expression, such as *corridos*, moral camps and the criteria that separate the good from the bad became dichotomized in melodrama. In the same way, the actors derive from overflowing boundaries of passion, of definitive loves and hates, of admiration or disdain, of loyalty or betrayal. In melodrama, affective worlds break through domestic spheres to be performed in public spaces and are revealed directly to the view of others. Before those diffuse publics, the wounded soul, the broken heart, or the shattered dream are shamelessly exposed. Also revealed are the men and women responsible for the pain, the traitor and traitoress who have coldly delivered the blow or ragged slash. In the same way, the sublimated traits of the woman (or man) producing the amorous excess are constructed through the song.

I have pointed out that the ranchera song gains meaning in the spheres where our country's popular cultures are defined. It is within the field of production of popular meanings that forms of expression are made possible and are repeatedly defined from the expressive field of those from below: of the poor; of those outside; of those lacking thrones and queens; of the shameful detractors of *damn worthless money*; of those who assume with pride having been born *in the most humble barrio;* and of those who dignify poverty with an ethic that evolves into ludic decree in the face of the deprivation: *I travel through life, very happy with my poverty.* In short, popular culture and rancheras allow us to identify the borders between *the children of the people* and those who belong to *false society.*

Nevertheless, central components of the popular cultures of postrevolutionary Mexico are recreated in the articulations of mass communication and new social experience. Consequently, Martín Barbero situates melodrama "at the turning point of the process which moved from the popular to the mass. Melodrama provided a point of arrival for the narrative memory and gestural forms of popular culture and the point of emergence of the dramatization of mass culture. That is, melodrama is where the popular begins to be object of a process that erases local cultural frontiers, a process that takes off with the constitution of a homogenous discourse and with the unification of the images of the popular, a unification that is the first form of mass culture"(1993, 113).[2]

In Mexico, melodrama, as apex of the popular and the masses, found in the ranchera song one of its privileged expressive forms, and Pedro Infante, Jorge Negrete, Lucha Reyes, Lola Beltrán, Javier Solís, Lucha Villa, Cuco Sánchez, and José Alfredo Jiménez are some of its time-honored interpreters.

In her analysis of the ranchera song, Nájera focuses on the work of the singer and composer from Guanajuato, José Alfredo Jiménez, without doubt one of the essential figures among those men and women who gave it prominence. Carlos Monsiváis (1998) calls José Alfredo "the spokesman of cantina lyric," "creature of tradition," and "poet of marginal desolation." The rain of images that Monsiváis offers about José Alfredo defines the linkages that the singer forms with "the people." For Monsiváis, José Alfredo "is not strictly a 'product of an era'; that is what the industry of cultural nationalism makes possible and that depends on what an era dictates: the invention of a people and of a national style. But José Alfredo transcends his formative environment and his 'Mexicanness,' even though it constitutes him, it is mainly a decorative element, and it is neither an obstacle for the force of his songs nor for his success in the Spanish-speaking world"(13).

I agree with Monsiváis that José Alfredo does not question the fundamental values of his medium. His popular philosophy and his songs are elements of mediation of the quotidian experience of millions of Mexicans whom he allows to be converted into protagonists of the songs: to participate in their stories; to be hurt by their tragedies and emotional setbacks; to celebrate their amorous victories while thinking of their own sentimental biography; to burst with shouts that confirm that we sing our own history and we add to it the elements that make it ours all the more.

From the Monsiváisian perspective, José Alfredo is a marginal antihero who "lives in the mythology of sedentaranism and vertigo: drunken revelry, implacable destiny, adoration with no limits to unfaithfulness, self-compassion assumed with the pleasure of triumph." One is more truthful in defeat: "I am proud to have been born in the most humble barrio, far from the bustle of false society." Because of that, Monsiváis affirms that in José Alfredo's marginal antiheroism, "poverty is the peak of moral values," with its essential popular singers: Tomás Méndez, Cuco Sánchez, José Alfredo Jiménez, Rubén Fuentes, following the tradition of Tata Nacho, Manuel Esperón, and Chucho Monge. In this way, rancheras are a thematic continuation of the melodrama of "the Golden Age" of Mexican cinema.

BECAUSE WHETHER YOU LIKE IT OR NOT, YOU BELONG TO ME

Notwithstanding the strong misogyny that runs through rancheras, as in almost all genres produced by patriarchal societies, the absence of their own space allows women to appropriate songs, providing them with hybrid components from which the borders, where the exclusivity of the male experience is entrenched, are dissolved. Women sing the same songs deconstructing the original meanings but maintaining their emotional charge, their sordid settings, their painful *ayes* (cries), and their fits of joy.

The emergence of woman in masculine discourse disrupts the original meanings, making possible the transgression of environments where she was merely the object of the rage, passion, disdain, or love of man. Monsiváis also notes this condition: "usually *ranchera* singers are impersonal, so to speak, and seize masculine spirit so as to sing to the woman who takes the bull by the horns, the fugitive, the love of their life. No one even thinks about other sexual inclinations, machismo does not allow it. And that is why singers integrate man's perspective and woman's skills" (1998, 36).

Within this transgressing field wild women stand out, temperamental women that dare to sing of their desires, pains, and passions without inhibitions. They also proclaim songs of love and indifference, where man evolves into the subject-object of love, of feminine desire. Roles are reversed; women gain a voice. Some of the singers of rancheras and ambassadors of pain, joy, and feminine desire are Lucha Reyes, Lola Beltrán, Lucha Villa, Amalia Mendoza, Chavela Vargas. They are pioneers of new expressive fields where women take the floor, and they will be joined by new voices and proposals that will directly present proposals that disrupt the perspectives that have been sheltered by machismo. Those that deserve mention are Irma Serrano, Paquita la del Barrio, Guadalupe D'alessio, Beatriz Adriana, Aída Cuevas, Eugenia León, and Guadalupe Pineda.

BECAUSE OUR SOULS ARE UNITED, WHO KNOWS UNTIL WHEN

Beginning with the elements considered here, we can recuperate Nájera's work to grant it the importance that it possesses. The perspective that the author offers acquires relevance in developing an interpretive direction that seeks to decodify the logic from which homogenizing and excluding masculine discourses reproduce forms of relations emerging from inequality. This condition, however, is not exclusive to rancheras but cuts across the collection of discourses that support patriarchal power. In another work I have shown how women's invisibility has been constructed in discourses about the Mexican nation (Valenzuela Arce 1999).

The subordinated representation of women is also found in other popular narratives, such as the corrido, where the logic of the participating men and women maintains strong gender differentiation and it is common for women to remain attributed with the images of the devoted mother, the femme fatal, the coquette, the repressed, or the unfaithful woman. In the corridos, the absence of a feminine protagonist stands out. The other dimension accentuated in them is the feminine image as countervalence or gauge of contrast where masculine qualities gain power, while the feminine condition acquires centrality only in pain, suffering, or abnegation—conditions that define a social position that denies her *being for herself* or limits her value to *being for another.*

Nevertheless, in new corrido production we also find diverse corridos where women take on protagonist roles, especially from the illegitimate occupations of drug trafficking or from the continual participation of women in social movements (Valenzuela Arce 1998, 2000; Herrera Sobek 1990).

The participation of women as protagonists in settings dominated by men and the deconstruction of masculine texts as elements that allow the active presence of women is one of the themes present in works like the one produced by Nájera. These analyses are interested not only in understanding the transgressions of narrative syntax, but in manipulating the articulations between text and context, in redefining the performativity of discourses, and in decodifying the discursive fields that reproduce and strengthen inequality. Mindful of that, and following Bauman and Briggs, Nájera analyzes the possibilities of the appropriation of the ranchera song by women—their possibilities of decontextualizing and recontextualizing it as a resource of control through which they are repositioned against the underlying patriarchal perspective. In appropriating these forms, women recreate rancheras and infuse them with new meanings, transgressing their masculinized, excluding, and *machista* dimension. It is from these elements that Nájera maintains that these appropriations and performances afford women the opportunity to take control of the text and convert it into their own subversive message.

NOTES

1. Translator's note: The literal translation of *campesino* as "peasant" or "farmworker" does not adequately convey its meaning in Mexican Spanish, which alludes to a history of social, cultural, and political relationships between people and the land.
2. Martín Barbero declares that "like the public marketplaces, the melodrama mixes a little bit of everything, social structures and the structures of feeling. The melodrama is much of what we are—fatalists, inclined to machismo, superstitious—and what we dream of becoming—stealing the identities of others, nostalgia, righteous anger. In the form of a tango, a soap opera, a Mexican film or a cheap crime story, the melodrama taps into and stirs up a deep vein of collective cultural imagination. And there is no access to historical memory or projection of dreams into the future which does not pass through this cultural imagination" (1993, 225).

WORKS CITED

Herrera Sobek, María. 1990. *The Mexican Corrido: A Feminist Analysis.* Bloomington: Indiana University Press.

Martín Barbero, Jesús. 1993. *Communication, Culture and Hegemony: From the Media to Mediations.* Trans. Elizabeth Fox and Robert A. White. London: Sage Publications.

Monsiváis, Carlos. 1998. "José Alfredo Jiménez: Les diré que llegué de un mundo raro." Pp. 13–38 in *Y sigue siendo el rey: Homenaje a José Alfredo Jiménez,* ed. Carlos Monsiváis and Emiliano Gironella Parra. México City: Fundación Cultural Artención.

Valenzuela Arce, José Manuel. 1998. *Nuestros piensos: Culturas populares en la frontera México-Estados Unidos.* México City: CONACULTA.

———. 1999. *Impecable y diamantina: La deconstrucción del discurso nacional.* Guadalajara, México: ITESO, El Colegio de la Frontera Norte.

———. 2000. *Jefe de jefes: Corridos y narcocultura en México.* México City: Raya en el Agua y Plaza y Janés.

CHAPTER SEVEN

Talkin' Sex: Chicanas and Mexicanas

Theorize about Silences and Sexual Pleasures

PATRICIA ZAVELLA

• • • • •

The inner process of meaning, perception and comprehension takes place in the word, in sound, in gesture, in the body.—Pavel N. Medvedev and Mikhail Bakhtin, *The Formal Method of Literary Scholarship: A Critical Introduction to Sociological Poetics*

Sometimes you don't know you feel something until you say it out loud.—Anonymous

Feminists have long critiqued the Mexican cultural framework regarding sexuality that poses oppositions of proper and shameful sexual practices for women, known as the virgin-whore continuum.[1] In this patriarchal logic there are culturally sanctioned discourses or practices of repressing women's sexual desires, whereby women should experience pleasure only in the context of institutional approval: through Church-sanctified marriage. Repressive practices include the multiple ways women's bodies are controlled, covered up, and their desires thwarted by parents, lovers, Church officials, teachers, partners, children, or even themselves. Under the logic of repression, when women break the silences they often engage in transgression and can produce an escándalo (scandal) of melodramatic proportions. Women who are branded an escandalosa—someone who flaunts the conventions of propriety, who disrespects or dishonors the family—occasionally find a sense of triumph, but also can experience a great deal of shame. In the literature on Chicana/Mexicana sexuality, there is a well-developed interpretive framework for understanding sexual repression, which I discuss below.[2]

Chicana lesbian theorists and creative writers have produced autobiographical essays and creative pieces illustrating their resistance to silencing and expressing their multifaceted desires, including spaces where women's yearnings are meaningful.[3] Extending their insights, I discuss how working-class Chicanas and Mexicanas, whose experiences span a continuum of heterosexual and openly lesbian relationships, theorize about desire in their own words.[4]

As I argued in "Playing with Fire: The Gendered Construction of Chicana/Mexicana Sexuality" (Zavella 1997a), Catholic-based repressive ideology should be seen as only a cultural template. Women's cultural poetics, the social meaning of sexuality, entails struggling with the contradictions of repressive discourses and social practices that are often violent toward women and their desires. Women contest or incorporate repressive notions into their sense of sexual selves and they use metaphors of juego y fuego (play and fire) to express bodily pleasure. That is, in discussing their intimate relationships, playing was a recurring metaphor that signified women's experiences of teasing, testing, or pushing the boundaries of social convention. In women's discourse, fire had dual meanings: the repression of desire, where sanctions were "too hot," and the uncontrollable force of the erotic, where passion consumed them. Women, then, sometimes "got burned" in transgressing social conventions, even as they sought sensations and imaginaries of the body enflamed (Zavella 1997a).

This essay is situated within this framework of cultural oppositions, particularly as women move through the life cycle, and explores the meanings of silences as well as pleasures. However, I emphasize that discourse that silences women's desires is a means of control that goes beyond repression and must be interrogated for social meaning. As Foucault reminds us, "Silence itself—the things one declines to say, or is forbidden to name, the discretion that is required between different speakers—is less the absolute limit of discourse than an element that functions alongside the things said" (1990, 61–62). My interpretation also builds on the framework by Ginsburg and Rapp (1995), who argue that social reproduction—of which gender and sexuality are central—should be seen as local expressions of transnational inequalities. In the context of transnational social inequality, individuals imagine and enact cultural logics and social formations through personal struggle, generational mobility, social movements, and the contested claims of powerful religious and political ideologies (2).

My interpretation of women's views of sexuality as a social firestorm incorporates systems of power based on class, race, and gender. Contesting —or accepting—the Mexican cultural script of virgin-whore, women also grapple with their working-class origins, racialized bodies, traditional gender expectations, and sexual orientation. Women construct their sexuality in a historically specific time frame during which feminist, gay/lesbian, and Chicana/o social movements have created new discourses about sexuality and Chicanas' rights as racialized women. Further, they reveal the production of complex local knowledges and cultural practices regarding sexuality that reflect women's lived experiences in a regional political economy, and respond to global considerations other than migration—notably, the AIDS pandemic and transnational popular culture.

Building on this framework, I discuss how, despite the obvious differences one would expect between those who grew up in Mexico and those who were reared in the United States, Mexican immigrants and Chicanas share a repressive heritage that is not unique but is particular to Mexican culture. I analyze culturally sanctioned silences as a key expression of gendered power relations in which women are subject to social control and through which they reclaim human agency.[5]

Closely related to the project of understanding the cultural specificities of control is the discourse that Chicanas and Mexicanas construct in response to silencing. Here I am referring not only to the language women create but the pleasure they express through their body, what Amber Hollibaugh and Cherríe Moraga (1983) call "what we're rollin' around in bed with." This project requires a whole new set of lenses, a move from control to the relatively uncharted realm of creativity. To capture women's views on control and desire, I conducted life histories in which I aimed for a conversational format where my questions seemed like the talk women have with those they trust. Nonetheless, I was struck with their tension in talking about sex—the embarrassed looks or hunched shoulders, giggles, stutters, or other bodily indicators of discomfort which, as they told stories or anecdotes, often gave way to a sense of wonder: "Gosh, I never thought I'd tell this to anyone," said one, and "I thought I had forgotten all this." Further, women often code-switched between English and Spanish to reveal the nuances of meaning. I use "talkin' sex" to convey the sense of awkwardness women often felt in describing feelings, experiences, sensations they rarely articulated except in occasional safe spaces with kin, intimate friends, lovers, or therapists. I argue that through their actions and language, women configure carnal desire in ways that embody contradictions of acquiescence *and* contestation.

Talkin' sex during our interviews became a discursive space constructed in collaboration between the subjects and me, inevitably colored by their perceptions of my project and me. I tried to be as clear and open as possible about the purposes of my research and how I would use the interview data, and I promised full confidentiality. Thus, the names I use are pseudonyms, with the exception of María Pérez, an out lesbiana, who insisted that I use her real name.[6]

I asked women to refer me to other women, which means that to the new interviewee I had been vouched for in some sense by the first. Attempting to mediate the power relations involved when interviewers intrude into people's private lives, I made it clear that they could stop the tape recorder at any point, could ask the purpose of any question, and could ask me questions about my life. Most women assumed that I was heterosexual, although several expressed their curiosity in coded ways; the most frequent question was whether I had children. As a middle-aged woman with children, I was open about my own multiple relationships, although mercifully, no one asked for details or I might have been as uncomfortable as the women I interviewed. None of these women refused to answer any questions; however, some responded metaphorically, as we see below. Finally, we must recall that these instances of talkin' sex were social constructions, verbal expressions of individual cultural memories that define women's identities and the meaning of Mexican culture in their own terms.[7]

I base my analysis on life histories with seventeen women of Mexican origin, six born in the United States and eleven born in Mexico.[8] The women's ages ranged from 21 to 56. Generally, these Chicanas and Mexicanas were socially located differently from one another. However, I do not want to reify these social categories, for there was variation within each group (Zavella 1994).[9] These data are part of a larger project, where my purpose is to understand how cultural expectations about gender and sexuality are configured in relation to race, poverty, and gender subordination in opportunity structures in Santa Cruz County.[10] Thus, all of the women I interviewed had low income and were situated in the working class or among the poor.

Most of the women I interviewed who had migrated from Mexico had not completed an elementary education and came from rural villages in Michoacán, Jalisco, Guanajuato, and Oaxaca. Two women, however, were from Mexico City and held degrees from Mexican universities. Some women migrated to the United States because of labor displacement; others were seeking refuge from abusive male kin or lovers or were merely seeking adventure. All of the Mexicanas migrated between age 15 and 30—none were reared in the United States—and they were predominantly Spanish speakers. These women usually identified themselves ethnically as Mexicanas, but occasionally one would use another term, such as Hispana or Hispanic.

The women born in the United States identified themselves ethnically in various terms, including Chicana, Mexicana, Mexican American, or Hispanic, and all were born in states in the Southwest. These women cannot be seen as culturally homogeneous, as they vary from the woman who identified herself as Hispanic and those at the other end of the cultural spectrum who considered themselves very Mexican in their cultural outlook. All of the Chicanas had completed high school and several had vocational training or some college. These Chicanas were the daughters of immigrants, that is, they were second generation; hence, most were bilingual although a few spoke very little Spanish.

This sample reflects globalizing processes particular to northern California. The settlement of Mexican immigrant women began in large numbers after the end of the Bracero Program (post 1964) and increased dramatically beginning in the 1980s. That the Chicanas are from the second generation, whereas the Mexicanas migrated as adolescents or adults within the past thirty years is a product of a particular migration history from Mexico to Santa Cruz County that is different from other regions such as Los Angeles or la frontera, which have longer settlement histories.

THE CULTURAL CONTRADICTIONS OF SEXUAL CONTROL

Mexican cultural logic includes severe control over sexuality *and* more openness for women's intimacy with other women. For example, research on traditional gender roles in rural Mexico indicates that sexuality and marital relations were largely taboo topics in peasant communities during the first half of the twentieth century, even between mother and daughter. The control over young women was so strict in rural areas that they were confined to their home to avoid being kidnapped for marriage or establishing illicit relationships (Mummert 1994, 195). Between the 1930s and industrialization, which began in the 1940s, the notions of virile macho men and self-sacrificing women—las mujeres abnegadas—were constructed in popular culture (Gutmann and Porter 1998). As late as the 1950s young couples often engaged in robo, a ritual "robbing" of the young woman (who may have actually consented or even helped plan the event) and elopement to circumvent parental control of children's choice of mate (Foster 1979, cited in Sánchez 1993, 31).[11] During this time, the ideal of female chastity prior to marriage was an indicator of social class, with upper-class young women being monitored and controlled more closely. Thus, working-class women were less restricted by the ideal of female virginity at the time of marriage, yet their variance from chastity was also seen as evidence of their inferiority to upper-class women (Sánchez 1993, 33).

Since the 1950s, Mexico has experienced rapid urbanization, feminization of the labor force, including in rural areas, increased migration within Mexico and to the United States, and the expansion of popular culture (influenced by the United States and other nations), including sexual liberation of women.[12] Research on sexuality in Mexico in the late twentieth century finds much regional variation in sexual practices. Xóchitl Castañeda argues, "In Mexico, to speak of sexuality . . . one should take account of the heterogeneity of the country, the particular circumstances of place and the different sectors of the population, and especially gender inequality. The historical, economic, and social processes engendered by globalization have varied significance in different regions of the country" (Castañeda et al. 1997a, 55; my translation).[13] Nevertheless, despite regional, ethnic, and class differences, the research on sexuality indicates that there are important gendered patterns regarding sexual experimentation prior to marriage. In one survey that was administered in rural and urban regions, 89 percent of young men first had sexual intercourse by age 15, but only 13 percent of the women had sexual intercourse by age 15. Moreover, the use of condoms varied significantly by region, with fewer living in the more rural area of Chiapas using condoms compared to the more urban Morelos, and women in the rural area had virtually no use of condoms (Castañeda et al. 1997b). This research indicates that we should expect variation in actual practice by Mexicanas who have migrated to the United States.

Moreover, in Mexican society it is quite acceptable for women to express affection through verbal display and touching. Sisters and female kin are often very close, as are women friends, and it is not unusual for women to sleep in the same bed, walk arm-in-arm or dance together in public, or embrace and kiss one another on the cheek in greeting or when departing. Indeed, the acceptability of women's intimacy is one of the attractions of Mexico for lesbians, who can be openly affectionate with lovers in ways that would be socially unacceptable in the United States. Mexican popular culture has become more open publicly, especially with the figure of the prostitute or sexually liberated woman permeating Mexican folk songs, movies, and literature.[14] Finally, women who are considered "artists" (regardless of type of performance or art form) are accorded more freedom to be openly suggestive regarding sexuality (Yarbro-Bejarano 1997).

The research on sexuality in contemporary times on the U.S. side of the border finds contradictory patterns for women of Mexican origin as well. Some research confirms the continuing importance of Catholic ideology in repressing women's desires and supporting the double standard for women (Espín 1984; Pavich 1986; Alonso and Koreck 1989; Padilla and Baird 1991). Perhaps Ana Castillo provides the most eloquent example of the cultural repression argument. In "La Macha: Toward a Beautiful Whole Self," Castillo points out that repression is counteracted through social expression in daily life:

> Sexuality surfaces everywhere in our culture, albeit distortedly, due to the repression of our primordial memories of what it truly is. We experience it in the hip gyrating movements of our cumbias and the cheek-to-cheek twirling tension of the Tex-Mex polka (both dances are commonly danced by women together as well as men and women); in the blood merging reflected in our mixed heritage as mestizas; in the stifling of emotions by the Church, its hymns and passion for the suffering of Jesus Christ (passion derives from extreme feeling and here it arises as a result of the repressed erotic and psychic sensations). Mexican erotica is charged by all our senses: in the traditional strict costuming of each gender: low cut dresses, tight Mariachi charro pants, open-toed pumps and pointed, dapper cowboy boots; in sum, our culture is infamous for its intensities. (1991, 34)

Similarly in "The New Mestiza," Gloria Anzaldúa theorizes how women are alienated from homophobic, hegemonic Mexican culture: La new mestiza is "caught between *los intersticios,* the spaces between the different worlds, she inhabits" (1987, 20). According to Anzaldúa, the borderlands, la frontera, is more than a geographic space; it exposes the dominant power that Mexican culture holds over what is considered "normal" or acceptable. Ironically, despite a relatively liberatory environment with highly sexualized popular culture, a vocal feminist movement, and access to contraception and abortion in the United States, women often feel constrained about openly expressing affection with other women.

On the other hand, despite having a high percentage who identify as Catholics, Mexicans in the United States often ignore Church doctrine when it comes to decisions about contraception or abortion (Alvirez 1973; Darabi, Dryfoos, and Schwartz 1986). For example, Hispanic teenagers are just as likely to have an abortion as black and white teenagers, and among highly educated Chicana academics and white-collar workers, there is overwhelming support for the right to choice (Pesquera and Segura 1993).

These theories of repression and marginalization expose attempts at control over what Carla Trujillo (1991) calls "the girls our mothers warned us about": "loose women" and lesbians. For some Chicanas and Mexicanas, however, the silence regarding sexuality was so complete that our mothers only warned us about men, and lesbianism was not even discussed. These silences left open questions about which pleasures were acceptable and how lesbianism is constructed.[15]

THE CONTEXT OF SILENCE DURING CHILDHOOD

My interview data provide no evidence for a cultural continuum where Mexicanas are more repressed about sexuality and Chicanas more liberated. Instead, despite many differences in experience based on being reared in two different societies at different points in time, Chicanas and Mexicanas often shared a repertoire of discursive practices about gendered sexuality, making statements about sex that were uncanny in their similarities.

For instance, both Chicanas and Mexicanas experienced childhood as a time when there was an overwhelming silence regarding sexuality. Consider the following typical statements by two women about the messages they were taught about sex as children: Vicenta Fernández, 56 years old, was reared in the 1940s in a small village in Michoacán and had no formal education whatsoever. Her family was so poor that Vicenta was sent to live with a *patrona* as a live-in cook, maid, and nanny. About her family of origin, she recalled: "Nunca hablaron de sexo, nunca. [They never spoke about sex, ever.]" Sara Rivas, a 22-year-old Chicana single mother attending a local community college, lived in the Santa Cruz region her whole life; her family had migrated from Mexico prior to her birth. She described how her family regarded sexuality when she was a child in the 1960s: "Sex you don't talk about. You just do not talk about sex."

In a similar vein, women received sanctions for sexual experimentation or play as young children that were often startling. Frida, an out lesbiana with a Mexico City college degree, recalled her childhood in the 1960s: "Nunca se podía uno tocar los genitales en frente (de la gente) porque (decían) 'déjate ahí, que haces allí, déjate ahí, no seas cochina.' [One could never touch the genitals (in front of others) because (they would say) 'Leave that alone, what are you doing there, leave that alone, don't be dirty.']" María Cabañas, a Mexicana from a small village, described an incident of childhood play that occurred during the 1950s: "Una vez que las niñas encueraban a los monitos y los acostaban, y me acuerdo que una vez lo pusieron encimados uno de otro. Mi mamá vino y vio eso y las corrió y no me dejó jugar con esas niñas. Y dijo, 'No te juntes con esas niñas porque son muy groseras.' [One time some girls undressed the dolls and they put them to bed, and I remember that one time they put one on top of the other. My mother came and saw that and she ran them off and would not let me play with them. She said, 'Don't get together with those girls because they are very crude.']"

Women's exposure to sex was sometimes violent. Dirana Lazer, a Chicana performance artist who had several years of university education, had been sexually molested by her uncle at age 4 in 1961. When her father found out he severely beat the uncle. Despite the highly charged nature of this conflict, the family never discussed the abuse or the beating until Dirana was an adult, and then the discussion was inadvertent and her sister asked that they never speak of it again.[16] In this context of denial, Dirana's family found sexuality in general difficult to discuss. When she was 7, her mother found Dirana masturbating and had a reaction that terrorized the child: "I remember she was screaming at my father, saying that my uncle made me like that, and so it was very clear: masturbation was a bad thing." Developmental psychologists maintain that children have moral values as early as age 4. These women's moral universe includes notions that sex is bad and carnal exploration or discussion is to be avoided (duCille 1996, 14).[17]

Despite having schooling experiences in different countries, Chicanas and Mexicanas had similar experiences with sex education. Minifred Cadena, a Chicana who attended school in southern California, recalled sex ed during the early 1960s: "In school we never talked about sex. The only time I learned about the female body was in Girl Scouts when we watched films." Frida recalled sex education in Mexico City during the early 1970s: "Del sexo empezamos ha estudiar eso el sexto año de primaria, y fue muy simple, muy básico, anatómico nada más. Nada de reproducción, ni de emocíones, ni de hormonas, ni de 'esto les va pasar y se van a sentir así' o 'es normal,' o no, nada. [We began studying about sex during the sixth year of elementary school, and it was very simple, very basic and anatomical, nothing more. Nothing about reproduction, nor about feelings, hormones, nor 'this is going to happen to you and you will feel like this,' or 'its normal,' oh no, nothing.]"

Menstruation is an important turning point for young women, and the lack of information they received about it was telling. Virtually no Mexicana received any warning that she was going to menstruate and several thought there was something wrong with them when it happened. María Cabañas, who began menstruating in the early 1970s, recalled: "Cuando tuve mi primera regla fue una experiencia muy fea para mi porque no me advertieron de eso tampoco. [When I had my first period it was a very ugly experience for me because they did not warn me beforehand.]" Thinking she had suffered an injury that would not stop bleeding, she had such a fright that she did not menstruate for three years. Some of the Chicanas received information via films, but only if their mother allowed them to sign up for sex education classes at school. Several immigrant mothers would not give permission, despite entreaties by older siblings. Thus, Chicanas too were often unprepared for the onset of menstruation. Sara Rivas, who began menstruating in the 1980s, recalled: "It just happened. I was in the bathroom, and like, 'Oh Mom!' and she comes in and she's, 'Oh, it's okay, it's okay, it happens to everybody.' And that's how I found out."

The silence around sexuality extended to same-sex relationships as well. Several women had heard about male homosexuals. Frida pointed out: "En México we always laugh at gays because there is the extreme of homosexuality. They're like queens . . . the ones who are not out, you never know— they might be married, they might be having children and all that and they can be gays en México. Los que más se ven son las transvestis o de plano, las reinas, así bien bien jototes. [Those who one sees more are the transgenders or the queens, those who are very very gay.]"

However, few of the Mexicanas had heard about lesbians as children. María Cabañas said: "Antes de casarme [en 1972] casi no se oían comentarios de las lesbianas; no supe mucho yo, nada más de esas mujeres jotas. [Before I married (in 1972) one did not hear comments about lesbians; I did not know much, nothing more about gay women.]" Chicanas experienced similar silence about lesbians. Sara Rivas recalled, "Yeah, my brothers talked about fags and sissies, but that was all." Dirana Lazer was one of the few women who had knowledge of lesbianism as an adolescent in the mid-1970s: "There was a lot of name calling—'oh she is just a dyke' or 'she's just a butch'—but that was because I was in an all-girl high school and that's how the other girls would refer to the gay girls. It was derogatory." Nowhere did these women hear notions of pleasure in relation to same-sex relationships among women.

Women did receive clear instructions about not losing their virginity, however, although sometimes the message was coded or opaque. María Cabañas recalled being told, "Como mujer, debe de ser respetada, siempre. Mi mamá especialmente decía que 'cuando te cases tienes que ser una señorita,' siendo virgen. [As a woman, one should be respected, always. My mother especially said, 'When you marry you have to be a young lady,' meaning a virgin.]" Chicana Monique Rodríguez, who became pregnant as a teenager and dropped out of high school, said: "My mom would explain it to us like this: 'You are like a flower or an apple right now, and if you are with somebody and they pick your flower or take a bite of your apple, then nobody is going to want you no more.' Even a kiss, she just said that 'you are dirty after you do that. You should wait until you get married.'" There was great variance, however, between the admonitions and the practice. In Mexico, these women lived sheltered lives prior to and after migrating to Santa Cruz County as adolescents. On the other hand, many Chicanas grew up in large households where both of their parents worked, and they had little after-school supervision. The assumption by parents was that the girls would obey the restrictions on their behavior and resist the temptations offered by American popular culture and the pressure of peers.

As an attempt to control their behavior, women were told that there was a whole array of signs that their body would display if they were to lose their virginity; for instance, women who were no longer virgins would walk differently—bowlegged or with their legs spread apart. Monique Rodríguez recalled that after she had sex with her boyfriend, her mother "read" her indiscretion on her body: "My mom told me that 'you don't walk right now, any more. You walk with your legs open.' So that's what she always told us." Women were told that their face or their eyes would become more "knowing," and, of course, the way young women dressed was an important indicator, for, as women were lectured, virgins do not dress provocatively. María Cabañas recalled: "Yo oí que cuando ya no son señoritas, las muchachas caminan diferente, y en la cara, siempre tienen vergüenza. [I heard that when they are no longer ladies, the girls walk differently, and by the looks on their faces, they seem ashamed.]" Some of the warning signs were downright bizarre. Monique Rodríguez continued: "And your ears, you can tell that they're yellow [when a woman loses her virginity], that's what she [her mother] said." Mexicana María Pérez recalled: "They told me that the backs of their knees would be different. And I was told that once you started, it never stopped, you know, you never stop after you have it [sex] for the first time, it will be kind of difficult to hold your desires." I could not help but chuckle and María responded: "That's ridiculous, but that's what they said to me."

The body, then, was seen as a map, a document to be read by others regarding women's possible transgressions and a source of betrayal if women did not control how they moved or displayed themselves in public. At the same time, women's bodies were seen as uncontrollable, subject to the whims of passion. Thus, women's bodies were policed, their reputations guarded, and the consequences for transgressions were severe. Sara Rivas, unmarried, became pregnant at age 17 with a black man, a student from the local university, which caused a big scandal in her family. She recalled this period of extreme tension: "It [sex] just wasn't talked about in this house, and if you did—that's when I was just considered a total slut. . . . My parents wouldn't talk to me when I was pregnant. I was just living here and they didn't talk to me. My mom was really worried what other people would think." Monique Rodríguez, who became pregnant at age 13 with a 15-year-old Chicano, recalled the tension in her family: "Because I had a baby, my dad kind of hated me for a lot of years. He never really talked to me. He was sad too. But he never confronted me. He could never, like, look at me and say anything."

Besides guarding their virginity and reputation, women heard admonitions that estranged them from their own body. There never seemed to be any let-up in the ways their body was objectified. Every woman believed that something was wrong with her body; most often, they told me they felt too fat, although the thin women regretted that they were too skinny.[18] Women who were not feminine in dress or demeanor or excelled in sports were teased for being tomboys and felt pressured to conform. Race politics intersected with these women's devalued bodies so that skin color, type of hair, and facial and body features became open to scrutiny and evaluation. For example, Dirana Lazer was beautiful and light-skinned but had dark hair and was chided by her blond mother for not being güera (blond). Her mother hoped that perhaps since her own green-eyed, red-haired European ancestry had skipped a generation with Dirana, these features would show up in her grandchildren. Because Dirana was overweight, her mother would not buy her clothes as a teenager, hoping she would be pressured into losing weight. It is not surprising that Dirana developed low self-esteem: "I would feel really bad because I'd go to school and, in comparison with the other girls who were traditionally Mexicanas, and were always made up and really clean, you know, that whole beauty enforcement that we get in our culture? I just couldn't even pretend because she wouldn't buy me anything."

MIXED MESSAGES

As these women made the transition to being teenagers, they found a new, difficult enforcement of modesty. They were no longer able to walk around in bathing suits or underwear, sit with their legs open, or play rough with brothers or other male kin, and they were discouraged from playing "boys' games." Adolescence was when many women noticed the marked gender privilege for the young men in their families: they had no curfews, got special meals, had no restrictions on displaying their body, and were entitled to seek carnal pleasures, including multiple partners. Dominique Ponce, for example, recalled her adolescence, which contrasted with that of her brother of a close age: "A guy does what a guy does; like it's okay for him to have sex or whatever. If you're a girl: 'No, you don't do that.'"

Along with these overt mechanisms of patriarchal control over women's sexuality, their families often celebrated the Mexican Catholic ritual of quinceañera for a young woman's fifteenth birthday. It is important to see a quinceañera as a tradition that is "an open, and sometimes chaotic terrain that is constantly reconfigured in everyday experience."[19] Nevertheless, in its most general features, la quinceañera is intended as an expression of gratitude to the Virgen de Guadalupe, a social debut that mimics a wedding, and a coming-of-age celebration of a young woman's purity. The celebrant wears a white dress (or, occasionally, pastel colored) and veil, and her fourteen female attendants dress in color-coordinated outfits, escorted by formally attired chamberlains. After a celebratory mass, the family often hosts a dinner or reception with a special cake and sponsors a large dance in which the attendants dance a waltz, although in families with fewer resources, the celebration can be more modest and include only extended family members and close friends who attend a dinner party. The celebrant often has an escort and, in contrast to prior strict monitoring of her interactions with men, it is permissible for the young woman to dance with her partner and friends. Often, mastering the waltz is the most time-consuming part of the preparation for a quinceañera, and the frequent practices are occasions for socializing. After the ceremony, the young woman is often allowed to date, although occasionally under the supervision of an adult. Increasingly, young Chicanas are also hosting quinceañeras, even when their family no longer has strong ties to Mexico.[20]

A quinceañera is an expression of ethnic identity and an event that transforms a girl into a Mexican Catholic woman through an ongoing process of negotiation (Dávalos 1996). La quinceañera carries significance regarding young women's sexuality as well, for it is often through the process of staging the event that parents withdraw some of their control over young women, and the women negotiate the terms of their adulthood. Among the women I interviewed, several did not have quinceañeras for varied reasons: not enough resources, disinterest, or, in the case of Frida, because "me daba pena [it bothered me]. I refused. I was ashamed of it. For me it was a waste. I didn't feel like I needed one. But we finally had a religious ceremony at the church and that's when I did my first communion too." Other women who did have quinceañeras had particular recollections. Sara Rivas, for example, recalled the significance of this ritual for her family in terms of her own autonomy: "It was really fun, and it meant I was a good little girl. It was a big event. I had everything, from the chambelánes, the whole works. That night my friends came over and there were guys there and I was dancing with a guy, and my parents were there and they didn't say nothing." Mirella Hernández recalled her quinceañera as representing "purity, your virginity," even though she thought she was one of very few virgins among her peer group (Zavella 1997a). All women who had full-scale quinceañeras recalled having a very good time; over and over they reported: "It was so much fun!" Regardless of the meaning the participants attributed to having or not having a quinceañera, it is the only Mexican ritual that focuses exclusively on young women, and it celebrates their purity.[21]

At the same time that young women were attempting to understand changes occurring in their body, the control against experimentation and exploration, and the changing messages they received at home regarding sexuality, these women were also enduring pointed messages at school, in church, and in their neighborhood. These messages were not just about how they regarded their body, but, in California, included questions about whether Mexican immigrants should receive an education and about tracking Mexicans and Chicanas into courses that did not prepare them for college. These women also struggled with teachers' questions about their abilities to perform academically or whether they fit into important social groups.[22] Minifred Cadena recalled wistfully her attempts to fit in with predominantly Anglos in her southern California school. Her immigrant parents came to this country "to be white, and they taught me white—everything was white on white." Not surprisingly, she remembered high school as a difficult period in her life. Adolescence was often when these women experienced a new interest on the part of men in their developing body and when the pressure to experiment with sex, drugs, or alcohol came from friends and kin their age. On top of these tensions and conflicts in the public arena, young women often had heavy household responsibilities, caring for younger siblings or, if living in farmworker households, subject to heavy work responsibilities themselves. It is not surprising, then, that many women felt besieged, as if they had little power or recourse other than to rebel in those arenas where they did have some freedom.

Several women's cultural poetics embodied struggle against the violent control of their desires. Occasionally that struggle became outright resistance. Sara Rivas moved very quickly from being her mother's favorite daughter at the time of her quinceañera to disgrace when she became a young single mother of two out-of-wedlock children at 17. She made her rebellion clear: "My mom said that she doesn't know why I did this to her.

She thinks that it's something against her, like I'm rebelling and stuff. And at first it was; they were just so strict, you know? And the more they would tell me that, the more I did it to hurt them. And that's what I still do sometimes now: they tell me not to do something, they make me mad, then I'll do it." Unfortunately, by having unprotected sex, Sara's rebellion eventually pushed her into circumstances in which she had very little autonomy.

PLAYING WITH FIRE AS ADOLESCENTS

Within this cultural and social context of pressure and the multiple attempts at silencing women's passion, how did they find pleasure in their body? Here women shed light on another facet of silence, the social space where women explore their feelings, relationships, or social taboos only with highly trusted friends, confidants, or lovers. Women's experiences with sexual experimentation are instructive and reveal how they "remapped" their body and ultimately transformed their subjectivity. Particularly regarding their initial sexual experiences, many women used metaphors related to playing (flirting, teasing, learning, or testing how far the relationship would go) and sexual pleasure as fire ("hot," "passionate," "boiling," "explosive") and, like uncontrolled flames, difficult to stop. The sanctions, if women were found out, were often a firestorm: "I got burned" or "Things got too hot at home."

Of the women who had been with only one sexual partner, all were reared in Mexico. For example, María Cabanas, now married with five children, was cloistered in her village, spending her time either in school or in the company of women kin, and thus had very little experience with men when she migrated at age 16. After courting for two years, mainly by telephone or with a chaperone, she was enticed alone to her future spouse's home. When I asked what had attracted her to Lucio, she recalled "su cuerpo [his body]," that he had a strong, trim, dark body. She described the couple's first sexual experience: "Para mi fue bonita, porque yo recuerdo que mi esposo decía que era muy inocente y que le gustaba verme. Se me hizo bonito, pues, haber aprendido todo de él. [For me it was beautiful, because I remember that my husband said that I was very innocent and that he liked to look at me. It was beautiful for me, well, to have learned everything from him.]" This couple considered their first sexual experience a commitment of marriage, and two months later went back to María's village in Guanajuato for a church wedding with the extended family and friends. Her relatives were unaware of her transgressions.

Not all of the women with one sexual partner had a marriage that lasted, however, and their limited sexual experience made them naïve regarding other prospects for courtship. Like the other Mexicanas, Frida had fairly limited sexual experience, only one male. Upon moving to Santa Cruz County, however, she encountered the possibility of a relationship with a woman: "I never thought about that, but I was seeing all these lesbians and it looked very normal to me. I started to experience some kind of feelings, excitement, especially with particular persons. So this woman approached me and I was like, my ego was big and I was like, 'OK!' There was never any direct communication, like 'Oh, you like me' or 'I like you,' but it was wonderful. I was exploring this side of myself. Then she kind of dumped me. But it was good because when that happened I came out to myself." Frida's initiation into lesbianism, only her second sexual relationship, was positive and resulted in her eventual commitment with another woman: "I knew that I liked women, that I was ready for a relationship with a woman." However, she remained closeted for quite some time.

Of the women in my sample who had many casual sexual partners, all were Chicanas with the exception of María Pérez, a highly educated Mexican immigrant who used her self-described "promiscuity" as a means of controlling her sexual partners (Zavella 1997a, 398–404). Often, Chicanas' devalued self-image became a factor in their sexual exploration. Minifred Cadena recalled: "The first time wasn't that pleasant. He didn't believe I was a virgin and then I kinda got flack for bleeding on the blanket. I remember that kind of made it very uncomfortable because I didn't even know that was to be expected. After that I got more promiscuous. I just felt like, well, I was ruined anyway and I was just like going for it. I felt pretty much like the black sheep of the family in a lot of ways, for other reasons too, but that was one of them. After that there were a lot of one-night stands; I don't know if I saw anybody twice: just experimenting, you know?"

In a similar fashion, Dirana Lazer had a negative first sexual experience. Bolstered by tequila, mushrooms, and marijuana, Dirana does not recall her first time: "I was devirginized at age 21. I was so drunk and so high, and I had such low self-esteem. Apparently we had sex." After that first relationship ended, she went through a phase of sexual experimentation while living in a big city: "I was sleeping with all kinds of different interesting men, whatever I could get my hands on. That sounds awful but that's the truth. I had lost that weight, and I looked good, and I felt like a million bucks. That's why I was seeing so many different guys." In her mind, Dirana was making up for her adolescence, in which she had felt "really ugly."

Several Chicanas who were coerced into sex the first time often had been drinking heavily and did not use birth control or condoms.[23] I asked

Sara Rivas what she had been thinking at the time, and she said, "Actually, I didn't think. I had that kind of attitude, like 'getting pregnant, it will never happen to me.'" Unfortunately, she did get pregnant, at age 17, which caused the tension in her household described earlier. In contrast, 13 years old at the time, Monique Rodríguez was totally unprepared for the effects of alcohol and being alone with her 15-year-old boyfriend. She said, "I'm a person that can't really say no to people," that is, she could not say no to the young man who pressured her for sex. When she became pregnant, Monique's parents were very upset.

EXPRESSIONS OF SEXUAL PLEASURE

After such troubling initial sexual experiences, how did women construct pleasure? As women described their sexual history after they lost their virginity, it became clear that each individual underwent a different process. When I asked women directly what gave them sexual pleasure, they often indicated that this was the point when they felt the most uncomfortable. This question came toward the end of the interview, after they had answered a number of questions about their experiences as children and adolescents and described their sexual history, sometimes in more detail than I had asked. I came to view the "pleasure question" as an important point of revelation, when women disclosed highly charged imaginaries or experiences—positive or negative. This was the point when women revealed transgressions, unfulfilled fantasies, sexual problems, or their play through language about sex.

Some women were attracted to certain "erotic scripts"—physical or social types or patterns in relationships—and if they had multiple partners, would return to that fantasy repeatedly. When the particular stereotype or script was problematic or promised more than real persons or circumstances permitted, then their relationship history was painful. Chicana Monique Rodríguez, for example, told me she was attracted to cholos. In her experience, these were men from Mexico who were very handsome, sexually aggressive, and flattering, who promised commitment and wanted children with her, but then had trouble with drugs and crime and became violent when things did not go their way. It was only after several of these relationships that she realized she needed to rethink her attractions, and that perhaps cholos were not the best type for her: "I don't like having sex, but I wish they'd just comfort me, sit with me or kiss me or stuff like that, but not have sex. . . . This life is crazy. You're not going to find a perfect guy."

Women's notions of sexual pleasure often included the common female request for more foreplay prior to intercourse, for partners to take the time so they could fully enjoy sex. For example, "I like a lot more foreplay than I usually get," said Minifred Cadena, who laughed as she characterized her current lover: "He's an animal. That [foreplay] doesn't always happen." Women also desired orgasms, variation in carnal exploration, and not to be pressured into sex when they were not in the mood. María Cabanas, married for twenty-three years to the same man, said, "Bueno, lo que a mi me gusta en verdad es siempre de satisfacernos y buscar la manera, sin preguntar, si tienes ganas. [Well, what I really like is to always satisfy ourselves and seek the means, without asking, if you are in the mood.]" Her tone indicated that this scenario did not happen every time. Dirana Lazer said: "I'd like orgasmic satisfaction. My pleasure would be doing it when I truly feel like doing it. Too often it is boom, boom, boom and it's done. I don't mind when it is aggressive sex. That is satisfying to me, that feels good. But I don't necessarily want to be having sex all the time. So my sexual fantasy is that it would be slower, longer, and more intimate, more affectionate. That would be nice, that would be a real treat. He knows that and he does try. We are not always in sync, but when we are it is nice." Note that pleasure and intimacy were seen as more romantic and thus preferable if they were spontaneous rather than subject to discussion or negotiation. As Frida observed, "Talking about sex has not been part of our cultural practice."

As women with low income, often the precarious circumstances of their lives had a negative effect on their sexual relations. Dirana Lazer had been unemployed for months and explained: "When I turn him away, I can see that at times it really hurts him, but I can't help it if I'm not in the mood. A lot has to do with our current situation, getting stressed out because of work and money. Those things affect me a lot. [But] when we do have sex, it is really, really good."

Other women who had less satisfaction with their sex lives nevertheless appreciated sexual intimacy or play. Dominique Ponce, for example, another Chicana who had been a teenage mother, admitted that she had never experienced an orgasm, yet found other pleasures in sex: "I don't care. It's nothing big. It's kind of funny and embarrassing. Somebody was telling me, 'It's probably better that you haven't [had an orgasm] because every time you're going to want it, and you can't.' But I like being close to somebody, I guess, and cuddling and having sex play. I enjoy that." After her divorce, Vicenta Fernández no longer had intimate relationships with men. However, I observed her taking pleasure by playfully bantering with her friends about a local wealthy, white widower. She speculated about whether he could stay awake long enough for courtship and joked that a shot (of tequila) would liven him up: "A ver si un trago lo anime."

In response to my question about sexual pleasure, there was another similarity between Chicanas and Mexicanas: how they talked about sex among women. Although only three women admitted having sexual relations with women, their language was downright gushing. Frida, for example, described a process of "coming home" with great aplomb:

> I feel it [having sex with a woman] was something that fulfilled my soul. It was like, "I feel *good.*" It's different from being with a man. A man can treat you soft but there is still something rough there and a woman can just change the whole thing. It's another way to see love. It's more kind. Me sentía llena [I felt full]. It's a little milimetro espace [tiny space] that wasn't fulfilled with men. Men could bring down the sky and give you the stars and all the universe [referring to an orgasm], and then, "OK, we're finished, that's it. I'm the man and you're the woman." With a woman I didn't feel that way, I felt like an *equal,* something more ritualistic, more spiritual. I reacted like, como si hubiera sido [as if I had been a] lesbian por años [for years], you know, like when you throw babies into water and they start swimming? I was in my element.

Dirana Lazer believed that everyone is bisexual but was closeted to her husband, and had similar superlatives regarding her one sexual experience with a woman. She batted her eyelashes and swished her hand as she recalled: " 'Lily' and I had one very intimate encounter; I guess you could say we *played* one afternoon. And I really liked it. It was a beautiful experience. I've never had as beautiful a sexual experience as I had with her. And that just leads me to believe that sexual experiences between women are much nicer than they are between men and women. I liked the softness, the sentiment. It's so different, the *essence* I get [she giggled]—I'm using all these deep words here. I was not threatened by her like I was with guys." These women found carnal pleasure in situations in which there was gender equality among women ("I felt like an equal," "I was in my element," "I was not threatened"), and the sensual aesthetic was familiar and pleasing. Regardless of whether they found pleasure with women or men in these politics of intimacy, women preferred that their desires were fulfilled on the basis of affection and respect, without resorting to open requests, negotiation, or struggle.

By historicizing these women's experiences, we see the transnational nature of discourse and practice that links second-generation Chicanas and Mexicana immigrants regarding sexuality. The pervading themes of silence and violence is clear. Women who are beaten or scolded for sexual experimentation as children and are taught to deny their own worth or sense of pleasure often find it very difficult later to take charge of their own desires—sexual or otherwise. Clearly, processes of silence can be devastating for those who have been sexually abused—every woman who disclosed abuse to me felt that she had been at fault or had done something wrong. This has a damaging effect on women's self-esteem and makes standing up for themselves when confronted with other systems of power very difficult, although not impossible. Further, young women who are subject to vigilance over their movement, comportment, and body, particularly when combined with heavy household responsibilities and racist, class-based constraints in public institutions, often feel disempowered and, not surprisingly, find ways to contest and perhaps even rebel. When that rebellion takes place through unprotected sex, women can become vulnerable to sexually transmitted infections, single parenthood, inadequate preparation for the labor market, and poverty.

We also see how women construe pleasure—whether with men or other women—by "playing" in multiple forms with complex notions of "fire," although the particular "gendered script" they enact or find attractive within those cultural poetics varies tremendously. Perhaps the one theme we see among women is their yearning for pleasure in relationships where there is equality, respect, and affection, that is, a safe space to play. Again, the nondiscursive appears in this realm of creativity, where open negotiation or struggle places a damper on passion. These women are "rollin' around in bed" with contradictory experiences and feelings derived from their multiple sources of structural subordination, against which they express their human agency. Their notions of carnal desire embody acquiescence *and* contestation of silencing discourses.

The similar discourse and practices experienced by Chicanas and Mexicanas are the product of my sample and the location where I am doing this research. Although I cannot claim that these findings hold for all women of Mexican origin, given the small sample size and lack of random sampling, clearly there are important cultural processes at work among these subjects. It would be very interesting to conduct this type of research in other regions—for example, in la frontera, where cultural border crossing happens daily, or rural northern New Mexico, where there is relatively little Mexican immigrant settlement and multiple generations of Mexican Americans live in relative isolation. We might find similar results along the border and very different ones in New Mexico—or vice versa. Clearly, these findings are only part of the total cultural repertoire of meanings and practices related to sexuality. I do not mean to suggest that these patterns of silencing and creating pleasure are the only ways in which Chicanas and Mexicanas experience sexuality.

In this regard, then, the Chicana feminist project related to sexuality becomes breaking the silence—theorizing the relative absence of discourse about sexuality, naming lesbianism, bisexuality, and transgendered subjects in our communities, challenging heterosexist assumptions and homophobia, and understanding the myriad ways in which women construe pleasure. We Chicana feminists must engage in the political work of moving sexuality from the realm of silence, repression, and control toward women's autonomy, empowerment, and creativity. We must create multiple spaces for women to continue "talkin' sex."

NOTES

I have been blessed with pointed and constructive criticisms from friends and colleagues who pushed me to clarify and refine this essay. Thanks to Gabriela Arredondo, Lionel Cantú, Xóchitl Castañeda, Gloria Cuádraz, Micaela di Leonardo, Ramón Gutiérrez, Aída Hurtado, Jim Jatczynski, Norma Klahn, Olga Nájera-Ramírez, and Caridad Souza for their intellectually stimulating discussions and very helpful comments. Thanks to the University of California Consortium on Mexico and the United States, which provided support for this research, and the Chicana Feminisms Research Cluster of the Chicano/Latino Research Center, University of California, Santa Cruz. I appreciate the research assistance by Francisca Angulo Olaíz and Esperanza Ocampo.

1. Situated in an honor-shame framework, theorists suggest that the history of Spanish conquest of indigenous peoples in Mexico set up the logic whereby sexual intercourse (chingar) is viewed as the metaphorical conquest of or violence toward women. For a full discussion, see Alarcón (1989) and Zavella (1997a, 402–18).

2. For a historical discussion of Mexican colonial notions of honor and shame, see Gutiérrez (1991). For works on contemporary sexuality, see Espín (1984, 149–64), Pavich (1986), Alonso and Koreck (1989), and Padilla and Baird (1991).

3. For autobiographical works on sexuality, see Alarcón, Castillo, and Moraga (1989), Anzaldúa (1987), Moraga (1983), and Trujillo (1991; 1992, 23–27). Also see Hurtado (1996, chap. 2), Pérez (1991, 159–84; 1993, 57–74), Ramos (1987), and the novel written by Pérez (1996).

4. Barbara Christian eloquently reminds us of the importance of ethnographic sources of information: "People of color have always theorized—but in forms quite different

from the Western form of abstract logic. And I am inclined to say our theorizing (and I intentionally use the verb rather than the noun) is often in narrative forms, in the stories we create, in riddles and proverbs, in the play with language, since dynamic rather than fixed ideas seem more to our liking. How else have we managed to survive with such spiritedness the assault on our bodies, social institutions, countries, our very humanity?" (1990, 336).

5. Kamala Visweswaran reminds us that at times, in constructing contradictory, multiple, and strategic identities, women resort to resistance through silence (1994, 50–51).

6. María Pérez viewed the disclosure of her name as part of her autonomy as an out lesbian (Zavella 1997a, 407).

7. For a discussion of collective cultural memories that narrates American identity in the face of traumatic events, see Sturken (1997).

8. In addition, I participated in five focus groups with a total of sixty-eight Mexican women, all immigrants, whose views on sexuality very much resonate with those expressed in the individual interviews.

9. Either I or a research assistant also interviewed men, but the cultural logic of their sexual practice differs considerably, so I do not discuss them here.

10. I analyze how, over time, the regional economy restructured and incorporated different racial groups in particular ways. Today in Santa Cruz County you can see a clear pattern of occupational segregation by race and gender in different sectors of the economy: Mexican immigrants in the worst-paying jobs such as busboys and maids, and Chicanas/os and whites in others, as part of the working poor or those who rely on social services (Zavella 1997b, 136–61).

11. However, during a much earlier era, Ramón Gutiérrez (1991) found discrepancies between village norms established by the state and the Church and the actual practices of young people who dated.

12. Beginning in the 1960s, Octavio Paz noted that Mexico had become "un país moderno" (a modern country) with an educated public who created demand for more books, and by the 1980s the boom femenino (female boom) had displaced popular male writers with a preference for women writers by a predominantly female reading audience (Kiddle 1985; D. Castillo 1998).

13. For other discussions of regional variation regarding sexuality in Mexico, see Taggart (1992) and Wilson (1995).

14. For a discussion of sexually liberated women in Mexican fiction or popular culture, see D. Castillo (1998). For a fascinating analysis of how Mexican prostitutes lead lives of "social schizophrenia" trapped in cultural oppositions of virgin-whore symbolized by la Virgen de Guadalupe and la Malinche, which becomes inscribed in day and night distinctions in their work, see Castañeda et al. (1996).

15. For a discussion of the acceptability of women's pleasures in work, see Alonso (1992).

16. There is no evidence that there are higher or lower rates of incest in Latino families when compared to other groups. Further, incest usually occurs in families that are physically abusive and is related to structural factors such as poverty, low education levels, and unemployment (Flores-Ortíz 1993, 1997; Russel y Rodríguez 1997). For a discussion of undocumented Latinas' vulnerability to domestic violence, see Anderson (1993) and Argüelles and Rivero (1993).

17. For two other ethnographic examples of violent sanctions toward women for sexual exploration as children, see Zavella (1997a).

18. In a study of female adolescents' body image, whites and Hispanics were more likely to worry about their weight than were blacks. The majority of the study's subjects describe the "perfect girl" as 5'7," 100–110 pounds, with a good figure, long blond hair, and blue eyes (Nichter and Vuckovic 1994).

19. For a discussion of the multiple perspectives on the meaning of quinceañera in the literature, by the Catholic Church, and by the participants themselves, see Dávalos (1996, 1997).

20. Jeanette Rodríguez (1994) finds that those women who have active, daily interaction with other Mexican Americans tend to refer to Our Lady of Guadalupe in more familial terms, such as "Our Mother," whereas those born in the United States and acculturated refer to her in more distant terms, such as "The Mother of Jesus." Her use of the acculturation model, however, is problematic.

21. Young men receive no coming-of-age ritual celebration (although there may be some encouragement of sexual experimentation), and other Catholic rituals include males and females.

22. For an interesting ethnographic study about social groups at a local high school in which Chicanas/os differed from Mexican immigrants, see Matuti-Bianchi (1986). For a discussion of how alienated Mexican American youth express their resistance to schooling, although not necessarily education, see Valenzuela (1997).

23. For a discussion of inexperienced drinking behavior by women, especially those from working-class or immigrant families, see Mora (1997).

WORKS CITED

Alarcón, Norma. 1989. "Traddutora, Traditora: A Paradigmatic Figure of Chicana Feminism," *Cultural Critique* 13: 57–97.

Alarcón, Norma, Ana Castillo, and Cherríe Moraga. 1989. "The Sexuality of Latinas." Special issue of *Third Woman*, no. 4.

Alonso, Ana Maria. 1992. "Work and Gusto: Gender and Re-Creation in a North Mexican Pueblo." Pp. 164–219 in *Workers' Expressions: Beyond Accommodation and Resistance*, ed. John Calagione, Doris Francis, and Daniel Nugent. Albany: State University of New York Press.

Alonso, Ana María, and María Teresa Koreck. 1989. "Silences: 'Hispanics,' AIDS, and Sexual Practices." *Differences: A Journal of Feminist Cultural Studies* 1: 101–24.

Alvirez, David. 1973. "The Effects of Formal Church Affiliation and Religiosity on the Fertility Patterns of Mexican American Catholics." *Demography* 10: 19–36.

Anderson, Michelle J. 1993. "A License to Abuse: The Impact of Conditional Status on Female Immigrants." *Yale Law Journal* 102(6): 1401–30.

Anzaldúa, Gloria. 1987. *Borderlands/La Frontera: The New Mestiza*. San Francisco: Spinsters/Aunt Lute.

Argüelles, Lourdes, and Anne Rivero. 1993. "Violence, Migration, and Compassionate Practice: Conversations with Some Women We Think We Know." Special issue on Latino ethnography. *Urban Anthropology* 22(3–4): 259–76.

Castañeda, Xóchitl, Victor Ortíz, Betania Allen, Cecilia García, and Mauricio Hernán-
dez-Ávila. 1996. "Sex Masks: The Double Life of Female Commercial Sex Workers in
Mexico City." *Culture, Medicine and Psychiatry* 20: 229–47.

———. 1997a. "Adolescencia, género y SIDA en áreas rurales de Chiapas." Editorial.
Pp. 55–83 in *Género y Salud en el Sureste de México,* ed. Esperanza Tuñón Pablos.
México City: ECOSUR, UNAM-PUEG, PORRUA.

———. 1997b. "Factores Socio-Culturales y de Género Asociados al Uso de Condon en
Adolescentes Rurales." Unpublished report.

Castillo, Ana. 1991. "La Macha: Toward a Beautiful Whole Self." Pp. 24–48 in *Chicana
Lesbians: The Girls Our Mothers Warned Us About,* ed. Carla Trujillo. Berkeley:
Third Woman Press.

Castillo, Debra A. 1998. *Easy Women: Sex and Gender in Modern Mexican Fiction.* Minneapolis: University of Minnesota Press.

Christian, Barbara. 1990. "The Race for Theory." Pp. 335–45 in *Making Face/Making
Soul: Haciendo Caras,* ed. Gloria Anzaldúa. San Francisco: Aunt Lute.

Darabi, Katherine F., Joy Dryfoos, and Dana Schwartz. 1986. "Hispanic Adolescent Fertility." *Hispanic Journal of Behavioral Science* 8(2): 157–71.

Dávalos, Karen Mary. 1996. "*La Quinceañera:* Making Gender and Ethnic Identities."
Frontiers 41(2–3): 101–27.

———. 1997. "*La Quinceañera* and the Keen-say-an-Yair-uh: The Politics of Making
Gender and Ethnicity Identity in Chicago." *Voces: A Journal of Chicana/Latina
Studies* 1(1): 57–68.

duCille, Ann. 1996. *Skin Trade.* Cambridge, MA: Harvard University Press.

Espín, Olivia M. 1984. "Cultural and Historical Influences on Sexuality in Hispanic/
Latin Women: Implications for Psychotherapy." Pp. 149–64 in *Pleasure and Danger:
Exploring Female Sexuality,* ed. Carol Vance. Boston: Routledge and Kegan Paul.

Flores-Ortíz, Yvette. 1993. "*La Mujer y la Violencia:* A Culturally Based Model for the
Understanding and Treatment of Domestic Violence in Chicana/Latina Communi-
ties." Pp. 169–82 in *Chicana Critical Issues,* ed. Norma Alarcón et al. Berkeley: Third
Woman Press.

———. 1997. "The Broken Covenant: Incest in the Latino Family." *Voces: A Journal of
Chicana/Latina Studies* 1(2): 48–70.

Foster, George M. 1979. *Tzintzuntzan: Mexican Peasants in a Changing World.* New
York: Elsevier.

Foucault, Michel. 1990. *The History of Sexuality. Volume 1: An Introduction.* Trans.
Robert Hurley. New York: Vintage Books.

Ginsburg, Faye D., and Rayna Rapp. 1995. Introduction. Pp. 1–17 in *Conceiving the New
World Order: The Global Politics of Reproduction.* Berkeley: University of California Press.

Gutiérrez, Ramón A. 1991. *When Jesus Came the Corn Mothers Went Away: Marriage,
Sexuality and Power in New Mexico, 1500–1846.* Stanford: Stanford University Press.

Gutmann, Matthew C., and Susie S. Porter. 1998. "Gender and Sexuality: 1910–96." Pp.
575–80 in *Encyclopedia of Mexico: History, Society and Culture,* ed. Michael S.
Werner. Chicago: Fitzroy Dearborn Publishers.

Hollibaugh, Amber, and Cherríe Moraga. 1983. "What We're Rollin Around in Bed With:

Sexual Silences in Feminism." Pp. 394–405 in *Powers of Desire: The Politics of Sexuality*, ed. Ann Snitow, Christine Stansell, and Sharon Thompson. New York: Monthly Review Press.

Hurtado, Aída. 1996. *The Color of Privilege: Three Blasphemies on Race and Feminism.* Ann Arbor: University of Michigan Press.

Kiddle, Mary Ellen. 1985. "The *Novela Testimonial* in Contemporary Mexican Literature." *Confluencia* 1(1): 82–89.

Matuti-Bianchi, Maria Eugenia. 1986. "Ethnic Identities and Patterns of School Success and Failure among Mexican-Descent and Japanese-American Students in a California High School: An Ethnographic Analysis." *American Journal of Education* 95: 233–55.

Medvedev, Pavel Nikolaevich, and Mikhail Bakhtin. 1985. *The Formal Method of Literary Scholarship: A Critical Introduction to Sociological Poetics.* Trans. Albert J. Wehrle. Cambridge, MA: Harvard University Press.

Mora, Juana. 1997. "Learning to Drink: Early Drinking Experiences of Chicana/Mexicana Women." *Voces: A Journal of Chicana/Latina Studies* 1(1): 89–111.

Moraga, Cherríe. 1983. *Loving in the War Years: Lo que nunca pasó por sus labios.* Boston: South End Press.

Mummert, Gail. 1994. "From *Metate* to *Despate:* Rural Mexican Women's Salaried Labor and the Redefinition of Gendered Spaces and Roles." Pp. 192–209 in *Women of the Mexican Countryside, 1850–1990*, ed. Heather Fowler-Salamini and Mary Kay Vaughan. Tucson: University of Arizona Press.

Nichter, Mimi, and Nancy Vuckovic. 1994. "Fat Talk: Body Image among Adolescent Girls." Pp. 110–28 in *Many Mirrors: Body Image and Social Relations*, ed. Nicole Sault. New Brunswick, NJ: Rutgers University Press.

Padilla, Amado M., and Traci L. Baird. 1991. "Mexican-American Adolescent Sexuality and Sexual Knowledge: An Exploratory Study." *Hispanic Journal of Behavioral Sciences* 13(1): 95–104.

Pavich, Emma Guerrero. 1986. "A Chicana Perspective on Mexican Culture and Sexuality." *Journal of Social Work and Human Sexuality* 3(spring): 47–65.

Pérez, Emma. 1991. "Sexuality and Discourse: Notes from a Chicana Survivor." Pp. 159–84 in *Chicana Lesbians: The Girls Our Mothers Warned Us About*, ed. Carla Trujillo. Berkeley: Third Woman Press.

———. 1993. "Speaking from the Margin: Uninvited Discourse on Sexuality and Power." Pp. 57–71 in *Building with Our Hands: New Directions in Chicana Studies*, ed. Adela de la Torre and Beatriz M. Pesquera. Berkeley: University of California Press.

———. 1996. *Gulf Dreams.* Berkeley: Third Woman Press.

Pesquera, Beatriz M., and Denise A. Segura. 1993. "There Is No Going Back: Chicanas and Feminism." Pp. 95–115 in *Chicana Critical Issues*, ed. Norma Alarcón et al. Berkeley: Third Woman Press.

Ramos, Juanita, ed. 1987. *Compañera: Latina Lesbians (an Anthology).* New York: Latina Lesbian History Project.

Rodríguez, Jeanette. 1994. *Our Lady of Guadalupe: Faith and Empowerment among Mexican-American Women.* Austin: University of Texas Press.

Russel y Rodríguez, Mónica. 1997. "(En)Countering Domestic Violence, Complicity, and

Definitions of Chicana Womanhood." *Voces: A Journal of Chicana/Latina Studies* 1(2): 104–41.

Sánchez, George J. 1993. *Becoming Mexican American: Ethnicity, Culture and Identity in Chicano Los Angeles, 1900–1945.* New York: Oxford University Press.

Sturken, Marita. 1997. *Tangled Memories: The Vietnam War, the AIDS Epidemic, and the Politics of Remembering.* Berkeley: University of California Press.

Taggart, James M. 1992. "Gender Segregation and Cultural Constructions of Sexuality in Two Hispanic Societies." *American Ethnologist* 19(1): 75–96.

Trujillo, Carla, ed. 1991. *Chicana Lesbians: The Girls Our Mothers Warned Us About.* Berkeley: Third Woman Press.

Trujillo, Carla. 1992. "Confessions of a Chicana Ph.D." *OUT/LOOK* (winter): 23–27.

Valenzuela, Angela. 1997. "Mexican-American Youth and the Politics of Caring." Pp. 322–50 in *From Sociology to Cultural Studies: New Perspectives,* ed. Elizabeth Long, Cambridge, England: Blackwell Publishers.

Visweswaran, Kamala. 1994. *Fictions of Feminist Ethnography.* Minneapolis: University of Minnesota Press.

Wilson, Carter. 1995. *Hidden in the Blood: AIDS in Yucatan.* New York: Columbia University Press.

Yarbro-Bejarano, Yvonne. 1997. "Crossing the Border with Chabela Vargas: A Chicana Femme's Tribute." Pp. 33–43 in *Sex and Sexuality in Latin America,* ed. Daniel Balderston and Donna J. Guy. New York: New York University Press.

Zavella, Patricia. 1994. "Reflections on Diversity among Chicanas." Pp. 199–212 in *Race,* ed. Steven Gregory and Roger Sanjek. New Brunswick, NJ: Rutgers University Press.

———. 1997a. " 'Playing with Fire': The Gendered Construction of Chicana/Mexicana Sexuality." Pp. 402–18 in *The Gender/Sexuality Reader: Culture, History, Political Economy,* ed. Roger N. Lancaster and Micaela di Leonardo. New York: Routledge.

———. 1997b. " 'The Tables Are Turned': Immigration, Poverty, and Social Conflict in California Communities." Pp. 136–61 in *Immigrants Out! The New Nativism and the Anti-Immigrant Impulse in the United States,* ed. Juan Perea. New York: New York University Press.

RESPONSE TO CHAPTER SEVEN

Questions of Pleasure

MICHELLE FINE

• • • • •

Querida Patricia:

If we had an evening, over dinner and wine, and the rare chance to talk across works, bodies, and our own stories, we might have a glorious conversation about "studying sex." To begin, let me just thank you. For decades you have created a series of essays in which you at once disrupt, stretch, and educate social science, cultural studies, Chicana studies, and feminist scholars through a lens of culture, gender, class, and sexuality. You elaborate with eloquence the yawning disconnect between academic discourses and talk on the ground. In the 1980s, you wrote on the problematic relation of feminism and Chicana studies. In 1996 you argued that "Feminist dilemmas begin at home, and we cannot take a cultural feminist stance in our approach to fieldwork. As we go through the process of talking with people like ourselves who are called 'other,' we should try to understand our own feminism and political struggles. Chicana feminist ethnography, then, would present more nuanced, fully contextualized, pluralistic self identities of women, both as informants and researchers" (154). Across essays you represent the ethical, theoretical, and political tensions that must surface in honest, self-reflexive research. My students at the Graduate Center, CUNY relish your texts, especially on insider-outsider dilemmas.

In this short commentary I want to try a virtual conversation between us, a correspondence about sexual fantasy and terror, about women's narratives and bodies, about culture and gender. I appreciate the chance to write with and to you about topics that cross our works, issues that incite, words that fill my mind. I appreciate, too, the opportunity to acknowledge the stunning theoretical and political advances in your essay "Talkin' Sex: Chicanas and Mexicanas Theorize about Silences and Sexual Pleasures."

Nevertheless, I begin with some mourning and regrets. Mourning for girls' and women's bodies abused and tortured, as their "entree" to sexuality, typically heterosexuality. Regrets for conversations never had, for stares endured, for uncles too close, for teachers who wouldn't dare to tell young women what they deserve to hear, for all of us adult women who have forsaken moments with girls when we could have introduced them to so much. I worry about the relentless self-blame narrated by the Chicanas and Mexicanas you spoke with, for violence brought to them by the hands of men. I can't stop thinking about how deeply reproductive most acts of female adolescent rebellion really, really are. And I am haunted that the missing discourse of desire I tried to describe in 1988 still remains, for most girls and women, simply missing (Fine 1993 [1988]).

With respect to the influence of culture and gender, as you maintain, local relations are indeed profoundly choreographed by global relations. So, too, in the area of violence against women. Although violence affects all women, poor and working class more than others, the details of local culture, class, and gender/family ideologies dramatically shape how women experience the violence: whether they leave or not, seek orders of protection, flee to a mother's or sister's home, call the police. In a study of life histories conducted with poor and working-class white, African American, and Latina women and men in the Northeast of the United States, Lois Weis and I, like you, found alarming rates of violence endured by girls and women across racial and ethnic groups. In *The Unknown City*, we report that over 90 percent of white girls and women had experienced either childhood abuse or domestic violence; over 80 percent of African Americans and Latinas. Where the women differed was not so much in their rates of experienced violence but what they did/felt they could do about it. White women typically told no one, rarely sought an order of protection, never went to a battered women's shelter, almost never called the cops. African American women were most likely to tell, seek protection from the state, flee to battered women's shelters. Latinas—primarily women from Puerto Rico— were the most self-blaming, the most likely to excuse the man's behavior, but were, to protect the children, quietly fleeing to safe spaces (Fine and

Weis 1998). No woman is immune to domestic violence. As you point out, most women resist in small and big ways. Chicanas and Mexicanas endure a particularly burdensome overlay of religion, culture, and Church sanctions for male violence that make it tough to flee. Working-class women who shiver in the face of immigration surveillance, who are denied or thrown off welfare, and who have not learned much English are sometimes hopelessly locked into violent homes. As the state sadistically celebrates a "reduction in the welfare rolls," these women endure, often in silence and with shame.

Moving, however, under the sheets into the theoretical (and the sexual) pleasures in your text, we learn that despite the uncles, the stares on the street, the state and Church-based surveillance, and the cultural silencing, women's desire endures. Women's "cultural poetics" dance between social control and "playing with fire." And yet, the clitoris—and the rest of the body—rises to the gendered and cultured occasion. All women seem to yearn and many delight. So much for the Church being fully embodied! The images of bodies enflamed, engulfed, feeling "full with a woman" (and "empty with a man!"—now there's a lovely feminist irony!) enrich your text. It is interesting to notice that more thrills were narrated by women who have been sexual with women!

I was taken by how much power (and danger) mythically attaches to the girl/woman who has "sinned." Despite the shame, the power renders the "sinning" almost appealing. As a consequence of one act, coerced, consensual, or somewhere in between, she now walks bowlegged, averts her eyes, takes up too much room, dresses provocatively, carries too much wisdom in her face. What does she now know? She knows what you call the "social firestorm" of sexuality. Women's power over men (and other women) grows refracted as a betrayal (of the patriarchy). I love your language: "The body, then, was seen as a map, a document to be read by others regarding women's possible transgressions and a source of betrayal if women did not control how they moved or displayed themselves in public."

From your essay, feminist understandings are enriched at the global nexus of gender, culture, immigrant status, and the body. You write on the power of transgressions, the force of surveillance, and the geography of sexual repression and how it does and does not fully "penetrate" the body. As you say, "Repression is counteracted through social experiences in daily life." And yet, methodologically you teach how awkwardly questions of pleasure can feel on the tongue of the interviewer, how hollow they may ring in the ears of the interviewed, how predictably those probes fall.

Otherwise giggly, chatty, can't-shut-em-up girls and women, when asked about pleasure, may suddenly apologize and explain, "I don't understand that question."

After I mourned and delighted, I allowed myself some dangerous thoughts. I now ask your indulgence and collusion: What if "we"—grown women who are so worried about sexually transmitted disease, pregnancy, and HIV—teach young girls about masturbation early, often, and regularly? Further, what if, instead of or in addition to *quinceañeras*, ritual celebrations of girls' purity, mothers, grandmothers, aunts, women with/without children, women across generations threw public and collective celebrations of sexuality for adolescent girls? With a smorgasbord of stories, sexual wisdom, and props, could we not feast on sexual delights, pleasures, titillations, entitlements, and dangers all displayed, gossiped about, stuffed into a piñata?

The reason I ask, of course, is because reading your essay, it becomes apparent that in the space of sexual knowledge and mother wit, we have left our collective daughters to learn on their own. We've sent them to the streets, learning the hard way with little in the way of sisterly, motherly, aunty guidance. We have probably had more conversations with them about crossing the street and bicycle helmets, maybe even pregnancy and venereal disease, than about pleasures, sexual entitlements, self-pleasuring, relations with women, and negotiated relations with men.

So here's the image: What if, on the same date, dotting the nation, in small towns and urban centers, our mothers, grandmothers, and aunts— especially the "loose women and lesbians" long shielded from the children—were to speak what Luis Moll would call their "funds of [sexual] knowledge"? What if they/we were willing to teach our daughters (collectively) as much about the politics and practices of sexual life as we were taught about cooking, keeping our legs crossed, petticoats, quiet voices, lipstick? What would our mothers and grandmothers tell us? What would we want young women to know? Could our generation sustain a conversation with young girls about pleasure and "just deserts" without tumbling into an avalanche (perhaps a necessary avalanche) about dangers?

Not to fuss over details, but where could we hold these feasts? Whatever made us think that schools would be able or willing to sponsor honest conversations that young women (and men) deserve? Much less churches? But what about community centers, open parks, libraries, dining room tables, youth magazines? How could we, respecting privacy, memory, dignity, and culture, nevertheless excavate with care the funds of sexual knowledge held by our mothers and grandmothers: stories of desire, affairs, disappointments, violence, thrills, pregnancies, abortions, babies given away and taken away, cross-race and -ethnic relations, sexual fantasies, lesbian relations buried inside women's souls gone forever with the death of each woman? Could women write and perform their own/other women's and girls' stories for a salon of young women? Dare we deliver this gift to our collective daughters?

At present, young women are going into bed usually unprotected, that is, without a feminist, angel escort. They may be "rollin' around in bed" with rich stories and delights, but whether they are lying next to a man or a woman, a boy or a girl, they deserve more from us, the women who (if we were lucky) "came" before them.

One last note: Jennifer Ayala (1998), one of my brilliant, creative doctoral students, is in the middle of a study interviewing young, adolescent Latinas in the Northeast and their mothers about how knowledge of culture, gender, and resistance moves across generations. In sharp contrast to the white/Anglo literatures on contentious adolescent daughter-mother relations, Ayala finds not only that young Latinas learn much from their moms but also that young Latinas teach their moms much about challenge, resistance, women's entitlement, and pleasure. And so, as a footnote, at our Fiesta de los Cuerpos de Mujeres: Body Talk across Generations of Girls and Women, we must remember that there is much we, too, will learn if only we listen to the girls.

Thanks, Patricia. I love your essay. What a contribution to feminist and Chicana studies and a gift to young girls. Let's have dinner again, soon.

NOTE

Many thanks to friends, students, colleagues, and anonymous girls and women waiting in family planning clinics and participating in sex education classrooms. Most particularly, I have learned from and been challenged by Jennifer Ayala, Aída Hurtado, Barbara Kamler, Rosemarie A. Roberts, Evelyn Shalom, and Stephanie Urdang.

WORKS CITED

Ayala, Jennifer. 1998. "Latina Mother-Daughter Relations." Master's thesis, Graduate Center, City University of New York.

Fine, Michelle. 1993 [1988]. "Sexuality, Schooling and Adolescent Females: The Missing Discourse of Desire." Pp. 75–99 in *Beyond Silenced Voices: Class, Race, and Gender in United States Schools,* ed. Lois Weis, Michelle Fine, et al. Albany: State University of New York Press. First printed in *Harvard Educational Review* 58(1): 29–53.

Fine, Michelle, and Lois Weis. 1998. *The Unknown City: Voices of Poor and Working Class Young Adults.* Boston: Beacon Press.

Zavella, Patricia. 1996. "Feminist Insider Dilemmas." Pp. 138–59 in *Feminist Dilemmas in Fieldwork,* ed. Diane Wolf. Boulder, CO: Westview Press.

CHAPTER EIGHT

Underground Feminisms: Inocencia's Story

AÍDA HURTADO

• • • • •

I keep before me the memory of Esperanza's laughter breaking the evening stillness whenever I would get too serious about trying to analyze what she was telling me. My aim is to work the dialectic between Esperanza's no-name feminism and my feminism of too many names, to go beyond the search for heroines on either side of the border.—Ruth Behar, *Translated Woman*

Writing about a Mexican street vendor in *Translated Woman* (1993), Ruth Behar notes that Esperanza acts, lives, and speaks as a feminist without ever calling what she does feminism or even being aware that her actions could be construed as feminist. The exclusion from scholarly attention of the lives of Women of Color, as well as the exclusion of the analyses of many scholars of Color, has resulted in the paradoxical dilemma identified by Behar in which mostly white academics have put forth many definitions of feminism but have failed to capture the experiences of poor Women of Color (Pesquera and Segura 1996, 231). The mainstream media have taken advantage of this confusion to announce, as *Time* magazine recently did, that feminism is dead. To emphasize the point, the cover featured the disembodied heads of Susan B. Anthony, Betty Friedan, Gloria Steinem, and Ally McBeal, signifying how "feminism has devolved into the silly" (Bellafante 1998, 58). The demise of feminism has not only been announced in the popular media, but scholarly analyses also debate whether younger women are committed to the ideals set forth in the second wave of the movement. However, feminism might look different if we were to expand its definition beyond the feminisms developed and defined by the academy. If we were to take into account women's lives and actions rather than restricting ourselves to theoretical definitions, we might find an answer for the apparent lack of feminist identification among women today (Griffin 1989).

In this essay I use a case study approach to demonstrate how gender, class, race, and ethnicity affected one woman's life choices and how she both accepted and resisted her subordination. From the very beginning, as I got to know Inocencia's life, I was constantly struck by how she did not fit many of the categories and frameworks I had studied in the social sciences.[1] She lives in a small border town in South Texas, a predominantly Mexican American area, known for its agricultural produce and the geographical area that produced Selena, the slain singer who popularized Tex Mex music. In spite of her rural surroundings and limited English skills, Inocencia is a sophisticated, cosmopolitan woman who kept track of national and international issues. During our interviews she would often weave her own personal narrative with what was going on in the popular media, both in the United States and Mexico. One of her favorite Mexican movie stars is the aging actress María Felix, who lives half the year in Paris and the other half in Mexico City with her much younger lover, a painter. She admired María Felix's independence and ability to rise above normative restrictions imposed on women to create her own life.

Inocencia lives in a humble house of only four rooms in the heart of the Mexican barrio. Yet, she paints her home once a year and takes great pride in decorating by sewing her own curtains and making tablecloths out of material she buys in the wholesale fabric store. Her home is filled with fashion magazines, from which she copies the latest fashions and takes the drawings across the border, where her favorite seamstress makes much cheaper versions. She gets her hair dyed often and splurges once in a while on a manicure. Her lack of money does not dictate a stark existence or a depressing one where there is no attention to aesthetic values. Her humor, conversation, and critical engagement with the public world is not what we read about in the social science literature when poor, immigrant, Mexican women are described. So it was with great anticipation and excitement that I got to know this woman and her amazing story of pain but also of survival.

In this essay, I heed Lamphere, Ragoné, and Zavella's call to show how women "resist subordination through their activities in everyday life, whether in renouncing the cultural prescriptions that control their bodies or rejecting pejorative self-perceptions" (1997, 6). Although Inocencia did not explicitly identify herself as a feminist, many of her actions violated the norms defined as appropriate for a woman who was also an immigrant, poor, and Mexican. The restrictions placed on her came from multiple sources, including her family and culture, but also from her structural position in this country, as a result of which she encountered racism, sexism, and classism. In fact, there were very few contexts in which she did not experience restriction. Yet her story is a testament to her use of wits, talent, and courage in not succumbing to these restrictions. Inocencia's strategies for resistance constitute a form of feminism that remains unlabeled and, for the most part, undocumented, beyond the reach of feminist theorizing (Saldívar-Hull 1991). Her life exemplifies what might be called "underground feminism"—forms of feminism that have not yet seen the light of the printed page to inform how we conceptualize women's oppression and liberation (Arguello and Rivero 1993; Zavella 1994).

I have constructed the following narrative of Inocencia's life history from a variety of sources. First and foremost are the interviews I conducted with her over a two-year period. I also interviewed her daughters, siblings, and other family members. In addition, her children and family members generously provided letters that she had written throughout her life and that elaborate many of the events referred to in the interviews.

INOCENCIA'S STORY BEGINS

Inocencia comes from a long line of migrants who moved to find economic opportunities to better their lives. Her parents met as young adults in the city of Veracruz, to which they had both come to find employment as adolescents from rural areas in Mexico. Inocencia and her siblings were born in Veracruz, and she remained there until 1952, when, at the age of 21, she married Agustino against her parents' wishes. Her parents' objections stemmed primarily from Agustino's lack of education and the fact that he came from the surrounding neighborhood, which they considered to be populated by drug addicts and men who were "good for nothing." But Inocencia was taken by Agustino's good looks and gentle demeanor. They got married in full regalia—white dress, Catholic Mass, *damas* (bridesmaids)—and the bill was footed by Inocencia's father. Immediately, the newlyweds moved to Potrero so that Agustino could get a job with Pemex, Mexico's national oil company. Inocencia considered this period her *luna de miel*

(honeymoon), although their living conditions were very harsh: "Al princi-
pio de la luna de miel, la pasé en Potrero cocinando con leña en la choza de
lodo y acarri[ando] agua y mol[iendo] el maíz. [The beginning of my honeymoon I spent in Potrero cooking with wood in a hut with a dirt floor, and
I had to carry water and grind corn.]"

Before long, the oil drilling slowed down in Potrero, so Agustino and
Inocencia moved briefly to Mexico City to live with her father's relatives.
According to Inocencia, "Nos fue muy mal en México . . . entonces de allí
nos fuimos a Poza Rica, dónde me embaracé . . . luego, luego. [Things did
not go well in Mexico City . . . so we then moved to Poza Rica, where I
got pregnant right away.]" They chose Poza Rica, a small village four hours
from Veracruz, because, like Potrero, it also had numerous oil fields owned
by Pemex where Agustino could find work.

The problems began almost immediately. Inocencia was in love, but her
parents did not take kindly to her living conditions, even though, according to Inocencia, they were considerably better than what they had been in
Potrero: "En Poza Rica pues ya teníamos casita, fue dónde le hice a mi hija
una cuna de mecate y en un cuartito chiquito una cocinita, y ya no cocinaba
con leña. [In Poza Rica, we had a little house, I made a cradle for my baby out
of burlap, and we had a little bedroom and a little kitchen and I didn't have
to cook with wood.]" Her parents, however, constantly reminded her of her
superior education and the bright dreams they had had for her before she
stubbornly decided to marry someone who, from their point of view, had no
future. Inocencia was torn between her feelings of love for her husband and
impending child and her loyalty to her parents. Her husband did not help
matters as he seemed pleased to work in the oil fields by day and hang out
in the local plaza with his friends at night, with no apparent plan for the
future. Nonetheless, Inocencia referred to these days as the most romantic
and happiest of her life. She was in love and largely content. Although she
experienced complications with her pregnancy late in the third trimester
and temporarily returned to her parents' home in Veracruz so she could
have her child in the hospital, she returned to Poza Rica once her daughter, Gabriela, was born. Agustino fell in love with their new child, taking
her everywhere and showing her off to his friends in the local hangout, a
combination of bar and restaurant.

These happy days came to an abrupt end when Inocencia became pregnant again fifteen months later. Agustino was not happy. They were already
under quite a bit of economic duress, and he felt that a second child would
be disastrous for them. Given Agustino's previous work history, Inocencia

realized that the economic survival of the family was now squarely on her shoulders, and she took control. She insisted that they move back to Veracruz to be close to her parents, who could help them. She approached her father and asked that he support her economically to finish her last year of nursing school, which had been interrupted when she got married. Her father was elated to do so but also did not miss this opportunity to berate Inocencia for her choice of husband.

Inocencia started her final year of nursing school two months pregnant and also took a job in the local *hospital civil* (public hospital).

> [Cuando regresamos a] Veracruz, empezaron los problemas porque, Gabriela tenía poco más de un año cuando volví a empezar a estudiar . . . me alivié un sábado y para el martes me fui a las clases en camión, fíjate. Fernando había pesado cuatro kilos y medio. Y así me iba a las clases. Mi papá siempre estuvo detrás de mi. [When we returned to Veracruz, that's when the problems started. Gabriela was a little over a year when I returned to school. . . . I delivered Fernando on a Saturday and by Tuesday I went back to classes, and I had to take the bus. Fernando weighed four-and-a-half kilograms. I still went to classes. My father always supported me.]

Inocencia's family obligations multiplied when her father fell ill with an appendicitis attack that required emergency surgery and intensive care after he left the hospital. Inocencia was the only one qualified to take care of him, so she moved him in with her family.

In spite of all of these hurdles, Inocencia continued her studies. Agustino supported her educational efforts by studying with her at night: "Poníamos una lámpara con un papel así, estabamos pobres, y yo empezaba a estudiar, luego le decía 'tómame la clase' y me ayudaba, sí me ayudaba. [We would sit by a lamp with paper around it to funnel the light. We were very poor, and I would start studying, then I would ask him, 'Help me memorize,' and he would help me. Yes, he would help me.]" Her hard work eventually paid off, and she graduated with honors in her class. She attended the graduation Mass, but she could not sit in the front of the church with her classmates because she was unable to buy the "Florence Nightingale" cape that all graduates were required to wear. Instead, she sat in the back of the church and cried as she watched her fellow students claim their diplomas and honors:

> Yo no tenía capa. [M]e dijo una muchacha que me iba a prestar [una capa], fui a conseguirla hasta su casa y no estaba. Total que no me pude formar

entre todas las que se graduaron porque no tenía capa. Y yo tenía mucho sentimiento porque había salido con calificaciones sobresalientes. Y me acuerdo que salí y mi papá iba con un bastón a verme porque todavía no podía caminar. . . . Y me dijo, "No, 'mija, usted no se apure, ¿para que quiere estar allí con ellas? Usted es la más inteligente." Consolándome, porque ni me retrataron ni nada. [I didn't have a cape. A friend said she was going to lend me one and I went all the way to her house and she wasn't there. So I couldn't line up with everybody else because I didn't have a cape. I was very hurt because I had earned outstanding grades. I remember my father came to the Mass using a cane because he was ill and he could hardly walk. . . . He told me, "Don't worry, why do you want to be up there with them? After all, you're the most intelligent one." He was trying to console me because they didn't even take my picture or anything.]

Unfortunately, in spite of her exemplary performance in school, Inocencia soon realized that a nursing degree was not sufficient to ensure her a substantial position in the local hospital. Again, she appealed to her father, this time to finance a specialization in midwifery. As a midwife, she would be able to open a small clinic in her neighborhood, stay close to home, and oversee her children. Her father agreed.

After she finished midwifery school, Inocencia began working full time and her marriage began to fall apart. While she was experiencing increasing success, Agustino's lack of formal education was preventing him from finding even the most menial of jobs. Inocencia's parents, her father in particular, kept pressing her about her husband's "irresponsibility" and lack of ambition, stressing her own superior abilities. Finally, she began to succumb to her parents' judgments. "Entonces fue una época muy dura porque mi papá empezo dale, dale y dale, entonces ya me fui a vivir con ellos, nos separamos. Y parecía que a Agustino no le importaba mucho, como ya casi ni nos veíamos. Como que no le importó mucho, ¿verdad? [It was a difficult time for me, because my father was constantly on me. So I went to live with them and we separated. It seemed like it didn't affect Agustino very much, and since we hardly saw each other, anyway. It seemed like it didn't matter to him (that I was gone).]"

Agustino and Inocencia finally got divorced in 1957, five years after they had married. They went to the local justice of the peace to get their final divorce papers. "Salimos de allí ya divorciados, nos fuimos a una cafetería que se llama Minerva en Veracruz y estabamos tomando la nieve y los dos empezamos a llorar porque, pues ya estabamos divorciados. [After we left there (the justice of the peace) already divorced, we went to a coffee shop called Minerva in Veracruz, and we were having some ice cream and we both started to cry.]"

Inocencia made yet another migration shortly after her divorce. Her younger sister, Lupe, had become pregnant without benefit of marriage, and the family was ashamed, especially because the two older daughters had left the paternal home *de blanco* (dressed in white). According to Inocencia, "Entonces mi papá cuando supo que estaba embarazada, yo estaba allí arrimada con ellos, le pegó mucho a Lupe, le dio una tranquiza. A mi me dio mucho coraje . . . y la corrió, y pues ¿a dónde iba? y le dije 'no yo me voy con ella.' [When my father found out about her pregnancy, he beat her up. . . . I got really angry. He threw her out, and where was she going to go? So I told him 'I'm going with her.']"

In the spring of 1958, just a few weeks shy of her twenty-seventh birthday, Inocencia took her pregnant sister, her children, and her few belongings and headed for the border. They arrived at the border city of Reynosa, Tamaulipas, six hours from Veracruz. Inocencia's plan was to work while her sister took care of her children until her own baby was born. But Inocencia failed to find a job in Reynosa, so she decided to try her luck in Matamoros, a neighboring border city about an hour away, near the coast. There, she quickly found a nursing position in a clinic and proceeded to rent an apartment for herself, her children, and her sister.

All was well for a few months. To Inocencia's great surprise, however, her sister, who at that point was on the verge of giving birth, by coincidence ran into Rodolfo, the father of her child. "Y se encontró con él unos días antes de aliviarse y ya él jamás se volvió a parar. Le dijo dónde se iba a aliviar y dónde vivía y jamás se volvió a parar. [They ran into each other just a few days before she delivered and he never came to see her after that. She told him where she was going to deliver and where she was living, but he never set foot in her house.]" Marcelino was born on November 10, 1958, and Rodolfo did not see his son until he was 3 months old. By this time, Inocencia had bought Lupe clothes so she could begin working as a teacher in a private school after she found child care for Marcelino. "[L]e iban a pagar muy bien. Pero luego se encontro a Rodolfo y ya no quizo trabajar. [They were going to pay her very well. But then she ran into Rodolfo again and she didn't want to work anymore.]"

Inocencia was rarely at home with her children and her sister because, as a midwife, she lived at the clinic and was on twenty-four-hour call for deliveries. This arrangement gave Rodolfo the opportunity to move in with Lupe without Inocencia's knowledge or consent. When Inocencia found out through a neighbor, she couldn't believe her sister's willingness to accept Rodolfo after he had abandoned her during her pregnancy. Although Inocencia continued to support her sister, Rodolfo's presence caused friction between them, especially because he did not contribute to the support of the household.

Soon after this, Inocencia learned that the owner of the clinic had decided to return to his hometown of Guadalajara, Jalisco, and she suddenly found herself without a job and with an entire family to support. Feeling defeated, she was riding the bus back to her sister's when, by sheer coincidence, she ran into a former nursing student who told her of a job in Mercedes, Texas, a small town across the border from Matamoros. However, Inocencia's *"tarjeta"* (card) allowed her only to go shopping in *"el otro lado"* (the U.S. side) and prohibited her staying longer than three days. By taking the job without proper immigration documents, she would run the risk of deportation and even jail time. Nevertheless, she decided it was more important to make a living than succumb to the fears of "La Migra" (the immigration service), so she sent her children to her mother in Veracruz and left for Mercedes. In the meantime, her sister's relationship with Rodolfo had become more solid, and they had decided to move in together in Matamoros, where Rodolfo had found a job with Pemex.

Inocencia's bad luck continued in her new job when several of her coworkers threatened to report her to the Immigration and Naturalization Service (INS) as an undocumented worker. Fortunately, the friend that helped her get the job in the first place alerted her and helped her find yet another job in a private clinic in the neighboring town of Harlingen. However, when Inocencia arrived, she saw that the clinic was in decline. The walls were dingy with peeling paint, the clinic was equipped with rusty equipment, and there were very few personnel. But instead of being daunted by her surroundings, Inocencia immediately jumped into action and became the "all-around handyperson," giving injections, tending patients, delivering babies, cooking meals, and doing the hospital's laundry. She was "interned" day and night and on twenty-four-hour call. Her intense work ethic gained her the respect of fellow nurse Laura, who also happened to be the clinic owner's mistress. When Laura finally asked Inocencia whether she was undocumented, Inocencia had to admit that she lacked the necessary papers to be working at the clinic. Laura volunteered to put in a good word with Dr. Pierce, the owner, to help her become legalized. Inocencia was grateful but diplomatically insisted that Laura include her two children in her appeal to Dr. Pierce.

CROSSING TO *EL OTRO LADO*

On December 2, 1959, roughly four months after her arrival at the Harlingen clinic, Inocencia and her two children crossed the border legally into Brownsville, Texas. By this time, she had become aware of irregularities in the clinic. To be sure, there were legitimate patients—mostly women from Mexico who came to deliver their children so they could be U.S. citizens— but there were also more mysterious goings-on. Inocencia eventually realized that the clinic was a source for illegal drugs. "Yo no tenía malicia de nada. Entonces llegaban gringos allí en los cuartos que tenía, disque iban a laboratorio y a tomarse un 'check up' ¿verdad? Resulta que iban y se drogaban allí. [I didn't have any malice about anything. White people would come and stay in the different rooms in the clinic. Supposedly they were coming to get lab work done and to get a 'check-up,' but it turned out they came to get drugs.]" Laura herself had become a drug addict. According to Inocencia, "A veces se encerraba en un cuarto y yo oía que gritaba mucho. Y le decía yo '¿Que tiene Laura?' 'No, es que le duele la cabeza.' [Sometimes she would lock herself in a room and I would hear her scream. I would ask, 'What's wrong with Laura?' (and others in the clinic would reply) 'She just has bad headaches.']" After awhile, Inocencia learned that Dr. Pierce would withhold drugs from Laura whenever they were having a dispute. That's when Inocencia would hear the pain of Laura's withdrawal: "[Entonces] no le daba la droga, se aventaba y gritaba en los cuartos. [That's when she would throw herself against the walls in the room and scream.]" Things got worse, and four months later the clinic closed.

Inocencia was without a job again. She next moved to the neighboring town of San Juan, Texas, and found work in another clinic. However, it was the same exploitive situation she had encountered before. She worked day and night as an all-around stand-in and got paid $25 a week (this was in 1960). When she heard from other workers in the clinic that jobs in *el Norte* paid much better, she concluded that she could find more economic stability and less exploitation if she joined the seasonal migrant stream. South Texas was, and still is, one of the biggest sources for seasonal migrant labor in this country. Families move to the Midwest in early spring to pick crops for a six-month period.

Soon Inocencia and her two children, who were now 5 and 7 years old, were moving again, this time to work as contracted labor for a major vegetable packing company. Together with fifty other people, they boarded buses leased by the company to drive them to Fostoria, Ohio, to work in the fields and packing operations of the firm. They were on the road for three days and two nights, stopping only for brief bathroom stops and to purchase food. In spite of all the migrations Inocencia had already experienced, this was the furthest she had ever been from her home. It was the spring of 1960 and she was 29 years old.

THE TURBULENT YEARS

Inocencia's arrival in Ohio was not auspicious. The bus unloaded close to a small cluster of buildings made of corrugated metal. These buildings constituted the "labor camp" in which all of the workers were housed. Inocencia was assigned a smaller unit because she had only two children, unlike other families who had as many as fifteen members. She walked into a hangar-like structure that had a cement floor and no internal walls. The furniture consisted of one large bed for her and the children, a small gas stove, and a small table with three chairs. There was no refrigerator, closets, or anywhere to store clothes. All of the bathroom and washing facilities were communal. Inocencia immediately went to work. She hung a strong rope where two walls met to form a corner and hung all of their clothes. She washed everything spotless and tried to make it as homey as possible. She didn't mind the living arrangements; her greater shock came when she was faced with the difficult and unfamiliar farm labor.

Every morning at six, the company trucks would arrive to pick up the workers—men, women, and children. They would pile in the back of the trucks and ride to the different fields, where they would weed the rows of cucumber plants with a long-handled hoe. Most of the families employed in the labor camps were skilled at this type of work and could finish a field within a few hours, but Inocencia was essentially by herself and had never handled a hoe before. Her lack of agility with the hoe forced her to take an inordinate amount of time with each furrow, and she would cry as she realized she was getting paid by the amount of work accomplished, not by the hour. Her children would trail behind her. Inocencia would often miss the target with her hoe and her older child, Gabriela, seeing her mother's distress, would replant the cucumber plant. Her little boy was younger and would get distracted. He would simply try to find a tree by the side of the field and sleep as much as possible.

Inocencia worked the entire summer, barely making ends meet and relying on the kindness of the surrounding families when she ran out of groceries at the end of the month. Then tragedy struck: she got deathly ill with peritonitis. She let the symptoms go untended for weeks because she couldn't afford a doctor, until one night she was screaming in pain. Terrified, her neighbors called the ambulance, and she was taken to the hospital. For the week that she was incapacitated, her children lived alone. She tried desperately to alert the hospital personnel about her children, but no one there spoke Spanish. She cried and prayed for the best. Upon her return from the hospital, she found her children safe and sound. Although they had stayed alone, the neighbors periodically brought them food and checked on them. Although Gabriela and Fernando were so young, they had taken care of themselves for an entire week.

By the time the season was over in September, Inocencia had befriended Max and Chora, a local Mexican couple from a family of twelve who offered their home to her. Inocencia was extremely grateful and helped with all of the household chores. She continued to work in the fields during the week, and on weekends she would do the laundry, cook, and clean for the entire family. "Y llegaba de la labor a hacer las tortillas. Los sábados que no trabajaba, a planchar toda la ropa de todos. [I would come from the fields to make tortillas. On Saturdays when I didn't work, I would iron everybody's clothes.]" In return, she was allowed to sleep in the living room with her children. This arrangement worked well, because she liked Chora and Max and got along very well with the entire family.

Chora was very proud of the fact that Inocencia was a nurse and kept telling people about her skills: "Chora le decía a todo el mundo que yo era enfermera, y que no tenía trabajo. Entonces una comadre de ella le dijo que ella tenía otra comadre en Chicago. [Chora would tell everybody that I was a nurse and that I didn't have a job. So one of her comadres told her that she had another comadre in Chicago.]" The comadre in Chicago told Chora that there was a possibility of a job in that city—although the job was unrelated to Inocencia's nursing skills—if Inocencia was willing to relocate. According to Chora's friend, Inocencia could work in a Mexican restaurant as a dishwasher and have her own room, where she and her children could live rent-free.

Habia dicho la señora que era un restaurant dónde yo iba a lavar los trastes, que les iban a dar escuela a mis hijos, que nos iban a dar un cuarto dónde vivir y todo muy bonito. Me acuerdo que empaqué en unas cajas de carton con mecates. Entonces fui y me compre un vestido a la segunda, presentable. [The lady said it was a restaurant and that I was going to wash dishes and that my children could go to school. They also said that they would give us a room to live in, and everything sounded very nice. I remember that I packed my things in boxes tied with a string. I went and bought myself a dress from a secondhand store so that I would look presentable.]

This proposition sounded very attractive to Inocencia, because she wanted a stable job so her children could start school as soon as possible. She accepted the promise of the job and, with her children, took the bus from Fostoria, Ohio, to Chicago, Illinois.

Inocencia had never seen such a huge city. Veracruz, where she had grown up, was definitely a city, but it was bright, sunny, and by the ocean, and its buildings were colonial, unlike the overpowering skyscrapers that lined the streets of downtown Chicago. As soon as she and her children arrived at the Greyhound bus station, she was struck with the dinginess of the place and the vacant looks of many of the individuals hanging around the waiting room. For the first time since her arrival in the United States, she was truly afraid for their safety. The rural settings of South Texas and the towns in Ohio had a friendliness about them, and she certainly never feared being physically harmed. Here, she felt she had to be careful.

A woman in her forties finally came to fetch her. She seemed friendly enough, but there was an air about her that Inocencia did not quite trust: "Entonces no me gustó cuando llegó la señora en un carrazo y muy pintada y el hijo de ella iba manejando el carro—muy pachuquillo así, verdad, pero dije, 'bueno,' y ya nos fuimos. [I didn't like the way the lady looked. She arrived in a big car and wore a lot of makeup. Her son was driving and looked very pachuqillo (like a gang member), but I said to myself, 'OK,' and we took off.]" They all got into the woman's big car, and her son drove them to the Mexican barrio in the inner city.

When they arrived, Inocencia immediately noticed that she wasn't going to work in a restaurant but in a bar. She protested when she realized that she wasn't going to be a dishwasher but a prostitute. "Y le dije pues yo nunca he trabajado en una cantina y no voy a trabajar. Entonces dijeron 'No, pues ahora nos debes el pasaje. . . .' Y como yo estaba bien tonta, que nos podían quitar el pasaporte. . . . Y el lugar que nos dieron para dormir era el cuarto de ella en el piso, allí los tres. Y yo lloraba, no sabía ni que hacer. [I told her I had never worked in a bar. Then they said, 'Well, now you owe us the money for the bus ride.' I was very naïve, I thought they could take my green card away. The place they gave us to sleep was on the floor of her room, all three of us. I cried and cried because I didn't know what to do.]"

The following morning the woman came to her room and told her, "'Vamos al centro,' y ya me compró tres vestidos. Ahora ya le debía tres vestidos. ['Let's go downtown,' and she bought me three dresses. Now I owed her for the three dresses.]" Upon her return from shopping, Inocencia found her son Fernando playing on the fire escape and she felt a dagger in her heart as she realized the implications for her children of taking this job: "Entonces estaba yo en la escalera sentada, me acuerdo como si fuera ahorita, andaba Fernando jugando. Allá en Chicago había mucho carbón, entonces traía los pantalones rotos y las rodillas llenas de carbón. Entonces yo no hallaba ni que hacer y me fui lloré y lloré rogándole a Dios que hiciera algo. [I was sitting on the fire escape—I remember as if it were right now. Fernando was playing. In Chicago there is a lot of soot, and his pants were torn and his knees were full of soot. I didn't know what to do and I cried and cried, praying to God to do something.]"

Late that afternoon, Inocencia went to the basement to do laundry, and an elderly couple, who were related to the bar owner's husband and visiting from Texas, followed her downstairs. They had seen Inocencia's distress and they offered her $20 to return to Fostoria on condition that she not tell the owners of the bar where she got the money. She agreed and left immediately. "Yo había sacado unas garras a lavar, en el sótano, y asi mojadas las agarré y las empaqué otra vez y nos salimos por el sótano, por la puerta que daba a la calle. [I took the wet laundry and I packed it, and we took off from the basement because there was a door that led to the street.]" She flagged a cab and handed the cab driver the note written by the elderly couple telling him to take them to the Greyhound bus station. She kept looking at the buildings whiz by on what seemed an interminable ride. "Iba marque y marque el esé [meter], y una ciudad tan grande, y yo rece y rece y rece que alcanzara para llegar. . . . A los autobuses, para irnos para Fostoria otra vez. Y le decía yo a mis hijos 'recen, recen para que nos alcance el dinero.' [The meter kept ticking and ticking, in a city so huge, and I was praying and praying that I would have enough money to get . . . to the bus station so we could go to Fostoria. And I would tell my children, 'Pray, pray that we have enough money.']" When they finally arrived at the station she owed the cab driver $8 and had only enough money left to buy three tickets to a town an hour away from Fostoria. She figured that once she arrived there, she would call Chora to pick them up. By this time, she had only a dime left for the phone call. She kept telling her children to drink water and to sleep, because she didn't have any money left to feed them. Unfortunately, even the bathrooms required money, so she would stay on the lookout while her children crawled underneath the bathroom doors to avoid the dime charge required to get in.

When they finally arrived at their destination, it was two in the morning and Inocencia felt uncomfortable waking Chora up. So they huddled on a bench at the bus station and slept until 8:30, when she finally called Chora, who came to get them. Chora was very apologetic for having mistaken the employer's intentions and renewed her commitment to finding Inocencia a job that was related to her training.

Not long afterward, another friend of Chora's, Velia, who worked in a Catholic hospital in the neighboring city of Toledo, Ohio, assured Chora that she could find Inocencia a job. Inocencia agreed to go with Velia and temporarily leave her kids with Chora and her family until she was settled.

A PEACEFUL RESPITE FOR THREE YEARS

The job turned out to be a dream come true. The nuns who ran the hospital were incredibly understanding and gentle with Inocencia's almost nonexistent English skills:

> Me pusieron en una sala de maternidad y yo no sabía ni gota de inglés. Cada vez que iba a trabajar nomás, me sentía como acorralada porque me pedían el cómodo y les daba agua, me pedían agua y les daba "Kotex" y asi nomás adivinando, pero las monjas fueron muy buenas conmigo, les pasaban a decir a las señoras que había una enfermera que no sabía inglés para que me tuvieran paciencia. [They placed me in a maternity ward and I didn't know a single drop of English. Every time I went to work, I felt like I was corralled because they would ask me for the bedpan and I would give them water, or they would ask me for water and I would give them a sanitary napkin (Kotex). I was just guessing, but the nuns were very nice to me. They would tell the patients that they had a nurse who didn't speak English, so they would be patient with me.]

Because her Mexican credentials did not meet the U.S. requirements and she did not speak English, Inocencia was hired as a staff member, not as a nurse. But, as usual, she distinguished herself with her indefatigable energy and commitment to work. She seemed to be everywhere at once and had a very pleasant professional demeanor, especially in her gentleness with patients. She immediately began taking English classes in the evening and tried to do the best job possible.

Within six weeks, she had saved enough money to rent an apartment right across from the hospital and was able to bring her children from Fostoria. She enrolled them in school, and for a short period of time things were relatively calm. Inocencia had some misgivings about the neighborhood because it was in transition as white families were moving out and African American families were moving in. In the midst of this ethnic and racial transition, there were only two other Mexican families, and they were caught in the conflicts that white flight was leaving in its wake. Inocencia had never lived in close quarters with anybody except Mexicans, and the language barrier contributed to her confusion about what was going on. Her younger child, Fernando, was especially vulnerable when he walked to kindergarten with his older sister, Gabriela. They were often accosted by African American kids, and whereas Gabriela was able to fend for herself with her belligerent verbal style, Fernando, who had always been shy, had a difficult time. He was often beaten up or intimidated by the older kids, and he began to express a desire to go back to Mexico.

In the meantime, Inocencia had cut off contact with her family because she was afraid to tell them about her trials. "Como en tres años mi mamá y papá no sabían de mí. . . . Yo no quería que supieran como andaba. [For about three years, my mother and father didn't know where I was. . . . I didn't want them to know all my troubles.]" Also, because her ex-husband had never helped her financially with the children, she felt no incentive to tell anybody in the "old neighborhood" about her life in el Norte. She had decided to make it on her own. And she did.

For the next year she made great progress in her life. She furnished her small two-bedroom apartment and was able to stay in her job, and her daughter did extremely well in school and became fluent in English. The only downside was that Fernando was having trouble coping with all of these transitions and with Inocencia's long hours at work. Her shifts began at seven in the morning, and she attended English classes at night. She tried as much as possible to get child care, but here again the dramatic cultural differences made things difficult. Most of the available sitters were German immigrants who did not speak English well and who were not very committed to her kids. As a result, Gabriela preferred to stay alone and read, and her little brother became more and more withdrawn. Finally, Inocencia decided to take drastic action, sending Fernando back to her ex-husband with a Mexican family from Toledo that was driving to Mexico for a vacation. This happened in 1961, at the beginning of the summer and the end of her first year in Toledo.

For the next two years, Inocencia continued to do well at work, although it was not an easy life. She earned enough for living expenses and even sent her parents some money. Her daughter was excelling in school. But the winters in Ohio were brutal, especially for someone coming from a tropical climate and without a car. Inocencia and her daughter would do their shopping and other errands by walking to the store and then "borrowing" shopping carts to bring their groceries home, trudging through the snow, often late at night after Inocencia's English classes.

Despite these hardships, Inocencia's gift for making friends paid off. She developed a network of friendships among the few Mexican families in the area, and she tried to have a social life by attending dances and other Mexican festivities. All in all, she felt fine about how things were going, but she continued to want a husband and greater economic security. She dated and had affairs with several Mexican men, but often they were married or simply did not want the responsibility of a family. Still, she persisted.

THE TURBULENT YEARS RESUME

Inocencia's respite came to an end during the summer of her third year in Toledo. Although she had grown up and lived in "rough neighborhoods" in Mexico, Inocencia's family had prided itself on avoiding all the vices available to them in the surrounding areas. Her family was not made up of saints, but they had never had any problems with the law and had placed great emphasis on education. Even her ex-husband's family, who supposedly did not have as much dedication to education as her own, were comerciantes (vendors) who believed in hard work and avoided illegal transactions. Inocencia's own scuffle with the bar owner in Chicago had reinforced her commitment to avoid compromising situations. Instead, she chose the route of hard work and dedication to get ahead and, for the most part, befriended like-minded people who were extremely poor but also extremely honest and proud.

And then she met Cornelio. Cornelio came from a Mexican family and had grown up in the Midwest. His mother, Cata, had six children without benefit of permanent (or even semipermanent) unions with men who were often in trouble with the law. Cata drank quite a bit, was extremely young for having such a large family, and did not adhere to any conventional morality. She enjoyed dressing in flamboyant ways that highlighted her eye-catching figure, wore a great deal of makeup, and was not much interested in fulfilling the normative demands of motherhood. Cata always had a man in the house, but he never stayed very long.

Inocencia met Cornelio at a Mexican dance. He was a trumpet player for the band and he cut quite an arresting figure. He was also four years younger than she. Even though she did not consider herself conventionally beautiful, Inocencia knew how to dress and conduct herself to maximize her looks; she had always looked younger than her age. She was also free of her mothering responsibilities, having, for the first time in three years, sent her daughter back to Mexico for the summer to visit her father.

Alone and lonely and in need of company and affirmation, Inocencia began seeing Cornelio in the summer of 1962 and had soon given herself over to him completely. Although Cornelio was a drinker and womanizer who had three young children of his own and did not believe in working or living in one place for very long, Inocencia was smitten with him. She suffered great fits of jealousy over his attentions to other women and finally insisted that he move in with her. Although Cornelio did not change his ways, he did move in with Inocencia and her daughter, who had by then returned from Mexico. Overnight, Inocencia's new family included three children between the ages of 8 and 12 in addition to her own 9-year-old daughter.

Also, for the first time, Inocencia began to miss work because of all-night fights and the constant moving from apartment to apartment owing to missed rent payments or the loud carrying-on of Cornelio and his buddies. At times, the rows resulted in Cornelio beating Inocencia severely enough that she ended up in the emergency room. But she never considered going to the police and never truly considered leaving him. In addition to the drinking, womanizing, and general conflicts, the children were not getting along, so Inocencia decided to send her daughter back to her parents in Mexico. As soon as Gabriela left, the situation with Cornelio worsened to the point that, for the first time in her adult life, Inocencia was unable to hold down a job. For a time, she, Cornelio, and his children bounced from apartment to apartment or from family member to family member.

Finally, Inocencia decided that having Cornelio's child was the only way to hold on to him. Julia was born on a chilly night in November 1964, when Inocencia was 33 years old. Julia's birth led to a short honeymoon between Cornelio and Inocencia, but afterwards the violence resumed. Finally, after a particularly brutal beating that culminated in Cornelio dumping Inocencia and Julia at the Greyhound bus station in the dead of winter, she took the bus back to Texas.

Inocencia settled in Brownsville, Texas, found a job in the local hospital, and moved into an apartment. Her mother joined her shortly to help take care of Julia. Not long after that, Inocencia contacted Cornelio, and he left his own children in Toledo with his mother and joined Inocencia in Brownsville. But reconciliation lasted only a couple of months, and when the conflicts resumed, Cornelio returned to Toledo. A month later Inocencia left her job, her furniture, and her apartment and followed him.

It was the middle of January when she, Gabriela, and Julia arrived at the Greyhound bus station in Toledo. It was about six o'clock in the evening, and Inocencia called Cornelio's mother to come pick them up. Cata told Inocencia that was impossible because Cornelio was no longer living with her. At a loss, Inocencia called Toña, a longtime friend with a family of five, who lived in the area. Toña agreed to pick up Inocencia and her two girls. When they arrived at Toña's modest home, Inocencia proceeded to track down Cornelio. She finally found him and set up a meeting with him at his mother's house. It turned out that Cornelio had found someone else in Inocencia's absence—someone much younger and, according to him, not as demanding as Inocencia. Inocencia said that what happened next was like something in a dream. She grabbed a knife and lunged at Cornelio, injuring him on the shoulder. Other family members pulled her back, but Cornelio was already bleeding profusely. Then she ran out of the house, and someone followed her and took her to Toña's house.

The following day, after Toña's kids had left for school, Gabriela and Julia were in the small kitchen with Toña and Inocencia, who was wearing a brand new pink robe with an elaborate ribbon at the neck. At some point, she looked down at her robe and suddenly lost control. She handed Julia to Gabriela and proceeded to the unheated living room, where she began to tear her robe to pieces with her teeth. She kept repeating that she had bought the robe when she had a home and that now it was gone. She pulled her hair, threw the sofa cushions against the wall, and tore more and more of her robe. In a panic, Toña called the fire station down the road while the kids cried and tried to grab on to their mother. Inocencia seemed oblivious to everything except her own reality.

The firemen arrived, calmed her down, and put her on a stretcher. They took her to the local mental hospital, where she remained for four months. As Inocencia got better, she was allowed to stay at Toña's during the weekends. Fortunately, Cornelio never tried to contact her. For her part, Inocencia was scared that she was going to be prosecuted for the knife attack and that her green card would be revoked; this last worry was an incentive to stay away from him. Finally, she got well enough to contact her parents in Mexico. Soon after, Toña received a letter from them with a check for $300, which they had obtained by selling their house. They pleaded with Toña to bring Inocencia and the children to the border town of Matamoros, where they could pick them up. Toña waited until the school year was over and then took Inocencia and her children to Mexico.

Inocencia's parents broke down crying when they saw their daughter. She was 35 years old, but she looked twice that age. She had the glassy look of those who have been institutionalized, and the medication she was taking made her hands shake. Her arms bent at the elbow as if in a permanent state of reaching out for an embrace. Her parents did not recognize in this woman before them the vivacious, intelligent, and rebellious daughter who had left for el Norte.

HOME ONCE AGAIN

Inocencia spent the following three months recuperating with her parents. She slowly became her old self and started to look for work in one of the local hospitals. Her father helped her put the word out: "Gente que iba al taller le decía que tenía una hija enfermera y que no tenía trabajo. [He would tell clients that would go to his (painting) shop that he had a daughter who was a nurse and needed a job.]" Eventually, she was able to get a temporary position at the Hospital del Seguro Social, the hospital in charge of dispensing socialized medicine. Inocencia's mother took care of her kids while she worked and she even got to see her little boy once in a while.

In her position at the Hospital del Seguro Social, Inocencia's hard work and dedication again distinguished her from the other employees, so much so that the head nurse told her that if she were willing to relocate to Matamoros, Tamaulipas (ironically, where she had started out) she could get a permanent position. Inocencia did not hesitate. She was still looking for economic stability and didn't see any future in temporary contracts. So she left her children with her parents and took the bus to Matamoros, the city to which she, her kids, and her sister Lupe had fled nine years earlier.

Just before she left Veracruz, Inocencia had started seeing Agustino again. He was not pleased that she had come home with a new child, but he was trying to be open-minded, especially because Inocencia had impressed on him how much Gabriela and Fernando needed two parents. The appeal to his fatherhood had an effect on Agustino, and he slowly grew closer to her. Once in Matamoros, Inocencia began to press him to join her, but he was determined to remain in his beloved Veracruz, where he had family, friends, and baseball (he was the local president of the amateur league). Although he did not have a very lucrative or very prestigious job, he had been working for the past eight years in the largest auto parts store in Veracruz. He was well liked, and he had his routine. He still lived in the same neighborhood with his mother and three adult, unmarried siblings, and everybody got along very well. Unlike Inocencia, he did not believe in the constant search for a better life. His life might not have been what others desired, but it fit him just fine.

Still, there were the kids. Inocencia kept insisting that if they moved to the border, the children could commute and benefit from schooling in the United States. They already had the coveted green card that everybody in their old neighborhood desired. This could be their ticket to becoming professionals, and, so far, both children had distinguished themselves with outstanding performances in school. This was the hook that prompted Agustino to consider leaving his life in Veracruz.

Finally, in 1968, when Inocencia's children were 15, 13, and 4 years old, Agustino agreed to move to Matamoros and bring the children. They didn't have much money, so in the beginning they lived on the outskirts of town. Agustino had a distant cousin who lived in a very modest house on a large plot of land, and he let Agustino and his family live in the back in a small shed with two rooms, no windows, and a dirt floor. That's where Inocencia and Agustino started their family life together again, eleven years after their divorce.

INOCENCIA RESUMES HER FAMILY LIFE

Once her family was settled in Matamoros, Inocencia focused on stabilizing their economic situation. She quickly contacted old friends to find out the process by which her husband could become a temporary worker at the local Pemex Oil site, the best-paid unskilled labor around. Pemex had an elaborate union system that gave its workers lifetime guarantees. Inocencia obtained the number of Agustino's ficha (union credential) from their days as newlyweds in Poza Rica and approached the union officials. The union at Pemex was and remains an elaborate patronage system in which high union officials give their friends first dibs on 30-, 60-, and 90-day contracts in return for regalitos (small gifts), which amount to kickbacks. Agustino, although he always accompanied Inocencia, was too ethical and shy to approach these union officials. It was Inocencia who would push, cajole, charm, and simply insist on meeting the appropriate authorities. She also realized that, although she now had a permanent job in the hospital, the rate of pay was not comparable to that in the local Pemex hospital. Again, she quickly set out to find a way to obtain a position there.

> Pedí permiso en el seguro un año porque me aseguraron trabajo por un año. . . . Y como siguió el trabajo fui a pedir otro año y me dijeron que ya no, perdía la planta. Y me arriesgué a perder la planta para irme de

transitoria allá [hospital Pemex]. Y la mayor parte del tiempo estuve de transitoria aunque me ascendían a supervisión y me dieron los cursos de supervisión porque era partera. [I asked for a leave from the Social Security hospital because they (Pemex) assured me of work for a year. . . . The work continued, so I asked for another year (of leave), and they said no, that I would lose my permanent job. I took the risk of losing my permanent job and instead became a temporary worker over there (at the Pemex hospital). For almost the entire time I remained there, I was a temporary worker, although they trained me to be a supervisor because I had a certificate in midwifery.]

NEGOTIATING THE BORDER

The first five years of their resumed life together were turbulent ones for Inocencia and Agustino. Since the divorce, Agustino had not had a relationship with another woman (although there were rumors of flirtations with a variety of women in the old neighborhood). He had lived with his widowed mother and his siblings and, as the eldest son, had a great deal of authority in the household. He never abused his authority, but he was not accustomed to negotiating decisions with an equal partner. Inocencia, in her thirty-seven years, had seen more and suffered more than most people. She had always had a strong personality, and she thrived on making her own decisions. Her adolescent children were not easy, either. Both they and Agustino resented leaving the beauty and ambiance of Veracruz for this godforsaken, dusty border town that, from their perspective, had little to offer.

During this rocky time, Agustino and Inocencia argued constantly, and there were enormous pressures around money. Eventually, Inocencia realized that she had to move her family to the U.S. side of the border if their children were going to have a shot at an education in the United States. She argued that it would be better if she and Agustino commuted to work on the Mexican side. Again, Agustino resisted. All of the family was "legal" with the exception of Agustino; that meant he alone ran the risk of harassment and possible imprisonment for living in the United States even though he worked in Mexico. However, Inocencia earlier had convinced Agustino to marry her again in the United States, and she now quickly applied for citizenship papers. Within a year and with arduous study, Inocencia passed the naturalization test and Agustino went into the queue of U.S. spouses, a quicker avenue to legalization.

But still the pressure was enormous, because Agustino—who, in spite of his poverty, had always taken pride in working and abiding by the law—

now had to deal with the border patrol on a daily basis. Further, because he was a recent union worker, he was assigned to work the night and afternoon shifts. That meant he would finish his shift at either midnight or eight in the morning, both dangerous times to cross the border (the evening was obviously associated with illegal activities, and the morning was when undocumented day workers crossed the border for work). He often slept in his car until it was late enough that he could pass as a "day shopper." Inocencia was also at the bottom in her temporary job at the Pemex hospital and had to take the hours she was offered. Consequently, when their shifts did not coincide, Inocencia and Agustino might not see each other for days. But still, they limped along, trying to build a life together—a life that at times seemed like it was going to come apart at the seams.

Things finally came to a head in 1970, when Inocencia discovered she was pregnant again. She was 40 years old and thought she was beginning menopause. She wanted an abortion, especially because she knew that given her age, there was a high probability that the baby would be born with birth defects. But Agustino was insistent that they could handle whatever happened. The fights intensified, but finally Agustino won and Inocencia agreed to follow through with the pregnancy.

Lupita was born in June 1971, just a few weeks before Gabriela finished her junior year in high school. The baby had an important effect especially on Agustino, who acted with Lupita the way he had acted with Gabriela when she was born. He took over the care of Lupita while Inocencia returned to work immediately, often taking on double shifts to increase their income. Inocencia also tried to work the graveyard shift as often as possible because it paid more (and, because it was the least desirable shift, there wasn't as much competition for it).

By now, Agustino had finally gotten his green card, and Inocencia insisted that he begin looking for a job in Brownsville rather than commuting to Mexico every day. But Agustino lacked the fearlessness that had always characterized Inocencia. Although he did not speak English and had only a third-grade education, he was a self-educated man (muy educado) who read voraciously and was extremely articulate. Moreover, he hated the aggressiveness and lack of gentility in the United States, and he was often at a loss as to how to elbow his way into the low-paying, competitive, unskilled jobs that his qualifications restricted him to. However, he found a semipermanent job in a vegetable packing shed where he worked eight months out of the year and was laid off and collected unemployment the rest of the time. He remained at this job for the next seventeen years, never earning more than minimum wage, with no medical, retirement, vacation, or other benefits. The only advantage was that he could take care of Lupita during the summer months, when he was laid off. He loved taking care of the baby, and it helped them economically by avoiding child care costs. Agustino remained loyal to this job and never missed a day. He also provided Inocencia and his children with a stability they had never had before, because, once settled, he refused to move. In addition, he managed the family's money so wisely and with such discipline that eventually he and Inocencia were able to buy the humble three-room house they had first rented when they came to live in Brownsville.

Inocencia also settled down with the arrival of Lupita. She was a bit jealous of the attention that Agustino doted on their new daughter, but she also felt confident that now he would never leave her. From the time her daughter was born in 1971 until 1987, Inocencia lived in relative calm and happiness with Agustino and their children.

At the age of 56, however, Inocencia became a widow when Agustino died unexpectedly of a heart attack at the age of 59. She was devastated, but she struggled to continue with her life. She refused to give up her home and move close to her grown children. Instead, she stayed where she and Agustino had spent seventeen years of their life together and eventually retired. Today, at the age of 68, she lives alone in the same house and is economically self-sufficient, thanks to her Social Security checks and the small pension she gets from her job (which eventually became permanent) at the Pemex Oil Company's hospital. She owns her car and her home. She has a large network of mostly women friends whom she visits on a regular basis. She enjoys going across the border from Brownsville to Matamoros for grocery shopping, doctor's appointments, and social visits. She takes trips to Mexico to visit her sisters, whom she still helps with gifts of clothes and money. Her brother lives a mile away from her in Brownsville; she brought him and his family, illegally, into the United States and then helped them get their green cards. She still occasionally delivers babies in her home to make extra money, especially for women who come across the border to have their children.

Inocencia visits her children once or twice a year. She loves them dearly but has never quite felt comfortable not being in charge or having something to do, and when there, she misses the border that enables her to exist in two cultures. Chicana feminists have written eloquently about the political, cultural, and psychological complexity of living *en la frontera* (Cantú 1995; Anzaldúa 1987); as Rosa Linda Fregoso notes, "By reenacting a continual crossing of frontiers, the *transfrontera* subject operates within and outside of traditions and communities" (1998, 328). Less explored, however, are the economic realities that tie many people to this region. In 2002, Inocencia lived on an income of about $6,000 a year. Her ties to the borderlands are not only cultural but economic. Nowhere in the United States could she have the lifestyle the border affords her by allowing her to shop and get health care and entertainment in Mexico and yet reside in the United States. She has eked out a cultural and economic existence that meets her material as well as her emotional needs.

After her turbulent life, Inocencia has found some kind of peace, and her children have, for the most part, forgiven her all of her transgressions, which they did not understand when they were young. She didn't understand them herself; mostly she was just trying to survive and provide for her family as best she knew how, at the same time that she was trying to provide something for herself.

INOCENCIA'S "NO-NAME" FEMINISMS

In her ethnography of Esperanza, the Mexican street vendor, Ruth Behar reminds us of the difficulty of a "feminist translation," particularly because Esperanza was a "transgressive woman whose social position does not make it possible for her to own the words 'patriarchy' and 'feminism' "(1993, 276). Similarly, Inocencia does not have a well-developed political framework to make sense of her life. Like most people, she lives as best she can within the restrictions that her class, gender, ethnicity, and race impose on her and on those she loves. The significance of her struggles, I believe, lies in her ability to use her intelligence, humor, and heart to resist these restrictions. It is in the analysis of these acts of resistance (Scott 1985) that we feminists may find some important lessons to enhance our own notions of feminism.

Assuming Agency

Throughout the two-year period I interviewed her, I was consistently struck by how much responsibility Inocencia assumed for responding to the problems around her. Whether she was addressing problems in her family or in the economic realm, she consistently assumed she could do something about them. From helping her sister during her unplanned pregnancy to helping her husband find better employment to pushing her children through school, she never allowed an obstacle to keep her from fighting back. She also did not express regret or see herself as a victim. In narrating her life, Inocencia recounted events and traumas as part and parcel of what every individual experiences; the goal is to negotiate all that life hands you. There was a total lack of self-pity in her recounting of her life history.

Well-justified critiques of "everyday forms of resistance" have charged that they do not necessarily lead to structural and political change (Gutmann 1993). Theoretically, however, we do not know how these everyday actions might lead to more structural political mobilizations later on. A case in point is the work by Mary Pardo (1998) and Patricia Zavella (1985), in which they document how working-class Chicanas started either with a family concern about their neighborhood or as friends of other women in a union and ended up being activist organizers on behalf of larger political issues. In Inocencia's case, she was periodically involved in union struggles in Mexico as she worked as a nurse and certainly has helped women take charge of their own medical care as she advised them about the best course of action in making decisions about medical procedures. She also raised three daughters who consider themselves feminists and who actively fight for social change in their own professions. Inocencia's goals of economic stability and education might be considered fairly "conventional," but hers is no Horatio Alger story of becoming middle class and unconcerned with those less fortunate than herself. Instead, in spite of her below-poverty existence, she is known for helping not only her family but those who come in contact with her, and she never, even at the age of 68, simply accepts what is dished out to her.

Allegiance to Family in the Context of Struggle
Even though Inocencia existed within a very well-developed patriarchal structure, she did not comply with it at all times. She was especially susceptible to her father's influence and judgment, but ultimately she rebelled. She did marry Agustino against her father's wishes, and although later she succumbed to the pressure to divorce him, this was not simply a result of her father's influence, for Agustino did lack the ambition to find a better situation for his family and felt very comfortable taking a back seat to Inocencia's initiative. She also violated her parents' wishes when she remarried Agustino, and certainly her transgressions in el Norte were not in compliance with the normative standards held by her parents or her community. In fact, she was perceived by her entire family as being a "difficult" person who always got her way and never let any barriers discourage her from her objectives.

Nonetheless, Inocencia always helped her family members and still does. When her father became ill after a long battle with diabetes, he lived with her and her family in Brownsville. By this time, her father was only a shell of his former self, suffering a leg amputation and the slow loss of his mental faculties. Inocencia hired somebody to take care of him while she worked, but it was she who was responsible for bathing him, feeding him, and taking him to the doctor. This was in the midst of tending to a troubled marriage and raising teenage children. Again, her loyalty and commitment to her immediate, as well as extended, family has never wavered.

Valorization of Self

In spite of the fact that Inocencia worked and still works for her family, she is very clear about her individual needs. In her family she is legendary for how well she takes care of herself physically—always wearing stylish clothes and makeup and doing things that please her, like maintaining a large network of mostly female friends. She is certainly not la madre sufrida often written about in Chicana feminist literature (Behar 1993, 271; Trujillo 1991, 188).

One of the demands Inocencia made of Agustino, in spite of their meager resources, was to go on vacation in Mexico every couple of years. In addition to organizing a big Christmas celebration with dinner and dancing every year, she attended weddings, baptisms, and work celebrations and was always one of the snappiest dressers at these gatherings. Agustino would often joke that when Inocencia turned into a "blue-haired old lady, she was still going to have un pico colorado [a red beak]." Even now, she looks at least ten years younger than her age, and Agustino's death has not dampened her enthusiasm for living or for enjoying her pleasures.

Rebellion against Physical and Mental Abuse

Although Inocencia suffered a great deal of physical and psychological abuse from Cornelio and other men in her life, including her father and Agustino in the early years of their marriage, she never took it without protest. Of course, the protest often resulted in intensification of the abuse. In her father's case, when she was in her late teens, it was still an accepted practice to beat children if they did not comply. Inocencia related how her father took a belt to her because she "spoke back to him," and how he told her he would not stop hitting her until she cried. Nevertheless, she withstood the beating and refused to cry until her mother intervened out of fear that Inocencia would end up in the hospital.

The situation was similar with Cornelio: Inocencia stated that he would often hit her precisely because she would not remain silent in the face of his abuse. Still, she always spoke up and never withheld what was on her mind. This cost her, but she did not give up. Eventually, the men who abused her would leave her because they could not domesticate her. Fighting back proved a successful strategy with Agustino; late in their marriage they reached a loving equality that persisted until his death.

Feminist Lessons for Her Daughters

All three of Inocencia's daughters are very much like her: they are competent, outspoken, friendly, professional women. Although her daughters did not always have a tension-free relationship with her, Inocencia taught them by example and through sheer imposition of her will when she thought it was necessary. She did not physically abuse her daughters, but she did direct their lives and impose her values on them. For example, as a teenager her third child disobeyed her once by going to a public dance without her permission. "Una vez se me fue al baile al Cívico, tenía como 13 o 14 años pero estaba muy grandota. Siempre que llegaba yo del trabajo, cuando estaba de día, que llegaba en la tarde me decía la señora que me ayudaba 'pues ella nomás llega y avienta los libros y se va y a mi no me dice dónde.' [One time she went to a dance in the civic center. She was about 13 or 14 years old but she was very developed. I would get home from work in the afternoon, when I was on the day shift, and the baby-sitter told me, 'She just comes and throws her books and she leaves without telling me where she's going.]" Inocencia went directly to the dance and forced her daughter to come home: "Que me voy para alla, y apenas iba Julia entrando que le volaban las mechas para adentro risa y risa. No que me bajo y que la pepeno. . . . 'Ay condenada muchacha, ándele vamonos para la casa.' Y ya se fue muy sumidita y ya la heche al carro, pero yo andaba bien enojada porque se me iba. [I went to the dance. She was just going in to the dance, her hair blowing in the wind, and she was laughing. I got out of the car and I grabbed her . . . (I told her,) 'Damn kid, let's go home.' And she left with me very quietly and I put her in the car, but I was really angry that she would go out without my permission.]"

Inocencia knew there was a price to be paid for enforcing her rules. She often experienced her children's strong resentments and, for short periods of time, even their outright rejection. But she did not regret her actions. She felt her "iron fist" was necessary because of the dangerous neighborhoods and schools their economic situation restricted them to. Agustino was not very helpful in this regard. He would often complain to her privately about things he did not like in his children's behavior, but rarely would he discipline them. Not surprisingly, the girls adored their father and resented their mother, who acted as the disciplinarian.

As her girls grew up and became successful, however, they were much kinder in their judgment of Inocencia. Again, she never denied what she had done to them. She never denied the damage she had caused Gabriela by exposing her to Cornelio. She felt she tried her best to repair the damage by fighting for Gabriela's right to fulfill her dreams of pursuing a profession.

Inocencia also taught her daughters the value of friendship with women. Men were always there, but it was the women who got things done. She taught them that survival depended on women helping other women. She gave her daughters ample evidence of this: Inocencia's sisters helping her with child care, her female friends connecting her with jobs, Laura helping her get her green card, Chora opening up her home to her, Velia finding her a job in Toledo, Toña taking care of her kids while she was in the hospital, and numerous other women helping her throughout her life. Even now, Inocencia visits several of her women friends in rest homes and those who are ill but still living in their homes and has Sunday brunch with—as she calls them sardonically—*las muchachas* (the girls). This group of ten women, mostly in their sixties, see each other every Sunday, visit each other when they are sick, help each other through family deaths and disappointments, and, most of all, share laughter and the triumphs of their children.

CONCLUSION

It is important to recognize that there are many feminisms and that their definitions are currently in flux. Griffin (1989) and others argue that the definitions of feminism, feminist identity, and feminist consciousness should remain flexible to maximize the inclusion of a diversity of women's experiences. I would also argue that the inclusion of the cultural, artistic, and scholarly productions of Women of Color are essential to informing these evolving definitions. The story of Inocencia's life, as well as those of the lives of many other women like her who do not have access to the academy and are not the usual topics of study, needs to be an integral part of the process of definition and inclusion.

EPILOGUE

In *Memoirs of a Geisha*, Arthur Golden notes, "A memoir proves a record not so much of the memoirist as of the memoirist's world. . . . Autobiography, if there is really such a thing, is like asking a rabbit to tell us what he looks like hopping the grasses of the field. How would he know? If we want to hear about the field, on the other hand, no one is in a better circumstance to tell us—so long as we keep in mind that we are missing all those things the rabbit was in no position to observe" (1997, 1–2).

Inocencia's story is told from her perspective, and in the "telling" (Sánchez 1995) she constructs her subjectivity and allows us to see what the rabbit saw as she was hopping through her life. All in all, as Inocencia reaches the twilight of her life, she is satisfied with the outcome of her struggles. She likes to recite the famous lines of the Latin American poet Amado Nervo:

Muy cerca de mi ocaso, yo te bendigo, Vida,
porque nunca me diste ni esperanza fallida
ni trabajos injustos, ni pena inmerecida;
porque veo al final de mi rudo camino
que yo fui el arquitecto de mi propio destino;
que si extraje las mieles o la hiel de las cosas,
fue porque en ellas puse hiel o mieles sabrosas;
cuando planté rosales coseché siempre rosas.
Cierto, a mis lozanías va a seguir el invierno:
¡mas tú no me dijiste que mayo fuese eterno!
Hallé sin duda largas las noches de mis penas;
mas no me prometistes tú sólo noches buenas;
y en cambio tuve algunas santamente serenas . . .
Amé, fui amado, el sol acarició mi faz.
¡Vida, nada me debes! ¡Vida, estamos en paz!

[In the twilight of my life, I bless you, life,
because you never gave me false hope
or unjust work, or undeserved pain
because I see at the end of my rough road
that I was the architect of my destiny;
if I extracted the honey or the vileness from things
it was because I put either vile or delicious honey in them;
when I planted rose bushes I always harvested roses.
True, my spring will be followed by winter:
but you never told me that May was eternal!
Without a doubt I found my nights of pain eternal
but you never promised me only good nights;
in return I had some celestially serene ones . . .
I loved, I was loved, the sun caressed my face.
Life, you owe me nothing! Life, we are at peace!]
(1982, 118–19; my translation)

NOTE

1. All of the names of individuals and geographical areas have been changed to protect confidentiality.

WORKS CITED

Anzaldúa, Gloria. 1987. *Borderlands/La frontera: The New Mestiza.* San Francisco: Spinsters/Aunt Lute.

Argüelles, Lourdes, and Anne M. Rivero. 1993. "Gender/Sexual Orientation, Violence, and Transnational Migration: Conversations with Some Latinas We Think We Know." *Urban Anthropology* 22(2–4): 259–76.

Behar, Ruth. 1993. *Translated Woman: Crossing the Border with Esperanza's Story.* Boston: Beacon Press.

Bellafante, Ginia. 1998. "Feminism: It's All about Me!" *Time* 151(25): 54–62.

Cantú, Norma E. 1995. *Canícula: Snapshots of a Girlhood en la Frontera.* Albuquerque: University of New Mexico Press.

Fregoso, Rosa Linda. 1998. "*Sacando los trapos al sol* [Airing dirty laundry] in Lourdes Portillo's Melodocumystery, The Devil Never Sleeps." Pp. 307–29 in *Redirecting the Gaze: Gender, Theory, and Cinema in the Third World,* ed. Diana Robin and Ira Jeffe. Albany: State University of New York Press.

Golden, Arthur. 1997. *Memoirs of a Geisha.* New York: Vintage Books.

Griffin, Christine. 1989. "'I'm not a women's libber, but . . .': Feminism, Consciousness and Identity." Pp. 173–93 in *The Social Identity of Women,* ed. S. Skevington and D. B. Baker. London: Sage.

Gutmann, Matthew C. 1993. "Rituals of Resistance: A Critique of the Theory of Everyday Forms of Resistance." *Latin American Perspectives* 20(2): 74–92.

Lamphere, Louise, Helena Ragoné, and Patricia Zavella. 1997. *Situated Lives: Gender and Culture in Everyday Life.* New York: Routlege.

Nervo, Amado. 1982. *Antología poética.* Madrid, Spain: Biblioteca EDAF.

Pardo, Mary S. 1998. *Mexican American Women Activists: Identity and Resistance in Two Los Angeles Communities.* Philadelphia: Temple University Press.

Pesquera, Beatriz M., and Denise A. Segura. 1996. "With Quill and Torch: A Chicana Perspective on the American Women's Movement and Feminist Theories." Pp. 231–47 in *Chicanas/Chicanos at the Crossroads: Social, Economic, and Political Change,* ed. David R. Maciel and Isidro D. Ortíz. Tucson: University of Arizona Press.

Saldívar-Hull, Sonia. 1991. "Feminism on the Border: From Gender Politics to Geopolitics." Pp. 203–21 in *Criticism in the Borderlands: Studies in Chicano Literature, Culture, and Ideology,* ed. Hector Calderón and José D. Saldívar. Durham, NC: Duke University Press.

Sánchez, Rosaura. 1995. *Telling Identities: The Californio Testimonios.* Minneapolis: University of Minnesota Press.

Scott, James C. 1985. *Weapons of the Weak: Everyday Forms of Peasant Resistance.* New Haven: Yale University Press.

Trujillo, Carla, ed. 1991. *Chicana Lesbians: The Girls Our Mothers Warned Us About.* Berkeley: Third Woman Press.

Zavella, Patricia. 1985. "'Abnormal Intimacy': The Varying Work Networks of Chicana Cannery Workers." *Feminist Studies* 11(3): 541–57.

———. 1994. "Reflections on Diversity among Chicanas." Pp. 199–212 in *Race*, ed. Steven Gregory and Roger Sanjeck. New Brunswick, NJ: Rutgers University Press.

RESPONSE TO CHAPTER EIGHT

Grounding Feminisms through La Vida de Inocencia

GABRIELA F. ARREDONDO

• • • • •

In a powerful and insightful essay, Aída Hurtado relates the life of Inocencia, a complex woman who navigates her own resistance to and acceptance of class, race, and gender subordinations. As she weaves the story of this woman's life, of her choices and their outcomes, Hurtado is constructing a pointed critique of current academic conceptions of feminism. Through Inocencia's story, Hurtado argues for the centrality of the expressions and productions of Women of Color in understanding the variety of feminisms that exist in the lives of seemingly subjugated women. Inocencia's experiences as a poor Mexican woman force awareness of previously unrecognized human agency even in reactive and impetuous acts. This awareness then highlights the transgressiveness of the lived experiences of women like her, women who are actively deconstructing their own subjugation while continually battling racializing, gendering, and classing subordinations. Moreover, Inocencia's experiences of these constraints in Mexico and in the United States underscore some remarkable similarities in the way class, race, and gender subordinations work across national borders in transnational lives.

Inocencia's life choices have been acts of survival that have an ironic blend of acceptance and resistance of constraints and norms. She wanted a husband and economic security, equating one with the other. Yet she continually fought to align these desires with her own independence and drive for "a better life." She chose to marry against her parents' wishes yet ultimately found her long-sought stability with the very man her family had discouraged her from marrying. In the interim, she lived a tumultuous life that so challenged normative prescriptions of her family and culture that when she finally settled down with Agustino, in her family's eyes he no longer seemed so wrong for her. As a mother of four children, she embodied motherhood, yet she subjected her children to the unrest and dire circumstances of her life. In spite of the turmoil through which they lived, she fought continually for them to obtain the best possible education.

The fearlessness and independence that drove Inocencia throughout her life were also punctuated by intense moments of dependence on support networks of female friends and family. In this we see the importance of other people in her ability to resist and contest her circumstances. With the economic support of her father, she trained in nursing and later recovered after her stay in the mental hospital. With Toña's help she escaped a dangerous and oppressive job and had her children well cared for. Yet her friends and family were also fundamental to creating the very constraints against which Inocencia constantly struggled, as in the case of her father, who lashed her as a young girl and disapproved of her choices.

Throughout the telling of Inocencia's life, Hurtado highlights the moments of resistance and the strategies for survival that Inocencia employs. Building on the work of Women of Color, Hurtado argues that these acts of resistance that make up what she terms "no-name feminisms" *must* inform the many academic definitions of feminism that have failed to capture the experiences of poor Women of Color. That is, everyday acts of resistance by poor Women of Color must inform our "named" feminisms.

In this spirit, Aída Hurtado presents the concept of "underground feminisms," "forms of feminism that have not yet seen the light of the printed page" and that need "to inform how we conceptualize women's oppression and liberation." Rather than working to name the unnamed, however, I encourage Hurtado to embrace the more radical reformulation she is beginning to outline: not only the underground nature of some feminisms but also the need to ground feminism itself!

By bringing "the feminisms developed and defined by the academy" down to earth, so to speak, she would be forcing them to be grounded in the everyday and in the diversities of women's lives. Such a grounding would *necessitate* recognizing the multiplicity of lived experiences and the fundamental ways women's lives are constrained and prescribed by racial, economic, gendered, and sexualized boundaries. Foregrounding these boundaries would also clarify those spaces in which women like Inocencia create openings for themselves that disrupt the borders of norms, prescriptions, and expectations. I suggest that a critical aspect of grounding feminisms involves situating them historically in order to move beyond either essentializing them or getting lost in qualifiers, which are somehow meant to capture specific actions or moments but that instead run the danger of privileging particular forms of feminism.

Framing feminisms within their historical moments serves several functions. First, it frees us to recognize a historiography of feminisms, named and unnamed, while opening entire chasms of time, vast eras in which women's actions *were* contestatory, self-conscious, independent moves toward bettering their own lives in response to and at times in opposition to the social, economic, and political constraints of their historical moment. In this light, Inocencia's story joins a trajectory through time of mujeres like Soledad Cruz (Photo 1) and Ramona Velasquez (Photo 2), women who are linked in their struggles, albeit marked by the distinctiveness of their historical moments. Or take, for example, the life of María Paniagua, a Mexicana who also traveled similar roads as Inocencia later did, a mujer who lived for a time in the early 1920s in the railroad camps in the stockyards area of Chicago (Mary McDowell Settlement House Papers, "Mexican Work Reports, 1920–21," Chicago Historical Society). She moved with her husband from San Antonio to Des Moines to Kansas City to Detroit, where he deserted her in 1923 with three children. Like Inocencia, she struggled to provide for her children alone. Like Inocencia, she relied on a network of female friends who helped her get to Chicago, where there were more jobs available. Like Inocencia's friend Toña, María helped other mujeres with child care, cleaning, and laundry to allow them to work in the factories. They, in turn, provided her with food and friendship. María's life, like that of Inocencia and thousands of other mujeres, is linked also through time in these networks of women in the "valu[ing] of friendship with women." Even in the too brief mention of "las muchachas," we see the ongoing importance of such networks in Inocencia's life.

Second, developing a historiography of these feminisms, named and unnamed, would allow us to embrace those mujeres who have struggled and continue to struggle in the academy by working to deconstruct subjugating knowledges and to value the lived experiences of Women of Color. Historians Antonia Castañeda (1993), Miroslava Chávez (1998), Deena González (1999), Emma Pérez (1999), Vicki Ruiz (1987, 1998), Rosaura Sánchez (1995), Elizabeth Salas (1990), and Shirlene Soto (1990), among others, have chronicled several of these lives and the networks that were integral to them. These scholars have been at the forefront of using Chicana and Mexicana

PHOTO 1   Soledad Cortés de Cruz entered the United States from Mexico in 1930 and moved through Brownsville, Texas to Hartford, Michigan before settling in Chicago to work as a sewing machine operator. After eighteen years of marriage and seven children (five born in Mexico, two in the United States), she divorced her husband in 1932. The children remained in Chicago with her and by 1940, she worked full-time in a sewing-factory. Petition Number 210114, Naturalization Records of Chicago Circuit Court, National Archives and Records Administration, Great Lakes Region, Chicago, Illinois. Special thanks to archivist Scott Forsythe. Reprinted with permission.

life stories to challenge academic conceptions of history, of evidence, and of feminism. In voicing Inocencia's story, Hurtado participates in this exciting historiographical move and ties herself and Inocencia into the trajectory of mujeres struggling and working through time.

Third, framing feminisms within their historical moments also argues against popular media and some academics who bemoan the demise of feminism, for it suggests that feminism as such may no longer be recognizable by them *precisely* because their own historical moment has changed.

PHOTO 2 Ramona Santillan de Velazquez entered the United States from Mexico in 1926 accompanied by her husband and four children. Together they eventually settled in Chicago, where she gave birth to her fifth child. Within ten years she was separated from her husband, raising all her children in Chicago, and working as a dressmaker. Petition Number 209588, Naturalization Records of Chicago Circuit Court, National Archives and Records Administration, Great Lakes Region, Chicago, Illinois. Special thanks to archivist Scott Forsythe. Reprinted with permission.

Women's resistances of their subjugations, then, haven't stopped; they have simply taken different forms.

Finally, grounding feminisms historically allows us to counter the laments of scholars and others who worry "whether younger women are committed to the ideals set forth in the second wave of the movement." The lives of younger women are circumscribed by necessarily different factors and forms of subjugation than those who went before them. To look for the ideals of "the second wave" in the next generations is to come dangerously close to essentializing the very prescriptions of feminism against which Women of Color have been fighting for decades. Inocencia's choices and circumstances were not those of her mother or of her daughters. That her daughters identify themselves as feminists speaks eloquently to her success in preparing them to continue to disrupt prescriptions, to challenge norms, and to resist subordination. Inocencia's daughters came of age at a particular historical moment in which their life choices and resistances of their own subjugations took forms distinct from their mother's. Their own ability to recognize their mother's acts of resistance and everyday acts of survival in a very different historical moment, however, underscores the strength of generational connections in the networks of mujeres, while recognizing the specificity of their historical circumstances and possibilities. Inocencia, like her daughters who followed, was "just trying to survive and provide for her family as best she knew how, at the same time that she was trying to provide something for herself." In those everyday choices Inocencia's experiences as a poor Mexican woman clearly define transgressive human agency, that is, actively challenging subjugation in the midst of ongoing subordination. Indeed, the power of those challenges is evident in the close bonds between Inocencia and her daughters, particularly in the ways her daughters' lives are animated by Inocencia's resilience.

In sum, Hurtado presents us with the outlines of an exciting and deliciously disruptive commentary. The tensions of transgression in the midst of subordination reflect the contradictions many mujeres live as they make choices that are potentially exquisitely empowering *and* self-destructive. Through Inocencia's life story Hurtado has introduced us to a fascinating woman who has lived through the racial, economic, and gendered constraints in her life while continually transgressing them, a mujer who has carved out a valuable life for herself and her children. I am thankful to Hurtado for Inocencia's story and am honored to be able to meet Inocencia through this telling of her *vida.*

WORKS CITED

Castañeda, Antonia. 1993. "Sexual Violence in the Politics and Policies of Conquest: Amerindian Women and the Spanish Conquest of Alta California." Pp. 15–33 in *Building with Our Hands: New Directions in Chicana Studies,* ed. Adela de la Torre and Beatríz Pesquera. Berkeley: University of California Press.

Chávez, Miroslava. 1998. "Mexican Women and the American Conquest in Los Angeles from the Mexican Era to American Ascendancy." Ph.D. diss., University of California, Los Angeles.

González, Deena. 1999. *Refusing the Favor: The Spanish-Mexican Women of Santa Fe, 1820–1880.* New York: Oxford University Press.

Pérez, Emma. 1999. *The Decolonial Imaginary: Writing Chicanas into History*. Bloomington: Indiana University Press.

Ruiz, Vicki. 1987. *Cannery Women, Cannery Lives: Mexican Women, Unionization, and the California Food Processing Industry, 1930–1950*. Albuquerque: University of New Mexico Press.

———. 1998. *From Out of the Shadows: Mexican Women in Twentieth Century America*. New York: Oxford University Press.

Salas, Elizabeth. 1990. *Soldaderas in the Mexican Military: Myth and History*. Austin: University of Texas Press.

Sánchez, Rosaura. 1995. *Telling Identities: The Californio Testimonios*. Minneapolis: University of Minnesota Press.

Soto, Shirlene. 1990. *Emergence of the Modern Mexican Woman: Her Participation in Revolution and Struggle for Equality, 1910–1940*. Denver: Arden Press.

CHAPTER NINE

Domesticana: The Sensibility

of Chicana *Rasquachismo*

AMALIA MESA-BAINS

• • • • •

In trying to establish a context for understanding the work of Chicana artists, I have responded as both an artist and a scholar, attempting to develop theory from the understanding of practice. This dialectic of knowledge began in the early 1980s, when I used oral histories as a tool in research in psychology to examine the issues of identity, culture, and gender
(Mesa-Bains 1983). After this foundational work, establishing the regional,
familial, and sociopolitical perspectives on Chicana artists, it became important to situate the forms of Chicana art making within the already developing theories of aesthetic production. Throughout the years of relationship and community building among Chicana artists, I had begun to
observe and also create artwork rooted in the everyday or vernacular so
much a part of our shared working-class backgrounds.

The pioneering work of Tomás Ybarra-Frausto (1989) on the sensibility of
rasquachismo delineated the vernacular of the downtrodden in the resilient
struggles of everyday life. In his seminal work, Ybarra-Frausto begins to
codify the details of the aesthetics of survival. His work draws together the
barrio stance and style, from the theater tradition of *carpa* and yard shrines
to the found objects of contemporary Chicano/a art. Often misunderstood
as a form of kitsch, rasquachismo has become a debated term associated
with the working classes. This essay is a response to the oversimplification of Chicano/a art reflective of popular culture as a form of kitsch, a

critique that had begun to collapse together the work of Cuban and Chicano/a artists. Scholars like Celeste Olalquiaga (1996) have begun to place together Chicana, Puerto Rican, and Cuban work without the distinction of rasquachismo. Olalquiaga attributes a calculated and self-conscious approach and fails to understand the unbroken tradition of home altars common to working-class Chicanas and, more important, the Chicano/a innovations on the traditional Days of the Dead *ofrendas*, or offerings. Although she reads the Chicana contestation of the patriarchal, she misses the aspect of tension in the spiritual affirmation, cultural reclamation, and feminist interrogation of just the practices that have given meaning to Chicana communities. The inability to situate the complex aspects of spirituality, colonialism, aesthetic preference, and internalized class phenomenon in these comparisons is troubling and invites response.

In this discourse on kitsch and rasquachismo it has become significant to mark out the aspects of the vernacular central to the work of Chicana artists whose own domestic sites of home, family, and labor influenced their aesthetic production and intention. It had already become clear early in the Chicano art movement that serious differences and distinctions were being made among men and women of the movement. The theorizing on feminist aspects of rasquachismo evident in the work on Chicana artists was an important step in distinguishing the sensibilities, strategies, and forms of art particular to women. These strategies were, in part, a way of calling into question the patriarchal control in the domestic sphere and subverting its representation through their visual practices.

Vernacular, vulgar, inferior, tasteless, and insensible are all terms associated with kitsch. The discourse on kitsch and its relationship to the postmodern avant-garde has been marked by multiple definitions. The work of Gerardo Mosquera (1984)[1] in particular has placed kitsch in a recuperative setting, where the Cuban artist who stands outside the everyday embellishments of kitsch can employ the "inferior" to speak of the arbitrary definitions of the "superior." The examination is expanded to make distinctions between mass-produced objects and the intimate expressions of sincere decoration in the domestic space. Kitsch, often defined as bad taste or false art, is also associated with the economic conditions in which the cheap, mass-produced object replaces genuine folk art and is a sign of modernization in many Third World countries. For the professionally trained Cuban artist, the appropriation of these kitsch materials can be seen as a relationship with a class experience or sentimentality that is no longer linked to the original folk form or lived experience of the artist. The use of the kitsch material may be a curiosity or a recognition of that which is lost. As Mosquera points out, there is a need for greater classificatory information and a more specific definition of these phenomena. In this process of clarification, meaning and usage become even more crucial. When is kitsch recuperated, by whom, and for what aesthetic intention? Many of these concerns for meaning and usage can be brought to bear on the Chicano phenomenon of rasquachismo, or the view of the downtrodden. Ybarra-Frausto elaborates: "Very generally, *rasquachismo* is an underdog perspective—*los de abajo* . . . it presupposes a world view of the have not, but it is a quality exemplified in objects and places and social comportment . . . it has evolved as a bicultural sensibility" (1989, 7).

In rasquachismo the irreverent and spontaneous are employed to make the most from the least. In rasquachismo one takes a stance that is both defiant and inventive. Aesthetic expression comes from discards, fragments, even recycled everyday materials such as tires, broken plates, plastic containers recombined with elaborate and bold display in yard shrines *(capillas),* domestic decor *(altares),* and even embellishment of the car. In its broadest sense it is a combination of resistant and resilient attitudes devised to allow the Chicano to survive and persevere with a sense of dignity. The capacity to hold life together with bits of string, old coffee cans, and broken mirrors in a dazzling gesture of aesthetic bravado is at the heart of rasquachismo. The source of rasquachismo rests in the everyday, the domestic sites of home and community.

For Chicanos emerging from a working-class sensibility, the political declaration of working class and underdog resonated with the sense of defiance against a dominating Anglo society. Raised in barrios, many Chicano artists have lived through and from a *rasquache* consciousness. Even the term Chicano, with all its vernacular connotations, is rasquache. As the *movimiento* model of cultural workers called on Chicano/a artists to dedicate themselves to anti-elite practices that would bring affirmation and pride to the community, the artist engaged in a cultural reclamation through which the traditions of the past could be reanimated in innovative styles. Artists working with meager resources in the early movement relied on the wit and strategies of their class through rasquachismo. The sensibility of rasquachismo became a tool of artist activism, a form of resistance to the false categorizations and hierarchies of folk and fine associated with art making. The intention was to provoke the accepted "superior" norms of the Anglo-American with the everyday reality of Chicano cultural practices. In the act of affirming the values of Chicano/a culture, artists sought to visually record the everyday, the familial, and the familiar. Whether through extensions and reinterpretations of the domestic settings, the car, or the personal pose, rasquachismo is a worldview, which provides an identity, which contests the Anglo concepts of culture. Unlike the Cuban recuperation of kitsch, in which artists of the educated class could borrow from the working class, rasquachismo is for the Chicano artists a facet of internal exploration that acknowledges the meaning imbedded in popular culture and practices. Rasquachismo then becomes for Chicano artists and intellectuals a vehicle for both culture and identity. This dual function of resistance and affirmation are essential to the sensibility of rasquachismo.

In the counterpoint between kitsch and rasquachismo two major differences are apparent. First, kitsch serves as a material or phenomenon of taste through mass-produced objects or style of personal expression in decoration; rasquachismo contains individual material expressions but, more important, a personal stance or attitudinal position. Consequently, the meaning of each is inherently different. Second, its usage reflects a radically different position for the artists. The recuperation of kitsch as a material expression is the act of an artist who stands outside the lived reality of its genesis. In the case of Cuban art being discussed here, kitsch is the sign of meaning for another class that can be employed for its sentimental or ironic values. For the Chicano/a artist rasquachismo is a gesture of survival, affirmation, and resistance to a dominant class from within a shared barrio sensibility. One can say that kitsch is appropriated, whereas rasquachismo is acclaimed or affirmed. Rasquachismo is an integral worldview, which serves as a basis for cultural identity and sociopolitical practice.

As such, rasquachismo has not been limited to the visual arts but in fact has been used as a major sensibility in theater, music, and poetry. The tragicomic spirit of barrio life, as Ybarra-Frausto details, has been a form present in the early *actos* of Luis Valdez's Teatro Campesino, in the poetry of Jose Montoya, and in the works of the Royal Chicano Air Force (RCAF), a conceptual artists' collective. It has been an aesthetic device in the urban street pageantry of ASCO of Los Angeles, and in the border spectacle of Guillermo Gomez-Peña. Rasquachismo can thus be seen as a redemptive sensibility linked to a broad-based cultural movement among Chicanos. As the first generation of their community to be educated in universities (after hard-fought battles in the civil rights period), these artists employed a bicultural sensibility. Operating as an internally colonized community within the borders of the United States, Chicanos forged a new cultural vocabulary composed of sustaining elements of Mexican tradition and lived encounters in a hostile environment. Fragmentation and recombination brought together disparate elements, such as *corridos* (Mexican historical ballads), images of Walt Disney, Mexican cinema and mass media advertising, and even Mexican *calendario* graphics and American Pop Art. This encounter of two worlds could be negotiated only through the sensibility of rasquachismo, a survivalist irreverence that functions as a vehicle of cultural continuity. In many respects, the rasquache defiance of Chicano art production has served as an anecdotal history for a community repudiated and denied in institutional history within the nation as a whole.

In the visual arts, rasquachismo as a sensibility has been a major force. The regional discourse in Chicano rasquache has been both rural and urban. For example, the hubcap assemblage of David Avalos has fused the amulets of Catholicism with urban car art in a new icon, the *Milagro Hubcap.* The rural ethos has been essential to the rasquache sculpture series of *Chiles in Traction* by Chicano artist Ruben Trejo. The innovation of traditional material is a hallmark of rasquachismo.

DOMESTICANA

In pursuing the meaning of rasquachismo in opposition to kitsch, I have reflected on the way Chicanas have expressed the rasquache defiance and tried to locate it within both the domestic and the interrogation of the patriarchal. To look within the rasquache production of Chicano/a art and to locate the work of women requires a description of both the barrio and family experience and an examination of its representation. The understanding of this visual production necessitates the application of feminist theory. The sense of survival, irreverence, and affirmation in the work of women plays against the tension of domination and control. The vernacular of the domestic is played out amid the contradictions of working-class women whose histories in labor activism and struggle would indicate an independence no longer bound by the patriarchy of the home and family. Yet the tension remains between the lived reality of resiliency and capacity and the submission to the culturally ascribed role of the female in a male-dominated context.

For the Chicana artist, the position of the underdog and the strategy of making do is situated in the domestic. She employs the material of the domestic as she contests the power relations located within it. The visual production emerges from the everyday practices of women's life with style and humor. I have chosen to define this feminist rasquachismo as *domesticana.* I chose the term because it satirizes the tourist art that stereotypes the Chicano/a, the genre called Mexicana. The play on domestic and Mexicana refers to the stereotyping of Chicanas within their own culture. Domesti-

Detail from *Emblems of the Decade: Borders Installation,*
mixed media by Amalia Mesa-Bains.

cana carries with it the charge of subversion, interrogation, and deconstruction.

The day-to-day experience of working-class Chicanas is replete with the
practices of the domestic space. The sphere of the domestic includes home
embellishments, home altar maintenance, healing traditions, and personal
feminine pose and style. Establishing the nutrient sources from which the
women draw their critique is important to the understanding of rasquachismo as a feminist practice. For many, the affirmation of the family domestic practices of the home altar and yard shrine was a sign of the power
of community. These strategies of art making were touched by the aesthetic
preferences developed from years of familial spiritual devotion. The origins of the ceremonial present in spirituality, religiosity, spectacle, and pageantry have left their mark in the prevailing Mexican aesthetic dimension.
Established through continuities of spiritual belief, pre-Hispanic in nature,
the family altar functions for women as a counterpoint to male-dominated

rituals in Catholicism. Often located in bedrooms, the home altar is the permanent, ongoing record of the family history and spirituality.

Women who exercise a familial aesthetic create arrangements of bric-a-brac, memorabilia, devotional icons, and decorative elements. Certain formal and continuing elements include saints, flowers (plastic, dried, natural, and synthetic), family photos, mementos, historic objects (military medals, flags, etc.), candles, and offerings. Characterized by accumulation, display, and abundance, the altars allow a commingling of history, faith, and the personal. Formal structures often seen are *nichos* (niche shelves), *retablos* (box-like containers highlighting special icons), and innovative uses of Christmas lights, reflective materials, and miniaturization. Set in domestic sites, altars become the domain of women and are a powerful tool in expressing the family's spirituality. The image of the Virgen de Guadalupe, a female deity, is a common icon in the home altar and creates a connection to women in their role of spiritual leadership.

As an extension of this sacred home space, the front yard shrine or *capilla* (little chapel) is a larger-scale, more public presentation of the family's spiritual aesthetic. Capilla elaboration can include cement structures with mosaic mirror decoration and makeshift use of tires, garden statuary, fountains, lighting, and plastic flowers. In both the home altar and capilla, the transfiguration relies on an almost organic accruing of found objects and differences in scale that imply lived history over time. For many Chicanas the development of home shrines is the focus for the refinement of domestic skills such as embroidery, crochet, flower making, and hand painting. The public nature of the yard shrine allows the work of women to cross the threshold of the private family space to one in which presentation and display are powerful expressions.

Related to the creative functioning of the domestic sacred space is the ongoing practice of healing skills. Special herbs, talismans, religious imagery, and photos of historical faith healers are essential to this cultural tradition. Young women learn from older women practices such as *limpias* with burned herbs and the application of homeopathic cures. Regional context contributes to the healing discipline, particularly in the Southwest. The *polvos* and limpias are also a testament to the cure from love and domination in such herb mixtures as *Contra Celo*.

In the larger area of domestic decoration the use of *artesanías* such as paper cutting, carving, and hand painting is prevalent. Added to the use of folk objects is the widespread popularity of *almanaques* or Mexican calendars and movie posters. The centrality of family life directs the sensibility of domesticana, and Chicanas are frequently raised in hierarchical roles of male over female, old over young. The emphasis on gender stratification creates boundaries in family roles in which women gain responsibility for child rearing, healing and health, home embellishment, and personal glamorization. This traditional picture is enlarged in families in urban centers but nonetheless remains relatively consistent. Chicana rasquache (domesticana), like its male counterpart, has grown not only out of resistance to majority culture and affirmation of cultural values but from women's restrictions within the culture. Defiance of an imposed Anglo-American cultural identity and of restrictive gender identity within Chicano culture have inspired a female rasquachismo or domesticana. Domesticana comes as a spirit of Chicana emancipation grounded in historical activism, advanced education, and, to some degree, Anglo-American expectations in a more open society. With new experiences of opportunity, Chicanas were able to challenge existing community restrictions regarding the role of women. Techniques of subversion through play with traditional imagery and cultural material are characteristic of domesticana. To this body of work we can begin to apply critical viewpoints of feminist theory.

FEMINIST THEORY

To understand domesticana Chicana, it is necessary to impose a criticality that understands art not as a mirror to society but as an agent of societal construction, as Griselda Pollack helps us to understand (1988, 30–31). Art production can be seen not as reflection of ideology but as a vehicle by which ideologies can be constructed. Art becomes a social reality, through which particular worldviews and identities can be lived, can be constructed, even reproduced, redefined, and redistributed. The construction of the feminine through patriarchy relies on a network of psychosocial relationships that produce meaning. Such meanings are created by the ways patriarchy positions us as wives, daughters, sisters, and mothers. Pollack elaborates: "The meaning of the term woman is effectively installed in social and economic positions and it is constantly produced in language, in representation made to those people in those social and economic positions—fixing an identity, social place and sexual position and disallowing any other" (1988, 31).

In this way, the domestic sphere, with all its social roles and practices, remains fixed in patriarchy unless representation of that world calls into question such practices and thereby contributes to its change. In particular, the feminine is charged with this potential for emancipation. The bedroom and the kitchen convey a centrality but also an imprisonment. With the advent of the modern metropolis, the polarity of public (male) space and private (female) space has taken on a split intensified by urbanization. In addition, the rural traditions within the Chicano community have encapsulated the private restricted domain of women in a unique fashion while strong kinship patterns in extended families have deepened the psychosocial network of female roles. The domestic chamber thus has become a space imbued with both a sense of saliency and isolation. Once again, Pollack's work on feminine space in representation becomes a critical frame: "The spaces of femininity operate not only at the level of what is represented in the drawing room or sewing room. The spaces of femininity are those from which femininity is lived as positionality in discourse and social practice. They are a product of a lived sense of social relatedness, mobility and visibility. Shaped within sexual politics of looking they demarcate a particular social organization of gaze which itself works back to secure a particular ordering of sexual difference. Femininity is both the condition and the effect" (1988, 31).

This condition and effect remain in place unless the representation of language relocates or repositions the feminine. In this ordering of space, both public and private, only spatial ambiguities and metaphors can function to shake the foundational patriarchy through challenging works in art. The Chicana strategies of domesticana that emerge from the spaces of femininity, such as the bedroom, the kitchen, and the yard, retake the gaze, the centrality for its own meaning and begin to reposition the Chicana through the reworking of feminine space.

CHICANA DOMESTICANA

The work of Chicana artists has long been concerned with the roles of women, questioning of gender relations, and the opening of domestic space. Devices of paradox, irony, and subversion are signs of the conflictual and contradictory nature of the domestic and familial world in the work of Chicana artists. In domesticana Chicana, the creation of a familial site serves as a site for personal definition for the artist. For Chicana artists taking the rasquache stance, their work takes on a deeper meaning of domestic tension, as the signs of making do are both affirmation of the domestic life and resistance to the subjugation of women in the domestic sphere. The domestic tension signifies the contradiction between the supportive aspects of the feminine and the struggle to redefine restrictive roles. Cherished moments stand side by side with examinations of self, culture, and patriarchal history in visions of a domestic chamber that is both paradise and prison.

Characteristics of domesticana include an emphasis on ephemeral, site-specific works. The emphasis arises from Chicano survivalist responses to the dilemmas of migration, dislocation, and the impermanence of community celebrations. Most of the work elaborates on traditional forms such as the reliquary, capilla, domestic memories of bedroom altars, vanity dressers, ofrendas (offerings for the Mexican Day of the Dead), and everyday reflections of femininity and glamour. The extension of these forms through domesticana serves as a retrieval of memory, capturing in permanent imagery the remembrance of things past.

Critical to the strategy of domesticana is the quality of paradox. Purity and debasement, beauty and resistance, devotion and emancipation are aspects of the paradoxical that activate Chicana domesticana as feminist intervention. Chicanas make use of assemblage, bricolage, miniaturization and small box works, photography, text, and memorabilia to create a mimetic worldview that retells the feminine past from a new position. Narratives of domesticity and ruin are presented in a redemptive enunciation in the language of domesticana. Artists use pop culture discards, remnants of party materials, jewelry, kitchenware, toiletries, saints, holy cards, and *milagros* (toy doll limbs) in combined and recombined arrangements that reflect a shattered glamour. Chicana artists working in domesticana may use hyperfeminization juxtaposed with destruction and loss in a persistent reevaluation of the domestic site. The works act as devices of intimate storytelling through an aesthetic of accumulation of experience, reference, memory, and transfiguration. Artists whose work embodies domesticana Chicana include Santa Barraza, Carmen Lomas Garza, Celia Muñoz, Patricia Rodriguez, and Patssi Valdez.

The rasquache works by Rodríguez, Valdez, and myself posit an approach to feminine space in the contemporary that reconstructs aspects of the domestic, the sacred, and the personal. In response to what is sometimes called the master narrative, we enunciate in our own voice a domesticana that, unlike kitsch, seeks not an appropriation of low over high but in fact a state from within Chicano/a culture. Moving past the fixation of a domineering patriarchal language, our domesticana is an emancipatory gesture of representational space and personal pose.

Patricia Rodríguez was one of the founding members of Las Mujeres Mural-istas, whose work was groundbreaking in the gender battles in the Chicano movement. In the years after Mujeres Muralistas, Rodríguez turned to a much more private and intimate form, yet one deeply marked by the cere-monial and enduring memories of her rural childhood. She moved from the public dialogue of mural work to a smaller, more private strategy of nicho or box work. A leading figure in the genre, Rodríguez elevated the tradi-tion of found objects and the feminine space. Elaborating the aesthetics of discard, the artist recalled her happiest moments gathering with her grand-mother the bits and pieces of the leftover and the discarded. Her sophisti-cated juxtapositions and assemblages bring intimacy and interrogation to the role of woman. Her retablo box pieces have formed part of a new genre of culturally encoded work. Her references to domestic space are part of feminist positioning, calling into question the restricted and privatized do-mestic sites of Chicana resistance. Using domestic markers like the dresser, the bedroom, and the jewelry box, Rodríguez expands them to include a psychological critique of women's roles, particularly the private world of women's wisdom. Her box pieces contain what is valuable to be saved and cherished and symbolize the insularity and controlled space of the home.

Through the use of assemblage, found containers, and discarded objects, Rodríguez has created very particular works using memory, history, and the feminine. The rasquache attitude of making the most from the least in dazzling displays of popular art decoration marks much of her work. Simi-lar to the functioning of home altars, Rodríguez's ceremonial works serve to document, accrue, and narrate events and the familial through arrange-ments often characterized by a subtle sense of the seductive, the veiled, and the contained. Her retablo- and nicho-style enclosures maintain a tradition of domestic space. The use of miniaturization and folkloric forms are reflec-tive of the Mexican traditions of religious art and home altars. Like small stage sets, they present themes of passion, death, healing, ancestry, and the everyday and serve as narrative junctures for broader cultural themes.

The representation of private space in public discourse is manifested in Rodríguez's small box work. The retelling of childhood festivities, rural celebrations, and patterns of kinship and community are elaborated in satirical staging in the small box tableaux. Memory as a device of emanci-pation is a persistent characteristic. Using the presentation of containers, Rodríguez's *Sewing Box* mixes the predictable elements of feminine por-traiture such as threads, bits of fabric, and milagros.

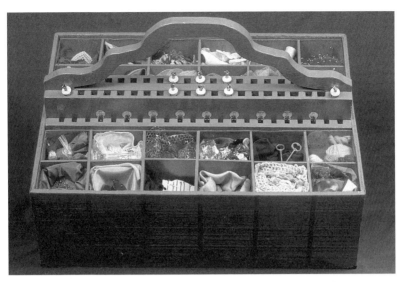

The Sewing Box: Women by Women, mixed media by Patricia Rodríguez.

Compartmentalized in their distinct enclosures, with drawers partially opened, the *Sewing Box* offers in juxtaposition the dominating patriarchy of small plastic soldier figurines. We are reminded of those segregated roles of girl and boy, of nurturing and aggression, through the phenomena of discarded experience. Tokens of love, narratives of domesticity and ruin are all presented as a secret directed by a gaze, which we are offered and from which we are ultimately excluded.

The tradition of box art has been a strong genre among both Chicano and Chicana artists, where earlier, pre-Hispanic and Catholic traditions of venerated reliquaries persist. As Ybarra-Frausto describes, "These sacred objects were venerated religious items such as a supposed thorn from the crown of the crucifixion, a piece of the true cross or vials of blood or mummified anatomical parts of a holy personage displayed behind glass in elaborate containers. As worshipers touched or venerated them, their aura or power was transferred to the supplicant" (1988, 11). The extension and innovation of these reliquaries through domesticana serve as a retrieval of memory, capturing in permanent imagery the ephemeral and temporal remembrance of things past. In assemblage, bricolage, miniaturization, and small sculpture, Rodriguez has created a mimetic worldview, which retells her feminine past with new positionality.

The artist's self-portrait piece consists of a small dresser of domestic chambers, the bedroom. A form of self-reliquary, the miniature dresser

Detail from *Emblems of the Decades: Borders Installation*,
mixed media by Amalia Mesa-Bains (close-up).

positions the woman as a domestic space herself, as receptacle, protector, and safekeeper of the domestic experience. Drawers partially open, drawers shut, small mirrors, and memorabilia constitute a satire of desire, privacy, exposure, and self-containment. The satire does not obscure the anguish of a space never safe from unwanted intrusions and demanding responsibilities. Rodríguez occupies a particular place among Chicana domesticana as one of the earliest practitioners of box work in the greater Chicano/a movement.

AMALIA MESA-BAINS

My own work on altar installation began in 1975 at the Galeria de la Raza and has been ongoing for over twenty-five years. Influenced by my upbringing as a Catholic and exposed to home altars with my grandmother and yard shrines with my *madrina*, I have interpreted, merged, and innovated on the tradition of altares and ofrendas. My works have crossed the boundaries from community settings to the institutions of fine arts, such as museums.

To write of my own work requires a distance not always possible, but necessary in the context of continuity as an artist. The emphasis on the ephemeral solely in site-specific shrine work arises from my early commitments to accessible work founded on the affirmation of our families and their histories. I have pursued strategies based on the survivalist position of shifting locations and community celebration that have been impermanent and ever changing. The Dia de Los Muertos tradition provided a foundational role for my sustained effort to respond to ceremonial needs. Like Patricia Rodríguez's, my work has centered on the duality and flux between private and public space. The domestic tension this holds for us reflects the ambiguities of metaphor between the carnal and the spiritual.

As a result of established themes of life and death, my altars have mediated a pantheon of female figures. The stance of representation I have utilized has functioned to rehistoricize women through works on Frida Kahlo, Dolores del Rio, Sor Juana Inés de la Cruz, Santa Teresa de Avila, and my grandmother, Mariana Escobedo. This canonization of icons counters the power of the Church and makes use of popularization through acclamation. Using accumulation, fragmentation, and dispersal, the shrines have created the dislocation of boundaries in space through their allegorical devices. The viewer is drawn against limitations of the temporal and spatial. Interior and exterior are challenged in the use of organic materials such as earth, leaves, twigs, and waste. Mirrors, broken and fragmented, act on the viewer to fissure illusion and gain states of receptivity. Aspects of feminine glamorization and the Catholic baroque in turn augment the works and reposition the spectacle within the marking off of ceremonial space.

Much like the capilla, the altar for Dolores del Rio in the Grotto of the Virgins is both familial space and serves as an interstice for a personal definition and patriarchal challenge. The installations serve as devices of intimate storytelling through an aesthetic of accumulation, experience, reference, memory, and transfiguration. Historical works such as the Dolores del Rio altar contextualize a domestic icon of the cinema within the Hollywood/Mexicana dual worlds and act as well for my personal narrative of life events and the relations of power between women and society.

The development of my domesticana is a merging of the home altar and the ofrenda to the dead in a context of examination and spiritual journey. I have chosen to create offerings to those women whose lives and work struggle against the power and domination of a masculine world. The struggles of these women reflect the iconic battles of women and religion, women and society, and, ultimately, women and the domination of patriarchy. In my work I have recalled Sor Juana Inés de la Cruz and the padres of the church, Frida Kahlo and Diego Rivera, Dolores del Rio and the conventions of the *gente decente* of her age, and my grandmother, Mariana Escobedo, and the men who sought to control her. The Chicana altares and ofrendas as contemporary art also stand against a museum system born of a colonial patriarchy that seeks to distinguish between the artist and the artisan, the masterpiece and the artifact, the folk and the fine. My domesticana is a resilient defiance both in my own culture and in the broader definitions society holds for women, art, and culture.

PATSSI VALDEZ

Patssi Valdez walked out of Garfield High School in the Chicano blowouts of 1969 at the age of 17 and two years later became a founding member of the legendary performance art collective ASCO (nausea). These early years framed an aesthetic exploration that would lead to her later work in installation and painting. Valdez has been both an icon and an icon maker through photographs, performance, installation, and painting. Her work has marked a transformation from persona to self-portraiture, from narratives of domestic ruin to images of regeneration. A persistent inquiry into the feminine has been the basis for her work for over twenty-five years. What began as an individual self-examination has come to signify a collective urban tale of Chicana life.

Valdez started her life in ASCO as both an object of beauty and a collaborative participant in costume, pose, and performance. Her development as an artist is rooted in a generation that came of age in an urban spectacle of racial conflict and cultural change. Despite the collaborative nature of ASCO, Valdez asserted control over her own image by determining the dress, makeup, and gaze for each photograph and later produced her own photographic montages, installations, and paintings. For over twenty-five years she has produced art that embodies a struggle for self-representation that questions the condition of women. Making her way through a turbulent life in Los Angeles, Valdez has created a visual autobiography filled with domestic tension and miraculous hope.

The early work of Patssi Valdez was integrally tied to the work of the urban conceptual art group, ASCO. Raised in the inner city of Los Angeles, Valdez faced many of the problems common to the urban condition: poverty, violence, sexual trauma, alienation and family fragmentation. Like other members of ASCO, she sought to define a domestic and personal space in this impoverished and sometimes dangerous section of Los Angeles. As the only woman in the conceptual group, her image became a material reality in an objectified image of glamour within the influential cinema landscape of Hollywood. Valdez's emancipation from object to subject required a development of her own visual language beyond ASCO.

Her collaboration in ASCO resulted in living street murals, pageantry,

Installation, mixed media by Patssi Valdez.

and urban spectacle, but it has been her own installation work that contributes to domesticana. Valdez's sensibility has been influenced by phenomena such as store display, Chicano theater, dress-up, domestic residue,
Pop Art, and surrealism situated in the struggle for identity. Her themes
of ruin and glamour can be interpreted through the accumulation and dispersal of make believe and illusion: party supplies, discarded movie sets,
detritus from the edges of downtown Los Angeles, and bits and pieces from
the bazaar and *mercado.* Valdez resists the patriarchal call to innocence and
submission and instead defies the image of the good woman, replacing her
with the gesture of turmoil and unruliness. It is just in this spirit of defiance in Valdez's dazzling women's domesticana that we sense the tension
among glamour, beauty, and ruin. The techniques of accumulation, adorn-
ment, abundance, and dispersal give the sense of chaos and motion central
to her installations.

The ephemeral construction of Valdez's pieces continues the Mexican
cultural practice of the impermanent. The fugitive nature of the work creates an acute sense of the momentary, when the permanent risks extinc-
tion. The temporary quality of the work gives it its fragile power. Ruin
is both the form and content, as Valdez contests the illusion of perma-
nency. The installations retain an arbitrary and ephemeral quality, rather
like something left behind. The works appear to be sites of an escape, a
fugitive space that has been recycled.

In her work *Vanitas,* Valdez presents a site-specific homage to the Black

Virgin. Utilizing the "Ave/Eva" polarities of purity and debasement, she establishes a hyperfeminization through pop culture discards: remnants of party material and gestures of the glamorous such as jewelry, toiletries, kitchenware, saints, holy cards, and milagros. They are combined and recombined to create an internal diary of festivity, destruction, and loss. In the tradition of the baroque vanitas, we are confronted through the specter of death with our own mortality in her staging of the coffin. Valdez offers us a sincere sensibility that balances on the edge of an impending irony. She situates us in the fragile and imponderable as we experience the precariousness of the ephemeral gestures of the glamorous. Her work projects the mythic and the private within the spectacle of the modern metropolis.

Throughout the tour of the seminal exhibition "Le Demon des Anges: Sixteen Chicano Artists from Around Los Angeles, 1988–1990," Valdez innovated on the theme of the dark Madonna with new materials gathered from each European site, elaborating a chapel and a garden with papier-mâché statuary. In a simulacrum of religiosity, classical imagery, and Chicana invention she challenged the real with the faux in a magical realism. Throughout the development of this visual context, the urgency of urban destruction and loss haunted the meaning of the work. It is as if the inevitable chaos of urban survival lingers outside the image, hastening the sense of temporality and extremity. Glamour is a façade that holds back the unavoidable ruin in Valdez's world. Domesticana in Valdez's work presents a world of sincere and innocent longing for beauty and festivity that is always in danger of fissure and chaos. The temporary quality of the work gives a fragile power as she contests the illusion of stability and permanence. The juxtaposing of patriarchal polarities of the good and bad woman transgresses the control of the masculine gaze that brings a redemptive enunciation to the language of domesticana. Valdez fashions domesticana as both product and pose in the attitudinal stance of rasquachismo.

SUMMARY

The expansion of a feminine rasquachismo as domesticana has been an attempt to elaborate intercultural differences between Cuban kitsch and Chicano rasquachismo, as well as to establish the sensibility arising from the struggle for identity, sexuality, and power. The understanding of kitsch as a sensibility of tastelessness and sentimentality appropriated as an ironic curiosity in the works of Cuban artists is contradicted by Chicana domesticana, born of sincere sources held in question by the strategies of inquiry. It is the domestic tension in domesticana that sets it apart from the kitsch statements of the Cuban genre. The tension is a sign of the struggle between that which is affirmed and that which must be contested.

This essay has tried to begin the dialogue on the aspects of rasquachismo centered on women's work. As in all explorations, terminologies must remain porous, sensibilities never completely named, and categories shattered. As Victor Zamudio-Taylor reminds us, Chicana domesticana "shatters the reified universe and breaks the monopoly of the established discourse to define what is real and true" (1988, 18). The redefining of the feminine must come from the representational vocabularies of women if we are to undo the wounds of patriarchy and colonization. That is the challenge of new views of space, of the new domesticana defiance.

NOTE

1. Interestingly, my work in regard to the kitsch/rasquachismo debate began in the late 1980s, when Mosquera's assistant, Celeste Olalquiaga, approached me to contribute to a book Mosquera was doing on kitsch. I completed the preliminary text, which serves as a basis for this current version of domesticana, but the book never materialized and I later learned that Olalquiaga was writing her own work on Chicanas and kitsch. I see this misunderstanding of the distinctions between kitsch and rasquachismo as a reflection on the gap between the class experience of some Latin American intellectuals and the working-class background of many of us who have tried to bring insight to the tension in our own cultural production.

WORKS CITED

Mesa-Bains, Amalia. 1983. "A Study of the Influence of Culture on the Development of Identity among a Group of Chicana Artists." Ph.D.diss., Wright Institute, Graduate School of Psychology.

Mosquera, Gerardo. 1984. "La Buena Forma de las Formas Malas." Union, Havana, Cuba.

Olalquiaga, Celeste. 1996. "Holy Kitschen: Collecting Religious Junk from the Street." Pp. 270–88 in *Beyond the Fantastic: Contemporary Art Criticism from Latin America.* Cambridge, MA: MIT Press.

Pollack, Griselda. 1988. *Vision and Difference: Femininity, Feminism and Histories of Art.* New York: Routledge Press.

Ybarra-Frausto, Tomás. 1988. "Ceremony of Memory: New Expressions in Spirituality among Contemporary Hispanic Artists." Exhibition catalogue. Santa Fe, NM: Center for Contemporary Art.

———. 1989. "Chicano Aesthetics: Rasquachismo." Movimiento Artistico del Rio Salado (MARS) exhibition catalogue, Phoenix.

Zamudio Taylor, Victor. 1988. "Ceremony of Memory: New Expressions in Spirituality among Contemporary Hispanic Artists." Exhibition catalogue. Santa Fe, NM: Center for Contemporary Art.

Invention as Critique:

Neologisms in Chicana Art Theory

JENNIFER GONZÁLEZ

· · · · ·

It is a pleasure to see the publication of Amalia Mesa-Bains's *"Domesticana: The Sensibility of Chicana Rasquachismo,"* both in *Aztlán* (1999) and in its expanded form here. I first encountered this document in 1992, when the artist kindly gave me an early, unpublished version to aid in my own writing about Chicana art. Even in its unfinished state, it was clear that the essay would make an important contribution to a new critical vocabulary delimiting the particular significance of what might be called a Chicana materialist iconography.

Since that time the essay has become a timely contribution to contemporary art theory and analysis. In particular, the essay encourages other writers and scholars to think carefully about the role of neologisms in art theory, the importance of subtle distinctions between descriptive terms such as *kitsch* and *rasquachismo,* the role of feminism in Chicana art practice, and the importance of reading across different artistic media in the construction of a theory of representation. There are also parts of the essay that could be further developed or explored by future scholars. The term "resistance," for example, remains somewhat opaque in its present use. What does it mean for an art work to have a "resistant" attitude? As a feminist practice, *domesticana* for Mesa-Bains is tied largely to the familial structure of the Mexican American household. How might the term relate to other feminist art practices, and why is it important to distinguish among different feminist vocabularies? How might the use of the term change over time, or be constrained by shifts in family structure, immigration, aesthetic norms? Below I offer a series of brief responses to each of the issues I find provocative in the text.

Domesticana is a neologism—a new or invented word. What does it mean to add this vocabulary to scholarship on Chicana art and life? If language shapes or dictates relations between people, their mode of communication, and even their relations to the material world, then to change the shape of that language is indeed a radical act. Malcolm X and Chicano activists understood the political significance of self-naming. In the face of social and economic oppression it becomes imperative to transform one's relationship not only to hegemonic stereotypes, but also to the language by which and through which this power is maintained. This is no less the case in the art world than in the barrio.

The creation of new descriptive terms is essential to writing about innovative contemporary art practices that cannot be adequately assessed within a traditional analytic or aesthetic lexicon. One might wish to explain the work of Amalia Mesa-Bains, Patricia Rodríguez, or Patssi Valdez by citing earlier examples of installation, assemblage, or even performance art, but this explanation alone will never encompass the richness of their unique contribution to art practice. In other words, nothing less than the innovative quality of the work is at stake when scholars attempt to address the specificity of the conceptual and aesthetic choices made. If the analytic vocabulary used by art critics and theorists is too narrow, the art may be read as merely derivative of other genres or may be misunderstood as a simple presentation or description of "identity." Works by these artists and others of traditionally marginalized populations have been, and will continue to be, misread by the mainstream press as long as they are judged by aesthetic standards or within cultural paradigms for which they were never intended. By creating a neologism, Mesa-Bains participates in a necessary form of self-naming that can also provide a new conceptual framework for future critics, scholars, and artists.

In addition to defining the concept of *domesticana*, Mesa-Bains explains the process by which she arrived at its use. She thus offers to her readers a method for the further reconceptualization of critical writing about art. Combining the word *Mexicana* (used to describe cheap tourist art from Mexico) with the *domestic* (culture of everyday home life), Mesa-Bains follows an activist tradition of deconstructing stereotypes by redefining them. Two terms that would otherwise be pejoratively marked along lines of class and gender—particularly in a patriarchal art discourse—are conjoined in a feminist recuperation and reversal. I see little merit in the indiscriminate proliferation of neologisms for every artistic innovation, but I find Mesa-Bains's essay to be an important contribution to scholarship on Chicana artistic practice and an example of the importance of carefully conceived innovations in the language of art theory.

CLAIMING DISTINCTIONS

There is a tendency in art museums, art galleries, and art scholarship, just as in mainstream popular culture in the United States, to generalize about Latinos. The cultural differences among Chicanos, Cubans, Puerto Ricans, Dominicans, Mexicans, Guatemalans, and others are frequently elided or homogenized into a general "Latino" category. Another key contribution of Mesa-Bains's essay is its careful critique of this generalizing tendency in the writings of other scholars. Her critique of Olalquiaga's (1992) theory of kitsch that appeared in *Megalopolis* is an effort to correct what she sees as the oversimplification of Chicano/a art practice. Although she is willing to concede that other artists (i.e., those described by Mosquera) may have a purely ironic, calculated relation to the mass culture they incorporate in their works as kitsch, she finds it imperative to distinguish this activity from the working process of the Chicana artists she discusses. This kind of differentiation is not a question of splitting hairs, but a crucial clarification of artistic goals and methods. What makes this clarification refreshing is that it demonstrates the conceptual and aesthetic differences *within* "Latino" art practice and, in the process, begins to work toward a critique of this homogenizing category itself.

There is a certain amount of courage involved in demonstrating the weak points in the arguments of scholars who support one's own work. Mesa-Bains takes a risk in her critique of Olalquiaga and in her efforts to develop an alternative critical vocabulary to that which is currently in vogue. In this era of niche marketing, where films and television programs, census forms and government funds, art exhibitions and museum collections are geared toward special interest groups (e.g., "teenagers" or "Latinos"), it is both dangerous and necessary to disrupt the hegemony of such categories. What one may lose in terms of a collective voice and visibility, one gains in historical accuracy. This kind of risk is crucial if scholarship is to become more sophisticated and precise. For Mesa-Bains the choice is clear when developing a new vocabulary for analyzing Chicana art practice.

Distinguishing between kitsch and rasquachismo, for example, allows for a shift away from a German terminology that recalls the useful but culturally limited readings of art by Clement Greenberg and his postmodern critics, to an everyday Mexican American vocabulary that recalls not only a bicultural sensibility but also a critical worldview. As Mesa-Bains points out, kitsch designates a quality of taste that can be appropriated, whereas rasquachismo designates both a set of material expressions and an attitude of irreverence that can be affirmed. It is a significant distinction not only because it emphasizes practice over product, but because it allows for a critique of the idea of taste more generally. Indeed, "taste" is not the central concern of most politically motivated art—perhaps because the idea of taste has always had its own culturally specific politics and local regimes of enforcement. A sense of taste that evolves through years of formal education in a specific social milieu is rejected here precisely because it is always clear for the "underdog" or "outsider" that there is more than one social milieu to which aesthetic signs accrue and that "good taste" is a relative term. In short, taste as an idea attached to education and breeding, to discrimination and sensibility, is inherited from a presumption of cultural homogeneity and privilege. Mesa-Bains's essay makes a timely and incisive distinction between the ironic "insider" use of kitsch as a critique of taste and the critical "outsider" position of rasquachismo.

REDEFINING FEMINISM

Much has already been written about the differences and parallels between the Anglo-American middle-class feminist movement and Chicana feminism of the 1970s. Instead of rehearsing this history, Mesa-Bains reveals how Chicana artists of the time developed a unique visual vocabulary that was both critical of patriarchy in their own communities and recuperative of the power of domestic space for women. In some respects, Mesa-Bains's celebration of domesticana seems to contradict other feminist efforts to reject the confines of domestic space as historically oppressive for women. For Mesa-Bains the strategy of domesticana is characterized by paradox: the artists employ the traditional materials of domestic spaces while contesting the traditional power relations of domestic roles. Of course, employment outside the home, whether in agriculture or industry, was always a matter of necessity and never of choice for working-class Chicanas. Thus, for many women, domestic practices such as altar building and the display of souvenirs and family mementos were methods of maintaining local power in a world where their social power was generally denied. Through traditional domestic arts, women gained access to status and respect within the family and community. Chicana artists who borrow from these arts are both participating in a long tradition and redefining it. Mesa-Bains argues that it is in this redefinition that the feminist impulse of domesticana lies.

In large-scale collaborative art projects such as *Womanhouse* (Judy Chicago et al.) a stark and almost surreal view was produced of the entrapment that domestic labors of cooking, cleaning, washing, ironing, birthing, and mothering produced for middle-class women. Freedom, for many middle-class Euro-American feminists of the 1970s, meant freedom from domestic labor and the right to work outside of the home. Although the relation to home life was significantly different for these feminist artists and the Chicanas about whom Mesa-Bains writes, there are important parallels that should not be overlooked. Despite ethnic and class differences there is a similar critique of the interlocking forces of patriarchy and domestic labor, a similar attention to the social roles available to women, and a similar recuperation and elevation of traditional women's crafts. Feminist artists such as Martha Rosler were playfully disrupting the "semiotics of the kitchen" while others such as Miriam Schapiro and Faith Ringgold were committed to claiming traditional women's work, such as sewing and quilting, for the fine arts.

There remain two key differences, however, that are tied precisely to the political goals and "outsider" status of Chicano/a art of this time. First, because Chicanas were working to address ethnic and class discrimination as well as gender discrimination, much of their work foregrounds this combination of political concerns. Unlike other feminist artists, whose primary focus was the gender discrimination of mass culture and the art world, Chicanas sought to celebrate their own ethnic traditions as a mode of social criticism in parallel with their feminist goals. Second, the anti-elitist focus of domesticana emphasized by Mesa-Bains runs counter to the impulse on the part of other feminists to raise domestic crafts to the realm of fine arts. It was the rarefied and limited scope of the art world that Chicana artists self-consciously rejected, Mesa-Bains suggests, in favor of community-based and locally legible works of art. The degree to which the conditions of exhibition have changed for Chicana artists would be interesting to explore further.

One of the factors that makes the term domesticana particularly useful for scholars of Chicana art, as I have suggested above, is its emphasis on a sensibility or practice rather than on a specific form or medium. Although Mesa-Bains focuses on the visual and performing arts in her essay (sculpture, painting, installation, and street art), her suggestion that domesticana is a "feminist rasquache" suggests that even works of literature and poetry, music, and spoken word might exemplify the same principles: a critique of gender roles, bricollage, paradox, irreverence, and a bicultural aesthetic. Hence, domesticana can be appropriated for critical analyses in a variety of disciplines and should prove useful to younger scholars researching a variety of media.

LOCATING ARTISTIC RESISTANCE

The idea of "resistance" is central to Mesa-Bains's essay, and indeed to much writing about Chicano/a art generally. One of the primary texts in the field (Griswold Del Castillo, McKenna, and Yarbro-Bejarano 1991), the comprehensive catalogue for the exhibition CARA: Chicano Art, Resistance and Affirmation, sets the tone for further analyses of this political art movement. Echoing the basic assertions of this text, Mesa-Bains argues in several places that domesticana is a form of resistance and/or affirmation. She writes, "The sensibility of rasquachismo became a tool of artist activism, a form of resistance to the false categorizations and hierarchies of folk and fine associated with art making." Elsewhere, she suggests that it is "resistant and resilient attitudes" that allow Chicanos and Chicanas to "survive and persevere with a sense of dignity" in the face of a "dominant class" or "majority culture." About her own artworks she writes that they produce a "resilient defiance" of definitions society holds for women, art, and culture.

What exactly is meant by the term "resistance"? Do forms of political resistance necessarily produce resistant texts? What can we discover if we examine more closely the assertion that artworks and/or cultural sensibilities (rather than individual people) perform a kind of resistance? In short, can art "resist," and, if so, what is it resisting?

If rasquachismo is an attitude as much as a form, and domesticana is a feminist rasquachismo, then Patssi Valdez's choice to perform in one body the contradictory boundary positions that society has ascribed to women is to take on just such an attitude. One might say the performance of this contradiction is a way of "resisting" the narrow range of female roles with which the artist is invited to identify. However, it is also possible to read the work as a reinscription of these roles, as a capitulation to the demands of society that women be *both* "good" and "bad."

Patricia Rodríguez's accumulations of objects in her box art projects, drawing on an iconography of household bric-a-brac and Catholic reliquaries. In some cases, her works gather together objects that represent different aspects of domestic life or personal memory. In the works of Mesa-Bains, there is a glorification or canonization of female figures who have played an exceptional role in a patriarchal or religious context: Frida Kahlo, Sor Juana Inés de la Cruz, Santa Teresa de Avila, and others. In one sense or another, these famous women "resisted" the structure of social institutions such as the family and church to follow their own intellectual goals. As works of art, the installations by Rodríguez and Mesa-Bains revive a forgotten history. In the context of the art establishment, these pieces can also be accurately described as portraits or self-portraits. They do not resist assimilation into the museum and gallery system, even if they successfully critique it. Perhaps it is the act of forgetting itself that is resisted in their historical recuperation.

Works of art are only resistant to the degree that they perform a material rhetoric—a visual argument—that counters another material rhetoric. But resistance is not a quality located *within* or *performed by* the work of art. Instead, it is a semantic transformation performed by the artist and agreed upon by the audience. By rereading signs in the world and ascribing to them a new meaning, by rejecting the constraints of one semiotic system in favor of another, by reconstructing the frames of reference through which one is defined and by which one is given access to power, these artists create a space for others to examine their own frames of reference, their own ideologies. This is what I see as the resistant element of domesticana.

QUESTIONING THE LIMITS OF DOMESTICANA

If scholars are to embrace the concept of domesticana there are a few questions that we might want to consider about its present and future use. I therefore end my response with a series of open questions that I hope others will take up and explore.

Is domesticana applicable only to Chicana art of a particular time period or generation? If domesticana relies on the notion of an "unbroken tradition" of domestic arts inherited from Mexico, what happens when new art practices by Chicana feminists break with this tradition? Is irony inherently incompatible with domesticana, as Mesa-Bains suggests, or does it in

fact have a role to play? Can there be a middle-class practice of domesticana? If domesticana relies on a shared barrio sensibility, how can one rely
on the homogeneity of this sensibility over time? Does the concept of domesticana constrain the critical discourse on Chicana art to the home? Are
other neologisms needed for an expanding analysis of Chicana art? If so,
what might they be?

WORKS CITED

Griswold Del Castillo, Richard, Teresa McKenna, and Yvonne Yarbro-Bejarano, eds.
    1991. *Chicano Art: Resistance and Affirmation, 1965–1985*. Los Angeles: Wight Art
    Gallery.
Mesa-Bains, Amalia. 1999. "*Domesticana:* The Sensibility of Chicana *Rasquache.*"
    Aztlán 24(2): 157–67.
Olalquiaga, Celeste. 1992. *Megalopolis: Contemporary Cultural Sensibilities*. Minne-
    apolis: University of Minnesota Press.

CHAPTER TEN

Reproduction and Miscegenation on the Borderlands:

Mapping the Maternal Body of Tejanas

ROSA LINDA FREGOSO

• • • • •

In writing this critical essay on the film *Lone Star*, I would like to open with Toni Morrison's observations about the subaltern presence in U.S. culture. In *Playing in the Dark* she writes, "The imaginative and historical terrain upon which American writers journeyed is in large measure shaped by the presence of the racial other" (1992, 46). There is no denying what Morrison calls "the Africanist presence" in U.S. culture, yet, until very recently, the "Mexicanist presence" was rarely acknowledged as also shaping "the imaginative and historical terrain upon which American writers [and, I would add, musicians and filmmakers] journeyed." In fact, John Sayles's *Lone Star* (1997) figures as one of those rare instances in the history of U.S. cinema in which the Mexicanist presence is positioned center stage.

It is no small accomplishment to feature prominently the entwinement of Anglos and Mexicans in questions of U.S. national (or regional) identity and citizenship, particularly because the disavowal of the Mexicanist presence in definitions of U.S. citizenship and identity has been one of the major mechanisms for the consolidation of colonialist rule in states like California, New Mexico, and Texas during the nineteenth century and for the maintenance of a dominant racial order throughout the twentieth century. Purposefully forgetting that this land was under Mexican colonial rule prior to the Anglo invasion puts a new spin on dominant interpretations of

Mexican "illegals" as *the* foreign invaders. For remembering a prior Mexicanist presence calls into question white nativist claims to the region.

It is in this context that a film like *Lone Star* captures the attention of cultural critics like myself who are tracking the Mexicanist presence in U.S. history and cultural politics. Sayles's portrayal of the entwinement of Mexicans and Anglos, as both agents and subjects of domination and complicity, as collaborators in the nation-building enterprise, is a welcome corrective to decades of erasure and to the politics of disavowal, which informs in undeniable and prevailing ways the texture of U.S. culture. Overwhelmingly, *Lone Star* has been praised by mainstream film critics and, to some extent, the Tejana/o intelligentsia for its representation of multiculturalism and alternative perspective on race relations. It is Sayles's tenth and most ambitious film, following a series of films tackling sensitive subjects.[1] Also a novelist and a script doctor who recently rewrote *Apollo 13*, Sayles perfects his storytelling techniques with *Lone Star*, rendering a richly layered and complex narrative with multiple story lines and the shifting points of view of at least ten substantial characters. Yet, despite its narrative and thematic intricacies and the filmmaker's elaborate account of multiracial Texas, something is terribly awry in Sayles's vision.

Informed by a feminist cultural studies perspective, my inquiry grapples with what is amiss in *Lone Star*. I am interested in exploring how a seemingly radical discourse around multiculturalism is enabled by and works within hegemonic relations of power, reaffirming racial hierarchies. As I will demonstrate, the film's vision of a new multicultural nation is filtered through a white patriarchal gaze, which marginalizes the point of view of the racialized woman in the narrative. My interest is in making visible the cinematic strategies, the racial and patriarchal structures used in relation to female representation. Despite what I show to be its flawed multiculturalism, *Lone Star* has captured the imagination of a number of scholars, including the anthropologist José Limón, who has celebrated the film's enlightened portrait of race relations. Limón's (1998) recent analysis responds to my earlier published critique of the film, and in my current analysis I address the limitation of his ethnographic reading in terms of its failure to address the cinematic mechanisms of spectatorship and identification that structure visual discourse. I end with a critique of *Lone Star*'s portrayal of motherhood as a "missed opportunity," for the film denies spectators an identification with the relationship between mother and daughter.

I remember someone once saying that behind every intellectual project, one finds an autobiography. In a similar vein, the point of departure for my feminist critique is an autobiographical insertion into the text, which begins with *Lone Star*'s narrative closure, when the lead female character, Pilar Cruz, utters the film's final words: "Forget the Alamo."

MEMORIES OF THE ALAMO

I first heard the phrase "Forget the Alamo" thirty years ago. It was my father's antidote to the official versions of Texas history taught in the public schools of Corpus Christi. Although we confronted prejudice on a daily basis, it was in those required eighth-grade Texas history courses that Chicanas/os received the officially sanctioned lesson in Anglo racism and contempt for Mexicans. Sitting in Oakland's Grand Lake Theater in 1996 next to my 13-year-old son, who is disturbed by the film's incest theme and critical of its "too many plot lines," I found myself transported back to my own childhood in Texas, sitting in Mrs. Roy's history class, which was adorned with the six flags over Texas and the haunting legacy of the battle of the Alamo.

For weeks, I was captivated by her petite hourglass shape, her crimson hair, and those red dots speckling her flesh and framing her marble-blue eyes. Mrs. Roy gave interminable, heart-wrenching lectures, re-enacting with melodramatic detail Anglo-Mexican struggles for Texas's independence. A devotee of the historian Walter Prescott Webb, Mrs. Roy passionately perpetrated his views about the "cruel streak in the Mexican nature." She had mastered the skill of counterpoint pedagogy, detailing history in terms of binary opposition: the noble letter-writing campaign of Stephen F. Austin versus the "bloody dictator" Santa Ana's wrath; the memorable deeds and bravery of Travis, Crockett, and Bowie versus the atrocities of the "treacherous" Mexicans; the high-powered artillery rifles and cannons of the "villainous" Mexicans versus the handful of muskets, revolvers, and bowie knife of the heroic Anglos. I can still see her there, pacing excitedly before us, diligently pointing at the maps of Texas, its flags, and charts. She gazed at me, the only Tejana in the class, and I felt her whiteness overpowering me each time she mentioned "the cruel streak in the Mexican nature."

Thirty years later, the shame I felt then turned to anger as I screened the 1915 film *Martyrs of the Alamo* during a research trip to the Library of Congress film and video collection. Directed by W. Christy Cabanne, *Martyrs of the Alamo* was supervised by D. W. Griffith, whose unmistakable imprint is etched in the narrative. The five-reel feature is shot in 35mm and replicates Griffith's "system of narrative integration," especially in its liberal use of "stylistic techniques—from composition to editing—to articulate an ideology of race that positions 'whites' as superior and 'non-whites' as deviant and inferior" (Bernardi 1996, 104). As the intertitle makes evident, Mexicans, under the command of Santa Ana, figure as the invaders in a world of "liberty-loving Texans who had built the Texas colony."

The articulation of style and race in the story is reinforced through characterization and cinematic techniques such as mise-en-scène, editing, and shot composition to the extent that crosscutting and parallel action render racial differences between Anglos and Mexicans. Mexicans are caricatured as dark, ominous, and physically aggressive. Medium and close shots depict the psychological depth of Anglo characters, whereas the camera remains distant from the Mexican characters. Filmed mostly outdoors and framed through distant and long shots, Mexicans are portrayed as a mass of bodies with faces that are indistinguishable from each other. And Mexican females fare no better, playing folkloric "cantina girls" whose sole purpose in the narrative is to dance for Mexican men. Yet, the most disturbing aspect of *Martyrs of the Alamo* is the way filmmakers reroute the historical conflicts in Texas through the discourse of sexual degeneracy.

The intertitle keeps looping through my head: "Under the dictator's rule, the honor and life of American women was held in contempt." The film is informed by an offensive, yet predictable racial narrative, namely, the colonialist fantasy of white womanhood under siege. *Martyrs* is, as Herman Gray writes of *Birth of a Nation*, a "scandalous representation" of nonwhite masculinity, embodying white anxieties about miscegenation (1997, 87–88). Following in the tradition of Griffith's racialized family drama, *Martyrs of the Alamo* recasts late nineteenth-century pseudo-scientific theories of degeneracy and miscegenation. The film positions Mexicans as sexually hungry subaltern men, predators devouring the angelic female with their looks, teasing a white mother with baby, touching white women's blond locks. The film thus draws from a repertoire of racial and imperial metaphors to construct the view of Mexican sexual degeneracy as a threat to the virtue of white femininity and racial purity. Santa Ana epitomizes Mexican degeneracy as the final segment of the film creates the myth about his out-of-control libido. The intertitle, "An inveterate drug fiend, the Dictator of Mexico also famous for his shameful orgies," is followed by a scene depicting Santa Ana in a drunken stupor, surrounded by four Mexican women dressed exotically in dark mantillas, vests, and skirts, dancing before him. Narrative resolution around Santa Ana's capture rewrites the political struggle over Texas as a defense of white femininity and, by extension, the white nation, thereby rationalizing the Anglo takeover of

Texas. At the end of this film, I am furious because, even though *Martyrs of the Alamo* is the most extremist, xenophobic account of the Texas conflict I have ever seen, its discursive effects lingered on fifty years later, haunting me in that Texas history class.

I return to earlier memories and place myself in the body of a 13-year-old girl, listening anxiously in that classroom. It is 1967. I imagine the harshness in the looks of my Anglo classmates, burning my flesh. By the time Mrs. Roy delivered her final soliloquy, reciting the climactic battle for Texas's independence, the primal scene that has so obsessed the Anglo-racist imaginary and is reenacted in countless colonialist films, including *Martyrs of the Alamo*, I was interpellated into her historically distorted, chromatically tainted universe inside the walls of the Alamo on what Anglo-Texans reconfigure as a purely Anglo side of the line. I would later buy a bowie knife from a mail-order catalogue. In the eighth grade, I had internalized the elision of Tejanos and the racist-colonialist gaze — a self-hatred equal to the hatred Anglo teachers of Texas history felt for Mexican Texans.

I still own that copy of Rafael Trujillo Herrera's book, *Olvídate de "El Alamo"* (Forget "the Alamo"), published in 1965 and given to me by my father in 1967 to temper my fulmination against the Mexican oppressors of Anglo freedom fighters. As the title makes evident, *Olvídate de "El Alamo"* is a diametrically opposed version of the battle for Texas. Told from a Mexican point of view, it renders the struggle in Texas less in terms of liberation and more from the perspective of conquest. Like Mrs. Roy's history lessons, Trujillo's text failed to account for the political intricacies of nineteenth-century Tejas, including the important fact that Tejano landowners joined Anglos in the fight against the centralist government of Santa Ana and that some Tejanos died alongside the Anglos inside the Alamo. I read *Olvídate de "El Alamo,"* understanding bits and pieces, but more important, the book ignited a life-long passion for oppositional discourse and counter-knowledges. Besides this introduction to Mexican nationalist discourse, in his customary proverbial wisdom, my father would further disorder Mrs. Roy's teachings. "Just imagine that one day you invite guests into your home," my father explains. "And you allow them to live in your home on the condition that they follow certain rules. Then one day, your houseguests decide that they don't agree with your rules and so they decide to take your house and kick you out. That's how it happened in Tejas."

Thus, while racist powers produced, marked, and incised my body as a historically specific, racial, and gendered subject of Texas, an oppositional force, metaphorized in the phrase *olvídate de "El Alamo,"* reoriented the

Pilar (Elizabeth Peña). Photo by Allen Pappé.
Courtesy of Castle Rock Entertainment.

terms of my inscription. This is the countermemory of Tejas that Pilar
Cruz's final words enable, putting me in touch with a long tradition of opposition to racist discourse, with popular forms of knowledge, transgressive
tales of resistance, subaltern practices of suspicion of official versions of
history. It is through these social practices and counterdiscourses that I, as
an actual, historical spectator, negotiate my reception of the film. However,
in contrast to Mrs. Roy, Pilar Cruz portrays a new breed of Texas history
teachers: a Tejana on the borderlands, belonging to a cultural formation
that refuses the absolutism of binaries and recounts the stories of Texas
in terms of their profound ambivalences, in tales of complicity, resistance,
and domination. And this is the cultural formation I embrace, for it constructs my spectator position and informs my deconstruction of *Lone Star.*

THE MULTICULTURAL FANTASY

Lone Star is set in Frontera (literally, Border), Texas and details the story
of Rio County Sheriff Sam Deeds's (Chris Cooper) investigation after the
discovery of skeletal remains on the outskirts of town. The remains are
believed to belong to Charley Wade (Kris Kristofferson), a racist and corrupt sheriff who mysteriously disappeared in 1957 after waging a campaign of bigotry and terror against the local Tejano and black communities.
Sam Deeds's father, the legendary Sheriff Buddy Deeds and Charley Wade's

former deputy, becomes Sam's prime suspect. In the course of his investigation, Sam rekindles an interracial romance with his teenage sweetheart, Pilar. Shot in Eagle Pass, Texas, Sayles captures the feel of Texas visually, filming in super 35mm, which gives the film its wide-screen look. While the murder mystery provides the film its major plot line, Sayles portrays a multigenerational drama, rendered through the life histories of an Anglo sheriff, a Chicana teacher, and an African American colonel. *Lone Star* can best be characterized as a blurred genre, combining elements from the Western, mystery, thriller, and romance. The film is also the latest in a long line of border films, for also on the screen prominently featured for its iconic significance is the figure of the border.[2]

Since the early days of silent cinema, U.S. filmmakers have made hundreds of films about the Mexico-U.S. border.[3] In fact, an obsession with borderlands is not the sole purview of U.S. cinema, for, beginning in the 1930s, the border also captured the imagination of Mexico's film industry, which in one decade alone released over 147 films in the border genre (Iglesias 1991). In the cultural imaginary of both the United States and Mexico, the border figures as the trope for absolute alterity. It symbolizes eroticized underdevelopment, an untamed breeding ground for otherness, and the site of unrepressed libidinal energies. Its inhabitants are coded as outcasts, degenerates, sexually hungry subalterns, and outlaws. In both Mexican and U.S. cinemas, the representation of the border as otherized territory is symptomatic of a colonialist and racist imaginary. The product of a Western gaze, this representation of frontier territories as abject serves both to define the United States and metropolitan Mexico and to shape their national identities.

In contrast, Sayles's portrait of the borderlands captures the complexity, nuances, and multidimensionality of the terrain. In fact, at first glance, *Lone Star* reads like an application of Chicana/o borderlands theory. Sayles invokes the Mexico-U.S. border as a paradigm for his own analysis of U.S. social relations: "There's a kind of racial and ethnic war that has continued. That continuing conflict comes into the clearest focus around the border between Texas and Mexico" (in West and West 1996a, 14). For John Sayles, *Lone Star* is a "film about borders," and the border operates as the signifier for the borders of everyday life: "In a personal sense . . . a border is where you draw a line and say 'This is where I end and someone else begins.' In a metaphorical sense, it can be any of the symbols that we erect between one another—sex, class, race, age" (14).

And Sayles did his homework on Chicana/o studies cultural critiques and border theories, reading Americo Paredes's *With a Pistol in His Hand,* screening Robert Young's filmic adaptation, *The Ballad of Gregorio Cortez*, listening to border corridos and studying their lyrics closely.[4] Furthermore, like much Chicana/o border writing, *Lone Star* is set on the borderlands region—the 2,000-mile strip of land, roughly twenty miles wide, separating Mexico from the United States. Sayles portrays the region as a transborder contact zone, a third country that is neither Anglo nor Mexican but rather multilingual, intercultural, and multiracial. And the film thematizes literal and figurative border crossings, cultural and social relations of accommodation and negotiation within and between the inhabitants on the borderlands. Exploring the racial, cultural, economic, and familial conflicts on the borderland, *Lone Star* candidly depicts tensions between Texans and Tejanas/os, Anglos and blacks, Mexicanos on this side of the border and on the other side, as well as the relations of complicity between the Texan Anglo and the Tejano Mexicana power elite. For example, Mercedes Cruz (Miriam Colon) is a successful restaurant owner who calls the border patrol on seeing desperate Mexican immigrants run across her yard and tells her immigrant employee, "In English, Enrique. This is the United States. We speak English." Jorge is a member of the Frontera elite, and Ray is portrayed as a Tejano deputy who plans to run for sheriff in the next election with the support of the local power structure. Thus, throughout the film, relations of power and privilege are nuanced, figuring centrally in both individual and group transactions. In this respect, *Lone Star* renders the experiences of continuity and discontinuity that mark daily life, namely, ongoing as well as incoherent encounters among various social groups, reference codes, beliefs, and linguistic and cultural systems.

The film, in fact, reads like an alternative lesson in Texas history. Sayles attempts to situate the figures of the border and borderlands as central elements of a historical revisionist project as well as in efforts to reclaim an alternative racial memory of the borderlands. The filmmaker challenges the prevailing historical amnesia and the ideology of "presentism" of society in his efforts to illuminate how past histories weigh incessantly on present circumstances and how the mythic legacy of the past clouds the present's truths. Sayles underscores the political project of showing the bearing of the past on the individual's present through an effective use of the cinematic techniques of seamless editing in the flashback sequences.

Contesting exclusionary formulations of a monocultural Texas history, *Lone Star*'s racial memory differs from two extremes: the Anglo colonialist erasure of Tejana/o subjects in Texas history (e.g., *Martyrs of the Alamo*) and also the Chicano protonationalist reversal of that exclusion, namely, Tejanos as the victims of conquest, the "good guys" in a them-versus-us binary revision of Texas history. Sayles portrays race relations in terms of an exercise of race and class power, in particular configurations and connections as well as in terms of singularities. Anglos and Mexicanos, Tejanos and Texans figure as both agents and subjects of domination and complicity. And the film's revision of Texas history goes beyond its documentation of Anglo-Mexicano relations of negotiation and accommodation, for *Lone Star* also reflects the filmmaker's "need to document" the history of multiculturalism in this country.[5] This is what he has to say: "As I said, [the United States is] not increasingly multicultural, it's always been so. If you go back and turn over a rock you find out, for example, that maybe a third or more of African Americans are also Native Americans and a much higher percentage of African Americans are also white Americans" (in West and West 1996a, 15).

Sayles celebrates a new social order, painting a tapestry of an interracial, postcolonial Texas, reviving a textured story of racial entwinement and complexity on the borderlands—a pluricultural transborder contact zone comprising Native Americans, blacks, Tejanos, and Anglos. The Mexico-U.S. borderlands in Sayles's universe is hybrid and multilingual; it is a tutored and refined view, which destabilizes traditional formulations of U.S. race relations (i.e., the black and white paradigm). Yet, despite its overture to multiculturalism, the film's narrative is, on closer inspection, driven by a deeply colonialist and phallocentric project.

Genuine multiculturalism, that is to say, the redefinition of the nation and a reconfiguration of center-margin power relations, insists on the interplay of multiple and plural identities. Truly questioning the border demands as well the interrogation of the boundary markers of race, class, gender, and sexuality. For in reconfiguring the nation in terms of multiculturalism, the center is no longer defined by the myth of racial purity, sameness, and singularity but by hybridity, difference, and plural identifications. If Sayles's multiculturalist project is to truly represent a new social order, to make a dent in the predominant monocultural, ethnocentric vision of society, it must decenter whiteness and masculinity. Even though multiculturalism always involves relations of power, neither whiteness nor maleness nor heterosexuality nor Europeanness functions as a universal in a multicultural world.

However, as Sayles's words make evident, maleness is the key, privileged signifier of the narrative: "For me, very often the best metaphor for history is fathers and sons. Inheriting your cultural history, your hatreds and your alliances and all that kind of stuff, is what you're supposed to get from your father in a patriarchal society" (in West and West 1996a, 15). Thus, a masculine-centeredness permeates the film, for while the border figures as the symbol for multiculturalism, crossings, intercultural exchanges, and hybridity, history is metaphorized in a patriarchal patrimony. On the surface, *Lone Star* attempts to rewrite the social order to encompass difference for a multicultural nation; however, the white father–white son structure of the story keeps the center intact and multiplicity at the margins of the story world. By reinscribing the centrality of the Oedipal narrative and the voice of white racial privilege, the film reaffirms the masculinist borders of whiteness, containing difference and regulating the disruptive aspect of otherness.

Whereas the plot is driven by the son's, Sheriff Sam Deeds's, search for truth, the son is motivated by a repressed hatred for his father, the legendary, benevolent patriarch of Rio County, Sheriff Buddy Deeds. Like Westerns and border genre films, *Lone Star* literalizes the symbolic structure of the Law, rendering the father-son as the embodiments of "civic law," as both are county sheriffs. Patrimony guarantees the cinematic reproduction of the symbolic Oedipal structure insofar as the son, Sam, assumes the place of the father, Buddy, literally as the sheriff of Rio County but also symbolically in the order of the phallus, the law of the father. The usual Oedipal scenario is further reinforced textually by the father-son conflict generated within the film. Namely, the son is driven by a desire to kill the father, not literally, because Buddy is already dead, but figuratively, for he is the prime suspect in the murder investigation. Instead of honoring his father's name, the son's investigation camouflages an obsessive desire to prove his father's culpability, to taint his father's reputation, thus destroying his name.

As in the best mystery thrillers, the plot twists and suspense of *Lone Star* yield a surprise and unexpected resolution to the murder investigation. Whereas all the evidence pointed to the father as the prime suspect, Sam discovers that the murder was in fact committed by Hollis Pogue, the current mayor of Frontera, who was not only the fledging deputy of the notorious Wade but also the horrified witness to Wade's racist atrocities. Narrated in a seamlessly edited flashback, the murder of Charley Wade is the central motif in the film's revisionist project. Wade is murdered by the young deputy Hollis to prevent the murder of Otis Payne, the owner of Big O's Roadhouse and mayor of Darktown. Emblematic of a white benevolence on the Texas frontier, the murder of one white man by another to save a black man's life rewrites race relations in Texas, resituating the history of black-white cooperation, resistance, and collusion against white racism.

Despite this revisionist endeavor, narrative closure around the son's discovery of the father's innocence further reinforces and consolidates whiteness as well as the patriarchal structure of the film.

The extent to which this film is driven by the patriarchal Oedipal narrative is additionally made evident by a secondary father-son antagonism between Otis Payne (who is black) and his son, Colonel Payne. Whereas anthropologist José Limón has argued that this racialized twist on the classic Oedipal drama actually decenters "the otherwise 'white' paradigm" of masculinity (1998, 155), I propose that blackness in fact "colors" the Oedipal drama but ultimately leaves patriarchy intact.[6] Patriarchy is consolidated through one of the film's major subplots, namely, the fact that all intergenerational conflicts implicating male characters (young and old, black and white) are resolved, whereas those involving the female characters, Mercedes and Pilar as mother-daughter, are not. And, as I show later on, this elision of the mother-daughter relation serves to further reaffirm the masculinist, Oedipal undertones of the film. In the end, the Oedipal conflict is resolved for white as well as for black masculinity. And in the case of the lead character, Sam, clearing the father's name allows the son to assume his rightful place, the place of the father in the symbolic order, guaranteeing thus the reproduction of patriarchy.

It is precisely this patriarchal structure of the Oedipal narrative that contains Tejana and Tejano subjectivities and points of view but also enables them to emerge. The structuring of information in the film positions Sam Deeds as the center of consciousness and the filter for narrative information. The stitching of present events with past memories through flashback sequences allows the filmmaker to provide characters with complex subjectivities. And while both Pilar's and her mother's subjectivities are constructed through this mode, Pilar's flashback is linked by seamless editing with Sam's flashback about their teenage rendezvous.

Thus, with the exception of Mercedes Cruz's flashback, each of the seven flashback sequences is mediated by the presence of the main hero, so that the memories of interracial conflict are structurally folded into the son's quest to dethrone the "legend" of the father. The unearthing of Texas's racist past and the revision of a multicultural social order are always already subsumed and contained within the point of view of whiteness and masculinity that is privileged in the narrative. It is the son's attempt to slay the father that ultimately authorizes the emergence of other points of view. As the vehicle for dominant racial and gender discourse, the white masculine subject also circumscribes the parameters of racial memories of conflict and collusion, thus marking the impossibility of a Tejana and Tejano psychical interiority and corporeality outside of the framework of an Oedipalized white masculinity.

Whiteness is also privileged as the mediating term for interracial contacts, both between people of color and between the sexes. Whites have meaningful interactions with blacks and whites interact with Mexicans, but blacks and Mexicans have no contact outside of whiteness, insofar as each racial group interacts with its "own kind" and there is no evident relationship between the groups. And while the whiteness privileged in *Lone Star* is no longer the white racist masculinity that framed race relations in a previous era, a new benevolent patron, *amigo* of Mexicans and blacks, is figured in the personas of Buddy and Sam Deeds.

THE SEDUCTION OF JOSÉ LIMÓN

In his appraisal of *Lone Star*, my Tejano paisano, the anthropologist José Limón, celebrates the film's novel and distinctive iconography. I would like to state from the outset that I have chosen to respond in these pages to Limón's disagreement with my earlier reading of the film in the spirit of furthering a lively and intellectually rigorous debate. Besides reinscribing a heteronormative definition of citizenship, Limón's recent book, *American Encounters* (1998), declares the biracial (Mexican Anglo) heterosexual couple as the allegory for race relations in this country. Limón is interested in exploring "the emergence of a new social order" through what he postulates as the "good marriage" between Anglos (usually males) and Mexicans (in most cases females): a "politics of negotiation and conflict" that is "beyond domination, inequality, iconographies and ambivalences" (154).[7] Exemplary of the degree to which things have changed in postcolonial Texas, *Lone Star* also demonstrates the "transformation of traditional iconography" and a reconciliation between Mexicans and Anglos. Limón adds: "The expressive events I have discussed here may be evidence of what historian David Montejano first identified as a developing rapprochement between Anglos and Mexicans in Texas—the genesis of a new mestizo mainstream, if you will—a rapprochement that works in part in transformational relation to a series of images that in the past have ratified Anglo domination" (161).

I do not want to quibble with the class origins of this positive assessment of the "new mestizo mainstream," for recent events in Jasper, as well as the growth of the punishment industry, paint a less favorable "rapprochement" for the Mexican and black working class of Texas.[8] Even so, the relationship between film and social reality is just not as transparent as Limón makes it out to be. Part of the problem with his analysis stems from the fact that he approaches film as empirical evidence for social transformations and fails to acknowledge the mechanisms that have historically structured vision in general and, more specifically, his own way of seeing.

Missing from Limón's analysis is a more nuanced and complicated understanding of the narrative economy of cinema. For example, one of his points of contention with my analysis stems from the following claim I make: "The unearthing of Texas's racist past and the revision of a multicultural order are always already subsumed and contained within the point of view of whiteness and masculinity which is privileged in the narrative" (Fregoso 1998, 183). Limón disagrees, noting that "it does not follow that there is a singular 'whiteness' which is uniformly privileged and by extension underwrites the unchanging social order" (1998, 158). Although I do, in fact, make a distinction between the forms of whiteness articulated by the film, my reference to "point of view of whiteness" does not refer to the ontological realm. Rather, I am referring to the realm of the cinematic, where, in the case of this film, point of view is indeed overwhelmingly circumscribed by whiteness and masculinity.

In places, Limón appears to recognize that he is dealing with the level of the discursive or with the representational realm of social reality. Yet often he slips back into a naïve view of film as a transparent reflection of the "real world." There is a long debate in film theory and history that has already established that film is neither a simple representation of social reality nor a transparent reflection of the social world. With this in mind, it is difficult to use *Lone Star* as ethnographic evidence for progress in turn-of-the-millennium Texas, as Limón attempts to do. The film is first and foremost a cinematic text, a cultural production, someone's (John Sayles's) reconstruction and vision of the social world. Like most artistic texts, it is intersected by multiple cultural discourses, various competing histories and representational traditions and, at this level, is organized by the cinematic apparatus, including institutionally and historically determined codes, conventions, modes of address, mechanisms of vision, viewing subjects, and points of view. Thus, my use of "point of view of whiteness" refers to the point of view that is constructed by the film and through the process of viewing this film. As even Limón (contradicting his earlier position) later acknowledges, this point of view happens to be that of Sam Deeds, who is the white masculine subject in the film. Proving my point, Limón makes the following observation: "Through his discovery of both the Oedipal conflict in his life and the true history of his town, he—and we—are able to bracket, deconstruct, and ultimately reject the Texas, truly 'white' and racist 'heroic' father figure" (159). Limón, however, does not explain just how the "he" and the "we" happen to come together. With this statement he does indeed disclose his investment in dominant mechanisms of visibility through which a white, heterosexual male subject comes into being. Just as significant, these words hint at Limón's uncritical assimilation of the cinematic apparatus as well as his lack of understanding of spectatorship in cinema.

In feminist film criticism, questions regarding female representation revolve around the cinematic mechanisms of spectatorship and identification. There are two, often conflated notions of spectatorship relevant to my analysis of the white patriarchal gaze in the cinematic discourse of *Lone Star*. The first involves what feminist film critics term the "hypothetical" or "textual" spectator, which is a concept used to refer to the textually inscribed position in the text, the position that the film offers as its "ideal" viewing position. The second notion of spectatorship is often called the "historical" or "empirical" spectator, that is, the spectator as an "actual" social subject who views the film at a particular moment in history. Whereas the spectator in the text (the hypothetical spectator) represents the "ideal" or favored position for reading the film, the historical spectator is more variable, determined by her social identity, context, and intersecting social discourses (Mayne 1993; Stacy 1994; Kaplan 1984). According to film theorist E. Ann Kaplan, "There is a delicate negotiation in any textual reception between the hypothetical spectator offered by the novel/film and the reading formations of the reader/viewer. . . . Depending on the social practice through which this reader/viewer is constructed, she or he will be more or less receptive to the hypothetical spectator position of the novel/film" (1992, 13).

In his appraisal of *Lone Star*, Limón ignores the distinction between these forms of spectatorship available to viewers. What he moreover fails to grasp is that the "we" is not a subject position preexisting the moment of enunciation. The "we" is a subject position constructed through the film's strategies. It is the site of the hypothetical spectator representing the viewing position the film offers. The film's mechanisms are what construct the "we," what make "us" identify as spectators with the camera's look, which is in turn aligned with Sam Deeds's point of view. As a historical spectator, namely, a specific Tejano male spectator, Limón is "receptive to the hypothetical spectator position" the film offers and is unable to resist the film's mechanisms, identifying unproblematically with the character Sam Deeds and his point of view.

And herein lies the fundamental difference between our readings. What is at stake with our opposing readings is much more than matters of contrary interpretations of the film. As a historical spectator, formed by a critical feminist antiracist consciousness, I refuse to participate in the patriarchal and racial structures of vision that inform this film. I refuse the spectator positioning the film offers me: an identification with Sam Deeds. On the contrary and despite Limón's critical consciousness, he remains seduced by the patriarchal visual economy of the film.

With narrative closure, *Lone Star*'s colonial and patriarchal structures of knowing and seeing remain firmly in place. Narrative resolution takes place in an abandoned drive-in theater, reminiscent of another film, *The Last Picture Show* (1971). It is at the eroticized site of the Vaquero Drive-in, that weathered relic of the '50s now overtaken by Johnson-grass weeds and the turbulent memories of Pilar and Sam's adolescent rendezvous, where Sam divulges the truth of his and her existence, namely, that they share the same father. Pilar's response, "We start from scratch? Everything that went before, all that stuff, that history—the hell with it, right? Forget the Alamo," provides the film's narrative closure. Yet, this climactic scene, a tribute to the petrified remains of a bygone social order, resurrects a repressed interracial narrative lodged deep within the national imaginary, unmasking further the legacy of disavowal on the borderlands.

Since the nineteenth century, the Texas myth of origins has been saturated with the racial politics of exclusion and a discourse of racial purity that disavowed social relations between the races. In fact, the identity of Texas is shaped by a deliberate repression of interracial political, social, and sexual relations. The Anglo denial of the history of Tejano/a-Texan entwinement is disturbed with Sam's discovery of his father's long-term illicit affair with Mercedes Cruz, the owner of the Santa Barbara Café who also happens to be Pilar's mother. In the process, the film makes evident the ways in which sexuality is a transfer point as much of power as of history and social relations. In this respect, the transborder "contact zones" on the borderlands are not only linguistic, cultural, and social but marked as well by sexual crossings and mixings. By unearthing the hidden history of miscegenation, the repressed history of interracial social and sexual relations, *Lone Star* appears to rewrite the new social order on the borderlands as racially mixed at its core, in sharp contrast to the Anglo Texan imaginary that constructs citizenship and/or membership in the Texas "nation" in terms of racially pure subjects. The filmmaker appears to provide viewers with a new, more enlightened vision of race relations. However, the discovery of this illicit love affair between an Anglo male and a Mexican female does not, as Limón contends, call "into question the cultural totality of the ruling order" (152). On the contrary, it serves to reaffirm colonialist masculinity, for the film is structured by a very old racial narrative, the story of miscegenation as a model of social inscription, whereby the white man's access to the brown woman's body is naturalized and in which the nation is grafted and etched onto the body of a woman.

There is a long tradition in Western thought of fixing the body of woman as allegory for land and nation, and it is by reading the motif of "forbidden love" in the film through this form of embodiment that we can gauge the significance of interracial love and sibling incest for cultural politics. The notion of the nation as "mother country" engenders the nation as female and further naturalizes woman in her reproductive role as mother (Shohat 1990). In the nation-building project, women's bodies mark the allusive boundaries of the nation, the race, the family insofar as the patriarchal imaginary utilizes women's bodies symbolically and literally to shape national, racial, and familial identities. There is, however, a dramatic alteration in feminine representation for white femininity, as the embodiment of the nation has now been supplanted by this new mestiza. *Lone Star* follows in the patriarchal tradition of engendering the nation as female, but in this instance it is a new fantasy of a multicultural nation figured on the body of a mixed-race mestiza. However, the film also extends the symbolic fantasy to encompass racialized sexual relations. Just as the body of woman figures as allegory for the nation, so too does sibling incest function as allegory for race relations in Texas.

The reunited lovers serve as allegories for Mexican and Anglo race relations. Yet, to the extent that Pilar and Sam share the same father rather than mother, the film recodifies race relations in Texas yet again in patriarchal terms, for the siblings derive the truth of their existence from the same father lineage, from a history metaphorized in patriarchal patrimony. And although the film attempts to render the truth of the entwinement of Mexicans and Anglos through this allegorical brother-sister relationship, it is a partial and mystifying truth, privileging the father while rendering the mother invisible in the reproduction of Texas history.

The film therefore envisions sexuality as a transfer point of phallocentric power insofar as miscegenation is grounded in the patriarchal colonialist fantasy of authorizing and privileging the white man's access to brown female bodies. For it is white men who cross racialized borders of gender, as in Buddy's illicit affair with Mercedes. Women in this narrative universe represent the subjects of hybridity, mixing, and sexual crossings on the borderland. The film further recycles racist, colonialist fantasies of interracial sexual relations, first by naturalizing and normalizing white male access to brown women's bodies while simultaneously prohibiting relationships between nonwhite men and white women. By excluding and denying the history of other forms of sexual relations, namely, those outside of the white male–woman of color paradigm, the film rearticulates and reaffirms the racist, colonialist interdiction against mixed-race unions between racialized men and white women. As we know from the history of race relations, antimiscegenation laws were aimed primarily at nonwhite men and, in the guise of protecting white femininity from these "sexual predators," these legal statutes were designed to ensure the racial purity of the white nation.

Ultimately, the narrative not only reproduces white masculine privilege but also maintains whiteness intact, for unlike Pilar, Sam is not the product of miscegenation, of a sexual contract between a white father and a brown mother. Instead, Sam embodies the myth of racial purity. As we learn in this climactic scene, the burden of miscegenation rests on his half-sister/lover, Pilar. As the offspring of a white man and a brown woman, Pilar symbolizes the new social order of multiculturalism: the nation is indeed inscribed on her body. At the same time, from a feminist standpoint, this scene may be read as ambivalent because Pilar's revelation, "I can't have children anymore," affirms female libidinal energies and locates female sexuality in desire and pleasure rather than in reproduction. Despite her infertility, as the sole subject of mixed-race parentage, Pilar embodies the borderlands, serving as the allegory for hybridity, racial crossings, and mixings. White male access to the multicultural nation takes place through the body of a brown woman.

The filmmaker reaffirms social hierarchies by reinscribing the centrality of colonialist heteronormative masculinity in the script of the nation. Irrespective of its overture to multiculturalism, *Lone Star* resituates white masculinity as the mediating term that is able to cross racial and sexual boundaries while erecting the mythic borders of its own racial purity and masculine privilege. In many respects, the film's enthusiasts may very well contribute to the consolidation of hegemonic regimes of knowing and seeing inscribed in this new multicultural myth-making enterprise. For, as Norma Alarcón has argued in another context, in uncritically accepting the terms of the film's logic, critics like Limón continue "to recodify a family romance, an oedipal drama in which the woman of color of the Americas has no 'designated' place" (1995, 42). In these final pages, I trace the strategies used in relation to female representation, focusing on the textual moves that marginalize the point of view of this "woman of color of the Americas."

In sharp contrast to *Lone Star*'s hyperinvestment in patrilineage, we find a submerged maternal discourse in the film's narrative. The film portrays motherhood in racial assymetries, figured in the absent (white) angelic, pure mother (embodied by Sam's mother) and the overshadowing, haunting presence of a Mexican Tejana mother (embodied by Pilar's mother). And nowhere is the subordination of women of color in history more evident than in the racialized mother-daughter relationship, embodied in Pilar and Mercedes Cruz's estrangement, their conflicts and unresolved tensions. It is not so much that I was disturbed by this, for their mother-daughter conflicts triggered memories of my own conflictual relation as the link in the motherline chain. I, too, have had similar conflicts on both sides of the chain—as the daughter of an assertive, strong-willed, vocal, and independent mother and as a mother of an equally assertive, strong-willed, vocal, and independent daughter. Relationships between mothers and daughters who share similar personality traits are often riddled with conflicts. The reason is perhaps explained by Elizabeth Brown-Guillory's essay in the introduction to an anthology dealing with racialized mother-daughter relationships: "Studies also suggest that when a mother looks at her daughter, she sees herself. She is constantly reminded of her mistakes, yearnings, dreams, successes and failures. When a daughter looks at her mother she often sees herself and rejects the image in the mirror" (1996, 2). And if both mother and daughter are fortunate enough to weather the frictions, hang in there, and work through some of the resentments, blames, ill feelings, guilts, and judgments, their relationship usually blossoms into a life-long, indissoluble bond. Such has been my own experience with these two "take-no-prisoners" kind of women in my life.

And this is what troubled me most about Mercedes and Pilar's relationship, that the filmmaker/scriptwriter made no effort to heal their wounds nor to formulate an ending that left us with the lingering impression of an alternative outcome. I longed for at least some semblance of an emotional resolution between mother and daughter, an inkling of some future reconciliation. I would like to have left the theater with the sensation that, in the not so distant future, Pilar and Mercedes—as was the case with *Lone Star*'s fathers and sons—would somehow work things out, just as I did several years ago with my own mother and more recently with my own daughter.

In many ways, the filmmaker has created a situation of significant mirroring, given the fact that the similarities between mother and daughter are striking. Both are independent and assertive. Mercedes excels in the private sector as a successful restaurateur and as a public official in her role as a city councilwoman; Pilar is a prominent public figure, a teacher, and leader in public debates regarding the school curriculum. Both were/are single parents, widows of Mexican men, and subsequently both develop love affairs with Anglo men. Perhaps Mercedes looks at Pilar and "sees herself." Perhaps Mercedes "is constantly reminded of her mistakes, yearnings, dreams, successes and failures." Or maybe Pilar looks at Mercedes and "often sees herself and rejects the image in the mirror." Are these the wedges separating them? Are these the sources of their mutual disenchantment? I will never know, for the filmmaker marginalized the point of view of the woman of color.

Although the male and female lead characters (Pilar and Sam) are portrayed as social equals in their respective roles as teacher and sheriff, we have seen the extent to which the film's mechanisms (i.e., identification and positioning) create an inequality that transcends the fictional universe, reproducing and reaffirming racial and gender inequality beyond the frame. I turn now to other elements of cultural discourse that have similar repercussions for race and gender relations in the social realm. Inspired by Alarcón's observations, I propose that Pilar "is simultaneously presence/absence in the configurations of the nation state and textual representation" (1995, 43). As I have shown, the body of a mixed-race woman marks the allusive boundaries of race and, in this case, the multicultural nation. She is thus "present" as embodiment (object) of the nation but absent as its speaking subject. The key to this disfiguration resides in textual representation, where the maternal presence is alienated from the mixed-race woman's genealogy.

My reference to the maternal is inspired by Julia Kristeva's theoretical efforts to dislodge the concept of "mother" from its patriarchal limitations. As Kristeva maintains: "I am only a mother in relation to my child, not outside of that relation. It is precisely patriarchal culture that has essentialized and fixed the concept of 'Mother' to my being-in-the-world instead of permitting it to be a mobile part of my being that comes and goes depending on whether I am in relation or not to the child" (quoted in Kaplan 1992, 41). Interestingly, in *Lone Star*, the maternal body on the borderlands, this "mobile part" of female subjectivity, the part "that comes and goes depending on whether [she is] in relation or not to the child," is represented as characterization, in other words, by virtue of the fact that both Mercedes's and Pilar's maternity is but one aspect of their identity as women. But the maternal presence also drives a wedge between women of color. Because the idealized mother paradigm belongs to the white absent mother, in the case of Pilar and Mercedes motherhood is a relation riddled with tension, turning against these women and subordinating them within the cultural imaginary of the new multicultural nation.

Pilar's mother, Mercedes Cruz, embodies this contradiction within motherhood. As the embodiment of the maternal presence, she is mobile in relation to her various identities as lover, mother, business owner, boss, and public official. But in relation to her daughter, she is neither a friend nor a confidant but is fixed within the mother paradigm of the "over-indulgent, phallic mother" (Kaplan 1992, 48). There is no equivalent tension between Pilar and her own daughter, as is the case with the other male grandparent-parent-grandchild triangle. However, Mercedes's narrative treatment is not one-dimensional: she is simultaneously contained or limited by the demands of the text and endowed with a certain discursive power.

The racialized mother's discursive power is evident primarily through character development. As viewers, we come to know Mercedes and witness her transformation. Besides Sam, Mercedes is the only other character actively involved in "memory work," in remembering and producing links to the past through the seamless editing techniques of the flashback. And it is precisely this visual production of Mercedes's personal memory that makes available her interiority to spectators. Viewers will recall that the sins of Mercedes include denial of her national, racial, and class origins: she claims a Spanish (white) rather than a Mexican (mestizo) heritage; insists that in America, "you speak English"; refuses to travel with her daughter to Mexico; and disavows her own "illegal" border crossing years ago.

In her final performance on screen, Mercedes recovers from this racial amnesia, resurrecting a repressed racial memory—the shadow haunting her present-day existence. She remembers the symbolic (primal) scene that engenders her as a racialized subject. It is the scene of a young Mercedes Gonzales Ruiz crossing the border illegally and meeting her future husband, Eladio Cruz, whose extended hand welcomes her with the words "Bienvenida a Tejas." This border crossing transforms a former citizen into an undocumented immigrant. A scene transfiguring a legal subject of one nation (Mexico) into an "illegal alien" or nonsubject of another (United States) is also the primal scene marking her body as a racialized subject. By dislodging this primal scene of border crossings from the site of the repressed, the narrative permits Mercedes to ally her rediscovered identity with the Mexican immigrants she employs. A previously reluctant boss, Mercedes now turns to assist Enrique and his undocumented fiancée. In this manner the filmmaker portrays a character who is redeemed and transformed through her active involvement in recalling things buried deep in her past and long forgotten. Along with investing this character with an interiority, the filmmaker's depiction of her metamorphosis works as an effective mechanism for furthering character identification. However, given that the film's finale comes two scenes later, after she emerges as a "speaking subject in process," the film forestalls the potentially transformative effects of this emergent subjectivity.

We have thus arrived at the moment I initially called "the film's missed opportunity." If the filmmaker had further developed Mercedes's subjectivity in process, he would have truly decentered the point of view of white masculinity, opening up a space for the cinematic elaboration of various spectators and multiple identifications. Instead, narrative closure recuperates the "Oedipal family romance" insofar as it resolves the brother and sister's conflict with the all-powerful father while alienating the maternal presence from the mixed-race female, thereby occulting the mother-daughter relationship.

In writing about the cinematic representation of motherhood, Kaplan indicates that with the exception of commercially unsuccessful women's films, female identification with the mother's femaleness is rarely explored in cinema. And when female-to-female bonding is examined, it "is usually subordinated to patriarchal demands by the text's end" (1992, 48). *Lone Star* is no exception to this model of female inscription. In sharp contrast to the manner in which each and every father-son relationship is portrayed, the conflicts between Mercedes and Pilar as mother-daughter remain unresolved with narrative closure. Specifically, the visuals reenact their estrangement, emphasizing Mercedes's critical gaze at her daughter and Pilar's judgmental outlook toward her mother. Female-to-female resentments and conflicts sustain a patriarchal discourse that makes inevitable the abjection of the mother. And even though both Mercedes and Buddy are blamed for Pilar and Sam's predicament, Buddy is, in the words of his own son, "a goddam legend" who can "handle" such incriminations. The same does not hold true for Mercedes, whose portrayal is neither mythic nor grand but much more ordinary and whose precarious vulnerability is reinforced through the negative interactions she maintains with other characters. Unlike the father in *Lone Star*, the mother is a character who cannot bear the burden of her incrimination.

The tendency to blame the mother is, of course, not restricted to this film, for in the words of Lucy Fischer, "in many films the mother is blamed for her transgressions and the ills she visited upon her offspring" (1996, 30). Mercedes's ultimate transgression is not her illicit love affair with a white

Texan but her deceit. The film implies that Pilar has fallen in love with her half-brother because the mother has lied and hidden her past. Although Mercedes attempts to prevent incest on the part of the siblings, she does so dishonestly and in the end fails. Her failure is ultimately the film's success, given that not even the incest taboo can prevent the romantic demands of the plot. But the film is ambiguous in this regard, seemingly condoning a "love that conquers all," even incest, while blaming the mother for the daughter's transgressions. Clearly, the film portrays a daughter who follows in the mother's footsteps ("like mother, like daughter"), reinscribing what Fischer calls "the nefarious duplication between mother and daughter" (184).

In examining the tendency of patriarchal discourse to incriminate the mother, Kaplan explains the ways in which she represents "a figure in the design, out of focus; or if in focus then the brunt of an attack, a criticism, a complaint usually in the discourse of a child (male or female) or in that of an adult (male or female) concerned to attribute all ills to the mother" (1992, 3). Along with the film's depiction of a mother-daughter interaction that is predominantly hostile and venomous, the lack of closure around Mercedes and Pilar's bonding in effect recodifies a cultural discourse of matriphobia, a hatred for the mother that can be traced to Freudian psychoanalytic theories that were popularized in the United States during the 1940s and remain with us to this day.

Given the centrality of intergenerational conflict as a major subtext or plot in *Lone Star*, this failed resolution around female identification further solidifies the social homogeneity of the social order and the Oedipal family romance that critical counterdiscourses and oppositional practices have attempted to rupture. Without a female counterpart to the father-son theme of reconciliation, the effects of thematizing the alienation of woman from woman reverberates beyond the fictional universe of the film into the cultural and social spheres of our own historical moment. Consequently, much more is at stake than the textual production of an estrangement between mother and daughter, for in the end this pair has no meaningful interaction as women.

CONCLUSION

In *Of Woman Born*, Adrienne Rich writes: "The quality of the mother's life—however embattled and unprotected—is her primary bequest to her daughter because a woman who can believe in herself, who is a fighter, is demonstrating to her daughter that these possibilities exist" (1977, 250–51). The quality of Mercedes's life was certainly embattled, and not simply by her own internal demons. Unbeknownst to Pilar, but not to the rest of the town, Mercedes carried on an illicit love affair during a time when interracial liaisons were frowned upon. Undoubtedly, Mercedes lived an unprotected and difficult life, both as the "other woman" of a white man in segregated South Texas and as a single working mother. However, the tragic figure in this story is not the mother, but the daughter. Pilar is the film's bastard child. As Ramon Rivera-Servera pointed out to me during my talk at the Latino Graduate Training Seminar at the Smithsonian, Pilar's corporal estrangement is total, encompassing not just her matrilineage, as I have argued, but she is also estranged from her paternity. And it is this bastard child, bereft of a maternal presence, deprived of paternity, who represents the new subject of the multicultural nation.

Although *Lone Star* is the first film to represent the complexities of postcolonial Texas with some verisimilitude, much more is at stake than the film's agreement with a preexisting truth. The film ostensibly engages in historical revisionism, allegedly rewrites the primal myth of the nation, outwardly rejects the absolutism of the myth of pure and authentic culture and of racial binarism. However, this project also betrays its serious limitations insofar as the patriarchal and colonialist structures of knowing and seeing undermine the fictional representation of multiculturalism and of a new social order in the film. This "new social order," which critics like José Limón are celebrating as the "genesis of a new mestizo mainstream," positions racialized women in a troubling location. The abjection of the mother creates the corporal estrangement of the mixed-race woman from history. Her history is rendered invisible through practices of repression and incorporation within patriarchy. Yet the work of creating a more just and humane future demands not a denial nor an erasure of the past but its revision and reconstruction. Whereas the film works to revision and reconstruct the white man's past, so that he may enter a multicultural present and future, the racialized woman enters history as a blank slate. Ultimately Pilar, as the embodiment of the new multicultural nation filtered through white patriarchy, is left without her matrilineage, paternity, and, most significant, without the history lessons necessary to guide her into the future. At this moment in history, when white supremacy violently attempts to reassert its hegemonic power over the multicultural nation, she (we) cannot afford to simply "forget the Alamo."

1. For example, labor unions in *Matewan* (1987), lesbianism in *Lianna* (1983), race relations in *Brother from Another Planet* (1984), and corruption in a working-class city in *City of Hope* (1990).

2. In a book-length study, Norma Iglesias defines border cinema in terms of the following criteria: (1) the plot or significant portion of the plot develops on the Mexico-U.S. border region; (2) the plot deals with a character from the borderlands region, irrespective of the setting; (3) the film refers to the Mexican-origin population living in the United States; (4) the film is shot on location in the borderlands, irrespective of the plot; (5) the story makes reference to the borderlands or to problems of national identity (1991, 17).

3. The U.S. film industry has made hundreds, perhaps (if one counts all of the one-reel silent films) thousands of films dealing with the U.S.-Mexico border. While they are too numerous to list, among the better-known examples of border genre films are *Licking the Greasers* (1914), *Girl of the Rio* (1932), *Bordertown* (1935), *Border Incident* (1949), *Touch of Evil* (1958), *The Wild Bunch* (1969), *The Border* (1982), and *Born in East L.A.* (1987).

4. This information is contained in the press packet distributed by Castle Rock Entertainment.

5. This observation was made by my colleague, Sarah Projansky.

6. Much as Clarence Thomas "colored" the Supreme Court but left its conservatism intact.

7. I find this a curious conflation or rather a separation of the realms of politics and the discursive. In the late twentieth century it is virtually impossible to conceive of a politics that is not informed by iconography, given the predominance of visual culture (i.e., image, spectacle) in constituting social reality.

8. I am referring to the dragging death of James Byrd Jr., who was chained to a pickup truck by three white supremacists in Jasper, Texas on June 7, 1998.

WORKS CITED

Alarcón, Norma. 1995. "Anzaldúa's Frontera: Inscribing Genetics." Pp. 41–53 in *Displacement, Diaspora and Geographies of Identity*, ed. Smador Lavie and Ted Swedenberg. Durham, NC: Duke University Press.

Bernardi, Daniel. 1996. "The Voices of Whiteness: D. W. Griffith's Biograph Films (1908–1913)." Pp. 103–28 in *The Birth of Whiteness: Race and the Emergence of U.S. Cinema*, ed. Daniel Bernardi. New Brunswick, NJ: Rutgers University Press.

Brown-Guillory, Elizabeth. 1996. Introduction. Pp. 1–19 in *Women of Color: Mother-Daughter Relationships in 20th Century Literature*, ed. Elizabeth Brown-Guillory. Austin: University of Texas Press.

Fischer, Lucy. 1996. *Cinematernity: Film, Motherhood, Genre*. Princeton: Princeton University Press.

Fregoso, Rosa Linda. 1998. "Recycling Colonialist Fantasies on the Borderland." Pp. 169–92. In *Home, Exile, and Homeland*, ed. Hamid Naficy. New York: Routledge.

Gray, Herman. 1997. "Anxiety, Desire and Conflict in the American Racial Imagination."

Pp. 85–98 in *Media Scandals: Morality and Desire in the Popular Culture Marketplace,* ed. James Lull and Stephen Hiverman. Oxford: Blackwell Press.

Herrera, Rafael Trujillo. 1965. *Olvídate de "El Alamo"* [Forget "the Alamo"]. México City: La Prensa.

Iglesias, Norma. 1991. *Entre Yerba, Polvo y Plomo: Lo fronterizo visto por el cine mexicano.* Tijuana, México: El Colegio de la Frontera Norte.

Kaplan, E. Ann. 1984. "Dialogue: Ann Kaplan replies to Linda Williams' Something Else Besides a Mother: Stella Dallas and the Maternal Melodrama." *Cinema Journal* 24(2): 41–53.

———. 1992. *Motherhood and Representation.* New York: Routledge.

Limón, José. 1998. *American Encounters: Greater Mexico, the United States, and the Erotics of Culture.* Boston: Beacon Press.

Mayne, Judith. 1993. *Cinema and Spectatorship.* London: Routledge.

Morrison, Toni. 1992. *Playing in the Dark: Whiteness and the Literary Imagination.* Cambridge, MA: Harvard University Press.

Rich, Adrienne. 1977. *Of Woman Born: Motherhood as Experience and Institution.* New York: Norton.

Shohat, Ella. 1990. "Gender and Culture of Empire: Toward a Feminist Ethnography of the Cinema." *Quarterly Review of Film and Video* 13(1–3): 45–84.

Stacy, Jackie. 1994. *Star Gazing: Hollywood Cinema and Female Spectatorship.* New York: Routledge.

West, Joan, and Dennis West. 1996a. "Borders and Boundaries: An Interview with John Sayles." *Cineaste* 22(3): 14–17.

———. 1996b. "Lone Star." *Cineaste* 22(3): 34–36.

The Sterile Cuckoo *Racha:*

Debugging *Lone Star*

ANN DUCILLE

· · · · ·

Although he does not appear to be particularly well educated, Sam Deeds, the good-guy (as opposed to good-old-boy) sheriff in *Lone Star* (1996), understands the meaning of metaphor. This understanding is critical, because it is underneath the film's wonderfully seductive metaphors of self-recognition—a cast of characters who look like us—that its *rachas,* its flaws, crawl. When the white bartender at the local watering hole simultaneously declares both his liberal-mindedness and his distaste for interracial relationships, Sheriff Deeds demonstrates his own progressive bent by pointing out that the bartender is only as liberal as "the next redneck." Indeed, the exchange between the two men handily positions the bartender not only as a redneck but as a white supremacist concerned about the browning of his America. In his view, the sleepy little border town of Frontera, Texas, is in a state of crisis because "the lines of demarcation are getting fuzzy."

His immediate example of this blurring of the color line is the black-and-white couple sitting at the corner table. He sees their public show of affection as an affront to the natural order of things—a social infraction that Sam's father and predecessor, the legendary Sheriff Buddy Deeds, would not have tolerated. "Buddy woulda been on them two," the bartender says. "He'd a went ova there and give them two a warnin'." Not because he "had it in for the colored, but just as a kind of safety tip." The safety tip is necessary, the bartender explains, because "most folks don't want their salt and sugar in the same jar." There is something out of joint or off-color about the bartender's salt and sugar imagery, as Sam Deeds quickly points out. "If you mixed drinks as bad as you mix metaphors, you'd be out of a job," he tells the would-be philosopher behind the bar. Salt and pepper are the dialectics commonly used to represent white and black, the nationally recognized, if not universally regnant, signifiers of racial mixing. Yet, in what is by no means an innocent slip of an ignorant tongue, the bartender has substituted sugar for pepper. He has sweetened the pot—or, rather, the jar—so to speak, and sexualized it too, sugar. The dark-skinned black female half of the mixed couple—the pepper *cum* sugar—is an absent presence (or is it a present absence?) in his would-be mixed metaphor. But, then, as Rosa Linda Fregoso argues, this is a man's film—a Buddy picture, if you will—in which women are of little consequence except as types of punctuation.

That said, it's really not the bartender or his metaphor that's mixed up; it's the film. I want to suggest, in fact, that *Lone Star* invites intensely oppositional readings, such as those offered by Fregoso and José Limón, precisely because of its mixed metaphors. Limón finds in the film's figures, particularly its "clean-cut, moral, and earnest" Mexican American male figures, an "emergent social equality," a "gradual ending of the colonial order," and "the emergence of a new Texas Anglo-American rapprochement" (1998, 153, 166). Like Limón, Fregoso finds in the film a vision of "a new multicultural nation." But for her that vision is "filtered through a white patriarchal gaze which marginalizes the point of view of the racialized woman [Pilar] in the narrative." She questions how it is that "a seemingly radical discourse around multiculturalism" ultimately reaffirms and reinscribes the same racial hierarchies and hegemonic power relations it would seem to critique.

Fregoso's question is an important one that points to a common failing in progressive film and other popular culture venues that attempt to work a kind of deconstructive black magic through parodic play with metaphors and stereotypes of race and gender. I think of Benetton's multimillion-dollar "United Colors" advertising campaign, for example, or Warren Beatty's 1998 film *Bulworth*, though *Bulworth* arguably performs the deconstructive operation more effectively than other films of its kind, including *Lone Star*. In the case of *Lone Star*, I would take Fregoso's critique a step further and argue that it isn't only Pilar's perspective that is sacrificed to the white male gaze; it's every other Other. Like the imagined multicultural communities of *Star Trek* in its various generations, *Lone Star* offers an ethnically correct cast of characters. But all except perhaps Pilar are typecast bit players who strut and fret their seconds upon the stage, sometimes full of sound and fury, but ultimately signifying nothing new. Limón's clean-cut, moral, and earnest Mexican American males, for example, in a close reading emerge as nothing more than local color, straw men who strut "in the attire of civil society" but who actually do no more in the context of the film than make radical noise. If anything, the film questions, rather than affirms, the morality and earnestness of young politicos such as Ray, the deputy who would be sheriff, and Jorge, the mayoral candidate. Faced off against the moral superiority of Sam Deeds, these colored boys don't measure up. At various points in the film, Sam, in fact, suggests that this new breed is in league with the corrupt white power brokers who want to build a new jail for their own personal profit and political advantage. "Hey, look," he says to Jorge, "I'm not gonna campaign against your deal here, but if anybody asks me, I got to tell them the truth. We don't need a new jail." Moral authority is the province (and provenance) of Sam, the lone star of *Lone Star.*

Limón would share that moral authority with the black club owner, Otis Payne, the unofficial mayor of "Dark Town." I'm not convinced, however, that the film is that generous in its portrayal of Payne except in the most traditional ways. Limón's own words are telling on this point: "Finally, it is the wise, savvy, and historically informed African-American, Otis Payne, understanding the limits of biological and cultural essentialism, who draws on his historical knowledge and personal experience to provide the second of two thematic lines for the film: 'Blood only means what you let it' " (166). The language here is as stereotypical as the character it describes. It is the way African Americans have been portrayed, from Uncle Tom to Whoopi Goldberg as Guinan in *Star Trek: The Next Generation* and Della Reese as the flying mammy in *Touched by an Angel.* Otis Payne, in fact, is several stock black characters rolled into one "Big O": the jive black dude who in his youth tried to outsmart the evil redneck sheriff, Charlie Wade; the absentee black father who abandoned his wife and son and moved in with another woman three doors down; and the wise, savvy African griot who serves not only as the community's historian but also as the film's raisonneur of sorts.

Stereotypes die hard, especially when they are metaphorically brought to life in technicolor, even where the intention may be to expose and dispose of them. If such is the intent here, the film, in my opinion, fails miserably in large part because of the symbols through which it attempts to work its multicultural magic. I would argue, in fact, that a generous interpretation of *Lone Star* as signaling the "emergence of a new Texas Anglo-

Mexican rapprochement" is possible only if one misses or misreads the film's dominant metaphors, particularly the metaphor of sterility. Where some spectators may see equality, rapprochement, and brother/sisterhood, others will find decay, infertility, and incest. And it is not simply subjective, I think—not merely a matter of interpretation. There aren't enough trees for us to miss the blighted forest in the barren land of *Lone Star.*

The film opens, in fact, in a wasteland, a desert of dry earth that yields not buried treasure but disinterred bones. Cliff, the white army sergeant we first see cataloguing the flora and fauna, describes the former firing range around him as a "lead mine," a desert full of horsecrippler. Here, as throughout the film, both word and image convey death, decay, and sterility, from the human skull Cliff's friend Mikey unearths in the opening scene, to the longhorn skeleton and dried rattlesnake skin "on the road between nowhere and not much else," to the now abandoned drive-in theater where Sam and Pilar made love in their youth.

The most significant, and most troubling, image of sterility, however, is the one borne invisibly by Pilar's brown body. Sam is the one who is childless—the one with the barren, unadorned apartment—but it is Pilar, the mother of two, who conveniently turns out to be sterile. It is, of course, significant that it is the illegitimate mestiza daughter of the *querida* or *concubina* Mercedes Cruz (who, for all her wealth and power, is herself an "illegal alien") who is sterile and not the legitimate Anglo son, whose absent mother was a saint, by the way. Here the film so naturalizes (and masculinizes) the national history of incest and miscegenation that Pilar is grateful for her infertility, which, in her view, mitigates the taboo against sexual intercourse between siblings, allowing her to continue a sexual relationship with her half-brother.

To Fregoso's brilliant analysis of Pilar's deeply historical narrative function, I want to add one small point. The reproductive potential of the female has been critical to nation building since time immemorial. What does it mean for the emergent multicultural nation, which the coupling of Pilar and Sam supposedly represents, that its new-age earth mother is no longer fertile and thus incapable of making generations with Uncle—oops—Brother Sam? What does it mean that Pilar, the history teacher, says, "Forget history"? Aren't those who forget history doomed to repeat it? Historically, sterilization has been used to contain and control the growth of certain unpopular populations, including, if not especially, people of color. Is sterility also a containment strategy here, the perfect antidote for the redneck bartender's anxieties about the browning of American civilization? I can almost hear long-time game show host Bob Barker saying in the background, "Help control the Tejano population. Have your pet mestiza/o spayed or neutered."

To end with the beginning, when we first meet Pilar, we learn that she is a recent widow whose coworker is concerned about her loneliness. We soon come to understand that Pilar's longing is not for her lost husband but for Sam Deeds, the lost love of her youth. Spayed as she announces herself at the end of the film, Pilar is *Lone Star*'s most extended mixed metaphor, salt and sugar in the same jar. And like the mule and other mixed-breed animals, she cannot reproduce. If hers is the body on which the new multi-cultural nation is to be built, life in the Lone Star State will get even lonelier.

WORK CITED

Limón, José E. 1998. *American Encounters: Greater Mexico, the United States and Erotics of Culture.* Boston: Beacon Press.

CHAPTER ELEVEN

Anzaldúa's *Frontera:* Inscribing Gynetics

NORMA ALARCÓN

• • • • •

THE INSCRIPTION OF THE SUBJECT

In our time the very categorical and/or conceptual frameworks through which we explicitly or implicitly perceive our sociopolitical realities and our own subjective (private) contextual insertion are very much in question. There is a desire to construct our own (women of color) epistemologies and ontologies and to obtain the interpretive agency with which to make claims to our own critical theory. Theoretically infused writing practices, such as those found in anthologies like *This Bridge Called My Back: Writings by Radical Women of Color* (Moraga and Anzaldúa 1981); *All the Women Are White, All the Blacks Are Men, But Some of Us Are Brave* (Hull, Scott, and Smith 1982), and *Making Face/Making Soul: Haciendo Caras. Creative and Critical Perspectives by Feminists of Color* (Anzaldúa 1990), are salient testaments to that desire for inscription in a different register—the register of women of color.

The self that writes combines a polyvalent consciousness of "the writer as historical subject (who writes? and in what context?), but also writing itself as located at the intersection of subject and history—a literary and sociological practice that involves the possible knowledge (linguistic and ideological) of itself as such" (Trinh 1989, 6). Self-inscriptions, as focal point of cultural consciousness and social change, weave into language the complex relations of a subject caught in the contradictory dilemmas of race, gender, ethnicity, sexualities, and class, transition between orality and literacy, and the "practice of literature as the very place where social alienation is thwarted differently according to each specific context" (Trinh 1990, 245).

Self-inscription as focal point of cultural consciousness and social change is as vexed a practice for the more "organic/specific" intellectual as it is for the "academic/specific" intellectual trained in institutions whose business is often to continue to reproduce his hegemonic hold on cognitive charting and its (political) distribution in the academy itself. As a result, it should be no surprise that critics of color, in a context different from that of *Bridge* and thus differently articulated, nevertheless critique through their exclusion, their absence or displacement in the theoretical production and positions taken by Euroamerican feminists and African Americanists. "The black woman as critic and more broadly as the locus where gender-, class-, and race-based oppression intersect, is often invoked when Anglo-American feminists and male Afro-Americanists begin to rematerialize their discourse" (Smith 1989, 44). Thus, cultural/national dislocations also produce cognitive ones as the models that assume dominance increasingly reify their discourse through the use of nonrevised theories, thus resembling more and more so-called androcentric criticisms. In other words, Smith says, "When historical specificity is denied or remains implicit, all the women are presumed white, all the blacks male. The move to include black women as historical presences and as speaking subjects in critical discourse may well then be used as a defense against charges of racial hegemony on the part of white women and sexist hegemony on the part of black males" (44–45). Thus the "black woman" appears as "historicizing presence," which is to say that, as the critical gaze becomes more distanced from itself as speaker, it looks to "black women" as the objective difference that historicizes the text in the present, signaling the degree to which such theorists have ambiguously and ambivalently assumed the position of Same/I as mediated by current critical theories. In this circuitous manner, the critical eye/I claims Same/Not Same, an inescapability that itself is in need of elaboration through the narratives that incorporate the historical production of differences for the purpose of exclusion, repression, and oppression. The inscription of the subject takes place in a polyvalent historical and ideological context that demands larger frames of intelligibility than that of a self/other duality.

Insofar as the critical discourses of Euroamerican feminists transform white patriarchal thought via the critical infusion of gender and sexuality, and racialized men challenge a white supremacist patriarchy via the critical infusion of race, women of color who are minimally intersected by these are excluded from what become accepted critical discourses in institutions. Though it is no small critical achievement to transform conceptual frames of intelligibility through the inclusion of a culturally produced category of difference, the fact remains that women of color, by our mere existence and self-inscription, continue to question those critical hermeneutics that silence the very possibility of another critical practice that does not foreclose inclusion or at least reveals awareness of the exclusions that make the construction of our work possible. The work of women of color emerges through the critical and material gap produced by multiple exclusions in the silences of the text that further may implicitly suggest inclusion such that we *appear* to be working together in opposition to the "Name of the Father and the Place of the Law." Are we?

Smith goes on to affirm that as black feminist theorists emerge they challenge "the conceptualizations of literary study and concern themselves increasingly with the effect of race, class, and gender on the practice of literary criticism" (1989, 46–47). My intention here is not so much to produce a "literary criticism" for Chicanas, nor do I want to be limited by the reach of what are perceived as "literary texts." I want to be able to hybridize the textual field so that what is at stake is not so much our inclusion or exclusion in literary/textual genealogies and the modes of their production, which have a limited though important critical reach, but to come to terms with the formation and displacement of subjects as writers/critics/chroniclers of the nation and the possibility that we have continued to recodify a family romance, an oedipal drama in which the woman of color in the Americas has no "designated" place. That is, she is elsewhere. She is simultaneously presence/absence in the configurations of the nation-state and its narrative representation. Moreover, the moment she emerges as a "speaking subject in process" the heretofore triadic manner in which the modern world has largely taken shape becomes endlessly heterogeneous and ruptures the "oedipal family romance" that is historically marked white in the United States. The underlying structure of social and cultural forms in the organization of Western societies has been superimposed through administrative systems of domination—political, cultural, and theoretical—and subsequent counter-nation-making narratives have adapted such forms in the Americas that are now disrupted by the voice of writers/critics of color such as Chicanas, so that we must "make familia from scratch."

In an earlier essay, "Chicana Feminisms: In the Tracks of the Native

Woman" (1990), I appropriated as metonym and metaphor for the referent/figure of the Chicana the notion of the "differend" from Lyotard, which he defines as "a case of conflict between (at least) two parties that cannot be equitably resolved for lack of rule of judgment applicable to both arguments. One side's legitimacy does not imply the other's lack of legitimacy" (1988, 12). In part, her conflictive and conflicted position emerges as Smith affirms when the oppositional discourses of "white" women and "black" men vie for her "difference" as historical materialization and/or a shifting deconstructive maneuver of patriarchy, "The Name of the Father and the Place of the Law." Yet one must keep in mind that Lyotard's disquisition on the term doesn't negotiate well the transitions between textual and political/juridical representation. As Fraser and Nicholson have noted, "There is no place in Lyotard's universe for critique of pervasive axes of stratification, for critique of broad-based relations of dominance and subordination along lines like gender, race and class" (1990, 23). Relations of dominance and subordination arise out of the political economy and the ways the nation has generated its own self-representation in order to harness its population toward its own self-projection on behalf of the elite. As such, the formation of political economies, in tandem with the making of nations, provides the locations from which historical material specificity arises and generates its own discourses. These discourses philosophically may or may not coincide with theories of textual representation, which may be held hostage through a discipline. The shift from theories of symbolic self-representation to juridical and phenomenological ones is not seamless; indeed, the interstice, discontinuity, or gap is precisely a site of textual production—the historical and ideological moment in which the subject inscribes herself contextually. In other words, the located historical writing subject emerges into conflictive discourses generated by theories of representation, whether juridical or textual/symbolic. Each is rule-governed by different presuppositions, and a Chicana may have better fortunes at representing herself or being represented textually than legally as a Chicana. That is, the juridical text is generated by the ruling elite, who have access to the state apparatus through which the political economy is shaped and jurisprudence is engendered, whereas representation in the cultural text may include representations generated by herself. However, insofar as the latter are, as it were, "marginalia," they not only exist in the interstices, they are produced from the interstices. She, akin to Anzaldúa's "Shadow Beast," sends us in as "stand-ins," reinforcing and ensuring the interstitiality of a differend, as the very nonsite from which critique is possible. Her migratory status, which deprives her of the "protection" of "home," whether a stable town or a nation-state, generates an "acoherent" though cogent discourse that it is our task to revise and inscribe.

It is, I believe, in the spirit of the above remarks, which are as much produced by my reading of Anzaldúa as hers are produced by her "hunger of memory," and by a coming into "being," which Anzaldúa understands to be both the truth and a fiction, a truth as the Shadow Beast who is continually complicit with and resistant to the stand-in, conscious will, and who "threatens the sovereignty" of conscious rulership, that the Shadow Beast ultimately undermines a monological self-representation, because it kicks out the constraints and "bolts" "at the least hint of limitations" (1987, 16).

INSCRIBING GYNETICS

Gloria Anzaldúa is a self-proclaimed Chicana from Hargill, Texas, a rural town in what is known as El Valle, the Valley. It is an agricultural area notorious for the mistreatment of people of Mexican descent, African Americans, and displaced indigenous peoples. Indeed, many of the narratives that emerge from that area tell of the conflictive and violent relations in the forging of an anglicized Texas out of the Texas-Coahuila territory of New Spain as well as of the eventual production of the geopolitical border between Mexico and the United States. These borderlands are spaces where, as a result of expansionary wars, colonization, juridico-immigratory policing, and coyote exploitation of emigrés and group-vigilantes, formations of violence are continuously in the making. These have been taking place as misogynist and racialized confrontations at least since the Spanish began to settle Mexico's (New Spain) "northern" frontier of what is now the incompletely Angloamericanized Southwest. Subsequently, and especially after the end of the Mexican-American War in 1848, these formations of violence have been often dichotomized into Mexican/American, which actually have the effect of muting the presence of indigenous peoples yet setting "the context for the formation of 'races'" (Montejano 1987, 309).

Consequently, the modes of autohistoricization in and of the borderlands often emphasize or begin with accounts of violent racialized collisions. It is not surprising, then, that Anzaldúa should refer to the current U.S./Mexican borderline as an "open wound" from Brownsville to San Diego, from Tijuana to Matamoros, where the former are considerably richer than the latter and the geopolitical line itself artificially divides into a two-class/culture system; that is, the configuration of the political economy has the "Third" World rub against the "First." Though the linguistic and cultural systems on the border are highly fluid in their dispersal, the geopolitical lines tend to become univocal, that is, "Mexican" and "Anglo."

Of Hargill, Texas and Hidalgo County and environs, Anzaldúa says, "This land has survived possession and ill-use by five powers: Spain, Mexico, the Republic of Texas, the United States, the Confederacy, and the U.S. again. It has survived Anglo-Mexican blood feuds, lynchings, burnings, rapes, pillage" (1987, 90). Hidalgo is the "most poverty stricken county in the nation as well as the largest home base (along with Imperial Valley in California) for migrant farmworkers." She continues, "It was here that I was born and raised. I am amazed that both it and I have survived" (98).

Through this geographic space, then, people displaced by a territorialized political economy whose juridical centers of power are elsewhere, in this case Mexico, D.F., and Washington, D.C., attempt to reduce the level of material dispossession through the production of both counter- and disidentificatory discourses. That is, the land is repossessed in imaginary terms, both in the Lacanian and Althusserian sense. I return below to a more elaborate discussion of this proposition, which I also characterize as dialogically paradigmatic and syntagmatic, respectively, yielding a highly creative heteroglossia.

However, before turning to Anzaldúa's attempt to repossess the borderlands in polyvalent modes, let's quickly review one area of counteridentificatory or oppositional discursive productions that are based on a self/other dualistic frame of intelligibility. Thus, for example, Américo Paredes and now his follower José E. Limón claim El Valle as the site where the corrido originated. That is, in the Américas in the Valley of a landmass now named Texas a completely "new" genre emerged, the corrido. As such, Limón strategically moves the emergence toward a disengagement from claims of the corrido's origins in the Spanish romance—Spain's own border ballads. The Paredes-Limón move could be contextualized as a racialized-class-culture-based one, where "people" of Mexican descent mediate their opposition to Anglos via the corrido. The transformation and transfiguration in raced class-crossing remains unexplored (Limón 1992, chap. 1). That is, the metamorphoses of the Spanish ballad form are induced by the emergence of an oppositional hero in the U.S.-Mexico border whose race-class position is substantially different from Spanish ballad heroes, who are often members of the aristocracy. Limón's strategy is in contradiction to that of María Herrera-Sobek's in her book *The Mexican Corrido: A Feminist Analysis* (1990), where she aligns the corrido with the peninsular origins theory, in which border ballads also emerged in the making of Spain. Herrera-Sobek's lack of desire to disengage the formal origins from Spain in its Spanish-language form and relocalize them in Texas could be a function of an implicit feminist position. The representation of women, be it in the romance or the corrido, reenacts a spectacularly Manichaean or romantic scenario in patriarchal tableaux. Why claim a "new" genre when what we have is a "new" dispossessed figure with claims to becoming a hero for "his" people in a different formation—people of Mexican descent, Chicanos/as.

The point of my analysis, however, is to call attention to the need to "repossess" the land, especially in cultural nationalist narratives, through scenarios of origins that emerge in the self-same territory—be it at the literary, legendary, historical, ideological, critical, or theoretical level—producing in material and imaginary terms "authentic" and "inauthentic," "legal" and "illegal" subjects. That is, the drive to territorialize/authenticate/legalize and deterritorialize/deauthenticate/delegalize is ever present, thus constantly producing "(il)legal"/(non)citizen-subjects both in political and symbolic representations in a geographic area where looks and dress have become increasingly telling of one's (un)documented status (Nathan 1991). It should be no surprise, then, that the corrido in the borderlands makes a paradigmatic oppositional hero of the persecuted in the figuration of the unjustly outlaw(ed), the unjustly (un)documented—in Anzaldúa's terms, Queers.

Thus, also, in Anzaldúa's terms, the convergence of claims to proper ownership of the land "has created a shock culture, a border culture, a third country, a closed country" (1987, 11). Here, the "detribalized" and dispossessed population is not only composed of "females, . . . homosexuals of all races, the darkskinned, the outcast, the persecuted, the marginalized, the foreign" (38), but is also possessed of the "faculty," a "sensing," in short, a different consciousness, which is represented by the formulation of the consciousness of the "new mestiza," a reconceptualized feminist consciousness that draws on cultural and biological miscegenation.

If, however, Gregorio Cortés becomes a paradigmatic oppositional corrido figure of Texas-Mexican ethnonationalism, given new energy after the publication of Paredes's *With a Pistol in His Hand* (1971 [1958]), Anzaldúa crosscuts masculine-coded "Tex-Mex" nationalism through a configuration of a borderland "third country" as a polyvocal rather than univocal Imaginary and Symbolic. She says, "If going home is denied me then I will have to stand and claim my space, making a new culture—*una cultura mestiza*—with my own lumber, my own bricks and mortar and my own feminist architecture" (1987, 22). To the extent that she wavers in her desire for reterritorialization à la Gregorio Cortés's oppositional paradigm, the "third country" becomes a "closed country," bounded; to the extent that she wants to undercut the "Man of Reason," the unified sovereign subject of philosophy, she constructs a "crossroads of the self," a *mestiza consciousness*. Anzaldúa's conceptualization of the mestiza as a produced vector of multiple culture transfers and transitions resonates simultaneously with Jameson's version of the Lacanian preindividualistic "structural crossroads," that is, "in frequent shifts of the subject from one fixed position to another, in a kind of optional multiplicity of insertions of the subject into a relatively fixed Symbolic Order" (Jameson 1991, 354). It has resonance with Cornelius Castoriadis's version as well: "The subject in question is . . . not the abstract moment of philosophical subjectivity; it is the actual subject traversed through and through by the world and by others. . . . It is the active and lucid agency that constantly reorganizes its contents, through the help of these same contents, that produces by means of a material and in relation to needs and ideas, all of which are themselves mixtures of what it has already found there before it and what it has produced itself" (1987, 106). Notwithstanding the different locations of each theorist, Anzaldúa, Jameson, and Castoriadis, the resonance is inescapable. (As is the resonance with Trinh Minh-Ha, cited at the beginning of this essay.)

That transversal simultaneity is one where the speaking subject in process is both traversed "by the world and by others" and takes hold so as to exercise that "lucid agency that constantly reorganizes . . . contents" and works in what the subject has produced herself. Now, the relatively fixed Symbolic Order that Anzaldúa's text crosscuts is differently reorganized as she shifts the targets of engagement. It is now cutting across Euro-hegemonic representations of Woman, now Freudian/Lacanian psychoanalysis ("I know things older than Freud" [Anzaldúa 1987, 26]), through Jungian psychoanthropology and the rationality of the sovereign subject as she in nonlinear and nondevelopmental ways shifts the "names" of her resistant subject positions: Snake Woman, La Chingada, Tlazolteotl, Coatlicue, Cihuacoatl, Tonantzin, Guadalupe, La Llorona. The polyvalent name insertions in *Borderlands* are a rewriting of the feminine, a feminist reinscription of gynetics. Of such revisionary tactics, Drucilla Cornell says, in another context, "in affirmation, as a positioning, as a performance, rather than of Woman as a description of reality" (1991, 7). Because the category of Woman in the case of Chicanas/Latinas and other women of color has not been fully mapped nor rewritten across culture-classes, the multiple-writing, multiple-naming gesture must be carried out given the absence of any shared textualization. Thus, a text such as Anzaldúa's is the racialized "ethnic" performance of an implicitly tangential Derridean deconstructive gesture that "must, by means of a double gesture, a double science, a double writing, practice an *overturning* of the classical opposition *and* a general *displacement* of the system" (Derrida 1982, 329; his italics). That is, through the textual production of, and the speaking position of, a "mestiza consciousness" and the recuperation and recodification of the multiple names of "Woman," Anzaldúa deconstructs patriarchal ethnonational oppositional consciousness on the one hand, and its doublet, "the Man of Reason"—an oppositional consciousness, which, as stated earlier, is given shape through the dualism of self (raced male subject) and other (white male subject).

Insofar as Anzaldúa implicitly recognizes the power of the nation-state to produce "political subjects" who are now legal, now illegal, deprived of citizenship, she opts for "ethnonationalism" and reterritorialization in the guise of a "closed/third country." Although she rejects a masculinist ethnonationalism that would exclude the Queer, she does not totally discard a "neonationalism" (i.e., the "closed/third country") for the reappropriated borderlands, Aztlán. However, it is now open to all of the excluded, not just Chicanos, but all Queers. That is, the formation of a newer imaginary community in Aztlán would displace the ideology of the "holy family"/"family romance" still prevalent in El Valle and elsewhere in the Southwest, which makes it possible for many to turn away from confronting other social formations of violence.

The imaginary utopic community reconfirms from a different angle Liisa Malkki's claim that our confrontation with displacement and the desire for "home" brings into the field of vision "the sedentarist metaphysic embedded in the national order of things" (1992, 31). The counterdiscursive construction of an alternate utopic imagined community reproduces the "sedentarist metaphysic" in (re)territorialization. Malkki continues, "Sedentarist assumptions about attachment to place lead us to define displacement not as a fact about sociopolitical content, but rather as an inner, pathological condition of the displaced" (32–33). Anzaldúa has clear recognition of this in the very concept of a mestiza consciousness as well as in her privileging of the notion of migratoriness, the multiplicity of our names, and the reclamation of the borderlands in feminist terms that risk the "pathological condition" by representing the nonlinearity and the break with a developmental view of self-inscription: "We can no longer blame you nor disown the white parts, the male parts, the pathological parts, the queer parts, the vulnerable parts. Here we are weaponless with open arms, with only our magic. Let's try it our way, the mestiza way, the Chicana way, the woman way" (1987, 88). Indeed, the hunger for wholeness—*el sentirse completa*—guides the chronicles, and that hunger is the same desire that brings into view both the migratoriness of the population and the reappropriation of "home." In the Américas today, the processes of sociopolitical empire and nation-making displacements over a 500-year history are such that the notion of "home" is as mobile as the populations, a "home" without juridically nationalized geopolitical territory.

THE SHADOW BEAST MOVES US ON

The trope of the Shadow Beast in the work of Gloria Anzaldúa functions simultaneously as a trope of a recodified Lacanian unconscious, "as the discourse of the Other," and as an Althusserian Imaginary through which the real is grasped and represented (Lacan 1977; Althusser 1971). The Shadow Beast functions as the "native" woman of the Américas, as a sign of savagery—the feminine as a sign of chaos. The speaking subject as stand-in for the "native" woman is already spoken for through the multiple discourses of the Other as both an unconscious and an ideology. Thus, the question becomes: What happens if the subject speaks both simultaneously and, implicitly grasping her deconstruction of such discursive structures, proposes the New Consciousness? "This almost finished product seems an assemblage, a montage, a beaded work with several leitmotifs and with a central core, now appearing, now disappearing in a crazy dance. . . . It is this learning to live with *La Coatlicue* that transforms living in the borderlands from a nightmare into a numinous experience. It is always a path/state to something else" (Anzaldúa 1987, 66, 73).

The Lacanian linguistic unconscious sets in motion a triangulated paradigmatic tale of mother/daughter/lesbian lover. The Althusserian Imaginary, on the other hand, sets in motion syntagmatic conjunctions of experience, language, folklore, history, Jungian psychoanthropology, and political economy. Some of these are authorized by "academic"-type footnotes that go so far as to appeal to the reader for the authorizing sources that will "legitimate" the statement. Some of these conjunctions in effect link together multiple ideologies of racist misogyny as it pertains to Indians/mestizas. Simultaneously, the Shadow Beast is metonymically articulated with Snake Woman, Coatlicue, Guadalupe, La Chingada, and others and concatenated into a symbolic metaphor through which more figures are generated to produce the axial paradigm—the totalizing repression of the lesboerotic in the fabulation of the nation-state. The chronicle effect, however, is primarily produced through the syntagmatic movement of a collective text one may call "panmexican," yet relocated to the borderlands, thus making the whole of it a Chicano narrative. The indigenous terms and figurations have filtered through the Spanish-language cultural text; the code switching reveals the fissures and hybridity of the various incomplete imperialist/neocolonial projects. The terms and figurations preserved through the oral traditions and/or folk talk/street talk coexist uneasily with "straight talk," that is, standard Spanish and standard English, all of which coexist uneasily with scholarly citations. The very "Symbolic Order" that "unifies" in Anzaldúa's text the production, organization, and inscription of mestiza consciousness is granted the task of deconstruction of other symbolic structures.

In short, then, Coatlicue (or almost any of her metonymically related sisters) represents the non(pre)-oedipal (in this case non[pre]-Columbian) mother, who displaces and/or coexists in perennial interrogation of the "Phallic Mother," the one complicitous in the Freudian "family romance." Coatlicue is revised and released as non(pre)-oedipal and non–Phallic Mother: "And someone in me takes matters into our own hands, and eventually, takes dominion over serpents—over my own body, my sexual activity, my soul, my mind, my weaknesses and strength. Mine. Ours. Not the heterosexual white man's or the colored man's or the state's or the culture's or the religion's or the parents'—just ours, mine. . . . And suddenly I feel everything rushing to a center, a nucleus. All the lost pieces of myself coming flying from the deserts and the mountains and the valleys, magnetized toward that center. Completa" (Anzaldúa 1987, 51).

Anzaldúa resituates Coatlicue through the process of the dreamwork, conjures her from nonconscious memory, through the serpentine folklore of her youth. The desire to center, to originate, to fuse with the feminine/maternal/lover in the safety of an Imaginary "third country," the borderlands disidentified from the actual site where the nation-state draws the juridical line, where formations of violence play themselves throughout miles on either side of the line: "She leaves the familiar and safe homeground to venture into the unknown and possibly dangerous terrain. This is her home/this thin edge of/ barbwire" (Anzaldúa 1987, 13). The sojourner is as undocumented as some maquila workers in southern California. In this fashion, the syntagmatic narratives, as an effect in profound structural complicity with ideologies of the nonrational Shadow Beast, contribute to the discursive structuration of the speaking subject, who links them to figures (like Coatlicue) of paradigmatic symbolism recodified for ethical and political intent in our time, engaged in the search, in Anzaldúa's

vocabulary, for the "third space." Anzaldúa destabilizes our reading practices, as autobiographical anecdotes, anthropology, ideology, legend, history, and "Freud" are woven together and fused for the recuperation, which
will not go unrecognized this time around. In a sense, reconstitution of
completeness for the subject is a reweaving of the subject through "interdisciplinary" thinking, or, its inverse, "disciplinary" thinking has produced
a fragmentation of the most excluded subject in the Symbolic Order. The
(im)possibility that Anzaldúa presents is the desire for wholeness, or is it a
totalization for Queers?

When Anzaldúa says she knows "things older than Freud," notwithstanding the whispering effect of such a brief phrase, she is, I think, an-
nouncing her plan to re(dis)cover what his system and, in Lacanian terms,
the patronymic legal system displace. This is so especially with reference
to the oedipal/family-romance drama. The Freudian/Lacanian systems are
contiguous to rationality, the "Man of Reason," the subject-conscious-of-
itself-as-subject, insofar as such a subject is its point of their departure
(Lacan 1977). Thus, the system that displaces the Maternal Law substitutes
it with the concept of the "unconscious," where the so-called primal repression is stored so that consciousness and rationality may be privileged
especially as the constituted point of departure for the discovery of the "unconscious." Further, it constitutes itself as the science-making project displacing what will thereafter be known as mythological systems, that is, the
"unconscious-as-the-discourse-of-the-Other" 's multiple systems of signification to which the maternal/feminine is also imperfectly vanished.

In a sense, Anzaldúa's eccentricity—effected through non-Western
folk/myth tropes and practices as recent as yesterday in historical terms,
through the testimonies textually conserved after the conquest and more
recently excavated in 1968 by workmen repairing Mexico City's metro—
constructs a tale that is feminist in intent. It is feminist insofar as through
the tropic displacement of another system she re(dis)covers the mother and
gives birth to herself as inscriber/speaker of/for mestiza consciousness. In
Julia Kristeva's words, "Such an excursion to the limits of primal regression
can be phantasmatically experienced as a 'woman-mother'" (1980, 239).
However, it is not as a "woman-mother" that Anzaldúa's narrator actual-
izes the lesboerotic "visitation" of Coatlicue, but as daughter and "queer." In
contrast, Kristeva gives us a sanitized "homosexual facet of motherhood,"
as woman becomes a mother to recollect her own union with her mother.
Though in her early work Kristeva posited the semiotic "as the disruptive
power of the feminine that could not be known and thus fully captured by
the masculine symbolic," she has "turned away from any attempt to write

the repressed maternal or the maternal body as a counterforce to the Law of the Father" (Cornell 1991, 7). We are left instead with a theorization of the "maternal function" in the established hierarchy of the masculine symbolic (7). Anzaldúa's narrator, however, represents the fusion without the mediation of the maternal facet itself. In Kristeva's text the "sanitization" takes place on the plane of preserving rather than disrupting the Freudian/Lacanian oedipal/family-romance systems, not to mention the triadic Christian configuration (239).

Anzaldúa's rewriting of the feminine through the polyvalent Shadow Beast is an attempt to reinscribe, on the one hand, what has been lost through colonization. She says, "Let's root ourselves in the mythological soil and soul of this continent" (1987, 68). On the other hand, she wants to reinscribe it as the contemporaneous codification of a "primary metaphorization," as Irigaray has posited—the repressed feminine in the Symbolic Order of the Name of the Father and the Place of the Law as expressed in the Lacanian rearticulation of Freud and the Western metaphysic (Butler 1990). According to Irigaray (1985), the psychic organization for women under patriarchy is fragmented and scattered, so that this is also experienced as dismemberment of the body. "The nonsymbolization" of her desire for origin, of her relationship to her mother, and of her libido acts as a constant to polymorphic regressions (due) to "too few figurations, images of representations by which to represent herself" (71). I am not citing Irigaray so that her work can be used as a medium for diagnostic exercises of Anzaldúa's work as "polymorphic regressions." On another plane of interpretation this could be understood as a representation symptomatic of the histories of dismemberment and scattering, which have their own polyvalence in the present for Chicanas. Anzaldúa's work is simultaneously a complicity with, a resistance to, and a disruption of Western psychoanalysis through systems of signification drastically different from those of Irigaray herself. Yet the simultaneity of conjunctures is constitutive of Anzaldúa's text. Indeed, what Irigaray schematizes as description is the multiple ways the "oedipal/family-romance," whatever language form it takes, makes woman sick even as it tries to inscribe her resistance as illness already. The struggle for representation is not an inversion per se. Rather, the struggle to heal through rewriting and retextualization yields a borrowing of signifiers from diverse, potentially monological discourses, as Anzaldúa does in an effort to push toward the production of another signifying system that not only heals through re-membering the paradigmatic narratives that recover iconographic figures, memory, and history, but also rewrites and codifies the heterogeneity of the present. The desire is not so much a counterdiscourse as that for a disidentificatory one that swerves away and begins the laborious construction of a new lexicon and grammars. Anzaldúa weaves self-inscriptions of mother/daughter/lover that, if unsymbolized as "primary metaphorization" of desire, will hinder "women from having an identity in the symbolic order that is distinct from the maternal function and thus prevent them [us] from constituting any real threat to the order of Western metaphysics" (Irigaray 1985, 71) or, if you will, the national/ethnonational "family romance." Anzaldúa is engaged in the recuperation and rewriting of that feminine/ist "origin" not only in the interfacing sites of various symbolizations but on the geopolitical border itself— El Valle (Saldívar-Hull 1991).

Anzaldúa's Shadow Beast, intratextually recodified as Snake Woman, La Llorona, and other figurations, sends her stand-in forth as an Outlaw, a Queer, a "mita y mita," a fluid sexuality deployed through a fluid cultural space, the borderlands, which stand within sight of the patronymic LAW and where many, except those who possess it, are Outlaws, endlessly represented as alterities by D.C. and D.F. *Borderlands/La Frontera* is an "instinctive urge to communicate, to speak, to write about life on the borders, life in the shadows," the preoccupations with the inner life of the subject and with the struggle of that subject amid adversity and violation with the "unique positionings consciousness takes at these confluent streams" of inner/outer. An outer that is presented by the Texas-U.S., Southwest/ Mexican border "and the psychological borderlands, the sexual and spiritual borderlands" (Anzaldúa 1987, preface). A self that becomes a crossroads, a collision course, a clearinghouse, an endless alterity who, once she emerges into language and self-inscription, so belated, appears as a tireless peregrine collecting all the parts that will never make her whole. Such a hunger forces her to recollect in excess, to remember in excess, to labor to excess, and produce a text layered with inversions and disproportions, which are effects of experienced dislocations, vis-à-vis the text of the Name of the Father and the Place of the Law. Chicanas want to textualize those effects.

The contemporaneous question, then, is how this can continue to be rewritten in multiple ways from a new ethical and political position, and what it might imply for the feminine in our historical context, especially for women of Mexican descent and others for whom work means migrations to the electronic, high-tech assembly work on both sides of the U.S.-Mexican border.

WORKS CITED

Alarcón, Norma. 1990. "Chicana Feminisms: In the Tracks of the Native Woman." *Cultural Studies* 4(3): 248–56.

Althusser, Louis. 1971. *Lenin and Philosophy and Other Essays.* Trans. Ben Brewster. New York: Monthly Review Press.

Anzaldúa, Gloria. 1987. *Borderlands/La Frontera: The New Mestiza.* San Francisco: Spinsters/Aunt Lute.

———. 1990. *Making Face/Making Soul: Haciendo Caras. Creative and Critical Perspectives of Feminists of Color.* San Francisco: Aunt Lute Books.

Butler, Judith. 1990. "Gender Trouble, Feminist Theory, and Psychoanalytic Discourse." Pp. 324–40 in *Feminism/Postmodernism,* ed. Linda J. Nicholson. New York: Routledge.

Castoriadis, Cornelius. 1987. *The Imaginary Institution of Society.* Trans. Kathleen Blamey. Cambridge, MA: MIT Press.

Cornell, Drucilla. 1991. *Beyond Accommodation: Ethical Feminism, Deconstruction and the Law.* New York: Routledge.

Derrida, Jacques. 1982. *Margins of Philosophy.* Trans. Alan Bass. Chicago: University of Chicago Press.

Fraser, Nancy, and Linda J. Nicholson. 1990. "Social Criticism without Philosophy: An Encounter between Feminism and Postmodernism." Pp. 19–38 in *Feminism/Postmodernism,* ed. Nancy Fraser and Linda J. Nicholson. New York: Routledge.

Herrera-Sobek, María. 1990. *The Mexican Corrido: A Feminist Analysis.* Bloomington: Indiana University Press.

Hull, Gloria, Patricia Bell Scott, and Barbara Smith. 1982. *All the Women Are White, All the Blacks Are Men, but Some of Us Are Brave: Black Women's Studies.* New York: Feminist Press.

Irigaray, Luce. 1985. *Speculum of the Other Woman.* Trans. Gillian C. Gill. Ithaca: Cornell University Press.

Jameson, Fredric. 1991. *Postmodernism, or, the Cultural Logic of Late Capitalism.* Durham, NC: Duke University Press.

Kristeva, Julia. 1980. *Desire in Language: A Semiotic Approach to Literature and Art.* Ed. Leon S. Roudiez, Trans. Thomas Gora, Alice Jardine, and Leon S. Roudiez. New York: Columbia University Press.

Lacan, Jacques. 1977. *Ecrits.* Trans. Alan Sheridan. New York: Norton.

Limón, José E. 1992. *Mexican Ballads, Chicano Poems: History and Influence in Mexican-American Social Poetry.* Berkeley: University of California Press.

Lyotard, Jean-François. 1988. *The Differend: Phrases in Dispute.* Minneapolis: University of Minnesota Press.

Malkki, Liisa. 1992. "National Geographic: The Rooting of People and the Territorialization of National Identity among Scholars and Refugees." *Cultural Anthropology: Space, Identity, and the Politics of Difference.* Special issue ed. James Ferguson and Akhil Gupta, 7(1):24–44.

Montejano, David. 1987. *Anglos and Mexicans in the Making of Texas, 1836–1986.* Austin: University of Texas Press.

Moraga, Cherríe, and Gloria Anzaldúa. 1981. *This Bridge Called My Back: Writings by Radical Women of Color.* Watertown, MA: Persephone Press.

Nathan, Debbie. 1991. *Women and Other Aliens: Essays from the U.S.-Mexican Border.* El Paso, TX: Cinco Puntos Press.

Paredes, Américo. 1971 [1958]. *With a Pistol in His Hand: A Border Ballad and Its Hero.* Austin: University of Texas Press.

Saldívar-Hull, Sonia. 1991. "Feminism on the Border: From Gender Politics to Geopolitics." Pp. 203–20 in *Criticism in the Borderlands: Studies in Chicano Literature, Culture, and Ideology,* ed. Héctor Calderón and José D. Saldívar. Durham, NC: Duke University Press.

Smith, Valerie. 1989. "Black Feminist Theory and the Representation of the 'Other.'" Pp. 38–57 in *Changing Our Own Words: Essays on Criticism, Theory, and Writing by Black Women,* ed. Cheryl A. Wall. New Brunswick, NJ: Rutgers University Press.

Trinh, T. Minh-Ha. 1989. *Woman, Native, Other: Writing Postcoloniality and Feminism.* Bloomington: Indiana University Press.

———. 1990. "Not You/Like You: Post-colonial Women and the Interlocking Questions of Identity and Difference." Pp. 371–75 in *Making Face/Making Soul: Haciendo Caras. Creative and Critical Perspectives by Women of Color,* ed. Gloria Anzaldúa. San Francisco: Aunt Lute Books.

RESPONSE TO CHAPTER ELEVEN

Inscribing Gynetics in the Bolivian Andes

MARCIA STEPHENSON

• • • • •

Norma Alarcón's enlightening and nuanced reading of Gloria Anzaldúa's *Borderlands/La frontera* engages the theoretically charged writing practices of the Chicana subject. For Alarcón, the Chicana emerges at the interstices of cultural and national discourses that would deny her as a historical presence and as a speaking subject. Given Alarcón's attention to the woman of color's struggle for representation, her essay has particular relevance for someone working in such a culturally and racially diverse geopolitical area as the Andean region. In the pages that follow, I touch on some of the themes Alarcón elaborates in her essay and then briefly consider a few points of convergence with recent indigenous feminist scholarship from La Paz, Bolivia.

Norma Alarcón is already well-known for her influential contributions to Chicana feminist scholarship. In this latest essay, "Anzaldúa's *Frontera:* Inscribing Gynetics," she takes up the question of how the Chicana produces her own self-representation at the intersection of a series of conflictive and contradictory textual, symbolic, and juridical discourses. As Alarcón suggests, the Chicana's own historical and material specificity may generate discourses that do not coincide philosophically with Eurocentric theories of representation. Anzaldúa's text brings to light this process of cognitive charting as it engages in the effort to rewrite the feminine in the borderlands, a geopolitical space where, Alarcón explains, colonial, juridical-immigratory, and economic "formations of violence are continuously in the making."

Alarcón contends that Anzaldúa rewrites the feminine by constantly shifting the name and place of her resistant subject positions—Snake Woman, La Chingada, Tlazolteotl, Coatlicue, Guadalupe, La Llorona, and so on—thereby throwing into question the authority and coherence of the Eurohegemonic subject. By invoking signifiers from diverse symbolic systems, Anzaldúa's text reinscribes gynetics through the "textual production of, and the speaking position of a 'mestiza consciousness,' and the recuperation and recodification of the multiple names of 'Woman.'" In Alarcón's reading, Anzaldúa's mestiza consciousness refuses a linear and developmental notion of self-inscription by privileging multiple and migratory speaking positions. Consequently, Anzaldúa's text cuts across the monologic Symbolic Order, hegemonic representations of Woman, and Freudian and Lacanian psychoanalytic models.

Because predominant signifying systems disallow any designated political, cultural, and theoretical "home" for the Chicana, she figures as both presence and absence in textual representations as well as in prevailing discourses of the nation-state. Anzaldúa reclaims the borderlands by creating an imaginary utopic community or third space, a "home" that is open to the illegal, the displaced, the outcast, and the Queer. This third space also calls for a different way of knowing or sensing, what Alarcón describes as a "polyvocal rather than a univocal imaginary." For Alarcón, this reappropriation of "home" privileges the notion of migratoriness, multiplicity, and provisionality: "in the Américas today, the processes of sociopolitical empire and nation-making displacements over a 500-year history are such that the notion of 'Home' is as mobile as the populations, a 'home' without juridically nationalized geopolitical territory."

Anzaldúa's disidentificatory text further disrupts the Symbolic Order personified by the white phallic mother through its deployment of the trope of the Shadow Beast. The Shadow Beast symbolizes the nonrational Other, the native woman who was vanished by neocolonialism's system of ideas: "That is, the Shadow Beast functions as the native woman of the Américas, as a sign of savagery—the feminine as a sign of chaos." The native woman—Coatlicue, Tlazolteotl, Snake Woman—stands in for the non(pre)-Columbian mother now displacing, now coexisting with the Phallic Mother of the oedipal family romance. Alarcón argues that with the symbolic displacement of the Western oedipal romance-drama, Anzaldúa can reclaim the native mother and thus give "birth to herself as inscriber/speaker of/for mestiza consciousness."

I turn now to the Andean region, which, like the U.S.-Mexican border zone, is another geopolitical space where the violent practices of (neo)colonialism underpin the discourses of a modernity that is always already gendered (male) and raced (white). For example, in a country such as Bolivia, with a majority population of indigenous peoples, the idea of a mestiza consciousness takes on a different historical specificity that precludes the fluidity and polyvalence of Anzaldúa's counterdiscourse from the Southwest-Mexican borderlands. Instead, the term *mestiza* is primarily an urban identificatory category that has become synonymous with ethnic and political acculturation, foreclosing signifying systems other than those vested in the patronymic Law of modernization, civilization, and Westernization. Because modernization sanctions *mestizaje*, the native Andean woman continues to be excluded as a historical presence and as a speaking subject. Always the object of Eurocentric discourses such as anthropology, folklore, development, modernization, and religion, the native woman must continually contend with racism, sexual and physical abuse, hunger, and material and territorial dispossession. Laura Pérez (1997) has similarly observed that there is no social or political place in a country such as Bolivia for flesh-and-blood indigenous peoples. Native peoples are vital to the national economy only as folkloric objects; their folklorization "recodifies them in the national discourse as part of the historical *cultural* patrimony but not as living beings whose way of life and thought is relevant to the country's present" (91–92). Aymara intellectual María Eugenia Choque Quispe (1998) has argued that colonialism in Bolivia has led to the unrestrained exploitation of native peoples and the environment, a violence that has impacted particularly on indigenous women. Indeed, the native woman's sole value is seen as residing in her usefulness as raw material for the production of a new, whiter identity (12).

As I argued in an earlier study (Stephenson 1999), it is possible to establish a link between the native struggle for territory and dignity and the self-inscription of the indigenous woman as historical subject. Although (neo)colonial discourses have attempted to displace her from the nation-state, marking her as modernity's primitive, savage Other, a few notable Aymara women have begun to retheorize the feminine both within and against the national/ethnonational "family romance." In particular, I would call attention to Choque Quispe's (1998) important essay "Colonial Domination and the Subordination of the Indigenous Woman in Bolivia." Just as Alarcón observed in the case of Anzaldúa's writing, Choque Quispe is also engaged in the "recuperation and rewriting of the feminine/ist 'origin'" at the intersection of the mestizo/indigenous juridical and symbolic borders.

In the first half of her essay, Choque Quispe provides an overview of the (neo)colonizing practices that even today deny indigenous peoples their humanity. She devotes the second half of her essay to a historically important and unprecedented analysis of specific Andean cognitive categories that, even as they ostensibly declare the equality of men and women, effectively displace the native woman. Consequently, there is no place she can call "home" within either the dominant national or ethnonational sociosymbolic. Choque Quispe argues that even as indigenous peoples critique the (neo)colonial relations that govern their ties to the state and the prevailing mestizo culture, they have found "a discourse of social and economic homogeneity in [ethno]nationalist romanticism" (16). The well-known saying "In this world all things come in pairs [and are equal]" is heralded throughout the Andes to describe the complementary but egalitarian relationship between men and women (16). Choque Quispe argues, however, that the general acceptance of this maxim obscures the subordination of the indigenous woman (16). In marriage, the woman is considered "naturally" to be subordinate to the male, who achieves personhood (*jaq'i*) only when he leaves behind his own secondary status as son and subordinates a person (woman) from a different family group. "It is marriage that produces the fusion of man and woman into one person (*jaq'i*). However, the title of this social persona corresponds only to the husband. Andean marriage is the relationship between *jiliri* (man) and *sullka* (woman [*sullka* expresses a subordinate status]). Cultural and educational models are invoked to mold the woman and to accept and defend her status as *sullka*" (17).

A more productive approach to understanding the simultaneous presence/absence of the native woman, Choque Quispe suggests, is through the examination of the term *mayt'ata* (literally, "on loan, borrowed"). Through her discussion of this term, Choque Quispe draws a parallel between the precarious relationship underpinning the juridical ties linking the traditional Andean community to the state and those that link the Andean woman to her family. Here again we see the common themes as being those of dispossession and displacement or homelessness. According to the saying "*imill wawaxa jaqitak uywañakiwa*" (literally, "A daughter is raised for other people"), the daughter is perceived as belonging neither to herself nor to her family. Similarly, when a young woman marries she takes on the status of "daughter-in-law" rather than "daughter." If the husband or his family has problems with the new wife, she can be returned to her family. From this uncertain position comes the perception that a woman is a being who is only borrowed (19).

Women are not dispossessed only through the family structure and marriage. They are also denied full leadership status within the community, as Choque Quispe demonstrates through her analysis of two Aymara terms of authority: *chuyma* (literally, "heart") and *p'iqi* (literally, "head"). The meaning of these words in Andean culture, however, has greater signficance than their literal translation first suggests. "*Chuyma* and *p'iqi* are virtues that are acquired over a lifetime, generally through a system of obligations. Woman, in her condition of *sullka*, is deprived of both virtues, which are seen as exclusively male, even though life experience and the passing of time may grant her these benefits" (20). These virtues are associated with the intelligence, reasoning, and good administration that can be acquired solely from long experience. Therefore, only a few exceptional men ever acquire the status and privilege granted by the title *p'iqini* or *chuymani* (20).

Choque Quispe's struggle for leadership experience has worked for her, despite the odds, and clearly that experience has begun to change the predominant ethnonationalist discourse. Her writings and activism, alongside the work of other Aymara women engaged in similar endeavors, have enabled indigenous women to challenge those signifying systems that refuse the native woman any designated place in rural and urban communities.

This dialogue regarding the self-inscription of the woman of color underscores the fact that we cannot minimize her struggle for representation, nor the (ethno)nationalist resistance to that struggle. I argue that this endeavor to generate a site for subject insertion is common to both Choque Quispe's and Anzaldúa's work. Neither Choque Quispe's nor Anzaldúa's struggle for representation merely overturns Western ways of knowing; these texts, in Alarcón's words, also seek healing through "rewriting and retextualization." By making use of signifiers from different signifying systems, both Anzaldúa and Choque Quispe attempt to forge another symbolic system "that not only heals through re-membering the paradigmatic narratives that recover memory and history, but also rewrites the heterogeneity of the present. The desire is not so much a counterdiscourse as that for a disidentificatory one that swerves away and begins the laborious construction of a new lexicon and grammars" (Alarcón)—a new lexicon that, in the case of Anzaldúa, can recuperate the mother/daughter/lesbian lover. Given the historical context from which Choque Quispe is writing, we cannot say that her text recovers the lesbian lover. However, I think it is possible to argue that her analysis *queers* the Andean heterosexist symbolic that requires the subordination of the native woman. In this way, both Choque Quispe's and Anzaldúa's textual projects attempt to recuperate and rewrite the "feminine/ist 'origin'" at the intersection of multiple signifying systems as well as at the historically specific sites of the U.S.-Mexican border area and the Bolivian Andes.

WORKS CITED

Choque Quispe, María Eugenia. 1998. "Colonial Domination and the Subordination of the Indigenous Woman in Bolivia." Trans. Christine Taff with Marcia Stephenson. *Contested Spaces in the Caribbean and the Américas.* Special issue ed. Aparajita Sagar and Marcia Stephenson. *Modern Fiction Studies* 44.1: 10–23.

Pérez, Laura Elisa. 1997. "De lo rural a lo global: Martha Orozco y el reto del nativo del planeta." *Revista de Crítica Literaria Latinoamericana* 23(46): 89–100.

Stephenson, Marcia. 1999. *Gender and Modernity in Andean Bolivia.* Austin: University of Texas Press.

CONTRIBUTORS

• • • • •

NORMA ALARCÓN is Professor of Ethnic Studies, Women's Studies, and Spanish and Portuguese at the University of California, Berkeley. Her publications include "The Theoretical Subject(s) of *This Bridge Called My Back* and Anglo-American Feminism," in *Making Face / Making Soul: Haciendo Caras*, ed. Gloria Anzaldúa (1990); and "Chicana Feminist Literature: A Revision through Malintzin/or Malintzin: Putting Flesh Back on the Object," in *This Bridge Called My Back: Writings by Radical Women of Color*, ed. Cherríe Moraga and Gloria Anzaldúa (1981). She is also the founder of Third Woman Press, the most important press in the field of Chicana feminist studies.

GABRIELA F. ARREDONDO is Assistant Professor of Latin American and Latina/o Studies at the University of California, Santa Cruz. She received her Ph.D. in history from the University of Chicago. Among her most recent publications is "Cartographies of Americanisms: Possibilities for Transnational Identities, Chicago 1916–1939," in *Geographies of Latinidad: Mapping Latina/o Studies into the Twenty-First Century*, ed. Matt Garcia, Angharad Valdivia, and Marie Leger (Duke, in press). Her research interests include historical constructions of racial, gender, and national identities of Mexican women and men in what is now the United States, U.S. social history, Chicana/o histories, and comparative Latina/o histories.

RUTH BEHAR, Professor of Anthropology at the University of Michigan, is the author of *Translated Woman: Crossing the Border with Esperanza's Story* (1993) and *The Vulnerable Observer: Anthropology That Breaks Your Heart* (1996). She is at work on an ethnographic novel, *Nightgowns from Cuba*, and her recently completed documentary film, *Adio Kerida: A Cuban Sephardic Journey*, is being distributed by Woman Make Movies.

MAYLEI BLACKWELL, Assistant Professor of Women's Studies at Loyola Marymount University, began conducting oral history interviews with Anna NietoGomez and members of the Hijas de Cuauhtémoc in 1991 and has spent the past ten years researching the formation of women of color, political subjectivities, feminisms, and social movements. She completed her Ph.D. in the History of Consciousness Department at the University of California, Santa Cruz. Her dissertation analyzes how racial and sexual differences impact the possibilities and challenges of transnational feminist organizing. She is an editor of the Women of Color Resource Center's report to the United Nations World Conference against Racism, *Time to Rise: U.S. Women of Color—Issues and Strategies*, and has recently completed a collaborative article, "Encountering Latin American and Caribbean Feminisms," which appears in *Signs* 28, no. 2 (2002).

NORMA E. CANTÚ is Professor of English at the University of Texas, San Antonio. In addition to her scholarly work, she has published poetry, short fiction, essays, and a novel, *Canícula: Snapshots of a Girlhood en la frontera* (1995), that received the Premio Aztlán. She is completing *Soldiers of the Cross: Los Matachines de la Santa Cruz*, forthcoming from the Texas A & M University Press, where she is editor of the Rio Grande / Rio Bravo: Borderlands Culture and Traditions series. She is also writing a second novel, *Hair Matters*.

SERGIO DE LA MORA is Assistant Professor in Chicana and Chicano Studies at the University of California, Davis, where he teaches courses on transnational film and video, literature, and popular culture. His articles have appeared in *Jump Cut, Film Quarterly, Archivos de la Filmoteca, Journal of Film and Video*, and a number of anthologies.

ANN DUCILLE is the William R. Kenan, Jr. Professor of the Humanities at Wesleyan University, where she chairs the African American Studies Program and directs the Center for African American Studies. A Guggenheim Fellow, she is the author of *The Coupling Convention: Sex, Text, and Tradi-*

tion in Black Women's Fiction (1993) and *Skin Trade* (1996), which won the Myers Center Award for the Study of Human Rights in 1997. Her current research is on representations of race and gender in popular culture.

MICHELLE FINE is Distinguished Professor of Social Personality/Psychology, Urban Education, and Women's Studies at the Graduate School and University Center, City University of New York. Her research interests include participatory quantitative and qualitative research on approaches to issues of social injustice, focusing on public high schools, prisons, and youth in urban communities. Research publications include *Changing Minds: The Impact of College in Prison* (www.changingminds.ws) and *The Unknown City* (with Lois Weis, Beacon Press).

ROSA LINDA FREGOSO is Professor of Latin American and Latina/Latino Studies at the University of California, Santa Cruz. Her publications include *The Bronze Screen: Chicana and Chicano Film Culture* (1993), *The Devil Never Sleeps and Other Films by Lourdes Portillo* (2001), *Miradas de Mujer* (1998), edited with Norma Iglesias, and *meXicana Encounters: The Making of Social identities on the Borderlands* (2003).

REBECCA M. GÁMEZ is a doctoral candidate in Spanish Linguistics at the University of Texas at Austin. Her areas of research include women's speech, pragmatics, and the negotiation of power relations articulated through linguistic choices. Gámez has done translation work in the service of Acción Zapatista and other popular education groups in the Austin area. She is currently collaborating on a bilingual collection of stories by Subcomandante Marcos, spokesperson for the Ejército Zapatista de Liberación Nacional in Chiapas, México.

JENNIFER A. GONZÁLEZ is Assistant Professor of Contemporary Art and Visual Culture at the University of California, Santa Cruz. Her essays concerning installation art, material culture, history, and memory have appeared in *Visual Anthropology Review* (1993), *Inscriptions* (1994), *Frieze* (1996), and in anthologies such as *Prosthetic Territories* (1995) and *With Other Eyes: Looking at Race and Gender in Visual Culture* (1999).

ELLIE HERNÁNDEZ is Assistant Professor of Women's Studies at the University of California, Santa Barbara. Her research focuses on postnationality in Chicana/o and Latina/o cultures. One of the concerns of her dissertation, "Irreconcilable Histories: Postnationality in Chicana/o Literature and

Culture," takes as a point of reference the undoing of traditional dialectical readings in matters of gender and sexuality. Other scholarly interests include Marxist theory, cultural studies, and gender theory.

AÍDA HURTADO is Professor of Psychology at the University of California, Santa Cruz. Her areas of interest include the study of social identity (including ethnic identity), Latino educational issues, and feminist theory. Her publications include *The Color of Privilege: Three Blasphemies on Race and Feminism* (1996) and *Voicing Chicana Feminisms: Young Women Speak Out on Sexuality and Identity.*

CLAIRE JOYSMITH, born and raised bilingually and biculturally in Mexico City, earned her degrees in English Literature and Language at the Universidad Nacional Autónoma de México and at the University of London. She has worked as a translator and teacher for twenty years and is currently doing research on Chicana literature and culture at the Centro de Investigaciones sobre América del Norte. Her publications include (as editor) *Las formas de nuestras voces: Chicana and Mexicana Writers in Mexico* (1995), *Cantar de espejos / Singing Mirrors: Antología bilingüe de literatura contemporánea escrita por chicanas / Bilingual Anthology of Contemporary Chicana Literature* (in press) (as editor with Clara Lomas) *One Wound for Another / Una herida por otra: Testimonios de Latin@s in the U.S. Through Cyberspace (11 septiembre 2001–11 de enero 2003)* (in press); (as translator) *The Imaginary Networks of Political Power* by Roger Bartra (1992); *Sofia: Poems by Joanne Logghe* (1999).

NORMA KLAHN is Professor of Literature at the University of California, Santa Cruz. Her research and publications focus on the literatures and cultures of Mexico, Latin America, and Chicana/o / Latina/o expressions from a cross-border perspective. She is coeditor of several critical anthologies, including *Los novelistas como criticos* (1992) and, most recently, *Las nuevas fronteras del siglo XXI / New Frontiers of the 21st Century* (2000). Her book in progress, entitled *Resurgent Mexico*, is on the novel and the postnational condition.

AMALIA MESA-BAINS is an artist, scholar, and activist and is currently Director of the Visual and Public Art Institute at California State University, Monterey Bay. She is an internationally recognized installation artist whose works have been exhibited by the National Museum of American

Art at the Smithsonian in Washington, D.C., the Whitney Museum of American Art in New York, the Mexican Museum in San Francisco, and El Museo del Barrio in New York. She is a Distinguished MacArthur Fellow and is a former Commissioner of Art for the city of San Francisco.

OLGA NÁJERA-RAMÍREZ, Associate Professor of Anthropology at the University of California, Santa Cruz, received her Ph.D. from the University of Texas at Austin. Author of *La Fiesta de los Tastoanes: Critical Perspectives in Mexican Festival Performance* (1997), she also produced the award-winning video, *La Charreada: Rodeo a la Mexicana* (1997). Her most recent work is *Chicana Traditions: Continuity and Change,* coedited with Norma E. Cantú (2002).

ANNA NIETOGOMEZ is a licensed clinical social worker with a small private practice as a psychotherapist for victims of domestic violence at Centro Desarrollo de Familiar. Her specialty is adolescents. She presently works for the Department of Health Services in the Audits and Investigations Division, where she serves as the Section Chief of the Santa Ana Medical Review Branch.

RENATO ROSALDO is Lucie Stern Professor in the Social Sciences at Stanford University. He is the author of *Culture and Truth, the Remaking of Social Analysis* (1989) and a member of the American Academy of Arts and Sciences. He was awarded first prize in *El Andar* magazine's poetry contest for the year 2000.

ELBA ROSARIO SÁNCHEZ is cofounder of the literary journal *Revista Mujeres,* based at the University of California, Santa Cruz. A self-identified nopal-eating, cilantro-loving Xicana, born in Guadalajara, México, she transplanted to the barrios of northern Califas. Elba works with the Puente Project, UC Office of the President, and lives in Oakland. She has published her work in numerous chapbooks and anthologies and has her own collection of poetry, *Tallos de luna - Moon Shoots.* She is also featured on the spoken word CD, *When Skin Peels.*

MARCIA STEPHENSON is Associate Professor of Spanish and Interim Director of Women's Studies at Purdue University. She is the author of *Gender and Modernity in Andean Bolivia* (1999), which received the Southeastern Council on Latin American Studies' A. B. Thomas Award for Excellence.

Currently, she is working on a book manuscript about indigenous epistemologies and the development of an indigenous counterpublic sphere in twentieth-century Bolivia.

JOSÉ MANUEL VALENZUELA ARCE, Researcher and Director of the Department of Cultural Studies at Colegio de México in Tijuana, received his Ph.D. in the social sciences with a specialization in sociology from Colegio de Mexico, D.F. His research interests include culture and identity, social movements, and urban sociology. His recent books include *Impecable Diamantina: La deconstrucción del discurso nacional* (1999), *El color de las sombras: chicanos, identidad y racismo* (1998), *Nuestros piensos: Culturales populares en la frontera México-Estados Unidos* (1998), *A la brava, ese: identidades juveniles en México: cholos, punks y chavos banda* (1997), *Oyé cómo va. Recuento del rock tijuanense* (1999), and *Jefe de Jefes: Corridos y narcocultura en México* (2002).

PATRICIA ZAVELLA, an anthropologist, is Professor of Latin American and Latina/o Studies and Co-Director of the Chicano/Latino Research Center at the University of California, Santa Cruz. Her most recent publication is *Telling to Live: Latina Feminist Testimonios*, coauthored with members of the Latina Feminist Group (2001).

INDEX

· · · · ·

Index · 387

Library of Congress Cataloging-in-Publication Data

Chicana feminsims : a critical reader / edited

by Gabriela F. Arredondo ... [et al.].

p. cm   Includes bibliographical references and index.

ISBN 0-8223-3105-5 (cloth : alk. paper)

ISBN 0-8223-3141-1 (pbk : alk. paper)

1. Feminism—United States. 2. Feminist theory—

United States. 3. Mexican American women—

Social conditions. I. Arredondo, Gabriela F.

HQ1421.C492 2003   305.42'-973—dc21

2002154970